T0211155

Communications in Computer and Information Science 1481

More information about this series at http://www.springer.com/series/7899

Ladjel Bellatreche · George Chernishev ·
Antonio Corral · Samir Ouchani ·
Jüri Vain (Eds.)

Advances in Model and Data Engineering in the Digitalization Era

MEDI 2021 International Workshops
DETECT, SIAS, CSMML, BIOC, HEDA
Tallinn, Estonia, June 21–23, 2021
Proceedings

Springer

Editors
Ladjel Bellatreche ⓘ
ISAE-ENSMA
Chasseneuil, France

George Chernishev ⓘ
Saint-Petersburg State University
Saint-Petersburg, Russia

Antonio Corral ⓘ
University of Almería
Almería, Spain

Samir Ouchani ⓘ
LINEACT CESI
Aix-en-Provence, France

Jüri Vain ⓘ
Tallinn University of Technology
Tallinn, Estonia

ISSN 1865-0929   ISSN 1865-0937   (electronic)
Communications in Computer and Information Science
ISBN 978-3-030-87656-2   ISBN 978-3-030-87657-9   (eBook)
https://doi.org/10.1007/978-3-030-87657-9

This Springer imprint is published by the registered company Springer Nature Switzerland AG
The registered company address is: Gewerbestrasse 11, 6330 Cham, Switzerland

Preface

The Model and Data Engineering (MEDI) Workshops is an international forum for the dissemination of research accomplishments on the application era of modeling and data engineering. The MEDI Workshops provide a thriving environment for the presentation of research on systems modeling and analysis, and advanced applications of sensitive, modern and complex large-scale systems. The MEDI Workshops, ushered by researchers from different areas of expertise, also aim to strengthen the relationship between industrial, academic, and governmental institutions. The events DETECT, SIAS, BIOC, CSMML, and HEDA were held over three days during June 21–23, 2021, to create a large collaborative scientific network, and to develop emergent projects, and facilitate faculty/student exchanges.

The 4th International Workshop on Modeling, Verification and Testing of Dependable Critical Systems (DETECT 2021) tackled critical systems that are increasingly used in a variety of domains and in several forms (e.g., cyber physical systems, embedded systems, real-time systems). Such systems are becoming more and more complex as they are networked and composed of heterogeneous subsystems. Integration of components, contributed by respective domain experts, is one of the key challenges in engineering system architectures. Deploying cyber-physical and internet-of-things systems in disparate critical domains requires engineers to ensure the safety and dependability of those systems. The DETECT 2021 workshop focused on all aspects of model-based system engineering of critical systems. DETECT workshop series aims to create a common community from academia and industry to share best practice, tools, and methodologies, taking into account the functional and non-functional aspects (scheduling, performance, security, safety, etc.) of such systems.

DETECT 2021 received 12 papers from authors in seven countries (Algeria, Canada, France, the Netherlands, Russia, Tunisia, and the UK). The Program Committee selected four full papers (an acceptance rate of 33%). Each paper was reviewed by at least three reviewers and discussed afterwards by the reviewers and the Program Committee chairs.

DETECT 2021 invited Robert Armstrong as a keynote speaker. He is a senior scientist at Sandia National Laboratories, California, USA. He is developing applications of formal methods in high-consequence controls and his research interests are in complex dynamical systems. His presentation was entitled "A vision of an open source correct by construction tool-chain". DETECT 2021 would not have succeeded without the support and the cooperation of the Program Committee members and external reviewers, who carefully reviewed and selected the best contributions. We would like to thank all the authors who submitted papers, the reviewers, and the Program Committee members for contributing to the success of DETECT 2021.

The Symposium on Intelligent and Autonomous Systems presents theoretical and practical solutions related to the increasing challenges facing IAS, especially those applied in modern systems like smart cities and Industry 4.0. SIAS targets mainly data-driven and model-based techniques and solutions that are based on artificial intelligence and formal methods. SIAS 2021 received 24 papers from authors in nine countries and accepted nine papers categorized into three sessions: Computing & Networking Optimization, Security and Safety, and Data and Decision Support. Each paper was assigned to at least three reviewers and the acceptance rate was 37.5%. All papers were presented according to the workshop program.

The first workshop on Control Software: Methods, Models, and Languages (CSMML 2021) focused on the application of formal methods and domain-specific languages to improve the quality of industrial control software. In total, we received 15 submissions from authors in four countries, of which 12 were full submissions. Each paper was reviewed by at least two Program Committee members, and decisions were overseen by the Program Chairs. Following an online discussion, we decided to accept three full papers and one short paper, an acceptance rate of 33.3%. Accepted talks were divided into two sessions: "Logics in Control Systems" and "Domain-Specific Languages in Control and Telecommunications".

Blockchains for Inter-Organizational Collaboration (BIOC 2021) addressed recent research efforts in the field of blockchain technology use for cross-organizational collaboration. The workshop focused on the application of information and communication technology to enable organizational and governmental service provisions. The goal of BIOC 2021 was to promote, establish, and speed up blockchain technology-related research, and identify future research questions. In total, we received four submissions from authors in five countries that all resulted in full papers. Each paper was reviewed by at least two Program Committee members, and decisions were overseen by the Program Chairs. Following an online discussion, we decided to accept one full paper, an acceptance rate of 25%.

BIOC 2021 invited the prestigious international speaker Yuhong Liu, Associate Professor at the Department of Computer Engineering, Santa Clara University, USA, to give the keynote talk. The selected papers were presented by the authors after the keynote and discussions also took place.

The first International Health Data Workshop (HEDA 2021) functioned as an inspiring meeting place where academicians, practitioners, and other attendees could present their resent research findings, and discuss new problems in the domain of health data modelling, interoperability, and health data analytics. The event was especially focused on how to explore the potential for open secondary use and analysis of citizens' health data along with developing, evaluating, and facilitating solutions.

HEDA 2021 received, in total, 11 submissions from authors in five countries. Each paper was reviewed by at least three Program Committee members, and decisions were overseen by the Program Chairs. Following an online discussion, we decided to accept six papers for publication in the proceedings, an acceptance rate of 55%, in addition to three work in progress papers which were selected for oral presentation at the workshop.

HEDA 2021 started with a keynote session where three invited keynote speakers focused on the use of health data in a clinical setting in Germany, Norway, and Estonia. Björn Bergh, Chief Digital Officer of the Universtiy Hospital Schleswig-Holstein and Head of Medical Informatics at the Universtiy of Kiel, Germany, started the workshop by presenting the HighMed project and their data integration solution. Magnus

Alvestad, administrative leader of the NeuroSysMed research centre at the Haukeland University Hospital, Norway, was presented how they use systems medicine for neurodegenerative diseases at NeuroSysMed. The keynote session was concluded by Peeter Ross, head of the eMedLab of Tallinn University of Technology (TalTech), Estonia, who spoke about Estonian e-Health: the past, the present, and the future. The rest of the workshop was arranged in three sessions on Medical Data and Images, Languages and Models, and Tools and Software.

In recent years, MEDI has taken place in Toulouse, France (2019), Marrakesh, Morocco (2018), Barcelona, Spain (2017), Almerìa, Spain (2016), Rhodes, Greece (2015), Larnaca, Cyprus (2014), Armantea, Italy (2013), Poitiers, France (2012), Obidos, and Portugal (2011). The tenth edition of MEDI was going to take place in Tallinn, Estonia, during June 21–23, 2021. Unfortunately, the third wave of the COVID-19 pandemic broke out this year and we had to move to a virtual conference with no opportunity for face-to-face interchange with the MEDI community.

In these troubled times, we are grateful to all the authors who submitted their work to MEDI 2021. In addition, we would like to thank the PC members and the external reviewers who diligently reviewed all submissions and selected the best contributions. Finally, we extend our special thanks to the Local Organizing Committee members who contributed to the success of MEDI 2021, even though they will not take the pride in hosting the physical conference this year.

The EasyChair conference management system was set up for MEDI 2021, and it made straightforward all tasks in the conference organizing workflow.

June 2021

Ladjel Bellatreche
George Chernishev
Antonio Corral
Samir Ouchani
Jüri Vain

Organization

MEDI Workshops Co-chairs

Ladjel Bellatreche   ISAE-ENSMA Poitiers, France
George Chernishev   Saint-Petersburg University, Russia
Antonio Corral   Universidad de Almería, Spain
Samir Ouchani   Lineact CESI, France
Jüri Vain   TalTech, Estonia

DETECT 2021

Workshop Chairs

Colin Snook   University of Southampton, UK
Abderrahim Ait Wakrime   Mohammed V University in Rabat, Morocco
Yassine Ouhammou   LIAS/ISAE-ENSMA, France

Program Committee

Shaukat Ali   Simula, Norway
Youness Bazhar   ASML, The Netherlands
Mohamed Yassin Chkouri   Abdelmalek Essaâdi University, Morocco
Dana Dghaym   University of Southampton, UK
Rachida Dssouli   Concordia University, Canada
Mamoun Filali-Amine   IRIT, France
Abdelouahed Gherbi   ETS Montreal, Canada
Fahad Golra   Agileo Automation, France
Paul Gibson   Telecom SudParis, France
Emmanuel Grolleau   LIAS/ISAE-ENSMA, France
Geoff Hamilton   Dublin City University, Ireland
Jameleddine Hassine   King Fahd University of Petroleum and Minerals,
                            Saudi Arabia
Jérome Hugues   SEI CMU, USA
Akram Idani   ENSIMAG, France
Gwanggil Jeon   Incheon National University, South Korea
Slim Kallel   University of Sfax, Tunisia
Tomasz Kloda   Technische Universität München, Germany
Zakaria Maamar   Zayed University, Dubai, UAE
Karla Morris   Sandia National Laboratories, USA
Mehrdad Saadatmand   RISE SICS Västerås, Sweden
Laura Titolo   National Institute of Aerospace, USA
Faiez Zalila   CETIC, Belgium
Messaoud Abbas   El Oued University, Algeria

SIAS 2021

Workshop Chairs

Otmane Aït Mohamed	Concordia University, Canada
Samir Ouchani	LINEACT CESI, France
Mohamed-El-Amine Brahmia	LINEACT CESI, France

Program Committee

Shaukat Ali	Simula, Norway
Abbdelhafid Abouaissa	University of Haute-Alsace, France
Abdelhakim Baouya	Verimag, France
Ali Ahmadinia	California State University San Marcos, USA
Aris Leivadeas	École de technologie supérieure, Canada
Arunkumar Ramaswamy	ENSTA, France
Cihan Tunc	University of North Texas, USA
Christopher Fuhrman	École de technologie supérieure, Canada
Ernesto Exposito	Université de Pau et des Pays de l'Adour, France
Hugo Jonker	Open University of the Netherlands, The Netherlands
Gabriela Nicolescu	Polytechnique Montreal, Canada
Hanifa Boucheneb	Polytechnique Montreal, Canada
Haythem Banysalameh	Al Ain University, Abu Dhabi, UAE
Houria Oudghiri	Lehigh University, USA
Jamil Ahmad	Islamia College Peshawar, Pakistan
Karim Lounis	Queen's University, Canada
Michael Mrissa	University of Primorska, Slovenia
Mourad Benmalek	ESI, Algéria
Nasrine Damouche	ISAE-SUPAERO, France
Olga Gadyatskaya	Leiden University, The Netherlands
Salim Chehida	Verimag, France
Raphaël Khoury	Université du Québec à Chicoutimi, Canada

BIOC 2021

Workshop Chairs

Alex Norta	Tallinn University of Technology, Estonia
Anne Laurent	Université de Montpellier, France
Arnaud Castelltort	Université de Montpellier, France
Akram Hakiri	University of Carthage, Tunisia

Program Committee

Shaukat Ali	Simula, Norway
Clemens Cap	University of Rostock, Germany
Arnaud Castelltort	Université de Montpellier, France
Soren Debois	IT University of Copenhagen, Denmark

Rik Eshuis   Eindhoven University of Technology, The Netherlands
Aniruddha Gokhale   Vanderbilt University, USA
Jaap Gordijn   Vrije Universiteit Amsterdam, The Netherlands
Guido Governatori   CSIRO, Australia
Hanen Idoudi   ENSI, Tunisia
Benjamin Leiding   TU Clausthal, Germany
Sabra Mabrouk   Carthage University, Tunisia
Giovanni Meroni   Politecnico di Milano, Italy
Luise Pufahl   TU Berlin, Germany
Stefan Schulte   TU Wien, Austria
Volker Skwarek   Hamburg University of Applied Sciences, Germany
Tijs Slaats   University of Copenhagen, Denmark
Layth Sliman   Efrei Paris, France
Mark Staples   CSIRO, Australia
Ingo Weber   TU Berlin, Germany

CSMML 2021

Workshop Chairs

Vladimir Zyubin   Institute of Automation and Electrometry, SB RAS,
                          Russia
Natalia Garanina   Ershov Institute of Informatics Systems, Russia
Sergey Staroletov   Polzunov Altai State Technical University, Russia

Program Committee

Igor Anureev   A.P. Ershov Institute of Informatics Systems, SB RAS,
                          Russia
Thomas Baar   Hochschule für Technik und Wirtschaft, Germany
Sergei Gorlatch   University of Muenster, Germany
Damas Gruska   Comenius University in Bratislava, Slovakia
Paula Herber   University of Muenster, Germany
Dmitry Koznov   St Petersburg University, Russia
Alexey Lisitsa   University of Liverpool, UK
Alexandr Naumchev   Innopolis University, Russia
Horst Schulte   Hochschule für Technik und Wirtschaft, Germany
Nikolay Shilov   Innopolis University, Russia
Vassil Todorov   Université Paris-Saclay, CNRS, CentraleSupélec, LRI,
                          France
Valeriy Vyatkin   Aalto University, Finland
Vladimir Zakharov   Lomonosov Moscow State University, Russia

HEDA 2021

Workshop Chairs

Martin Leucker   University of Lübeck, Germany
Yngve Lamo   Western Norway University of Applied Sciences,
                        Norway

Organizing Chair

Gunnar Piho   Tallinn University of Technology, Estonia

Program Committee

Ezio Bartocci   Vienna University of Technology, Austria
Gayo Diallo   University of Bordeaux, France
Lukas Fischer   Software Competence Center Hagenberg GmbH,
                        Austria
Josef Ingenerf   University of Lübeck, Germany
Wendy MacCaull   St. Francis Xavier University, Canada
Peeter Ross   Tallinn University of Technology, Estonia
Ludovico Iovino   Gran Sasso Science Institute, Italy
Fazle Rabbi   University of Bergen, Norway
Adria Rutle   Western Norway University of Applied Sciences,
                        Norway
Vincenzo Ciancia   Institute for Information Science and Technologies,
                        Italy

Abstracts of Invited Talks

A Vision of an Open Source Correct by Construction Tool Chain

Robert Armstrong

Sandia National Laboratories, Livermore, CA, USA

Abstract. From recent headlines, it is clear that current digital systems are brittle and easy to subvert. There are a number of fundamental reasons for this: mostly having to do with complexity and the nonlinear dynamical system out of which a computer is made. Understanding the fundaments of complex dynamical computational systems helps to form the solution space. Formal verification of safety, security and reliability would seem to provide a path out of this predicament: dramatic successes of its application are not lacking. However, unlike traditional software development, no commonly accepted tool chain for correct-by-construction (C × C) development for practical software has evolved. Some speculation will be devoted to the requirements of such a tool chain and what shape it might eventually take. Currently, few languages have an accepted formal semantics let alone proof tools for verification. A reasonably well-accepted semantics for C is available and elements necessary for such a tool chain already exist. Some time will be spent on our own efforts to create a workflow for C × C of high-consequence controls in the C language. Using freely available tools and some commonly-used engineering-design applications, we have demonstrated a compelling, if incomplete answer. This effort may point the way to a more satisfying tool chain which could open the way to developing more reliable software.

New Developments in the IEC 61131-3 and 61499 Standards for Industry 4.0

James H. Christensen

Holobloc Inc., Cleveland Heights, OH 44121, USA

Abstract. The "HMS platform", proposed in 2003 after a 10-year study by the Holonic Manufacturing Systems (HMS) Consortium, may be considered a forerunner to the cyber-physical systems platform ("CPS-Plat-form"), which serves as a core technology of the Fourth Industrial Revolution ("Industry 4.0"). The HMS platform proposed the use of software agents to perform dynamic reconfiguration of machine control systems to achieve "agile" manufacturing systems that would be dynamically reprogrammable and reconfigurable, information intensive, and continuously changeable.

The required agility of the underlying control system of the HMS platform was to be provided by the IEC 61499 architectural standard, which was adopted in 2003. This standard defines an event-driven extension of the "function block" concept from the IEC 61131-3 PLC programming language standard. Event-driven function blocks are then used as the fundamental units of software encapsulation, reuse, deployment and reconfiguration in an agile distributed system architecture.

Since 2003, the emergence of cloud/edge computing architectures, with their associated containerization and the orchestration technologies and "TCP/IP every-where", have made high-level functionality such as AI and ML (Machine Learning), along with access to "big data", available to factory-floor systems. The event-driven nature of the IEC 61499 architecture now makes it an ideal match for integration with such systems in the formation of the Fourth Industrial Revolution. This talk concludes with a description of some of the related improvements being considered for inclusion in the upcoming Third Edition of IEC 61499, and future issues to be addressed in Compliance Profiles.

Contents

Control Software: Methods, Models, and Languages (CSMML)

Blockchain for Inter-organizational Collaboration (BIOC)

The International Health Data Workshop (HEDA)

moDeling, vErification and Testing of dEpendable CriTical systems (DETECT)

Refinable Record Structures in Formal Methods

Asieh Salehi Fathabadi$^{(\boxtimes)}$ ⓘ, Colin Snook ⓘ, Thai Son Hoang ⓘ,
Dana Dghaym ⓘ, and Michael Butler ⓘ

ECS, University of Southampton, Southampton, UK
{a.salehi-fathabadi,cfs,t.s.hoang,d.dghaym,m.j.butler}@soton.ac.uk

Abstract. State-based formal specifications benefit from data structuring mechanisms, which collate associated properties and efficiently declare complex types. For example, 'record' data structures, similar to those used in programming languages, can be built into the concrete syntax of a language as an enhancement over flat data relationships. While this is relatively simple to achieve for a single-level specification, it becomes significantly more involved when the specification language allows for progressive refinement of the data supporting the specification. Individual fields may be added to create sub-records within a refinement and replaced to create refined records during a refinement step. The impact on the ability to verify invariant and refinement proof obligations must be considered. Here we describe a record structuring syntax that includes notions of extension and inheritance that can be used in a refinement-based formal method. We illustrate the approach using extensions to the Event-B formal method.

1 Introduction and Motivation

Any formal language that relies on complex representations of a mutable state, benefits from data organisation to help the reader understand the semantic roles, associations and composition of its individual data objects. This can be done diagrammatically (e.g. class diagrams) or via textual syntactic structures that clarify the permitted ownerships between objects (e.g. records or structures) in terms of fields or properties. The latter is well-known from high-level programming languages (Fortran, Pascal etc.) as well as some formal specification languages (VDM). However, these languages do not support refinement and are not designed to facilitate verification by theorem provers. Verification by proof (rather than execution) has many benefits such as completeness and genericity, but tends to be hampered by features that support usability. Event-B [1] is a formal specification language designed for modelling discrete systems at an abstract level and supporting progressive refinement of detail. Event-B models are verified by automatic theorem provers. When the theorem provers do not succeed manual intervention is needed to determine whether a proof is possible or the model is wrong. To obtain the highest possibility for the automatic

© Springer Nature Switzerland AG 2021
L. Bellatreche et al. (Eds.): MEDI 2021 Workshops, CCIS 1481, pp. 3–15, 2021.
https://doi.org/10.1007/978-3-030-87657-9_1

theorem provers to succeed, a cautious approach was taken to featuring the modelling notation. Hence records are not available in Event-B and past attempts to add them have not entirely successful. Here we suggest a new approach to add records for Event-B in a way that will not hamper the verification of models. A central tenet of Event-B is that abstraction and subsequent refinement helps to clarify problems leading to useful and correct models. Any record notation that we introduce must therefore fully support the notion of data refinement and include record relationship operators to achieve this. In this paper we illustrate a new records feature that supports data refinement without impacting on provability. We previously [8] introduced the concept of this feature in brief. Here we expound the mechanisms by which records are extended and refined and illustrate their use by example. The concepts are general enough to be applied to other languages but illustrated throughout with our implementation in CamilleX [10] which is a textual front-end for the Event-B language, provided via a plug-in to the Rodin [2] platform.

The paper is structured as follows: Sect. 2 provides background on Event-B and the tooling. Section 3 reports on the syntax and transformation of record structure, followed by application of it in the voting system case study in Sect. 4. Section 5 compares with other data structuring methods. Finally Sect. 6 concludes.

2   Background

Event-B [1] is a refinement-based formal method for system development. An Event-B model contains two parts: *contexts* for static data and *machines* for dynamic behaviour. Contexts contain carrier sets s, constants c, and axioms $A(c)$ that constrain the carrier sets and constants. Machines contain variables v, invariant predicates $I(v)$ that constrain the variables, and events. Event-B uses a mathematical language that is based on set theory and predicate logic.

Event-B is supported by the Rodin Platform [2], an extensible open source toolkit which includes facilities for modelling, verifying the consistency of models using theorem proving and model checking techniques, and validating models with simulation-based approaches.

The records feature has been made available as part of the CamilleX editor [10]. CamilleX provides a textual representation of Event-B models, as opposed to the XML Rodin files. CamilleX supports two types of textual files *XMachine* and *XContext*, which in turn will be automatically translated to the corresponding Rodin Event-B components (machine and context). The records feature is also translated to standard Event-B, hence it is not required to be processed by the Rodin tools.

The records feature is based on the EMF framework for Event-B [4]. This framework does not only use the *Eclipse Modeling Framework* (EMF) [16] utilities, but also provides extension and translation mechanisms to extend the Event-B language. CamilleX uses the XText [7] framework to implement an editor and translation tool. XText is an eclipse-based open source framework for developing domain-specific languages. The CamilleX grammar is extended in accordance with the new records meta-model.

3 Record

3.1 Record Syntax and Semantics

Records and fields defined in an XContext are constants, whereas records and fields defined in an XMachine are variables. The syntax for defining a record in an Event-B XMachine or XContext text file is specified as below (keywords are shown in red):

record record_id
(field_id : [multiplicity] field_type)*

Each record has an identifier, *record_id*, and contains zero or more field(s). A record field has an identifier, *field_id*, an optional multiplicity, *multiplicity*, and a data type, *field_type*.

Multiplicity constrains the number of values associated with that field. There are three alternative multiplicity options for a field:

- one: the field has exactly one value.
- opt: the field has at most one value (optional).
- many: the field has zero or more values.

If no multiplicity option is specified for a field, it is considered to be one. While the one multiplicity is common, the opt and many multiplicities give flexibility in defining the cardinality associated with each field in a record.

Record relation types:
A record can optionally *inherit, extend* or *refine* another record using the following syntax:

record
[record_id inherits inherited_record_id] / [extended record record_id] / [refined record record_id]
(field_id : [multiplicity] field_type)*

Record relation type	Record name	Fields	Application
inherits	**new** record name	**add** field(s) (optional)	a new record inherits from an existing record in: • a **single**-level specification:
extends	keep record name	**add** field(s) (optional for refinement)	an existing record is extended with new field(s) in: • a **single**-level specification or • a super-position **refinement**
refines	keep record name	**add/remove** field(s)	an existing record is refined in: • a data **refinement**

Fig. 1. Record relation types

Figure 1 compares the three different types of relationships between records:

- **inherits:** defines a new record, with a distinct name, over a subset of an existing records domain. The new record inherits all of the fields of its parent and may add new fields. The inheritance is used in single-layer specification where the model is built as one flat level.
- **extends:** defines the refinement of an existing (abstract) record where all of the abstract fields are retained and some new fields may be added. Unlike in the case of **inherits**, the name of the record domain is retained. The **extends** is used in both single-layer specification and super-position refinement. Super-position or horizontal refinement is to extend the model with new requirements.
- **refines:** defines the refinement of an existing (abstract) record where some abstract fields are replaced by new fields (new fields may also be added). The refining relationship between records are applied to the data refinement. Data refinement or vertical refinement is performed when no more new requirements are needed for consideration. The same state space and transitions are refined to more discrete details.

Record Relation type	Application in Event-B (from "source" to "destination")
inherits	from a *context* to the *same context* (1) from a *context* to the *extended context* (2) from a *machine* to the *same machine* (3) from a *machine* to the *seen context* (4)
extends	from a *context* to the *extended context* (1) from a *machine* to the *seen context* (2) from a *machine* to the *refined machine* (3)
refines	from a *machine* to the *refined machine* (1)

Fig. 2. Record relation types in Event-B

Figure 2 describes how these record relationships are applied in Event-B to be used between or within Event-B components. As will be illustrated with the examples later, record inheritance is used to define subtypes at the same level of abstraction. Record extension is used to layer the definition of the fields of a record across context and machine layers. Record refinement is used to support define data refinement of record structures between machines at different abstraction levels.

Figure 3 describes these inter-/intra-component usages in more detail. The left-hand side of Fig. 3 shows the different uses of the inherits relationship, while the right-hand side presents extension and refinement relationships. Each box, representing an Event-B component, is divided into two: the top illustrates the semantic record relationship including implicit ownership of fields; the bottom shows the corresponding syntax needed to specify these record relationships in the XContext and XMachine text files (following the presented syntax rules above).

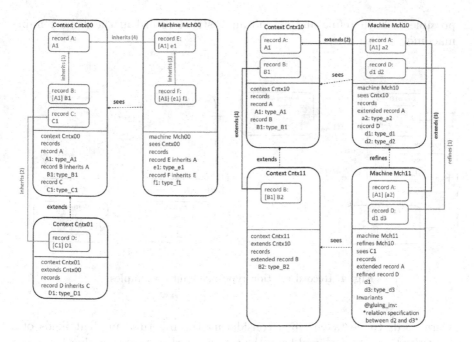

Fig. 3. Record relation types: semantics and syntax

- A record field is either an inherited/extended constant field (illustrated in square brackets in Fig. 3) or an inherited/extended variable field (illustrated inside brackets) or a locally defined field (constant in context or variable in machine). The first two are implicit and only the newly introduced fields are explicitly declared in the syntax (at the bottom).
- In a refined record, the fields to be retained must be explicitly listed as well as declaring any new fields. When listing a retained field of a refined record, the type is optional and should only be given if it is more restrictive (i.e. a proper sub-set of) the abstract type. When the type is not restricted, it is preferable to omit it since the generated invariant is already available from the abstract machine. When one or more abstract fields have been refined (i.e. not listed as retained), an invariant must specify the refinement relation between the refined abstract fields and the new refining ones. This so called, gluing invariant is similar to those used in Event-B data refinement but quantified over all instances of the record. For now, we have not added any syntax or automation to support this gluing invariant; it must be constructed by hand, including appropriate quantification, and added to the machine's invariants. In future work we will consider whether it is advantageous to provide a syntax for invariants within records.
- An extended record in a machine is a special type of refinement, where no field(s) are removed. Therefore a record from an abstract machine can be either refined or extended by another record in a refining machine. It is not

possible to both refine and extend an abstract record in the same refining machine.

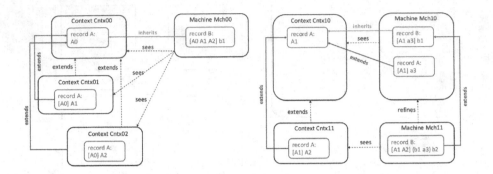

Fig. 4. Record relation types: semantic examples

Care needs to be taken when considering the inherited implicit fields of a record since they are gathered from the transitive closure of the inheritance but also depend on the scope of the component. Syntactically, an inheriting/extending record only specifies the newly added fields and a refining record specifies all of the fields retained from the parent record. Two examples are provided in Fig. 4. The fields [A1] and [A2] in the left example, and [A2] and (a3) in the right example, are fields which are implicitly inherited by the record but are not explicitly declared nor implicitly inherited from the parent record. In the left-hand example, [A1] and [A2] are implicitly inherited by record B in $Mch00$, since B inherits from record A in $Cntx00$ which is extended separately in contexts $Cntx01$ and $Cntx02$ which are seen by machine $Mch00$ and hence their extensions are visible from $Mch00$. In the right-hand example, [A2] is implicitly inherited by extended record B in $Mch11$ even though it has no direct relation to record A in $Cntx11$. This is because the abstract record B in $Mch10$ inherits record A in $Cntx10$ and A is extended in $Cntx11$ which is seen by $Mch11$. Also, variable field (a3) is implicitly inherited in record B of $Mch10$ and $Mch11$ even though record A appears disconnected from record B in $Mch10$. This is because the abstract record B in $Mch10$ inherits from record A in $Cntx00$ which is also extended to add (a3) in $Mch10$. Since this extension is visible, and nothing is refined away in $Mch11$ (due to using record extension), (a3) is implicitly retained in $Mch11$.

A record can inherit/extend/refine another record using several different modelling styles as discussed below, considering that static record data are specified in a context, while dynamic record data are specified in a machine:

– A record specified in a context/machine or extending context inherits a record specified in the same context/machine or parent context respectively (inherits number 1, 2 and 3 from Fig. 2). In this approach, we inherit fields of the parent record and can possibly add new fields (changed record name). This approach supports hierarchical definition of data structures where a generic record specifies shared fields while more specialised child sub-records add additional fields.

– A record specified in a machine, inherits/extends a record specified in a context that is seen by the machine (inherits number 4 and extends number 2 from Fig. 2). When a record needs both variable and constant fields, we can inherit the constant fields from a static record in a context, and add new dynamic variable fields either using inherits (changed record name) where a variable subset of the record domain is required, or using extends when the record remains based on the static record domain.

– A record specified in an extending context, extends a record specified in the parent context (extends number 1 from Fig. 2). In this approach, we extends fields of the parent record by new fields (same record name).

– A record specified in a refining machine, extends/refines a record specified in the abstract machine (extends number 3, refines number 1 from Fig. 2). This approach supports data refinement where fields can be extended (superposition) and/or replaced (data refinement) for an existing abstract record in a refinement level.

3.2 Record Transformation

When the CamilleX XContext/XMachine is saved, a Rodin context/machine file, including Event-B elements representing any records, is generated. The translated elements representing records, include sets, constants and axioms in a context and variables and invariants in a machine.

In a context:

- A record that does not inherit or extend is translated to a set:

  sets record_id

- An inheriting (child) record is translated to a constant and an axiom that specifies the record's domain type as a sub-set relation:

  constants record_id
  axioms record_id $\subseteq$ parent_record_id

- An extended record does not need any translation for the record's domain because the previously generated constants and axioms are in the scope of the extending record.

- Each field is translated to a constant and an axiom, specifying the field type:

  constants field_id
  axioms field_id $\in$ record_id ($\leftrightarrow$/$\leftrightarrow\!\!\!\!\rightarrow$/$\rightarrow$) field_type

There are three alternative relation types for a field depending on its multiplicity:

– "many": is translated to a relation ($\leftrightarrow$)

- "opt" (optional): is translated a partial function ($\rightarrow\!\!\!\!\!+$)
- "one": is translated to a total function ($\rightarrow$).

In a machine:
- A record in a machine must either inherit, extend or refine another record; due to the need for the invariant translation specifying a record type.
- An inheriting record is translated to a variable and an invariant, specifying the record type as a sub-set relation:

> variables record_id
> invariants record_id $\subseteq$ parent_record_id

- For an extending/refining record, the previously generated (abstract) variable is repeated in the Event-B machine (as part of a Event-B refinement structure).
- Each field is translated to a variable and an invariant, specifying the field type:

> variables field_id
> invariants field_id $\in$ record_id ($\leftrightarrow$/$\rightarrow\!\!\!\!\!+$/$\rightarrow$) field_type

4 Case Study: An Electronic Voting System

In this section we illustrate the use of records in part of a model of a voting system with a smart ballot box that only accepts legitimate paper ballots, the full development of the model is presented in [5]. We start by distinguishing between legitimate and illegitimate paper ballots. In machine m1 of Fig. 5, we introduce the record papers where each paper explicitly includes the voter's information; voter and their selected vote. Then to distinguish between the papers, we introduce two records legitimate and illegitimate where both inherit the fields vote and voter from papers. We also add invariant partition−papers to specify the disjoint property of the legitimate and illegitimate sub types.

In the next refinement m2, record papers is extended by introducing a timestamp field time for the paper ballot, and we also retain the records legitimate and illegitimate. Therefore both legitimate and illegitimate are extended records and (implicitly) inherit papers record in m2 (represented by dashed lines in Fig. 5).

In the last refinement m3, we data refine papers to ensure the privacy of the voter. We introduce encryption where the new field encrypted_ballot will replace the fields vote and voter. This will also be reflected in the inheriting records legitimate and illegitimate. In this case, we need a gluing invariant to relate the disappearing fields voter and vote with the new field encrypted_ballot. We introduce the gluing invariant gluing−legitimate−papers in m3. The gluing invariant ensures that when applying the encryption algorithm using the encryption key to the voters' information and selections, the result will be the encrypted paper ballot. This only applies to legitimate papers where the encryption key will be secretly shared with legitimate ballot issuing machines. The invariant for illegitimate ballots is the converse of the above, i.e., with inequality.

As presented in the previous section, all records specified in the CamilleX text file (Fig. 5) are automatically transformed to the standard Event-B language. As

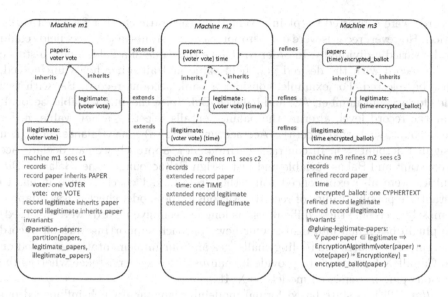

Fig. 5. Record relation types (Here, PAPER is a record, and VOTER , VOTE , TIME , and CYPHER_TEXT are carrier sets defined in the seen contexts.)

an example of transformation of record, in machine m1, an invariant is generated for the record field voter:

$$@\text{inv\_record\_paper\_voter: voter} \in \text{paper} \rightarrow \text{VOTER.}$$

In general, given a record recordName, the generated invariant related to its field fieldName is labelled inv_record_≪recordName≫_≪fieldName≫. This allows us to trace any undischarged proof obligations related to this invariant back to the source record and field.

In Event-B, proof obligations (PO) are generated to prove the correctness and consistency of the model. One kind of PO, invariant preservation (INV), ensures that events result in a state that satisfies an invariants. As an example of PO, for the event issues_paper, where a new paper is created, an invariant preservation PO is generated to prove that the event issues_paper is preserving the property specified in the invariant inv_record_paper_voter i.e., a paper can only have one voter. This PO is discharged by proving an action in the event issues_paper to set the voter field of the new record instance appropriately, i.e., @act: voter(p) := v, where p is a new paper to be created and v is an existing voter belonging to the set VOTER.

5   Comparison with Other Data Structuring Methods

Declarative Records in Event-B. A previous attempt [14] to provide support for records (based on [6]) extended Rodin Event-B to support records and fields.

Records were converted to 'plain' Event-B by the static checker for proof verification. However, records were only supported as constants and hence, fields could not be varied individually. In order to change the value of a field, a new instance of the record with the desired new field value and all other fields unchanged, must be selected. For example, consider a bank account record, BA with two fields for account number, Acc and balance, Bal. Since the only variable, account, is at the record level, altering the balance entails selecting a new value, n, for the account, such that $Acc(n) = Acc(account) \wedge Bal(n) = newBalance$, and then assigning $account := n$. In contrast, with our new approach we can declare Acc as constant and Bal as variable and just assign $Bal(account) := newBalance$. Difficulties were also experienced using the ProB model checker since it has to instantiate possible values of records. Although, the model checker was adapted to mostly overcome these difficulties (as long as recursive records were not used) the plugin has fallen into disuse. Our new approach supporting variable record structures, alleviates the tooling challenges and our implementation is based on the CamilleX framework to provide human-usable text persistence whereas the previous plug-in persisted models as XML.

Alloy [12] is a state-based formal modelling language which influenced our approach. Records are similar to Alloy *signatures*, with the same notion of extends and fields. We based our syntax for field multiplicity on Alloy multiplicities with some changes to the terms (lone = opt, one = one, some = many). Sibling signatures are disjoint by default and signatures can be marked as *abstract* indicating that their *subsignatures* form a partition. We did not include disjoint/partition features in records because it requires all siblings to be declared simultaneously in the same refinement. *Facts* can be added to constrain signatures with implicit quantification over the instances of the signature. For records, disjointedness, partition and additional constraints are specified separately by adding extra Event-B axioms or invariants. Alloy is a single level specification method, without support for refinement. Hence there is no need (or opportunity) to progressively develop record structures in the way that we do via record inheritance and extension mechanisms. Furthermore, Alloy is verified by model checking rather than theorem proof.

VDM [3] is one of the earliest formal modelling languages and has a sophisticated notion of structured data types for many decades. However, although theoretical work has been done on reification of data structures, tool support for refinement with theorem proving appears to be lacking. Hence it enjoys more user-oriented specification features, but less verifiable abstract modelling capabilities, than we present here for Event-B.

Z [11] is also a well-established formal specification language. Z 'schema' provide a mechanism for structuring data (and behaviour), allowing the schema to be extended and promoted (to a set of instances). In this sense Z schema go beyond simple data structuring. Z does have a notion of refinement, however, "it is well known that the operators of the Z schema calculus are not monotonic with respect to refinement, which limits their usefulness in software development" (Lindsay Groves [9]).

UML-B Class diagrams [13] provide a way to structure data in a similar way to records. Classes, attributes and associations are linked to Event-B data elements (carrier sets, constants, or variables) and generate constraints on those elements that reflect the data relationships. A class represents a set of instances as does a record and attributes or associations are similar to fields. However, class diagram models provide more options (e.g. multiplicity of fields, partitioning of subsets) than are required in records. Initially, we considered whether a clean human-usable text persistence for class diagrams might provide an efficient route to textual record structures. However, a human-usable text persistence is more than a view for editing. The idea is to use an elegant concrete syntax, free of machine parsing details (such as found in e.g. XML), for all purposes. This means that the human-readable elegant syntax must be capable of recording every detail of the model. The abstract syntax (meta-model) for class diagrams has been designed to support diagram editors. For example, associations are contained by the diagram root, not by a class. Since the additional options and structure differences of class diagrams must be accommodated in the persistence, they impact the concrete syntax for records. Therefore, while class diagrams remain an alternative option for data structuring, it is beneficial to provide a separate textual syntax and tooling for records in Event-B.

6   Conclusion and Future Works

In the Event-B formal language, record structures can be defined indirectly by using projection functions on a set to define fields, but there is no 'built-in' support for direct definition of record structures. Directly defined records improve the clarity of models without impacting on proving. Previous attempts [14] to add support for records were partially successful but have not endured. Here we contribute a new, improved approach to records, integrated within the CamilleX textual framework, that addresses some of the limitations of [14]. In particular, we have designed a new notation for extensible records, so that records can be smoothly extended and refined during the refinement process. Furthermore, record structures will help identify program data when generating code from Event-B models which is a future research direction [15].

The record syntax helps modellers to directly represent the semantics of the modelled data by collating associated data projections within their common domain. We have discussed how records can possess fields implicitly via their inherits, extends and refines relationships and how these scoping issues are affected by the visibility of the Event-B components via the normal Event-B component relationships (refines, sees and extends). Implicit visibility of data is not a new issue introduced by records, but is revealed when we start to consider the collation of associated data projections in records. Hence records lead us to address this visibility issue that already exists in Event-B. In future work we will consider tooling to help modellers, for example by providing contextual information about the fields that are implicitly in scope of a record.

We have been conservative in our approach, only introducing features for records when we feel there is a convincing need for them. In some areas, where we felt there were both pros and cons, we will assess the case in future work. One example of this is the possibility of providing a syntax for invariants inside records which would increase the localisation of information about the record and allow us to generate the 'lifting' quantification automatically. However, we would have to provide a mechanism for naming the quantification instance identifier (i.e. similar to 'self') and complications may arise when the property is not entirely encapsulated within the record. Therefore we have decided to defer this issue for further assessment and utilise standard Event-B invariants which provides maximum flexibility.

Acknowledgements. This work is supported by the following projects: - HiClass project (113213), which is part of the ATI Programme, a joint Government and industry investment to maintain and grow the UK's competitive position in civil aerospace design and manufacture. - HD-Sec project, which was funded by the Digital Security by Design (DSbD) Programme delivered by UKRI to support the DSbD ecosystem.

References

1. Abrial, J.-R.: Modeling in Event-B: System and Software Engineering. Cambridge University Press, Cambridge (2010)
2. Abrial, J.-R., Butler, M., Hallerstede, S., Hoang, T.S., Mehta, F., Voisin, L.: Rodin: An open toolset for modelling and reasoning in Event-B. Softw. Tools Technol. Transfer **12**(6), 447–466 (2010)
3. Bjørner, D., Jones, C.B.: Formal Specification and Software Development. Prentice Hall, Hoboken (1982)
4. Fritz, F., Snook, C., Iliasov, A.: Event-B and Rodin Wiki: EMF Framework for Event-B (2009). http://wiki.event-b.org/index.php/EMF_framework_for_Event-B. Accessed 01 Feb 2021
5. Dghaym, D., Hoang, T.S., Butler, M., Hu, R., Aniello, L., Sassone, V.: Verifying system-level security of a smart ballot box. In: Raschke, A., Méry, D. (eds.) ABZ 2021. LNCS, vol. 12709, pp. 34–49. Springer, Cham (2021). https://doi.org/10.1007/978-3-030-77543-8_3
6. Evans, N., Butler, M.: A proposal for records in Event-B. In: Misra, J., Nipkow, T., Sekerinski, E. (eds.) FM 2006. LNCS, vol. 4085, pp. 221–235. Springer, Heidelberg (2006). https://doi.org/10.1007/11813040_16
7. Eysholdt, M., Behrens, H.: XText: implement your language faster than the quick and dirty way. In: OOPSLA, pp. 307–309. ACM (2010)
8. Salehi Fathabadi, A., Snook, C., Hoang, T.S., Dghaym, D., Butler, M.: Extensible record structures in Event-B. In: Raschke, A., Méry, D. (eds.) ABZ 2021. LNCS, vol. 12709, pp. 130–136. Springer, Cham (2021). https://doi.org/10.1007/978-3-030-77543-8_12
9. Groves, L.: Refinement and the z schema calculus. Electron. Notes Theoret. Comput. Sci. **70**(3), 70–93. REFINE 2002, The BCS FACS Refinement Workshop (Satellite Eventof FLoC 2002) (2002)
10. Hoang, T.S., Snook, C., Dghaym, D., Salehi Fathabadi, A., Butler, M.: The CamilleX framework for the Rodin platform. In: Raschke, A., Méry, D. (eds.) ABZ 2021. LNCS, vol. 12709, pp. 124–129. Springer, Cham (2021). https://doi.org/10.1007/978-3-030-77543-8_11

11. Davies, J., Woodcock, J.: Using Z: Specification, Refinement and Proof. Prentice Hall, Hoboken (1996)
12. Jackson, D.: Software Abstractions: Logic, Language, and Analysis. The MIT Press, Cambridge (2012)
13. Snook, C., Butler, M.: UML-B: formal modelling and design aided by UML. ACM Trans. Softw. Eng. Methodol. **15**(1), 92–122 (2006)
14. Snook, C.: Event-B and Rodin Wiki: Records Extension (2010). http://wiki.event-b.org/index.php/Records_Extension. Accessed 01 Feb 2021
15. Sritharan, S., Hoang, T.S.: Generating SPARK/Ada from Event-B models. Submitted to iFM 2020 (2020)
16. Steinberg, D., Budinsky, F., Paternostro, M., Merks, E.: Eclipse Modeling Framework. The Eclipse Series. 2nd edn. Addison-Wesley Professional, Boston (2008)

Development of Critical Systems
with UML/OCL and FoCaLiZe

Messaoud Abbas(✉), Fatima Haloua(✉), and Ammar Boucherit(✉)

LIAP Laboratory, University of El Oued, PO Box 789, El Oued, Algeria
{messaoud-abbas,haloua-fatima,ammar-boucherit}@univ-eloued.dz

Abstract. Before the use of critical systems, they must be free of security threats described at the specification stage. On the first hand, high levels of safety highly recommend the use of formal methods to check such security requirements. On the other hand, most software development methods recommend graphical tools, such as UML (Unified Modeling Language) and OCL (Object Constraint Language), to visualize and specify system components at the first development stages. In this context, we propose a life-cycle development approach that combines UML/OCL and the FoCaLiZe formal environment for the development of critical systems. The combination of UML/OCL and FoCaLiZe facilitates the development of such systems and ensures the constraints imposed by standards. In this approach, we highlight the development stages, starting from UML/OCL model until the generation of secure code. In order to check security requirements, we use Zenon, the automatic theorem prover of FoCaLiZe. As an example of a critical system, we present the development stages of a theoretical (mathematical) system.

Keywords: Software engineering · Development life cycles · Critical systems · Formal methods · Verification · UML · OCL · FoCaLiZe

1 Introduction

We have already formalized most UML/OCL elements with FoCaLiZe [1], an object-oriented development environment using a proof-based formal approach. The static aspects were formalized in [2–4] and the dynamic aspects were formalized in [5,6]. These contributions have only defined transformation rules from UML/OCL to FoCaLiZe. However, such transformation rules have not been exploited in a general software engineering approach. The latter remains a future prospect in the aforementioned articles.

Therefore, As an application of our previous works, this paper presents a life-cycle development approach that combines UML/OCL and formal methods for the development of critical systems. This approach should cover most development life-cycle phases. In other words, the formal method itself must provide all development phases, from specification and design until code generation and maintenance. UML and OCL are used as a starting point for the development.

© Springer Nature Switzerland AG 2021
L. Bellatreche et al. (Eds.): MEDI 2021 Workshops, CCIS 1481, pp. 16–30, 2021.
https://doi.org/10.1007/978-3-030-87657-9_2

Through UML we design the model architecture and through OCL we specify its requirements. Then, the UML/OCL model is transformed into the target formal method that should maintain perfectly its architecture and specification. We should also allow an interactive process between UML/OCL and formal method to cover all life-cycle stages and facilitate software maintenance.

In the case of critical systems, software components have to be really compliant with the specified requirements. Here, formal methods are highly recommended for the specification, coding and verification of such systems. In fact, the development of safety critical systems have the greatest interest in terms of verification during all the development phases. Standards such as IEC-61508 [7] and Common Criteria for security evaluation [8] provide requirements about verification to be performed along each stage of the life-cycle.

Formal methods such as Event-B [9] and HOL-OCL [10] provide frameworks that cover most life-cycle development stages, from system specification until coding and maintenance phases. Formal methods are strongly based on mathematical and logical concepts, which makes them not favoured by developers. Contrary to UML/OCL, it is difficult to specify a system and design its architecture with formal methods, mainly in the first development stages where non specialized users may be involved. This is why most software development methods use UML (Unified Modeling language) and OCL (Object constraint Language) in the first stage of software development [11]. Note that, although OCL enables formal specification (well defined syntax), UML/OCL lacks formal bases to prove that OCL constraints are maintained within the development stages.

Thus, to consider the above life-cycle requirements, our choice naturally focused on FoCaLiZe. On the formal side, FoCaLiZe is inspired from Coq [12] and OCaml[1] and on the design and architecture side it is inspired from Object-Oriented programming paradigm. FoCaLiZe supports most of UML conceptual and architectural features such as encapsulation, inheritance (generalization/specialization), multiple inheritance, function redefinition, late-binding, dependency, templates and template bindings [2–4]. These features help to maintain UML/OCL model components and properties in the target formal model. However, the FoCaLiZe programming language is a purely functional language. Functional paradigm is also recommended for critical system development, to avoid any side effect aspects. For proof and verification, FoCaLiZe uses its own proof language (FPL) and its automated theorem prover Zenon [13]. The theorem prover Zenon makes the user intervention much easier since it manages to fulfill most of the proof obligations automatically. In addition, whenever such a proof fails, Zenon helps the user to locate the source of the inconsistency. When Zenon succeeds, it provides automatically a Coq code which will be checked by the Coq theorem prover. Coq will act as an assessor, not only on all the proofs contained in the development but also on the whole consistency of the model [14].

We illustrate our approach with the development of a theoretical algebraic example, the structures `Group`, `Ring` and `Field`. The example is sufficiently restrictive to comply with paper size limitations.

---

[1] Objective Caml programming language: http://ocaml.org/.

This document is organized as follows: Sects. 2 and 3 present FoCaLiZe and UML concepts. Section 4 describes the outline of our development approach. Before concluding, Sect. 5 shows a slight on related works.

2 FoCaLiZe Concepts

FoCaLiZe is a complete development environment that integrates a programming language, a requirement specification language and a proof language. A FoCaLiZe development is organized as a hierarchy of **species** that may have several roots. This hierarchy is built step by step (incremental approach), starting with abstract specifications and heading to concrete implementations using object oriented features such as inheritance and parameterization.

A **species** is the main brick in a FoCaLiZe development. It is a structure that resembles Object-Oriented classes and grouping together the carrier type of the species, functions to manipulate this carrier type, logical properties and proofs. The general syntax of a species (see Table 1) uses the following methods:

- The carrier type (**representation**), describes the data structure of the species. The representation of a species can depend on the representation of other species. It is mandatory and can either be explicitly given or delayed and has to be later on provided, through inheritance.
- Function declarations (**signature**), specify functional types that will be defined later through inheritance, no computational body is provided at the first specification stage.
- Function definitions (**let**), which are functional types together with computational bodies.
- Properties (**property**), statements expressed by a first-order formula specifying requirements to be satisfied in the context of the species. Their proofs are delayed and have to be provided through inheritance.
- Properties together with their proofs (**theorem**).

As we mentioned above, species have object-oriented flavors. We can create a species from scratch or from other species using (multiple) inheritance. Through inheritance, it is possible to associate a definition of function to a signature or a proof to a property. Similarly, it is possible to redefine a method even if it is already used by an existing method. The late-binding mechanism ensures that the selected method is always the latest defined along the inheritance tree.

A species is said to be **complete** if all declarations have received definitions and all properties have received proofs. The representations of complete species are encapsulated through species **interfaces**. The interface of a complete species is the list of its function types and its logical statements. It corresponds to the end user point of view, who needs only to know which functions he can use, and which properties these functions have, but doesn't care about the details of the implementation. When complete, a species can be implemented through the creation of collections. A collection can hence be seen as an abstract data type, only usable through the methods of its interface.

Table 1. The syntax of a species

spec	::=	**species** *species_name* [(*param* [{ , *param*}*])] =
		[**inherit** *spec_def* [{ , *spec_def*}*] ;]
		{*methods*;}* **end**;;
param	::=	*ident* **in** *type* | *ident* **is** *spec_def*
spec_def	::=	*species_name*
		| *species_name* (*param* [{ , *param*}*])
methods	::=	*rep* | *signature* | *let* | *property* | *theorem*
rep	::=	**representation =** *type*;
signature	::=	**signature** *function_name* : *function_type*;
let	::=	**let** [**rec**] *function_name* = *function_body*;
property	::=	**property** *property_name* : *property_specification* ;
theorem	::=	**theorem** *property_name* : *property_specification*
		proof = *theorem_proof*;

3   UML/OCL

UML and OCL are often adopted as a modeling standard in the software development life-cycles. UML helps to design, visualize and document the artifacts of a system. OCL is a formal declarative language that enables to specify UML model components. A UML model is a set of diagrams describing the static and the behavioral aspects of software systems. The current study supports the following subset of UML2 class diagram features:

- UML classes with attributes and operations;
- Inheritance and multiple inheritance with method redefinition and late binding;
- OCL constraints, and OCL constraints (multiple) inheritances.

The inheritance of OCL constraints means that the OCL constraints of a super-class are automatically propagated through simple and multiple inheritances to its sub-classes.

An **OCL Constraint** is a statement of the OCL language [15] which uses types and operations on types. We distinguish between primitive types (**Integer**, **Boolean**, **Real** and **String**), enumeration types, object types (classes of UML model) and collection types. For brevity, only OCL invariants are considered in this paper. An OCL **invariant** is a first order expression attached to class elements (attributes and/or methods) and must be true for all instances of that class at any time.

Example of a UML/OCL Model
We present here a theoretical (mathematical) example rather than an industrial example for two reasons. First, the used example allows for a more simple,

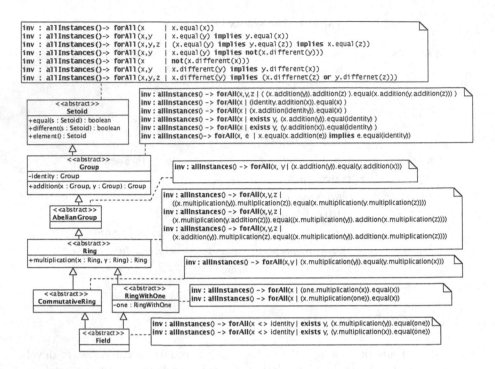

```
inv : allInstances()-> forAll(x     | x.equal(x))
inv : allInstances()-> forAll(x,y   | x.equal(y) implies y.equal(x))
inv : allInstances()-> forAll(x,y,z | (x.equal(y) implies y.equal(z)) implies x.equal(z))
inv : allInstances()-> forAll(x,y   | x.equal(y) implies not(x.different(y)))
inv : allInstances()-> forAll(x     | not(x.different(x)))
inv : allInstances()-> forAll(x,y   | x.different(y) implies y.different(x))
inv : allInstances()-> forAll(x,y,z | x.differnet(y) implies (x.differnet(z) or y.differnet(z)))
```

```
<<abstract>>
Setoid
+equal(s : Setoid) : boolean
+different(s : Setoid) : boolean
+element() : Setoid
```

```
inv : allInstances() -> forAll(x,y,z | ( (x.addition(y)).addition(z) ).equal(x.addition(y.addition(z))) )
inv : allInstances() -> forAll(x | (identity.addition(x)).equal(x) )
inv : allInstances() -> forAll(x | (x.addition(identity)).equal(x) )
inv : allInstances() -> forAll(x | exists y, (x.addition(y)).equal(identity) )
inv : allInstances() -> forAll(x | exists y, (y.addition(x)).equal(identity) )
inv : allInstances()-> forAll(x, e | x.equal(x.addition(e)) implies e.equal(identity))
```

```
<<abstract>>
Group
-identity : Group
+addition(x : Group, y : Group) : Group
```

```
inv : allInstances() -> forAll(x, y | (x.addition(y)).equal(y.addition(x)))
```

```
<<abstract>>
AbelianGroup
```

```
inv : allInstances() -> forAll(x,y,z |
    ((x.multiplication(y)).multiplication(z)).equal(x.multiplication(y.multiplication(z))))
inv : allInstances() -> forAll(x,y,z |
    (x.multiplication(y.addition(z))).equal((x.multiplication(y)).addition(x.multiplication(z))))
inv : allInstances() -> forAll(x,y,z |
    (x.addition(y)).multiplication(z).equal((x.multiplication(y)).addition(x.multiplication(z))))
```

```
<<abstract>>
Ring
+multiplication(x : Ring, y : Ring) : Ring
```

```
inv : allInstances() -> forAll(x,y | (x.multiplication(y)).equal(y.multiplication(x)))
```

```
<<abstract>>
CommutativeRing
```

```
<<abstract>>
RingWithOne
-one : RingWithOne
```

```
inv : allInstances() -> forAll(x | (one.multiplication(x)).equal(x))
inv : allInstances() -> forAll(x | (x.multiplication(one)).equal(x))
```

```
<<abstract>>
Field
```

```
inv : allInstances() -> forAll(x <> identity | exists y, (x.multiplication(y)).equal(one))
inv : allInstances() -> forAll(x <> identity | exists y, (y.multiplication(x)).equal(one))
```

Fig. 1. Example of UML/OCL model

practical, and detailed overview of the modelling and verification phases than an industrial example. Second, we have chosen an algebraic example whose basic properties have already been proven in FoCaLiZe libraries (basic properties on integers), which facilitates the proof of its theorems and make it comply with the page limit.

In mathematics, algebraic structures are strictly formal theoretical models. Each structure has its own elements and specifications and may be used as a basis for the definition of a new algebraic structures. So, at the first development stage, it is possible to use UML and OCL to design the architecture of algebraic structures and specify their requirements (properties) with OCL.

The model presented in Fig. 1 shows the UML architecture of the three algebraic structures **Group**, **Ring** and **Field**. The class **Group** (models algebraic groups) inherits the class **Setoid**. The latter is an abstract class that specifies any non-empty set with an equivalence relation on equality (the operation **equal**). The attached OCL constraints to the class **Setoid** specify the main properties of an equivalence relation (reflexivity, symmetry and transitivity):

- reflexivity: inv : allInstances()-> forAll(x | x.equal(x))
- symmetry: inv : allInstances()-> forAll(x | x.equal(x))
- transitivity: inv : allInstances()-> forAll(x | x.equal(x))

The other constraints specify the operation different (the inverse of equal). The closure operation addition is the group operation (internal composition law). The OCL constraints attached to the class Group specify the group properties (associativety, identity element and inverse element):

- Associativety:
  ```
  inv : forAllInstances()->(x,y,z |
  ((x.addition(y)).addition(z)).equal(x.addition(y.addition(z))))
  ```
- Identity Element (left and right):
  ```
  inv : forAllInstances()->(x | (identity.addition(x)).equal(x))
  inv : forAllInstances()->(x | (x.addition(identity)).equal(x))
  ```
- Inverse Element:
  ```
  inv : forAllInstances()->(x | exists y,
  (x.addition(y)).equal(identity))
  inv : forAllInstances()->(x | exists y,
  (y.addition(x)).equal(identity))
  ```

The class AbelianGroup specifies abelian groups, the closure operation (addition) is commutative:

- Commutativity:
  ```
  inv : forAllInstances()->(x,y |
  (x.addition(y)).equal(y.addition(x)))
  ```

The class Ring models Algebraic rings. It inherits all properties (attributes, operations and OCL constraints) of the class AbelianGroup and species its second closure operation multiplication. The latter must satisfy two properties (see their OCL specification in Fig. 1):

- Left and right distributivity of the operation multiplication over the operation addition.
- Associativity of the operation multiplication.

The class CommutativeRing models algebraic commutative rings, rings with commutativity of the second closure operation (multiplication). So, It inherits Ring with an additional property (see the attached OCL constraint in Fig. 1).

Similarly, the class RingWithOne models rings with neutral element for the operation multiplication. Here, the attribute one of the class RingWithOne plays this role. Finally, the class Field (see Fig. 1) models algebraic fields. Mathematically, a field is a commutative ring with neutral element that accepts inverse element on the second closure operation (multiplication). So, the class Field inherits all attributes, methods and OCL constraints of its super-lasses (multiple inheritance). In addition it specifies the existence of the inverse element with regards to multiplication (left and right), as follows:

- ```
  inv: forAllInstances()->(x <> identity |
  exists y, (x.multiplication(y)).equal(one))
  ```

- ```
  inv: forAllInstances()->(x <> identity |
  exists y, (y.multiplication(x)).equal(one)).
  ```

4 Development Process

Let's start with a general overview on the proposed development approach. Figure 2 shows the development framework that integrates a UML/OCL tool, the transformation rules (from UML/OCL into FoCaLiZe) and the FoCaLiZe environment. The proposed framework involves a development team with UML/OCL users and FoCaLiZe experts. Thus, to produce a secure code, starting from a UML/OCL model, we follow the steps:

1. Designing the UML/OCL model using a UML2 tool that supports the specification of OCL constraints. These UML/OCL tools export graphical UML/OCL models into textual specifications following the XMI (XML Metadata Interchange) standard [16]. In this framework we have used the Papyrus[2] tool.
1. Restructuring the generated XML document. This module modify the appearance order of XML elements (tags), according to the syntactic and semantic dependencies between UML classes. A UML class cn_i is syntactically and semantically dependent on another class cn_j if the class cn_i inherits from the class cn_j, the class cn_i is parameterized by the class cn_j, the class cn_i is dependent on the class cn_j or the class cn_i is a bound class generated by a binding relationship from the class cn_j. In such way, we construct a dependency graph that will guide the transformation of the UML class diagram into FoCaLiZe.
2. Generating a FoCaLiZe specification from the UML/OCL model. Here, we use the transformation rules described in [2–4]. The generated formal and abstract model reflects perfectly the original UML/OCL model with all its methods, properties, relationships and conceptual (specification) scope. All these features are maintained within a purely functional scope and with the possibility to check properties using the Zenon theorem prover. In the latest versions of FoCaLiZe, some test generation techniques are also available.
3. Completion of the generated FoCaLiZe code and specification. In this step, a FoCaLiZe developer implements all undefined methods (representations + function signatures), until reaching the final code. The implemented methods should ultimately satisfy all the properties (theorems) derived from the OCL constraints.
4. Integration of proof indications for the derived properties (from OCL constraints). Here, the developer organizes the proof in steps (using FPL). Each step provides proof hints that will be exploited by Zenon (the automatic theorem prover of FoCaLiZe) to handle the proof when compiling the FoCaLiZe code.
5. Compiling the FoCaLiZe code using the `focalizec` command. The latter invokes Zenon to find proof. When Zenon succeeds, it provides automatically a Coq code which will be checked by the Coq theorem prover. Coq plays the role of a third participant to assess all the proofs contained in the development and the whole consistency of the model [14].

---

[2] Papyrus homepage: https://www.eclipse.org/papyrus/.

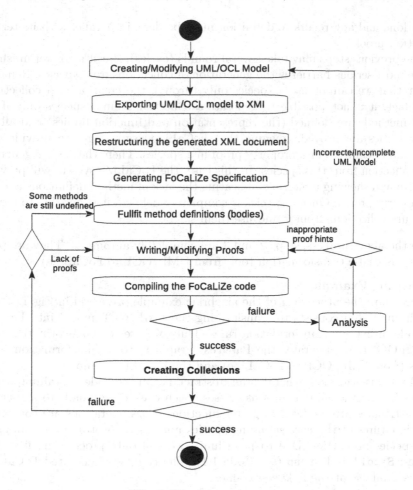

Fig. 2. Development process

When a proof fails, the FoCaLiZe compiler indicates the line of code responsible for the error. The FoCaLiZe developer (expert) interprets the error message. There are Two kinds of errors:

- The original UML/OCL model incorrect or incomplete.
- The proof hints (tactics) are not properly provided to lead the proof to
  its end.

In the first case, it is necessary to convey the message to UML users inorder to
correct and/or complete the UML model, and then restart the development
cycle again. In the socond case, the FoCaLiZe developer must modify his
original source file (FoCaLiZe source) to provide a tractable proof script for
Zenon.

Note that in addition to explicit proof obligation (derived from OCL properties), the FoCaLiZe compiler adds implicit proof obligations when analyzing
species. In particular, if one function is redefined, all related proofs must be

re-done and any recursive definition must be done in parallel with its termination proof.

7. The previous steps may take several rounds (cycles). But it's not yet finished, the most serious barrier is the generation of collections from species. Remember that we cannot use a species only through the creation of a collection. In fact, it is not possible to generate a collection from a species only if all its methods are defined (the representation and function bodies) and all its properties are proved. Imagine that FoCaLiZe users forget to provide one method definition or a property proof in a species. Then, they try to generate a collection from this species. In this case, the FoCaLiZe system will prevent them and showing a message indicating the lack of method definitions and/or property proofs. Once a species is completely defined, it is possible to create secure collections from it and use them safely.

In the above process, steps 2 and 3 are completely automatic. They are part of the automatic transformation tool (from UML/OCL to FoCaLiZe).

Processing Example

Let's see now the processing of the algebraic example presented in Fig. 1.

The first step consists to transforming the UML/OCL model into FoCaLiZe code, using our transformation rules. Thus, we use the transformation tool UML2FOC[3] that integrates the Papyrus[4] graphical tool, transformation templates (from UML/OCL to FoCaLiZe) and the FoCaLiZe compiler.

The transformation generates an abstract FoCaLiZe code containing seven species having the same names as classes. Each class corresponds to a species, class attributes are modeled as getter functions, class operations are converted into signatures of the corresponding species and OCL constraints are mapped into species properties. Due to page limit, we will only process the first two species: Setoid and Group (see Code 1.1). The complete generated FoCaLiZe code is available at the link: source-file.

Code 1.1. Transformation of the classes Setoid and Group

```
(*** The species Setoid ***)
species Setoid =
 signature element : Self;
 signature equal : Self -> Self -> bool;
 signature different : Self -> Self -> bool;
 property equal_reflexive : all x : Self, !equal (x, x);
 property equal_symmetric : all x y : Self,
    Self!equal (x, y) -> !equal (y, x);
 property equal_transitive : all x y z : Self,
    !equal(x, y) -> !equal (y, z) -> !equal (x, z);
 property same_is_not_different : all x y : Self,
    !different (x, y) <-> ~ (!equal (x, y));
```

---

[3] UML2FOC is a prototype that we have developed to validate the transformation rules from UML/OCL to FoCaLiZe: http://www.univ-eloued.dz/uml2foc/.

[4] Papyrus: https://www.eclipse.org/papyrus/.

```
property different_is_irreflexive: all x : Self ,
    ~(!different (x, x));
property different_is_symmetric: all x y : Self ,
    !different (x, y) -> !different (y, x);
property different_is_complete: all x y z : Self ,
!different(x, y)->(!different(x, z)\/!different(y, z));
end;;
(*** The species Group ***)
species Group = inherit Setoid;
(* The Group binary operation *)
signature addition : Self -> Self -> Self ;
(* Neutral element *)
signature identity : Self;
(* addition is associative *)
property associativity : all x y z : Self ,
    !equal( addition(x, addition(y, z)),
            addition(addition(x, y), z) ) ;
(* identity is right neutral *)
property identity_is_right_neutral : all x:Self ,
            !equal(!addition(x, !identity), x);
(* identity is left neutral *)
property identity_is_left_neutral : all x : Self ,
            !equal(!addition(identity, x), x);
(* Any element from group have an inverse *)
property inverse_right : all x:Self , ex y:Self ,
            !equal(addition(x, y), !identity);
property inverse_left : all x:Self , ex y:Self ,
            !equal(addition(y, x), !identity);
(* identity is unique *)
property identity_is_unique : all e : Self ,
  (all x : Self , !equal(x,!addition(x,e))) ->
                            !equal(e,!identity);
end;;
```

The generated FoCaLiZe code (Code 1.1) contains only signatures (no function bodies are provided yet) and properties (no proofs are provided yet). When users compile this code, no error message will be shown. But when they try to generate collections from the derived species (**Setoid** and **Group**), FoCaLiZe will prevent them and invite them to provide definitions (function bodies) to all methods and proofs to all properties.

Now it is the role of the FoCaLiZe user to complete the generated species. Some proofs could be handled based on the existing properties and signatures. However, some other proofs will be delayed until the implementation of the representation (the carrier type of species) and functions.

For example, see the proof of the property **identity_is_unique** of the species **Group** (Code 1.2). It uses the properties **identity_is_right_neutral** and **identity_is_left_neutral** of the current species (**Group**) as premises, but also the properties equal_transitive and equal_symmetric of the super species Setoid.

Code 1.2. Proof of the property identity_is_unique

```
species Group = inherit (Setoid).
 ...
 property identity_is_unique : all e : Self,
   (all x : Self, !equal(x,!addition(x,e))) ->
                       !equal(e,!identity);
 proof of identity_is_unique =
<1>1 assume e : Self,
   hypothesis H1: all x : Self, !equal(x,!addition(x,e)),
   prove !equal(e,!identity)
   <2>1 prove !equal(!identity,!addition(!identity,e))
       by hypothesis H1
     <2>2 prove !equal(e,!identity) by step <2>1
     property !identity_is_right_neutral,
     !identity_is_left_neutral, !equal_transitive,
     !equal_symmetric
     <2>3 qed by step <2>2
<1>2 conclude;
end;;
```

Here Zenon succeeds to find the proof. If the proof fails, the FoCaLiZe compiler will show a message highlighting the source of the error (see Fig. 2).

The Group $(\mathbb{Z}, +)$
In order to use the generated species Group, let us see the development of the concrete group $(\mathbb{Z}, +)$. It is the set of integers $(\mathbb{Z})$ equipped with integer addition $(+)$ and the neutral element 0. Thus, the FoCaLiZe user creates the species GroupZPlus that inherits the abstract species Group and defines all its undefined methods and prove all its unproven properties (see Code 1.3). Here, we use definitions and theorems from the standard FoCaLiZe library (basics) on integers.

Code 1.3. Creating the Group $(\mathbb{Z}, +)$

```
species GroupZPlus = inherit Group;
representation = int;
let identity = 0;
let equal = syntactic_equal;
let element = identity;
let addition = ( + );
proof of equal_symmetric = by definition of
               equal property basics#beq_symm;
proof of equal_transitive = by definition of
               equal property basics#beq_trans;
proof of equal_reflexive = by definition of
```

```
                 equal property basics#beq_refl;
proof of identity_is_right_neutral = by property
   basics#int_0_plus , equal_transitive , equal_symmetric ;
proof of identity_is_left_neutral = by property
   identity_is_right_neutral , basics#int_plus_commute ;
proof of associativity = by property
                basics#int_plus_assoc;
proof of inverse_right = by property
                identity_is_right_neutral;
proof of inverse_left =  by property
                identity_is_left_neutral;
end;;
```

After providing all definitions, the FoCaLiZe user could now pass the barrier of creating collections. The collection Zplus (see Code 1.4) implements the final species GroupZPlus. It is a final entity that can be safely exploited by final users.

Code 1.4. Creating Collections

```
collection Zplus = implement GroupZPlus ; end;;
```

At this stage, the FoCaLiZe user has defined all methods and prove all properties of the species GroupZPlus that inherits the species Group. The latter itself has already been inherited from the species Setoid. Then, he creates a collection in order to use the model in practice. Now to compile the FoCaLiZe source (*source.fcl*) succefully we use the command *focalizec* as follows:

```
focalizec source.fcl
Invoking ocamlc...
>> ocamlc -I /usr/local/lib/focalize -c source.ml
Invoking zvtov...
>> zvtov -zenon /usr/local/bin/zenon -new source.zv
Invoking coqc...
>> coqc -I /usr/local/lib/focalize -I /usr/local/lib/zenon source.v
```

As we can notice here, after verification of the syntax, we will get two generated files: *source.ml* (the OCaml code) and *source.zv* (the "pre-"Coq code). In its turn, the command *focalizec* invokes Zenon through the command *zvtov source.zv* which replaces the proofs written in the FoCaLiZe Proof Language by the effective Coq proofs found by the Zenon theorem prover. Coq code will be checked by the Coq theorem prover.

5   Related Work

We have already formalized most UML/OCL elements with FoCaLiZe, the static aspects [2–4] and the dynamic aspects [5,6]. These works have prepared the road to the proposal of this article. The transformation rules were formally checked and tested, using a denotational semantics [2].

The authors of [14] propose a development life-cycle approach adapted to the FoCaL[5] specificity and compliant with independent assessment requirements, through a complete example. The presented approach showed how the FoCaL development environment can help to fulfil requirements upon the development of critical systems. However, a complete development life-cycle should integrate a modelling graphical tool, such as UML, in the first development stages. Our proposal enhance the contribution of this article through the combination of UML/OCL and FoCaLiZe.

In [17], the authors describe how the FoCaLiZe environment can be used to formally express specifications and to develop through a progressive refinement the design and implementation of secure systems. Hence, they propose a modular implementation of a generic framework for the definition of security policies together with certified enforcement mechanism for these policies. Although the authors of this article talked about FoCaLiZe as an Object oriented programming environment, the first design stages are not familiar in software development. As we commented the previous work [14], it is useful to enhance the proposed policies with a pure Object Oriented graphical modelling tool for the first specification and design phases.

Other formal methods have also been used for the development of life cycle in critical system engineering. Among the closest formal methods to compare with FoCaLiZe is the B method [18] through its Event-B variant [9]. There are several proposals using Event-B in the development of critical systems. Among the most recent contributions is [19]. The latter shows a formal approach to rigorous development of critical systems using Event-B. Another recent contribution using Event-B [20]. demonstrates diagrammatic Event-B formal modelling of a hybrid, 'fixed virtual block' approach to train movement control for the emerging European Rail Traffic Management System.

As a comparison, FoCaLiZe has a better natural correspondence with UML class diagrams than Event-B which has no lifting mechanism (for specifying the characteristics of a set of instances). Event-B has strong support for refinement which is useful to support inheritance but the relationship to class inheritance has to be explicitly encoded via subsets of instances. Whereas, FoCaLiZe has specific (natural) support for inheritance between species. In fact, these features are required for stepwise design and architecture. Thus, when transforming an Object Oriented graphical model (UML/OCL) into Event-B, most Object Oriented features will be manufactured and then we can not reason similarly on both original and target models. However, Event-B has very good support for (mostly) automatic proof to verify constraints and refinement whereas FoCaLiZe requires more manual input to achieve the verification.

---

[5] FoCal is the previous name of the FoCaLiZe environment. Since 2009, the FoCal environment was rewritten from scratch and got the name FoCaLiZe. This rewriting mainly affected the syntax of the environment.

6   Conclusion and Perspectives

In this article we have proposed a development life-cycle for critical systems. Thus, we have combined UML/OCL as a graphical and visual tool and FoCaLiZe as a formal method. Thanks to FoCaLiZe features, the proposed approach covers all development stages: specification, design, architecture, implementation, test/verification/proof and maintenance. For a complete life-cycle, the proposed approach enables a coming and going between UML/OCL and FoCaLiZe, until the generation of secure usable components. The proposed process will be useful for any critical system modeled with a UML class diagram and specified with OCL constraints (class invariants). However, it is necessary to provide FoCaLiZe libraries for proofs relating to each new application domain. In this paper, we have used proofs on integer (to generate the concrete group $(\mathbb{Z}, +)$), which are already provided in the FoCaLiZe standard libraries.

In this article we have only used a small prototype (UML2FOC) to validate our proposal. As a future work, we plan to develop a complete framework that integrates UML/OCL tools, FoCaLiZe and transformation templates. To meet the high level safety/security requirements, this framework should be within a single formalism. All phases will be treated within this formalism to avoid any additional traceability when changing from one phase to another.

References

1. Hardin, T., Francois, P., Pierre, W., Damien, D.: FoCaLiZe: Tutorial and Reference Manual, version 0.9.2. CNAM/INRIA/LIP6 (2018). http://focalize.inria.fr
2. Abbas, M., Ben-Yelles, C.B., Rioboo, R.: Formalizing UML/OCL structural features with focalize. Soft Comput. **24**(6), 4149–4164 (2020)
3. Abbas, M., Ben-Yelles, C.B., Rioboo, R.: Formalizing UML/OCL multiple inheritance with focalize. In: 2018 International Conference on Smart Communications in Network Technologies (SaCoNeT), pp. 261–266. IEEE (2018)
4. Abbas, M., Ben-Yelles, C.-B., Rioboo, R.: Modeling UML template classes with FoCaLiZe. In: Albert, E., Sekerinski, E. (eds.) IFM 2014. LNCS, vol. 8739, pp. 87–102. Springer, Cham (2014). https://doi.org/10.1007/978-3-319-10181-1_6
5. Abbas, M., Rioboo, R., Ben-Yelles, C.B., Snook, C.F.: Formal modeling and verification of UML activity diagrams (UAD) with focalize. J. Syst. Archit. **114**, 101911 (2021)
6. Abbas, M., Ben-Yelles, C.B., Rioboo, R.: Modelling UML state machines with FoCaLiZe. Int. J. Inf. Commun. Technol. **13**(1), 34–54 (2018)
7. Brown, S.: Overview of IEC 61508. Design of electrical/electronic/programmable electronic safety-related systems. Comput. Control Eng. J. **11**(1), 6–12 (2000)
8. Public Key Infrastructure and Token Protection Profile: Common criteria for information technology security evaluation. National Security Agency (2002)
9. Abrial, J.R.: Modeling in Event-B: System and Software Engineering. Cambridge University Press, Cambridge (2010)
10. Nipkow, T., Paulson, L.: Isabelle HOL-the tutorial (2001)
11. Unhelkar, B.: Software Engineering with UML. CRC Press, Boca Raton (2017)
12. Coq: The Coq Proof Assistant, Tutorial and Reference Manual, version 8.4. INRIA - LIP - LRI - LIX - PPS (2012). http://coq.inria.fr/

13. Bonichon, R., Delahaye, D., Doligez, D.: Zenon: an extensible automated theorem prover producing checkable proofs. In: Dershowitz, N., Voronkov, A. (eds.) LPAR 2007. LNCS (LNAI), vol. 4790, pp. 151–165. Springer, Heidelberg (2007). https://doi.org/10.1007/978-3-540-75560-9_13

14. Ayrault, P., Hardin, T., Pessaux, F.: Development life-cycle of critical software under FoCal. Electron. Notes Theor. Comput. Sci. **243**, 15–31 (2009)

15. OMG: OCL: Object Constraint Language 2.4, January 2018. https://www.omg.org/spec/OCL/2.4/PDF

16. OMG: Xml metadata interchange (XMI) specification 2.5.1, June 2015. https://www.omg.org/spec/XMI/2.5.1/PDF

17. Doligez, D., Jaume, M., Rioboo, R.: Development of secured systems by mixing programs, specifications and proofs in an object-oriented programming environment: a case study within the focalize environment. In: Proceedings of the 7th Workshop on Programming Languages and Analysis for Security, pp. 1–12 (2012)

18. Abrial, J.R.: The B-Book: Assigning Programs to Meanings. Cambridge University Press, Cambridge (2005)

19. Singh, N.K., Lawford, M., Maibaum, T.S., Wassyng, A.: A formal approach to rigorous development of critical systems. J. Softw. Evol. Process **33**, e2334 (2021)

20. Dghaym, D., Poppleton, M., Snook, C.: Diagram-led formal modelling using iUML-B for hybrid ERTMS level 3. In: Butler, M., Raschke, A., Hoang, T.S., Reichl, K. (eds.) ABZ 2018. LNCS, vol. 10817, pp. 338–352. Springer, Cham (2018). https://doi.org/10.1007/978-3-319-91271-4_23

Systematic Assessment of Formal Methods Based Models Quality Criteria

Lorenzo Maldini[1]([⊠]) [iD] and Stephen Wright[2] [iD]

[1] ECS, University of Southampton, Southampton, UK
`hal1e20@soton.ac.uk`, `lorenzomaldini@vivaldi.net`
[2] Department of Engineering, Mathematics and Design,
University of West of England, Bristol, UK
`Steve.Wright@uwe.ac.uk`

Abstract. When presented with two fully proved formal methods-based specifications, how can a System Engineer decide which is superior when both models specify the same requirements, but in two different ways? This paper investigates and propose a methodology by which formal methods (using the specific example of the Event-B notation) can be differentiated in terms of their quality, using criteria that may be highly subjective in nature. Established complexity functions applied to software are not applicable to formal methods, thus the paper proposes a new function which quantifies the "quality" of a given model. Complexity is not the only factor involved in determining the quality of formal methods, the quality of system thinking involved also play an impactful role. We propose a quality function which uses the well-established properties of axiomatic systems in theoretical mathematics with the addition of a specifically formulated complexity function. The distinction criteria are based on evaluating how four main properties have been achieved: "Consistency", "Completeness", "Independence" and "Complexity". We base our approach according to the paradigm of; "if the formal specification looks visually complicated for a set-theory novice, then it is a poorly modeled specification". Furthermore, we explore the notion of Miller's rule (magic No. 7) to define what "good" should look like. We conclude that we need more than Miller's 7, we need 1, 2 and 3 to help us with defining what good quality looks like, by taking human cognitive capacity as a benchmark. This novel approach implies considerable further research, described in future work section.

Keywords: Formal methods · Systems engineering · System thinking · Event-B · Model based system engineering · Miller's rule · System complexity function · Information processing capacity

1 Introduction

Software engineers utilize various metrics that help them to decide whether a particular program is "good" or "bad" and are mainly focused on measuring the complexity of an algorithm [11]. Computational complexity theory is an essential part of computer science since it also informs the optimization of a given program to solve a certain

© Springer Nature Switzerland AG 2021
L. Bellatreche et al. (Eds.): MEDI 2021 Workshops, CCIS 1481, pp. 31–45, 2021.
https://doi.org/10.1007/978-3-030-87657-9_3

problem, or even whether the program is the right algorithm for the purpose. There are multiple software complexity measures, ranging from as simple as the number of lines of code to as detailed as the number of variable definitions/usage associations. Consequently, choosing the appropriate complexity measure can be a tedious exercise and criteria becomes essential to establish an order to help with choosing the right measure. One important criterion for metric selection is uniformity of application, known as "open re-engineering" [12]. The idea behind the latter concept is to draw a distinctive independence between concrete implementation and modeling abstractions. Abstractions enable meaningful complexity evaluation, while making concrete source codes and language specific quality metrics hinders the usability range.

As for formal methods, the challenge is different, in the sense that there is more than mere implementation complexity, there is the system thinking involved in the process. It is highly likely that a System Engineer could potentially compose two completely different formal methods interpretations of the exact same system specification. The question we ask, what would make the better solution. There is currently no specific method to allow formal methods practitioners to make an informed selection between the two. This paper proposes some criteria that can potentially contributes towards a research thread in quality metrics for formal methods. Each respective criterion is quantified by a given formula.

The main motivation behind this contribution emerged while we were trying to figure out how can we evaluate whether a formal specification, related to an aircraft landing gear case study, is a good or bad [18].[1] This pursuit had led us to realize that there may be no specific scheme available for formal methods, and formal methods practitioners make their own judgment on the size and complexity level, to be introduced as part of a solution, without the guidance of some systemic metric that can keep track how their formal design decisions they make impact systemically [13]. The main purpose of formal methods, from a System Engineering point of view, is to eliminate ambiguity of specification and check the validity of system requirements. System development process entails extensive communication activities, among various types of stakeholders, within which formal methods-based specification may need to be communicated and evaluated. Also, the process may include communication among formal methods practitioners and software engineers, therefore, having a quality metric that can be optimized supports maintaining a good practice in reducing un-necessary complexities that may result in counter-productive effort in translating specification into computer codes.

One of the challenges of Formal Methods in Systems Engineering practice is the excessive complexity connotation that is associated with it [13]. Therefore, providing a metric, with which formal methods quality can be classified and quantified, should assist developers to maintain the simplest form possible in describing a specification. Furthermore, quality quantification metrics can contribute towards a cost estimation process for formal design development. To give an arbitrary example; evaluating working hours taken to produce a given complexity level.

---

[1] This paper is produced as an output from Lorenzo Maldini's (previously known as Haider Al-lami) bachelor's degree thesis titled "The Application and Analysis of a Landing Gear System Formal methods in Event-B".

2 Literature Review

Complexity measures should have both descriptive and prescriptive elements. Descriptive measures relate to measuring how error-prone the software, how hard it is to understand, how hard it is to modify and test. While prescriptive measures identify operational steps to help control software, for instance splitting complex modules into multiple simpler modules, or indicating the amount of testing required on given modules. Furthermore, good complexity metrics are predictive, i.e. Correlate with something interesting. Specific complexity value should mean the same thing regardless of the programming language used for an application. The most basic complexity measure is the number of code-lines. The latter method does not meet the open reengineering criterion since it is sensitive to programming language, coding style and textual formatting of the source code. On the other hand, a cyclomatic complexity measure, which measures the amount of decision logic in a source code function is a better application of open reengineering criterion. The latter method is better known as McCabe complexity. Examples of current complexity measures [12]:

- Cyclomatic complexity v(G): Amount of decision logic.
- Essential complexity ev(G): Amount of poorly-structured logic.
- Module design complexity iv(G): Amount of logic involved with subroutine calls.
- Data complexity (sdv): Amount of logic involved with selected data references.

McCabe complexity is calculated using as the number of decision points $+1$ (for structured programming). For example, suppose an algorithm that has 5 decision nodes (if statements), then McCabe complexity number for this algorithm would be 6. McCabe complexity is also related to testability of a method/procedure but not the testability of a specific path. McCabe complexity does not take into consideration the feasibility of paths (in terms of whether there are specific values for the variables that force the execution through them) [16].

Contemporary software metrics mainly describe the software but cannot describe the comprehensibility of the software parts. Comprehensibility of the software parts can be related to the same psychological factor that limits people's ability to do mental manipulations of no more than 7 objects at the same time [17].

Function complexity is another method to define the complexity of a software. The idea assumes that the greater the distance in lines of code between related functions the more cognitive effort is required to be expended to understand the connections between functions during the initial stages of program comprehension. The function complexity is derived in two parts; by determining how many functions are called within a program and calculating the distance in lines of code that lie between a function call and functions' declaration, the following equation is used to describe FC (Function Complexity) [7]:

$$FC = \sum_{i=1}^{name} distance_i \tag{1}$$

Where, name represent the number of functions or procedures that are called, and distance represent the number of lines of code from functions' declaration. Spatial complexity term can then be defined as the total summation of the complexity ratings for each function it contains:

$$PC = \sum_{i=1}^{n} FC_i \qquad (2)$$

Where n is the total number of functions that exist within a program.

The Halstead metric [2] suggests several different measures that draw upon several different operators and operands that a program contains. Neither McCabe's cyclomatic complexity metric nor Halstead's proposal explicitly draws inspiration from the psychology of programming, nor takes into consideration human factors.

The methods discussed here, which focus on presentation of the detail of formal notations, are complementary to a range of other techniques developed to enhance understandability of formal methods via improvements to high level structuring. In the domain of Event-B, some techniques include provision of graphical interfaces based on the ubiquitous Unified Modelling Language (UML) [14]. The latter is a useful approach to handle the visual complexity of formal specification.

3 Visual Complexity

We could approach the problem through analyzing the underlying mathematical characteristics of proof obligations, the mathematical functioning of various operations, and employ something like Category or Graph Theory concepts to help us build some concise evaluation in a manner McCabe has done. However, the main difference between a source code (written in traditional programming language) and formal methods based language is that the latter is a concise description of high-level statements (I.e., requirements), while the source code is a procedural process to execute tasks instantiated from requirements. Therefore, formal methods approach focuses on the "what" while source code focuses on the "how" [11]. Hence, adopting an approach like McCabe's, may lead us to imprecise & unnecessary effort that could be simplified by mere adopting the connotation of "what looks aesthetically complex to a novice in set theory eye, is a complex model". The approach assumes that formal methods are intended to act as a proxy intermediate representation of requirements encoding to address the issue of ambiguity of requirements, source code and the traceability between them to a human reviewer.

In the literature review, we presented a notion suggested by [12] that complexity measures should have the following elements: descriptive, prescriptive, and predictive. We argue that a fourth element should be considered when complexity is evaluated directly relating to the cognitive ability of a human to digest the context. Since formal methods intrinsically address the "what", Visual Complexity beyond a certain level can easily defeat the human mind's ability to perform accurate interpretation of symbolic formulations, especially when combined with the technicalities of formal notation. Therefore, a fourth element may be added into the list of elements to be considered by any complexity measure which is "Perceived Complexity" or the "perceptive" criterion.

Current software complexity metrics do not directly consider such generic human Cognitive aspects related to source code comprehension [8]. Although, spatial complexity function provides an advancement towards consideration of human psychology, however mainly proposed to evaluate Object Oriented programming. The structure of formal methods is generally based on the concepts of abstraction and refinement and are generally declarative in nature with little emphasis on the explicit ordering of imperative commands familiar to conventional coding. For example, current complexity functions take into account the number of steps required to implement a solution to a given problem (typically implemented by imperative programming techniques), but formal methods typically define the nature of the problem itself, which may be unrelated to the complexity of the solution. Hence, to support our hypothesis we define Visual Complexity as the aesthetic complexity of written code to human perception.

One of the main reasons behind the introduction of bugs in any code is misinterpretation of the purpose of the code. Unless the written code is comprehensibly explanatory of its purpose, those who are going to read the code afterwards will have to spend time trying to figure out what the code is trying to achieve. One way to address it is through commenting which can be viewed as a method to manage complexity and may be could provide reviewers with some form of appreciation of how complex a source code is. As for formal modeling, relying on commenting alone to handle the understanding of formal system components usually accompany the implicit assumption that whatever the comment says, the formal code is the exact representation of it. What we really need is to see a simple formal code that we can easily verify the comment context against it rather than rely solely on trust that the specialist has done the job correctly. Hence, having a meaningful quality metric for formal methods can help reviewers to decide whether the specialist should work a bit harder to simplify further the formal code in-hand.

The practicality of addressing complexity of a written formal code can be stretched beyond mere quality improvement. Promoting a culture of neat, tidy, and easy to follow formal code writing style may also help to lessen the discouragement of newcomers to the realm of formal methods practice. Therefore, it is useful to have a complexity function and some quality metrics that takes into consideration the readability of the written code. When we address complexity and readability, we are specifying the reliability of design process to produce efficient formal specification. Therefore, the approach taken in this paper towards quantifying quality is mainly based on how reliable the formal modeling process involved in specifying systems.

4   Formal Methods Readability

The main purpose of formal methods techniques is to avoid mistakes at early stage of development lifecycles. Therefore, having a method which allows the formal methods designer to measure and monitor the development of complexity in the model becomes a very useful tool. For example, Fig. 1 shows only one fragment of some larger statement.

It can be noted how some practitioners choose to over-complicate formal specification. Such trend in synthesizing formal specification can have a counterproductive impact on addressing ambiguity of specification.

$$act31 \; : general\_EV\_func :\in (1..3 \rightarrow POSITIONS) \times (1..3 \rightarrow A\_Switch) \times$$
$$(1..3 \rightarrow (GEARS \rightarrow BOOL)) \times (1..3 \rightarrow (GEARS \rightarrow BOOL)) \times (1..3 \rightarrow$$
$$GEAR\_ABSORBER) \times (1..3 \rightarrow (DOORS \rightarrow BOOL)) \times (1..3 \rightarrow (DOORS \rightarrow$$
$$BOOL)) \times (1..3 \rightarrow BOOL) \rightarrow BOOL$$
$$act32 \; : close\_EV\_func :\in (1..3 \rightarrow POSITIONS) \times (1..3 \rightarrow A\_Switch) \times$$
$$(1..3 \rightarrow (GEARS \rightarrow BOOL)) \times (1..3 \rightarrow (GEARS \rightarrow BOOL)) \times (1..3 \rightarrow$$
$$GEAR\_ABSORBER) \times (1..3 \rightarrow (DOORS \rightarrow BOOL)) \times (1..3 \rightarrow (DOORS \rightarrow$$
$$BOOL)) \times (1..3 \rightarrow BOOL) \rightarrow BOOL$$

Fig. 1. An illustration of what we would classify as a very complicated model [6]

5   Methodology

The strategy we adopted in synthesizing the metrics mainly heuristic in nature. We underpinned the heuristics on the notion that formal methods (such as Event-B) are intrinsically application of axiomatic systems, with invariants (theorems & axioms), events, and guards being viewed as a system of lemmas. The rationale behind such assumption is that requirements essentially are predicates, that can be evaluated in a binary fashion. In a similar fashion, Ogleznev and Surovtsev [9] draw an analogy that government constitution is a form of an informal axiomatic system. The authors base this notion on the assumption that "Axioms are considered as contextual definitions of … concepts by means of which they are formulated". They argue that comparing a government constitution as an axiomatic system allows them to verify and validate its constructs against a well-founded criteria: Completeness, Consistency, and Independency. This is an interesting view on how formal modeling can contribute towards the verification and validation of new laws before they may introduce in the constitution. Albeit, the authors do not propose to formalize the constitution, it can be argued that laws have a systemic impact on human population livelihood. Since laws have a critical impact on societal livelihood and wellbeing, it would make sense to consider formal verification and validation of laws before being constituted as part of logical scrutiny process.

From such thought experiment, we draw the analogy that system requirements are like a constitution which the system must adhere to. Since formal specification describe mathematically those requirements, they too can be viewed as a rigorous representation of the system constitution.

In theoretical mathematics, axiomatic systems have a defined quality criterion. The term axiomatic system quality refers to how good and well-founded an axiomatic system is. The quality of an axiomatic system is defined by three main properties: Independency, Completeness and Consistency [4]. We attempted to further quantify each criterion and proposed the addition of "complexity function". We derived the quantification from a self-defined requirement on what each quality metric equation should inform the evaluation.

As for quantification of the metrics, it is important to know that we are not proposing a proving method of each criterion. Rather, we are proposing a methodology that quantify the manner each criterion is achieved during formal modeling development. For example:

- The meaning of Consistency and Completeness being done automatically or manually?
- Has the developer set all independent invariants to be non-theorems or has he kept the number of non-theorems to absolute minimum and utilized theorems?
- How complex formal methods are produced?
- How readable (explainable) expressions used?

6 Theoretical Mathematics: Axiomatic Systems (AS)

An axiomatic system is a list of a predetermined set of statements which are accepted as truths with no need for proof. A very good example of AS is; Euclidean Geometry and axioms of the natural numbers. One of the reasons why axiomatic systems are developed was the need to determine precisely which properties of systems can be deduced from self-evident properties [10]. Any set of axioms can be described by three main properties: consistency, independency, and completeness [3].

Typically, limiting axioms to include only statements simple-enough to be intuitive & self-evident is sufficient for practical purposes. Therefore, simplicity of proposed axioms can be identified as virtuous in axiomatic-invariants statements. David Hilbert, one of the most important mathematicians in the twentieth century, specified simplicity of axioms as the fourth property of a good and well-founded axiomatic system [5].

6.1 Consistency

The main characteristic of a valid axiomatic system is that axioms do not contradict each other. Consistency may be defined as: "An axiom system is said to be consistent if it is possible for all of the axioms to be true. The axiom system is said to be inconsistent if it is not possible for all of the axioms to be true" [3]. The definition refers to whether axiomatic statements (in the context of formal methods we map the term axiomatic statements to non-theorems type of expressions) include a contradiction.

Consistency is a useful and an important factor to consider as a qualitative criterion that requires to be examined, especially for practical engineering applications. As we argued earlier, it is essential for the engineer to be able to decide whether one solution he/she is developing is the optimum choice. Moreover, it is challenging to prove consistency of axioms, since axioms are put forward to be truths that are accepted without the need of proof. Sometimes, contradictory axiomatic systems may be consistent if any single statement is taken out. This means that entire system is inconsistent rather than one statement [3]. Relative consistency is another method can be used in mathematical logic to proof a consistency of a system [5].

6.2 Completeness

The system is said to be complete if and only if every single theorem is provable (or derivable) by the set of axioms introduced [4]. Completeness is an important property of axiomatic systems, however if a system is not complete, the damage is not as crucial as if it was inconsistent [5]. In retrospect, addressing completeness can be useful as a quality criterion for formal systems. In the sense that, if some model1 contains more Invariants (theorems) which are not derivable by its set of axioms (non-theorems) then it is inferior to some model2 that all of its invariants (of type theorems) are derivable from its axioms (non-theorems). In formal methods context, we see that Completeness can potentially go alongside with Consistency since the act of discharging proof obligations implies the proof of the axiomatic system used is fully consistent and complete.

6.3 Independence

Any axiom is said to be independent if and only if, it is not derived from another axiom [2]. An axiomatic system is called independent if each axiom is independent of others. In other words, redundancy is not desirable in an axiomatic system. Since axioms are statements that are accepted as truths, which is undesirable, we conclude that more redundant axioms imply a more undesirable specification of an axiomatic system. In the context of formal modeling we propose that independency can be managed by monitoring the number of non-theorems introduced relative to the number of theorems proved by them. In other words, if a developer set some invariant as non-theorem that had been proved by another non-theorem, the quality reviewer may invoke the question why such design choice? Consequently, establishing a deeper understanding on the quality of system thinking involved that may reveal some findings.

6.4 Simplicity, the Fourth Property

Simplicity, on the other hand, potentially plays an important part in reliability of formal methods-based specification development process. The property can be analyzed in a quantitative manner. In this paper, simplicity of a model will refer to how easily readable formal statements are. We induce the terms of the metric by evaluating the number of invariants, actions, guards, and number of operations types used in each machine or context.

7 Evaluating the Performance of Formal Specification Reliability

In essence, we are utilizing theoretical mathematics to inform formal specification development of what good modelling should look like. The philosophy we are applying is based on the notion that number of expressions (operations, invariants, actions etc.) compose an overall systemic visual complex. By including other factors such as completeness, consistency, and independency, we can build a view on how model designers approached problems in hand and attempted to improve output quality thus allowing us to evaluate the level of System Thinking involved.

We start with defining what we mean by Formal Model Reliability. A formal model is said to be reliable when it is synthesized with no malicious corner-cutting approach (such as axiomatization for the sake of discharging POs) or over complicating the specification unnecessarily. Reliable Formal Modelling depends on three main factors: Readability, Complexity and Critical System Thinking in proving correctness of specification. To quantify each factor, we will need to have some properties to test performance against.

Starting from Axiomatic Systems properties, we derived four potential properties that can help us with specifying each factor in formal methods-based specification.

Firstly, we studied independence of axioms, How introduced independent axioms impact on model reliability by the formal system designer. We stipulate that Independency test can inform us of what kind of System Thinking the designer adopted in modelling the system. For instance, if every single invariant is a non-theorem and more than 50% of them are redundant or derivable by other non-theorems, then the designer's mind-set can be said to be focused only on discharging proof obligations in expense of increased number of non-theorem invariants. Formal specification reliability increases by decreasing the number of derivable non-theorems. It also increases by decreasing the total number of non-theorems in the model. This can be a useful observation because it demonstrates that the designer could have decided to turn the 50% redundant axioms ratio into theorems to be proved. The designer then must justify why he or she made such design decision. In absence of such metric, it would be difficult to stipulate the number of redundant axioms across a large-scale model. The more redundant non-theorems are introduced, the poorer the proof of consistency claimed.

As for Consistency and Completeness, the main challenge we face is how to compare between two models whose completeness and consistency would have been fully proved and verified? In other words, when all proof obligations are discharged, inherently, the model is proved to be 100% complete and 100% consistent. Since proof obligations (such as feasibility PO) test the consistency of each statement with the given axiomatic invariants and whether the action statements maintain the invariants, thus, by the end of each model, the model will always be 100% complete and consistent. The problem arises: if this is the case, then how are the models can be compared in terms of completeness and consistency? The answer for this problem lies not on how complete or consistent the models are, rather on how completeness and consistency of the model were achieved. We propose the notion that any action, any axiom and theorem in the model should be completely provable automatically in the first instance by the tool used, for example Rodin.

Therefore, we propose that completeness and consistency test of formal modeling to be based on the ratio of the number of POs discharged automatically to the total number of POs discharged interactively. In essence, we are hypnotizing that designer's effort in discharging proof obligations is the quality measure of how reliable completeness and consistency was achieved. In other words, we define that when a designer manually discharges all proof obligations during the development phase, then we run into the risk that some POs may have been maliciously discharged.

Complexity on the other hands, can be influenced by how the above criteria performed. However, in this paper we will consider the factors that influence Visual Complexity as parameters for measuring formal methods systems complexity. We define inefficient complexity in formal modeling as the approach that specifies a simple system functionality in unreasonable number of formal codes and utilize unreasonable number of operational symbols across minimal number of refinements. By unreasonable we propose the consideration of the rule of anything above 3 [20]. In other words, a reasonable complexity of a given invariant, action, guard etc. should not exceed the utilization of 3 operations in one given expression. The rule of 3 is related to the cognitive comprehension of human mind in handling conceptual complexity at a given time. We argue that overloading human mind with excessive operations can potentially lead to mistakes, for example, in Fig. 1, a reviewer is likely be mentally unmotivated to go through a half page of formal specification. A reviewer may then base his/her review on trust that the associated comment is sufficient to explain what the formal code is intended to specify. This way we run into the danger that the designer may incorrectly specified the functionality and due to stress, he or she may have commented incorrectly.

7.1 Consistency and Completeness (1st Criterion)

We propose that the quality of achieving consistency and completeness (CC), composed together, can be evaluated by the ratio of the number of POs that are proved automatically $POAuto_i$ to the total number of POs PO_i in the model:

$$CC = \frac{\sum_{i=1}^{n} POAuto_i}{\sum_{i=1}^{n} PO_i} \tag{3}$$

The metric informs that the more POs are automatically proved, the more we can be assured that consistency and completeness of a model had been achieved reliably.

7.2 Independency (2nd Criterion)

We propose that model Independency (Ψ) can be accounted for by considering nontheorems in total rather than specifically for independent non-theorems only, since reducing the number of all axioms in general will be effective enough to ensure model reliability. For that, we will accept that axioms are independent as they ought to be. Since theorems are more desirable than non-theorems, as they need to be proved rather than to be accepted as undeniable truths, Therefore, we will specify reliability of a model, as a function of independency, by comparing the total number of theorems in a model $thrm_i$ to the number of total invariants (independent axioms & theorems) Inv_i.

$$\Psi = \frac{\sum_{i=1}^{n} thrm_i}{\sum_{i=1}^{n} Inv_i} \tag{4}$$

The metric should be interpreted that the more non-theorems are introduced in the model, the less useful the independency introduced for model reliability. The rationale behind this classification is based on observation that introducing excessive number of non-theorems means a poor System Thinking Approach. We can assume that the designer's aim is to discharge POs in the expense of model reliability.

7.3 Formal Methods Complexity (3rd Criterion)

We hypothesize that Formal methods Complexity increases as the total number of Operations and Expressions increase with respect to total number of refinement modules.

Therefore, the more refinements we introduce with lesser expressions and operations, the simpler the system is.

$$\omega = \frac{\sum_{i=1}^{n} P_i + \sum_{i}^{n} Ops_i + \sum_{i=1}^{n} Var_i}{\sum_{i=1}^{n} Ref_i} \tag{5}$$

Where n denotes the total number of occurrences, P denotes formal expressions (invariants, actions, guards etc.), Ops denotes the formal operations incorporated in the model ($\forall$, $\in$, $\Rightarrow$, $\wedge$ etc.), Var denotes the unique variables introduced in the model and Ref denotes model's refinements.

Another useful metric to approximate the density of operations ρ_{Ops} across expressions which could potentially allow for estimating the cognitive effort required to comprehend a model:

$$\rho_{Ops} = \frac{\sum_{i=1}^{n} Ops_i * \sum_{i=1}^{n} Var_i}{\sum_{i=1}^{n} P_i} \tag{6}$$

The above equation informs that to optimize model readability, developers may want to consider minimizing the number of operations per expression.

8 Formal Model Quality Performance Function

We interpret Quality Performance as how well the system designer manages to handle tradeoff among Readability, Complexity and System Thinking. The better System Thinking (i.e. CC & $\Psi = 1$) and the lesser operational density and complexity introduced, the higher the Quality Performance is:

$$Q_{fm} = \frac{\Psi * CC}{\rho_{Ops} * \omega} \tag{7}$$

9 Cognitive Capacity Benchmark; the Rule of 1, 2, 3, 7

Wright made a remark with regards how much complexity a formal methods practitioner should introduce in every refinement step. He argued that it should be no more than a head full however the task to quantify "how much is a head full" is an impossible endeavor [15]. Albeit, the latter argument may not be an absolute conclusion. It is an important notion to address, considering that comprehension error is a recognized risk that arises due to program complexity [1]. Since formal modeling main goal to reduce error due to ambiguity, creating ambiguous and excessively complex formal methods defeat its intended purpose. Therefore, by addressing the impact of information presented in models on human cognition, we can draw more concise view on what good simplicity looks like. Miler started the agenda of linking cognitive psychology and information theory to propose how much information which is manageable by a human mind [19]. He proposed the amount of data presented in each task that is manageable by human Short-Term Memory (STM) should be around 7 ± 2 items. Throughout the years, magic number 7 have been accepted by communication professionals to be the good guideline average to adopt. However, Doumont [20] argues that 7 is in fact too many. The latter also labels, in terms of human mind capacity to handle information, 3 as the simplest complexity. Furthermore, he argues that 1 to be the focus, the symbol of consistency. While number 2 is symbolic with simplest form of redundancy. We argue that both opinions can be useful for our definition of good formal modeling practices, hence we propose the rule of 1, 2, 3, 7.

Considering the unavoidable impact of complexity on comprehension errors, and what above theorists suggested of what good enough can be, we propose the following schema of what good simplicity in formal methods looks like:

- May be at least 7 levels of refinements for a given solution.
- For every given refinement ensure that no more than 1 new variable is introduced.
- For every given refinement ensure that no more than 2 invariants are introduced.
- Start the abstract machine with 1 variable, 1 invariant, 1 event.
- In every given formal expression ensure that no more than 3 operations are introduced.

The above guideline can be viewed as some instantiation of the rule of 1, 2, 3, 7. We observe that in order to keep complexity down, the number of refinements needs to be high hence we proposed to quantify a "head full" by number 7. In other words, 7 items of information (let it be operations, expressions, variables etc.) in any given presentation to a human mind is a "too-many" thus we should refrain from exceeding this number. However, in terms of complexity, given the inverse relation with number of refinements, 7 would be an appropriate choice to specify what good minimum is for simplicity. We also recognize that there is a trade-off with solution practicalities needs to be considered, for example 3 operations only in each expression may not be sufficient to precisely describe the intended functionality.

10   Case Study

For the case study we will use [6] To validate our proposed criteria. The model utilized Event-B and Rodin tool to formalize several requirements related to aircraft landing gear system. A total of 9 machines were developed and a roughly 11,236 operations (the total count of following operations types: $:=, \in, =, \Rightarrow, \wedge, >, \rightarrow, \mapsto, \rightarrow, x - 1, |, \forall, ()$, $\{\}, \times,.., []$) and roughly 47 unique variable. The model contains roughly: 92 invariants, 1397 actions, 1377 guards, thus the total of applicable formal expressions sum up to 2866 predicates. The developers do not specify how many of the invariants are set to non-theorems, thus invoking a useful question to ask as we won't be able to evaluate the second criterion without such information, in this case we will assume $\Psi = 1$. Moreover, developers specify a total 529 proof obligations, 448 of which discharged automatically. We are not counting the *Model Contexts* in this example due to their absence from the document, normally contexts are also included in the evaluation.

10.1 Consistency and Completeness (1st Criterion)

We can evaluate how CC is achieved by applying Eq. (3):

$$CC = \frac{448}{529} \approx 0.85 \tag{8}$$

The figure above informs the development team that model's Consistency and Completeness are 85% reliable. One of the reasons could relate to the excessive complexity introduced in the model. Therefore, a simpler model could achieve higher CC reliability.

10.2 Formal Methods Complexity (3rd Criterion)

By applying Eq. (5) we stipulate:

$$\omega = \frac{2866 + 11236 + 47}{9} \approx 1575 \tag{9}$$

We can clearly deduce that concentrating such amount of operations in only 9 refinements is rather excessively complex. If we want to reduce complexity down to 3 while keeping the number operations, predicates, and variables the same, we will need to spread the complexity over 4721 refinements. Either way, the formulae reveals a serious issue that would need to be revisited by the developers in how they could reduce the complexity of the model.

10.3 Operations Density Index

Applying formulae (6) estimate the average density of formal expression in the mode to be:

$$\rho_{Ops} = \frac{11236 * 47}{2866} \approx 184 \tag{10}$$

Given that we proposed value of 7 to be a head full (incomprehensible), we can conclude that model readability is more than a head full to be manageable. Thus, there is a high level of risk of comprehension errors. If we would want to reduce the risk down to a value of 3, the developers may want to spread the density of variables and operations over roughly 75441 optimized expressions. Considering that model developers may need to spread complexity over 4721 refinements, increasing expressions volume will result into increasing complexity from 3 up to 7. However, still far less complex than keeping it under 10 refinements. By evaluating optimized expressions total over optimized number of refinements, we conclude a maximum 16 expressions per refinement would suffice to keep complexity of the model at optimal level. Overall, we can conclude that the model produced by [6] needs further work to address quality issues, specially complexity and readability.

Given the above parameters, we evaluate the total Quality of formal model to be:

$$Q_{fm} = \frac{\Psi * CC}{\rho_{Ops} * \omega} = \frac{1 * 0.85}{184 * 1575} \approx 0.000003 \tag{11}$$

The result demonstrates [6] produced a poor-quality model to specify the landing gear system. Excessively dense expressions and excessively complex model. The System Thinking employed into designing the model is measured at 85% reliable, given the assumption of $\Psi = 1$.

11 Conclusion

We aimed to demonstrate the usefulness of having some quality metrics in order to optimize the quality of formal methods. Complexity functions related to software are not adequate to be applied on formal methods since the latter intrinsically focused on the "what" rather than the "how". We then attempted to produce a method to test the quality of formal methods based on axiomatic systems properties: Completeness, Consistency, Independency and Complexity (simplicity). We proposed several equations that could describe how each property is achieved and reveal some insight into the system thinking employed during the development of formal methods. We have also observed the link between human cognition and formal specification, and adopted the rule of 1, 2, 3, 7 to help with identifying what good model look like. Moreover, we understood that the term "Measure" we used in the report may be too ambitious to claim, as the question of quantifying quality is a hard problem to precisely answer. Therefore, we will argue the term "indicator" rather than "measurement" in future papers.

This leads us to draw an indication on follow up future work. An evaluation of the effectiveness of the method is needed. Also, examining more case studies are essential to validate its usefulness. One way to perform such evaluation is by conducting interviews and workshops with formal methods practitioners. What we have not considered in this paper is type-theory based formal methods, we narrowed the focus of the paper to set theory and Event-B for simplicity. The case study needs to be evaluated using other methods and compared with the proposed method. Furthermore, equations presented requires formal analysis to assure correctness. We used the term "complexity" because it is in alignment with common knowledge, from a system science point of view, complex does not equal complicated all the time, there are complexes that are not complicated for example a set of numbers from 0 to 1, it is a complex, but not complicated. In other words, we ought to say, "complication indicator" rather than "complexity measure", there is a difference in connotation between the two phrases which has an impact on precision of expression. An exploration of better ontology, that draws a distinction between "indication & measurement" & "Complexity & Complication", ought to be used according to System Science point view would be an interesting take on the issue of quality measurements.

References

1. Klemola, T., Rilling, J.: Modeling comprehension processes in software development. In: Proceedings First IEEE International Conference on Cognitive Informatics, Calgary, AB, Canada (2002)
2. Halstead, M.H.: Elements of Software Science. Elsevier, New York (1977)
3. Barsamian, M.: Introduction to Axiomatic Geometry. Ohio University, Athens (2017)

4. Partee, B.H., Wall, R.E., Ter Meulen, A.: Mathematical Methods in Linguistics. Kluwer Academic, Dordrecht (1990)
5. Corry, L.: David Hilbert and the Axiomatization of Physics (1898–1918): From Grundlagen der Geometrie to Grundlagen der Physik. Kluwer, Dordrecht (2004)
6. Méry, D., Singh, N.K.: Modeling an aircraft landing system in Event-B. In: Boniol, F., Wiels, V., Ait Ameur, Y., Schewe, K.-D. (eds.) ABZ 2014. CCIS, vol. 433, pp. 154–159. Springer, Cham (2014). https://doi.org/10.1007/978-3-319-07512-9_12
7. Douce, C., Layzell, P., Buckley, J.: Spatial measures of software complexity. In: Proceedings of the 11th Meeting of Psychology of Programming Interest Group (1999)
8. Douce, C., Durant, S.: Understanding program complexity: an approach for study. In: Psychology of Programming Interest Group Annual Conference (2011)
9. Ogleznev, V., Surovtsev, V.: The constitution as an axiomatic system. Axiomathes **28**, 19–232 (2018)
10. Lee, C.W.: Axiomatic Systems. University of Kentucky, Kentucky (1997)
11. Sommerville, I.: Software Engineering. Amsterdam Cape Town Pearson Education Limited, Boston (2016)
12. Watson, A.H., Mccabe, T.J.: Structured Testing: A Testing Methodology. National Institute of Standards and Technology, Gaithersburg (1996)
13. Romanovsky, A., Thomas, M.: Industrial Deployment of System Engineering Methods. Springer, Heidelberg (2013). https://doi.org/10.1007/978-3-642-33170-1
14. Snook, C., Butler, M.: UML-B: formal modeling and design aided by UML. ACM Trans. Softw. Eng. Methodol. **15**, 92–122 (2006)
15. Wright, S.: Formal construction of instruction set architectures. University of Bristol, Bristol (2009)
16. Hummel, B.: McCabe's cyclomatic complexity and why we don't use it. CQSE GmbH, Garchingbei München (2014)
17. Miller, G.: The magical number seven, plus or minus two: some limits on our capacity for processing information. Psychol. Rev. **101**(2), 343–352 (1956)
18. Al-lami, H.M.: The application and analysis of a landing gear. University of the West of England, Bristol, UK (2016)
19. Baddeley, A.: The magical number seven: still magic after all these years? Psychol. Rev. **101**(2), 353–356 (1994). https://doi.org/10.1037/0033-295x.101.2.353
20. Doumont, J.-L.: Magical numbers: the seven-plus-or-minus-two myth. IEEE Trans. Prof. Commun. **45**, 123–127 (2002)

Deriving Interaction Scenarios for Timed Distributed Systems by Symbolic Execution

Boutheina Bannour[1(✉)], Arnault Lapitre[1], and Pascale Le Gall[2]

[1] Université Paris-Saclay, CEA, List, 91120 Palaiseau, France
{boutheina.bannour,arnault.lapitre}@cea.fr
[2] Université Paris-Saclay, CentraleSupélec, MICS,
91192 Gif-sur-Yvette Cedex, France
pascale.legall@centralesupelec.fr

Abstract. In this paper, we propose a symbolic framework to analyze and debug communicating distributed models. We implement dedicated symbolic execution techniques for such models and use them to compute interaction scenarios satisfying a particular user coverage objective. These scenarios reveal emergent temporal and data correlations that are part of the system specification. To support the understanding and the analysis of such learned knowledge, our tooling allows for an intuitive annotated scenario visualization using sequence diagrams. As an application, we develop behavioral models for the so-called distributed Trickle algorithm which manages information dissemination in Wireless Sensor Networks (WSN). We select relevant scenarios which cover critical communications achieving an up-to-date or outdated state of the network.

1 Introduction

Context and Related Work. Symbolic Execution (SE in short) [10] is a powerful execution technique for analyzing programs or models. Its main principle is to execute a program or a model using variables instead of concrete values. SE collects for each explored path a set of logical constraints on the introduced variables for its execution, called Path Conditions (PC). Therefore, such a symbolic path represents a possibly infinite set of concrete paths. As such, SE is a systematic execution technique, which is valuable for the analysis of complex programs or models. Moreover, SE is gaining interest due to the availability of computing resources and the progress made in constraint solving.

SE has been increasingly used in the analysis of concurrent multi-process systems and more recently of distributed systems. Although we are positioning our work at the level of models of distributed systems, we will discuss related approaches dealing with programs [1,11,20,22,23,25] for their relevance and for having addressed early issues related to non-deterministic concurrent executions and/or asynchronous communications. In [1], authors use an object oriented modeling language for programs which allows objects to execute concurrently (or

© Springer Nature Switzerland AG 2021
L. Bellatreche et al. (Eds.): MEDI 2021 Workshops, CCIS 1481, pp. 46–60, 2021.
https://doi.org/10.1007/978-3-030-87657-9_4

synchronize) and to interact by asynchronous method calls. In [25], the Symbolic PathFinder [21] tool is extended to deal with bytecode of multi-threaded Java programs without communication primitives. Another work [18] still based on PathFinder proposes analysis of inter-process communications. In [11], concrete and symbolic execution are combined to provide an efficient analysis based on a fixed order of scheduling multi-threaded programs. In [22], authors implement SE of distributed systems on top of the KLEE tool [5] by unfolding a number of execution paths for some subsystems while keeping track of their communication history in terms of emitted/received network packets and then identifying pairwise states on packets emitting/recipient subsystems. While combinatorial interleaving is often bypassed by using exploration heuristic or partial order reduction techniques, the originality of this work is to come up with an alternative to interleaved execution of distributed subsystems. SE has been extended to models using variants of abstract labeled transition systems, namely Symbolic Transition Systems (STS in short) [6,12]. Timed STSs (or TSTS for short) which extend STS with clocks have been defined later in [3,26,27]. [26,27] are rather a merge of Timed Automata [2] and STS so that clock values represent convex abstractions, known as zones, while [3] uses symbolic techniques to homogeneously handle both clocks and other data variables. The DIVERSITY tool [17] implements the SE of TSTS [3,6] and also provides them with textual syntax and editing features.

Contribution. We adopt a compositional modeling approach based on TSTS like those in [3] for the purpose of modeling behaviors of distributed subsystems. A technical improvement is that we give a new definition of TSTS in which transitions are equipped with an expressive sequential statement language. This statement language mixes computations on clocks and other variables, and enables many steps of communications, guards and variable updates to be combined into a single (symbolic) execution step. The objective is to provide modeling facilities for different levels of detail that may appear in the specification of real distributed systems, such as in the specification of the Trickle case study [13,14,16] which has motivated the present work. We then define models of distributed systems as a collection of TSTSs. These are endowed with SE using asynchronous communication mechanisms for which we define time and data interdependencies. More precisely, our SE mechanisms collect all possible information linking data and time on the execution of distributed subsystems. Thus, we propose identification constraints to take into account that values received at a given port necessarily correspond to a value emitted at a port connected to it. Similarly, since a duration between an emission of a message a followed by a reception of a message b at a given location should be greater than the duration between the reception of a followed by the emission of b at a remote location, we consider constraints on delays separating events (emissions/receptions). As part of our contribution, we implement the proposed TSTS-based distributed models together with their SE in the DIVERSITY tool. Interactions between communicating subsystems can therefore be explored in the tool. In order to primarily assess these interaction behaviors, we propose a dedicated selection method that highlights the emissions and their corresponding receptions.

Structure of the Paper. Sect. 2 presents the motivating example of the Trickle-based information dissemination. Section 3 introduces TSTS and their associated SE mechanisms. In Sect. 4, we define TSTS-based models for distributed systems together with dedicated unfolding techniques applying correlated SE of the involved TSTS under asynchronous communication. Then, we show in the section how interaction scenarios can be selected from such models and discuss experimental results on the Trickle case study. Finally, we give some concluding remarks in Sect. 5.

2 Motivating Example: Trickle-Based Dissemination

Trickle [13,14,16] is the state-of-the-art distributed algorithm for the dissemination of information across a Wireless Sensors Network (WSN). This algorithm is provided as a standard library in TinyOS [15] and Contiki [8], two of the best known firmware Operating Systems (OS) for WSN. Trickle is also used in recently standardized WSN protocols namely the Multicast Protocol for Low Power and Lossy Networks (MPL) [9] and the Routing Protocol for Low Power and Lossy Networks (RPL) [28]. The dissemination of information across the network is through sensor-to-sensor short-range communications since such small devices can be equipped only with small radio antennas. In addition, such communications may be asymmetric: a node can send messages to another node without the opposite being possible. The network can be seen as a directed graph connecting nodes to their neighbors which can be reached by their transmissions. Trickle is a fully distributed algorithm. Each node applies a set of rules according to its state, i.e., the information it holds. The goal is to converge to an updated global state of the network where all nodes have the same information. The Trickle algorithm can be described as follows:

- each node maintains a current interval τ, a counter c and a broadcasting time t in current interval τ,
- global parameters to all nodes (same values) are k the redundancy constant, τ_l the smallest value for τ, and τ_h the largest value for τ,
- each node applies the following rules:
  1. at the start of a new interval a node resets its timer and counter c and sets at random t to a value in $[\tau/2, \tau[$,
  2. if the node receives a message consistent with the information it holds, it increments c,
  3. when its timer reaches t, the node broadcasts a message carrying the information it holds if $c < k$,
  4. when its timer expires at τ, it increases its interval length by setting τ to $\min(2 \cdot \tau, \tau_h)$ and starts a new interval,
  5. when a node receives a message that is inconsistent with its own information, then if $\tau > \tau_l$ it sets τ to τ_l and starts a new interval, otherwise it does nothing.

Each time an inconsistency is detected, the interval τ is set to τ_l, then τ is doubled up to τ_h. Note that the node transmits only if its neighbours are unlikely to be up-to-date, when $c < k$ given c counts receptions of consistent messages in the interval (k is fixed based on neighbours number). If $c \geq k$, the node suppresses the transmission. Moreover, since small intervals are considered immediately after the inconsistency, the frequency of transmissions is greater at the beginning (and decreases when approaching τ_h). This allows nodes to quickly share the same information. Now nodes are not necessarily synchronized, yet Trickle suggests choosing a random t (in $[\tau/2, \tau[$ together with imposing a listen-only period (first half of τ) in order to enhance the distribution of the transmission load between nodes in the interval (and hence energy cost).

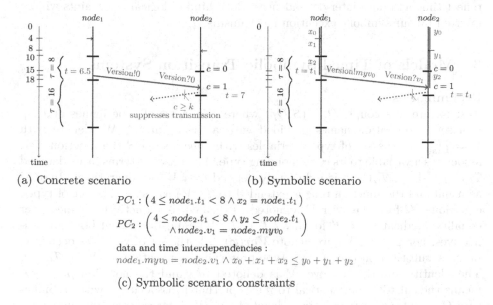

(a) Concrete scenario   (b) Symbolic scenario

$$PC_1 : \left(4 \leq node_1.t_1 < 8 \wedge x_2 = node_1.t_1 \right)$$

$$PC_2 : \left(\begin{array}{c} 4 \leq node_2.t_1 < 8 \wedge y_2 \leq node_2.t_1 \\ \wedge\, node_2.v_1 = node_2.myv_0 \end{array} \right)$$

data and time interdependencies :
$node_1.myv_0 = node_2.v_1 \wedge x_0 + x_1 + x_2 \leq y_0 + y_1 + y_2$

(c) Symbolic scenario constraints

Fig. 1. Illustration of Trickle scenarios

Figure 1 depicts a first scenario (Fig. 1a) between two nodes $node_1$ and $node_2$, each implementing the Trickle algorithm. The second scenario (Fig. 1b) is an abstract scenario that can be obtained by our symbolic execution for which the first scenario is a concretization. The scenarios illustrate the transmission suppress according to Trickle rules, the information being disseminated is a version number. Node $node_1$ emits a version number 0 on its port $node_1.Version$ (denoted by $Version!0$ on the message with source the axis of $node_1$). This version number is received later by node $node_2$ on its port $node_2.Version$ (denoted by $Version?0$ on the message with destination the axis of $node_2$). When $node_2$ receives the same version number as it holds, it increments its counter $node_2.c$ which reaches k ($k = 1$). This results in suppressing the transmission scheduled at the value stored in $node_2.t$ ($node_2.t = 7$) within the second half of the

τ-interval ($node_2.\tau = 8$). Executions at $node_1$ and $node_2$ are given by the following succession of delays and emissions/receptions:

$node_1$: "4, 6, 6.5, Version!0" and $node_2$: "8, 7, 5.5, Version?0"

Initial delays 4 and 8 are measured since a common fictitious time point denoted by 0 on the time axis. They correspond to elapsed time before respectively $node_1$ and $node_2$ are started. The small arrows indicate the start of the nodes on their respective axes. Introducing such delayed initialization is typical for distributed subsystems where there is no global clock. The symbolic scenario encodes such execution using (fresh) variables and logical constraints (Fig. 1c). Constraints $4 \leq node_1.t_1 < 8 \wedge x_2 = node_1.t_1$ and $4 \leq node_2.t_1 < 8 \wedge y_2 \leq node_2.t_1 \wedge node_2.v_1 = node_2.myv_0$ correspond to Path Conditions (PC). On the other hand, constraints $x_0 + x_1 + x_2 \leq y_0 + y_1 + y_2$ and $node_1.myv_0 = node_2.v_1$ reflect time and data inter-dependences. Both kind of logical constraints will be inferred by our symbolic execution mechanisms.

3　Models of Timed Symbolic Transition Systems

Preliminaries

A signature is a couple $\Omega = (S, Op)$ where S is a set of type names and Op is a set of operation names provided with a profile in S^+. We denote with $V = \coprod_{s \in S} V_s$ the set of typed variables with $type : V \rightarrow S$ the function that associates a variable to its corresponding type. The set of Ω-terms in V, denoted $T_\Omega(V) = \coprod_{s \in S} T_\Omega(V)_s$, is inductively defined over V and operations Op of Ω as usual and the function $type$ is extended to $T_\Omega(V)$ as usual. The set of typed equational Ω-formulas over V, denoted as $\mathcal{F}_\Omega(V)$, is inductively defined over equality predicates $t = t'$ for any $t, t' \in T_\Omega(V)_s$ and over usual boolean connectives. For $\varphi \in \mathcal{F}_\Omega(V)$, we denote $Var(\varphi) \subseteq V$ the set of variables occurring in φ. A substitution over V is a type-preserving application $\rho : V \rightarrow T_\Omega(V)$. The identity substitution over V is denoted id_V and the notation $\rho[x \rightarrow t]$ means the substitution identical to ρ except that it associates t with x. Signature Ω includes a particular type, denoted $time \in S$, for representing durations, and which is provided with usual operations, i.e., $<: time \times time \rightarrow Bool$ and $+ : time \times time \rightarrow time, \ldots$

An Ω-model is a set $M = \coprod_{s \in S} M_s$ with M_s a set of values for type s, hence inducing a mapping between each operation name $f : s_1, \ldots, s_{n-1} \rightarrow s_n \in Op$ and the corresponding concrete operation $f_M : M_{s_1} \times \cdots \times M_{s_{n-1}} \rightarrow M_{s_n}$. The set M_{time} is denoted D (for the set of durations) and is isomorphic to the set of non-negative real numbers ($\mathbb{R}_{\geq 0}$). An interpretation is an application $\nu : V \rightarrow M$ that associates a value in M to each variable $v \in V$, canonically extended to $T_\Omega(V)$ and $\mathcal{F}_\Omega(V)$ as usual. For $\nu \in M^V$ and $\varphi \in \mathcal{F}_\Omega(V)$, the satisfaction of φ by ν is denoted $M \models_\nu \varphi$ and is inductively defined w.r.t. the structure of φ as usual. We say a formula $\varphi \in \mathcal{F}_\Omega(V)$ is satisfiable, denoted $Sat(\varphi)$, if there exists $\nu \in M^V$ such that $M \models_\nu \varphi$.

A *TSTS-signature* is defined as a tuple $\Sigma = (\Omega, A, K, P)$, where $\Omega = (S, Op)$ is a signature, A, K and P are pairwise disjoint sets of variables representing respectively *generic data variables* (A), *clock variables* (K) and *ports* (P). Variables in A and P can take any type in S whereas variables in K (i.e. *clocks*) are limited to type *time*. So, each class of variables is partitioned w.r.t. types $s \in S$, hence $A = \coprod_{s \in S} A_s$, $P = \coprod_{s \in S} P_s$ whereas K can be reduced to K_{time}[1].

As glimpsed in the introduction, transitions of TSTS will be defined using sequential scheduling of statements like in programming languages.

Sequential Statements

A sequential statement (statement in short) *stm* is defined as follows:

$$stm ::= \textbf{skip} \mid p?x \mid p!t_1 \mid x:=t_2 \mid \textbf{newfresh}(x) \mid [\phi] \mid$$
$$stm_1;stm_2 \mid \textbf{if}(\phi) \textbf{ then } stm_1 \textbf{ else } stm_2$$

with $p \in P$, $x \in A \cup K$, $t_1 \in \mathcal{T}_\Omega(A \cup K)_{type(p)}$, $t_2 \in \mathcal{T}_\Omega(A \cup K)_{type(x)}$, and $\phi \in \mathcal{F}_\Omega(A \cup K)$. The set of statements over Σ is denoted by $Stm(\Sigma)$.

skip is the null statement; $p?x$ denotes the reception, on port p, of a value which is stored in x, whereas $p!t_1$ denotes the emission, on port p, of the value corresponding to the current interpretation of term t_1; $x := t_2$ assigns the variable x with a new value denoted by t_2; **newfresh**(x) randomly assigns x with a new value; $[\phi]$ denotes a condition on variables which enables the statement execution. Moreover, statements can be built using sequence (;) and condition (**if** ... **then** ... **else** ...).

Timed Symbolic Transition Systems (TSTS)

A TSTS over a TSTS-signature $\Sigma = (\Omega, A, K, P)$ is a triple $\mathbb{G} = (Q, q_0, Tr)$, where Q is the set of states, $q_0 \in Q$ is the initial state and Tr is the set of transitions of the form (q, stm, q') with $q, q' \in Q$, and $stm \in Stm(\Sigma)$.

For a transition $tr = (q, stm, q')$, q (resp. q') is the source (resp. target) state of the transition. *stm* is called the statement of the transition. We use the notations $src(tr)$, $tgt(tr)$ and $stm(tr)$ to refer to q, q' and *stm* respectively. For $\mathbb{G} = (Q, q_0, Tr)$ a TSTS, we use $States(\mathbb{G})$, $initSt(\mathbb{G})$ and $Trans(\mathbb{G})$ to respectively refer to Q, q_0 and Tr.

Figure 2 depicts a TSTS which models the behavior of a Trickle node, according to rules described in Sect. 2.

From the initial state q_0, the node assigns t with a new fresh value using the action **newfresh**(t), this new value for t is constrained by the guard $[\tau/2 \leq t < \tau]$. The clock[2] cl is initially reset, as glimpsed before it is used to activate the different Trickle events, that is when reaching t and starting new τ-intervals.

When node reaches the state q_1, it can receive a message (on port Version) from a neighboring node before reaching t (loop-transitions on q_1). Such message carries a version number. The message is processed as follows (see macro updateVersion): if the node is outdated, it updates its version number ($myv := v$). Trickle rule related to (in)consistency is then applied: if the neighbour is

---

[1] Variables in A_{time} are not of the same nature of those in K as they are only used to store terms of type *time*, while clocks are used to measure time passing.

[2] Any clock of a given node, here cl, evolves only if a transition of that node is executed: the clock is then implicitly incremented by a fresh duration.

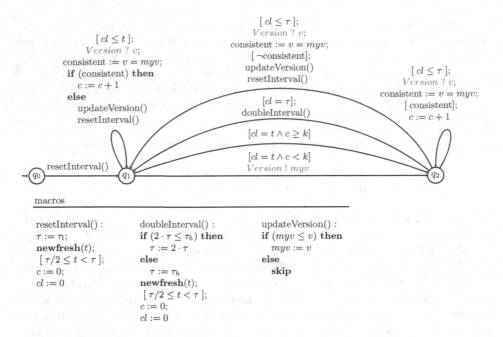

Fig. 2. Timed Symbolic Transition Systems (TSTS) modeling a Trickle node

up-to-date, i.e., the node and its neighbour agree the version number, then the counter c of the node is incremented; otherwise a new τ-interval is considered for the node where τ and c are reset, since additional little-spaced messages are needed for convergence. When $cl = t$, the transmission is scheduled only if $c < k$ in order to inform neighbors of version number the node possesses (horizontal transition $q_1 \rightarrow q_2$), otherwise the process does nothing (curved transition $q_1 \rightarrow q_2$).

At the state q_2, while $cl \leq \tau$ and messages are consistent (agree on version number), the counter c is incremented (loop-transition on q_2), upon the reception of inconsistent message (different version number) the node starts a new τ-interval by resetting both cl and c (upper transition $q_2 \rightarrow q_1$). When $cl = \tau$, the node increases the listening interval by doubling τ (up to τ_h) (lower transition $q_2 \rightarrow q_1$).

Symbolic Execution of TSTS

Given a TSTS signature $\Sigma = (\Omega, A, K, P)$, we introduce a set of so-called *fresh variables* (also called symbolic parameters) $F = \bigcup_{s \in S} F_s$ which is disjoint from both the data and clock variables of Σ (i.e. $F \cap (A \cup K) = \emptyset$). We write $F_t \subseteq F$ for the set of fresh variables of type *time* and $F_d = F \backslash F_t$ for the set of non-time fresh variables. In the following, we will refer to the signature $\Sigma_F = (\Omega, F, \emptyset, P)$ to define the symbolic execution of a TSTS which is defined over Σ.

Execution contexts (EC in short) are data structures used to store information characterizing logical constraints on symbols related to an actual execution of a TSTS. An EC of a TSTS $\mathbb{G} = (Q, q_0, Tr)$ is a tuple $ec = (q, \pi, \lambda, \theta, Act, pec)$:

- $q \in Q$ is the (current) state of $\mathbb{G}$,
- $\pi \in \mathcal{F}_\Omega(F)$ is a constraint that should be satisfiable in order to reach ec.
- $\lambda : A \cup K \rightarrow \mathcal{T}_\Omega(F)$ is a type-preserving substitution through which data variables of $\mathbb{G}$ are replaced by terms over variables in F,
- $\theta \in \mathcal{T}_\Omega(F_t)$ is a term denoting the sum of durations elapsed so-far since the beginning of the execution of $\mathbb{G}$,
- Act is a sequence of emissions and/or receptions that have occurred since the beginning (; ; stands for the empty sequence),
- and pec is the parent EC which allowed ec to be reached.

We distinguish initial execution contexts of the form $ec_0 = (q_0, true, \lambda_0, z_0, ; ; , self)$ such that λ_0 associates to each variable of $A \cup K$ a fresh variable in F verifying $\forall \theta \in K$, $\lambda_0(\theta) = z_0$ and $\forall x \neq y \in A$, $\lambda_0(x) \neq \lambda_0(y)$ and $\lambda_0(x) \neq z_0$."$self$" is a special identifier indicating that by convention, the parent EC of an initial execution ec_0 is itself. $Var(ec_0) \subseteq F$ is the set of all fresh variables occuring in ec_0. To refer to the constituents of an EC $ec = (q, \pi, \lambda, \theta, Act, pec)$, $q(ec)$ stands for q, $\pi(ec)$ for π, $\lambda(ec)$ for λ, $\theta(ec)$ for θ, $Act(ec)$ for Act and $pec(ec)$ for pec. We denote $\mathcal{EC}(\mathbb{G})$ ($\mathcal{EC}_0(\mathbb{G})$) the set of all (initial) execution contexts ec of $\mathbb{G}$ such that we have $Sat(\pi(ec))$. In order to take advantage that only some components of an EC are likely to be modified at each symbolic execution step, we will use a kind of additive notation which will point out the only modified components of ECs: for example, with ec an EC, $ec' = ec[Act \rightarrow Act; act]$ means that ec' coincides with ec except that the component $Act(ec')$ is $Act(ec); act$.

Symbolic Execution of Statements

Let stm and $\mathbb{G}$ be resp. a statement and a TSTS both defined over Σ and let $ec \in \mathcal{EC}(\mathbb{G})$. The set $SE(stm)_{ec} \subseteq \mathcal{EC}(\mathbb{G})$ of ECs reached from ec by symbolic execution of stm is defined as follows:

$$SE(\mathbf{skip})_{ec} = \{ec\} \tag{1}$$

$$SE(p?x)_{ec} = \{ec[\lambda \rightarrow \lambda[x \rightarrow y], Act \rightarrow Act; p?y]\} \quad y \in F_{type(x)} \tag{2}$$

$$SE(\mathbf{newfresh}(x))_{ec} = \{ec[\lambda \rightarrow \lambda[x \rightarrow y]]\} \quad y \in F_{type(x)} \tag{3}$$

$$SE(p!t_1)_{ec} = \{ec[Act \rightarrow Act; p!\lambda(t_1)]\} \tag{4}$$

$$SE(x := t_2)_{ec} = \{ec[\lambda \rightarrow \lambda[x \rightarrow \lambda(t_2)]]\} \tag{5}$$

$$SE([\phi])_{ec} = \{ec[\pi \rightarrow \pi \wedge \lambda(\phi)]\} \tag{6}$$

$$SE(stm_1; stm_2)_{ec} = \bigcup_{ec'_0 \in SE(stm_1)_{ec}} SE(stm_2)_{ec'_0} \tag{7}$$

$$SE(\mathbf{if}\,(\phi)\,\mathbf{then}\,stm_1\,\mathbf{else}\,stm_2)_{ec} = SE(stm_1)_{ec[\pi \rightarrow \pi \wedge \lambda(\phi)]} \tag{8}$$
$$\cup SE(stm_2)_{ec[\pi \rightarrow \pi \wedge \lambda(\neg(\phi))]}$$

Symbolic Execution of Transitions

Let $tr = (q, stm, q')$ be a transition of $\mathbb{G}$ and $ec = (q, \pi, \lambda, \theta, Act, ec)$ be an EC of $\mathcal{EC}(\mathbb{G})$. The set of ECs $SE(tr)_{ec}$ reached from ec by symbolic execution of tr is defined as the set of all $ec' = (q', \pi', \lambda', \theta + z, Act', ec)$ such that there exists $(q, \pi', \lambda', \theta, Act', pec)$ in $SE(stm(tr))_{ec[\lambda \to \lambda_0']}$ where λ_0' is defined as follows:

$$\lambda_0'(w) = \lambda(w) + z \text{ for } w \in K \quad \text{and} \quad \lambda_0'(w) = \lambda(w) \text{ for } w \in A \qquad (9)$$

with z a fresh variable in F_t, denoted as $delay(ec')$ in the sequel.

The set of ECs ec' reached from of a given EC ec by executing $tr \in Trans(\mathbb{G})$ is obtained in two steps. First, all clocks are increased by the same amount of time, denoted by the $time$-typed variable $z \in F_t$ which allows to obtain the intermediate substitution λ_0' (9). Second, transition statement $stm(tr)$ is evaluated from the newly built context, i.e., ec in which λ_0' replaces λ. ECs obtained then, characterize substitutions λ' reflecting data variables substitutions by new variables as defined by the statement symbolic execution.

Symbolic Execution of TSTS

The symbolic execution of a TSTS $\mathbb{G}$ from $ec_0 \in \mathcal{EC}_0(\mathbb{G})$ is the smallest set of ECs, denoted as $SE(\mathbb{G})_{ec_0}$, satisfying: $ec_0 \in SE(\mathbb{G})_{ec_0}$ and for any $tr \in Trans(\mathbb{G})$, $ec \in SE(\mathbb{G})_{ec_0}$ such that $q(ec) = src(tr)$, we have $SE(tr)_{ec} \subseteq SE(\mathbb{G})_{ec_0}$. This results in a tree structure en-rooted in ec_0.

4 Distributed Models and Interaction Scenarios Derivation

We use TSTS to specify Timed Distributed Systems (DS in short). A remote subsystem is characterized by a TSTS. Communications between subsystems TSTSs are specified by asynchronous data-passing over unbounded fifo queues.

Distributed System Model

A Distributed System model $Sys = (\mathbb{G}_1, \cdots, \mathbb{G}_m, \Gamma)$ is defined by:

- a family $(\mathbb{G}_i)_{i \in \{1,..m\}}$ of TSTS defined over $\Sigma_i = (\Omega, A_i, K_i, P_i)$ verifying that different sub-systems do not share constituents, i.e., $\forall i, j \leq m$ with $i \neq j$, $A_i \cap A_j = \emptyset$, $K_i \cap K_j = \emptyset$ and $P_i \cap P_j = \emptyset$,
- the function $\Gamma : P_{Sys} \to 2^{P_{Sys}}$ specifying connections between ports.

The set of all ports of Sys is denoted by $P_{Sys} = \bigcup_{i \leq m} P_i$. Besides, the set of all generic data variables (resp. clock variables) of Sys is denoted by $A_{Sys} = \bigcup_{i \leq m} A_i$ (resp. $K_{Sys} = \bigcup_{i \leq m} K_i$).

From now on, Sys will denote a generic DS model. We now define the symbolic execution of Sys over the signature $\Sigma_F^{Sys} = (\Omega, F, \emptyset, P_{Sys})$. Figure 3 depicts a DS for a grid topology of four Trickle nodes, each is associated with a TSTS.

System Execution Context. A *system execution context* (or a SC) of Sys is a tuple $ec_{sys} = (ec_1, \cdots, ec_m, \gamma, \chi, pec_{sys})$ where

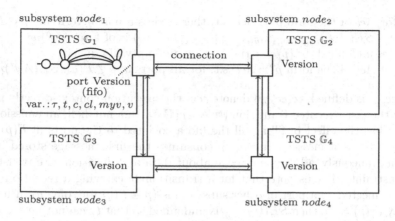

Fig. 3. Distributed System for a Trickle grid topology

- $ec_i \in \mathcal{EC}(\mathbb{G}_i)$ with $i \leq m$, is an EC over Σ_F^{Sys},
- $\gamma : P_{Sys} \rightarrow (T_\Omega(F_d) \times T_\Omega(F_t))^*$,
- $\chi \in \mathcal{F}_\Omega(F)$,
- and pec_{sys} is either the identifier $self$ or any other SC.

$\mathcal{EC}(Sys)$ is the set of all SC of Sys and we can access to components of ec_{sys} using notations $\gamma(ec_{sys}), \chi(ec_{sys})$ or $pec_{sys}(ec_{sys})$.

γ associates to each port the content of its fifo queue in terms of a received piece of data and its emission date. χ represents a constraint on time and data inferred from data exchanges in Sys. As in the unitary case, pec_{sys} gives access to the SC from which ec_{sys} has been built. Similarly, if $pec_{sys} = self$, ec_{sys} is then an initial SC. The symbolic execution of a DS-model consists in executing a transition of one of its component TSTS $\mathbb{G}_i$ and making execution contexts of Sys evolve accordingly. Intuitively, the evolution of the overall SC will essentially concern the EC relating to the TSTS $\mathbb{G}_i$ for which the transition is being executed.

Symbolic Execution of Transition in a DS-Model

For a $SC\ ec_{sys} = (ec_1, \cdots, ec_i, \cdots, ec_m, \gamma, \chi, pec_{sys})$, let tr be a transition in $\mathbb{G}_i$ such that $i \leq m$ and $src(tr) = q(ec_i)$. The symbolic execution $SE(tr)_{ec_{sys}}$ of tr from ec_{sys} is the set of $ec'_{sys} = (ec'_1, \cdots, ec'_i, \cdots, \gamma', \chi', ec_{sys})$ provided that all components of ec' are well defined according to the rules:

- $ec'_i \in SE(tr)_{ec_i}$
- for all $j \leq m$ such that $j \neq i$, $ec'_j = ec_j$
- $(\gamma', \chi') = SE(Act(ec'_i))_{(\gamma, \chi)}$ with $SE(Act)_{(\gamma, \chi)}$ inductively defined or undefined as follows:
  - for Act the empty sequence $(Act =; ;)$, (γ, χ)
  - for Act of the form $p!t; Act'$, $SE(Act')_{(\gamma[q \rightarrow \gamma(q).(t, \theta(ec'_i))]_{q \in \Gamma(p)}, \chi)}$

- for Act of the form $p?x; Act'$ s.t. there exists a port q verifying $p \in \Gamma(q)$,
  * $SE(Act')_{(\gamma[p\rightarrow w], \chi \wedge (\theta(ec'_i) \geq \theta) \wedge (x=t))}$ if $\gamma(p)$ is of form $(t, \theta).w$
  * undefined if $\gamma(p) = \epsilon$ (i.e. $\gamma(p)$ is an empty fifo queue)
- for Act of the form $p?x; Act'$ s.t. for all ports q, $p \notin \Gamma(q)$, $SE(Act')_{(\gamma, \chi)}$.

When ec'_{sys} is defined, $ec(ec'_{sys})$ denotes ec'_i the execution context directly modified by the last executed transition ($tr \in Tr(\mathbb{G}_i)$). In a nutshell, an emission on a port p has the effect of filling all the fifo associated to the ports of $\Gamma(p)$ and the reception of a message on port p consumes the first message stored in its fifo. Simultaneously, all the knowledge about data and durations are translated into constraints. Let us note that for a transition tr carrying a reception on a port p connected to a port of other subsystems ($p \in \Gamma(q)$ for some q), if its fifo is empty ($\gamma(p) = \epsilon$), then $SE(tr)_{ec_{sys}}$ is undefined so that tr cannot be executed in the current SC.

Symbolic Execution of a DS-Model
Let us introduce ec^0_{sys} an initial SC defined as a tuple ($ec^1_0, \cdots, ec^m_0, \gamma_0, true,$ $self$) where for all $i \leq m$, ec^i_0 is in $\mathcal{EC}_0(\mathbb{G}_i)$ and for all p in P_{Sys}, $\gamma_0(p)$ is the empty queue, i.e. is ϵ. The symbolic execution $SE(Sys)_{ec^0_{sys}}$ of Sys is the smallest set of SC containing ec^0_{sys} and all SC reached by symbolic executions of any $tr \in \bigcup_{i \leq m} Trans(\mathbb{G}_i)$ from any $ec_{sys} \in SE(Sys)_{ec^0_{sys}}$. A system symbolic path pa_{sys} is a sequence $ec^0_{sys} ec^1_{sys} \cdots ec^k_{sys}$ such that for all $0 < i < k$, $pec_{sys}(ec^{i+1}_{sys}) = ec^i_{sys}$, we denote $tgt(pa_{sys}) = ec^k_{sys}$, the target of pa_{sys}.

For any $ec_{sys} = (ec_1, \cdots, ec_m, \gamma, \chi, pec_{sys})$, we note $\pi(ec_{sys}) = (\bigwedge_{i < k} \pi(ec_i)) \bigwedge \chi$.

A symbolic path pa_{sys} is feasible iff $Sat(\pi(tgt(pa_{sys})))$.

Selection Method
Interaction scenarios will be selected based on the computation of a feasible path pa_{sys} from the symbolic execution tree of the overall DS model Sys. The method favors the selection of system paths with a high coverage of subsystems pairwise Emissions (**E**) and Receptions (**R**) in the spirit of the work [24] and that of our previous experimental work on Trickle [4,19]. The idea is to guide the SE of Sys with the objective to compute a system path pa_{sys} which covers sequences where an emission ($p!a$) of a piece of data a by some subsystem is followed by the corresponding reception ($q?a$) of a by another subsystem ($q \in \Gamma(p)$). The selection is implemented according to the *Send Receive Pair Coverage criterion (SRPC)* [24] by defining coverage sequences based on internal pairwise Emissions and Receptions. To cope with the potential combinatorial explosion due to asynchrony, we have integrated the SRPC criterion with some exploration heuristics available in the tool DIVERSITY [17].

Experimentation. Table 1 gives some metrics on symbolic exploration for the computation of updated/outdated scenarios on grid topologies T1 (Fig. 3) and T2 (T2 has a connection less). The results are obtained on a PC equipped with an Intel Core i7 processor and 32GB RAM. The outdated scenario given in Fig. 4 is the one described on line 5 of Table 1. We report on the size of all

Table 1. Experimentation for Trickle

Scenario	Exploration	($|\mathbf{E}|,|\mathbf{R}|$)	$|SC|$	Time	Coverage	Rate
Updated (T1)	Heuristic	(5, 11)	7239	1 m	100%	100%
Updated (T1)	BFS	(4, 9)	620120	1 h 0 m 34 s	72%	n/a
Outdated (T2)	Heuristic	(7, 15)	9156	23 s 650 ms	100%	100%
Updated (T2)	Heuristic	(8, 17)	13708	1 m 40 s 600 ms	100%	100%
Outdated (T1)	Heuristic	(3, 6)	1041	7 s 340 ms	100%	100%

$|\mathbf{E}|$: Emission events count, $|\mathbf{R}|$: Receptions events count in scenario, $|SC|$: count of System Contexts, Coverage: percentage of targeted coverage, Success rate for 20 trials of the selection heuristic
N.B., overall TSTSs size is 12 states and 28 transitions for both topologies T1 and T2

other generated scenarios in terms of number of Emissions and Receptions. We have used CVC4 solver to check the feasibility of logical constraints inferred for scenarios (system paths). We report on BFS (Breadth-First Search) in order to illustrate the exploration combinatorial. Even though left running for more than one hour, only partial coverage has been achieved with BFS. Then we have evaluated the coverage under the heuristic. Experiments show reduced running time. Given the overall short running time of our selection mechanism on the 4 asynchronous Trickle nodes, we expect it to be scalable to many other nodes. The reader can refer to [7, 29, 30] for some informative running time results on model-checking other Trickle case studies, yet in synchronous setting. Those first results need to be consolidated with further experiments.

Figure 4 depicts a sequence diagram of $node_4$ being outdated for some duration since the start of new version dissemination held by $node_1$ (Topology T1). The diagram has been adapted from the output generated by DIVERSITY. Neighbors of $node_4$, that are $node_2$ and $node_3$ are first updated by $node_1$ with a new version (green messages), they hence reset their interval to τ_l. After that, $node_4$ sends its version (old with respect of that of $node_1$) and gets them to reset their interval (blue messages). Thus, the transmissions of $node_2$ and $node_3$ are postponed; this gives time to $node_1$ re-transmit its version again and saturate their counters (orange messages); therefore they suppress their transmissions for $node_4$ respectively at $y_4 + y_5 = node_2.t_3$ and $z_4 + z_5 = node_3.t_3$ (last logical constraints in the scenario). Beyond highlighting such atypical scenarios, the symbolic execution of the model has allowed us to better understand the complex concurrency between nodes, which are ruled by non-trivial time constraints.

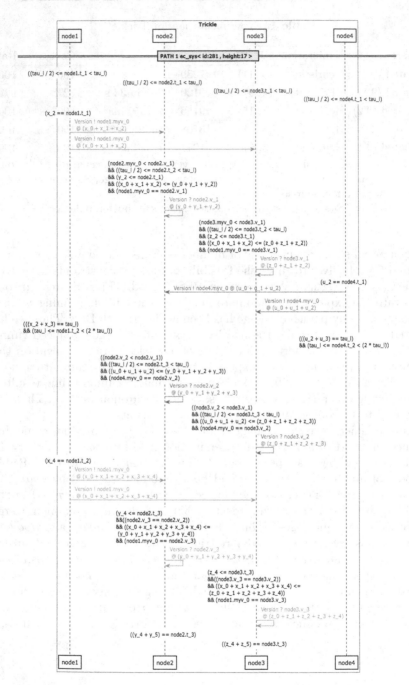

Fig. 4. A Trickle scenario for the topology of Fig. 3

5   Conclusion

We have provided a symbolic execution framework for timed distributed models fitted with feasible scenario selection mechanisms. Our framework has been completely implemented in the DIVERSITY tool and applied successfully on the distributed Trickle case study models using a heuristic approach. We believe that efficient novel partial order reduction techniques under the time setting -that we plan to develop in the near future- can leverage on this selection mechanism in order to accelerate the targeted selection for wide Trickle topologies.

References

1. Griesmayer, A., Aichernig, B., Johnsen, E.B., Schlatte, R.: Dynamic symbolic execution for testing distributed objects. In: Dubois, C. (ed.) TAP 2009. LNCS, vol. 5668, pp. 105–120. Springer, Heidelberg (2009). https://doi.org/10.1007/978-3-642-02949-3_9

2. Alur, R., Dill, D.: A theory of timed automata. J. Theor. Comput. Sci. **126**(2), 183–235 (1994)

3. Bannour, B., Escobedo, J.P., Gaston, C., Le Gall, P.: Off-Line test case generation for timed symbolic model-based conformance testing. In: Nielsen, B., Weise, C. (eds.) ICTSS 2012. LNCS, vol. 7641, pp. 119–135. Springer, Heidelberg (2012). https://doi.org/10.1007/978-3-642-34691-0_10

4. Bannour, B., Lapitre, A., Le Gall, P.: Exploring IoT trickle-based dissemination using timed model-checking and symbolic execution. In: Georgiou, C., Majumdar, R. (eds.) NETYS 2020. LNCS, vol. 12129, pp. 94–111. Springer, Cham (2021). https://doi.org/10.1007/978-3-030-67087-0_7

5. Cadar, C., Dunbar, D., Engler, R., Klee, D.: unassisted and automatic generation of high-coverage tests for complex systems programs. In: USENIX (2008)

6. Gaston, C., Le Gall, P., Rapin, N., Touil, A.: Symbolic execution techniques for test purpose definition. In: Uyar, M.Ü., Duale, A.Y., Fecko, M.A. (eds.) TestCom 2006. LNCS, vol. 3964, pp. 1–18. Springer, Heidelberg (2006). https://doi.org/10.1007/11754008_1

7. Dong, J.S., Sun, J., Sun, J., Taguchi, K., Zhang, X.: Specifying and verifying sensor networks: an experiment of formal methods. In: Liu, S., Maibaum, T., Araki, K. (eds.) ICFEM 2008. LNCS, vol. 5256, pp. 318–337. Springer, Heidelberg (2008). https://doi.org/10.1007/978-3-540-88194-0_20

8. Dunkels, A., Gronvall, B., Voigt, T.: Contiki - a lightweight and flexible operating system for tiny networked sensors. In: LCN. IEEE (2004)

9. Hui, J., Kelsey, R.: Multicast protocol for low-power and lossy networks, request for comments: 7731. Technical report, Silicon Labs, February 2016

10. King, J.C.: Symbolic execution and program testing. Commun. ACM **19**, 360248 (1976)

11. Sen, K., Agha, G.: CUTE and jCUTE: concolic unit testing and explicit path model-checking tools. In: Ball, T., Jones, R.B. (eds.) CAV 2006. LNCS, vol. 4144, pp. 419–423. Springer, Heidelberg (2006). https://doi.org/10.1007/11817963_38

12. Frantzen, L., Tretmans, J., Willemse, T.A.C.: A symbolic framework for model-based testing. In: Havelund, K., Núñez, M., Roşu, G., Wolff, B. (eds.) FATES/RV -2006. LNCS, vol. 4262, pp. 40–54. Springer, Heidelberg (2006). https://doi.org/10.1007/11940197_3

13. Levis, P., et al.: The emergence of a networking primitive in wireless sensor networks. Commun. ACM **51**(7), 99–106 (2008)
14. Levis, P., Clausen, T., Hui, J., Gnawali, O., Ko, J.: The trickle algorithm, request for comments: 6206. Technical report, Internet Engineering Task Force (IETF), March 2011
15. Levis, P., et al.: TinyOS: an operating system for sensor networks. In: Weber, W., Rabaey, J.M., Aarts, E. (eds.) Ambient Intelligence. Springer, Heidelberg (2005). https://doi.org/10.1007/3-540-27139-2_7
16. Levis, P., Patel, N., Culler, D., Shenker, S.: Trickle: a self-regulating algorithm for code propagation and maintenance in wireless sensor networks. In: NSDI. USENIX Association (2004)
17. Arnaud, M., Bannour, B., Lapitre, A.: An illustrative use case of the DIVERSITY platform based on UML interaction scenarios. Electr. Notes Theor. Comput. Sci. **320**, 21 (2016)
18. Shafiei, N., Mehlitz, P.C.: Extending JPF to verify distributed systems. ACM SIGSOFT Softw. Eng. Notes **39**(1), 1–5 (2014)
19. Nguyen, N.M.T., Bannour, B., Lapitre, A., Le Gall, P.: Behavioral models and scenario selection for testing IoT trickle-based lossy multicast networks. In ICST Workshops. IEEE (2019)
20. Dustmann, S.O., Sasnauskas, R., Wehrle K.: Symbolic system time in distributed systems testing. In: ICST. IEEE (2012)
21. Pasareanu, C.S., Rungta, N.: Symbolic pathfinder: symbolic execution of java bytecode. In: ASE. ACM (2010)
22. Sasnauskas, R.S., Dustmann, O., Kaminski, B.L., Wehrle, K., Weise, C., Kowalewski, S.: Scalable symbolic execution of distributed systems. In: ICDCS. IEEE (2011)
23. Sasnauskas, R., Kaiser, P., Jukic, R.L., Wehrle, K.: Integration testing of protocol implementations using symbolic distributed execution. In: ICNP. IEEE (2012)
24. Robinson-Mallett, C., Hierons, R.M., Liggesmeyer, P.: Achieving communication coverage in testing. ACM SIGSOFT Softw. Eng. Notes **31**(6), 1–10 (2006)
25. Khurshid, S., PĂsĂreanu, C.S., Visser, W.: Generalized symbolic execution for model checking and testing. In: Garavel, H., Hatcliff, J. (eds.) TACAS 2003. LNCS, vol. 2619, pp. 553–568. Springer, Heidelberg (2005). https://doi.org/10.1007/3-540-36577-X_40
26. Von Styp, S.C., Bohnenkamp, H., Schmaltz, J.: A conformance testing relation for symbolic timed automata. In: Formal Modeling and Analysis of Timed Systems - 8th International Conference, FORMATS Proceedings, pp. 243–255 (2010)
27. Andrade W., D. L. Machado P., Jéron T., Marchand H. Abstracting time and data for conformance testing of real-time systems. In: ICST Workshops. IEEE (2011)
28. Winter, T., et al.: Rpl: Ipv6 routing protocol for low-power and lossy networks, request for comments: 6550. Technical report, Cooper Power Systems and Cisco Systems and Stanford University (2012)
29. Woehrle, M., Bakhshi, R., Mousavi, M.R.: Mechanized extraction of topology antipatterns in wireless networks. In: Derrick, J., Gnesi, S., Latella, D., Treharne, H. (eds.) IFM 2012. LNCS, vol. 7321, pp. 158–173. Springer, Heidelberg (2012). https://doi.org/10.1007/978-3-642-30729-4_12
30. Zheng, M., Sun, J., Liu, Y., Dong, J.S., Gu, Yu.: Towards a model checker for NesC and wireless sensor networks. In: Qin, S., Qiu, Z. (eds.) ICFEM 2011. LNCS, vol. 6991, pp. 372–387. Springer, Heidelberg (2011). https://doi.org/10.1007/978-3-642-24559-6_26

Symposium on Intelligent
and Autonomous Systems (SIAS)

Energy Efficient Real-Time Calibration of Wireless Sensor Networks for Smart Buildings

Mads Mørk Beck[1], Jalil Boudjadar[2(✉)], and Yousra Chougui[3]

[1] ReMoni ApS, Aarhus, Denmark
[2] Aarhus University, Aarhus, Denmark
jalil@ece.au.dk
[3] VIA University College, Horsens, Denmark

Abstract. Wireless sensor networks (WSN) are becoming a pervasive technology integrated in most of real-time monitoring infrastructures and industrial control applications. Timeliness accuracy, performance and energy efficiency are key metrics to consider when deploying such WSN systems. Timeliness accuracy amounts to time-stamp collected data at sensor level in order to calculate an integrated real-time state of the monitored environment. It is usually achieved on the expense of energy consumption of sensors. Namely, such metrics are conflicting in a way that improving one metric deteriorates the other metrics. This paper proposes an energy-efficient time synchronization protocol to enable a high accuracy calibration for time stamping sensors data. The rational behind the protocol is to ensure that data is correctly time-stamped and time-relevant in order to operate the control loop managing the energy of the smart building. Our experimental results on an actual case study show that our protocol outperforms the state of the art protocols in terms of both time accuracy and energy efficiency.

Keywords: Wireless sensor networks · Time synchronization · Energy efficiency

1 Introduction

Sensor networks are widely used to monitor real-world phenomena and industrial control applications [8,19,20,22,23]. They are a key component to achieve high energy efficiency in smart buildings, particularly Nearly Zero Energy Buildings (NZEB) [2]. Wireless (clamp-on) sensors are sensors operating on limited integrated batteries and don't need a wired contact to the electric equipment to monitor [18]. A clamp-on sensor enables to measure voltage and current variations, which are the main parameters in calculating the energy consumption. Sampling data for both parameters, in real-time, from different sensors must be

---

Supported by FIE project *PowerClamp* and AU Industry 4.0 project *IntellECoSS*.

L. Bellatreche et al. (Eds.): MEDI 2021 Workshops, CCIS 1481, pp. 63–77, 2021.
https://doi.org/10.1007/978-3-030-87657-9_5

synchronized so that energy consumption is calculated at the given time point (timestamp) at which the data is sampled. Such sensors provide high flexibility compared to conventional sensors, however to make the battery lasting for longer time periods they have very limited computation resource to track the time progress. Thus, individual sensor timers can drift from the application physical time usually tracked by a master node sensor (gateway). To calibrate their local timers, sensors require to synchronize frequently with the master node.

For real-time monitoring applications built using Wireless Sensor Networks (WSN), physical time of the sensors often plays a crucial role given that a misalignment of the sensors through wrongly time-stamped data leads to inconsistent data, and thus confusing picture about the actual state of the monitored application [16]. This can cause an application controller to undertake inefficient, or even wrong, actuation actions [17].

As the EU states that all new buildings after 2021 should be nearly zero energy buildings (NZEB) [2], the need for smart grid monitoring systems is going to increase. The main reason behind this increase is related to buildings producing green energy on their own, are often self-sustained energy-wise without requesting power from the grid. The surplus energy can be sold to the grid. The cost-efficiency of making such a decision relies on the accuracy of buildings to measure their energy consumption (usually at appliance level) in real-time, e.g. a building may end up in a situation where it would sell power to the grid while needing the power to sustain itself creating potential risk of blackout.

Most of conventional energy monitoring solutions rely on collecting and processing massive data, which expensive with respect to sensors energy-consumption, data communication and processing. Such an approach is not practical when using WSN. Different time synchronization protocols have been proposed in the literature [3–7, 26, 27] to increase the practicality of WSN to monitor energy consumption and identify potential energy wastes in buildings. While trading off the synchronization accuracy and power efficiency, most of such protocols require that the sensor stay at *receiving mode* for most of its life time which drains the limited battery resource. In this paper, we propose an intelligent time synchronization protocol to calibrate sensors clocks. To increase battery lifetime, our protocol requires a minimal time duration within which the sensor is in receiving-mode while it secures a perfect synchronization with 0-delay drifts.

The rest of the paper is structured as follows: Sect. 2 introduces the overall WSN architecture. Section 3 presents the time synchronization challenge in WSN. Relevant related work is described in Sect. 4. Section 5 presents our newly proposed time synchronization protocol. Implementation and results discussion are provided in Sect. 6. Finally, Sect. 7 concludes the paper.

2   Architecture of Wireless Sensor Networks

For NZEB application domain, synchronous sensors are used to provide an accurate state of the building energy consumption at the same time points. Given that sensors have limited energy resources, having individual clocks is not practical. Rather, making sensors synchronize with a sink node is much more profitable, however achieving a perfect time synchronization is a challenging task due to many reasons such as communication bandwidth, messages loss, sensors failure, etc. The overall WSN architecture is depicted in Fig. 1. It consists of a set of sensors to sample the instantaneous current and voltage of the monitored home appliances and a dedicated node called *master node* where all data in dumped for processing and potential cloud communication. The master node runs also a control loop, calculating the current energy consumption and sending synchronization packets to sensors. In order for the control loop to be accurate, the data received needs to be a precise picture of the instantaneous energy consumption. As data is transmitted wirelessly, there is no guarantee for data to arrive at the same time point for each sampling. Thus, data is in fact timestamped by the source sensors so that the issue instant is considered rather then the data arrival time to the master node.

From a logic point of view, the system can be split into three different components: the hardware of the sensors itself, the firmware/software running on the sensors, and the software running in the main controller (sink node). In this paper the main control loop is implemented as a cloud service, enabling to provide data and processing to customers, thus the sink node functionality is only to maintain sensors synchronized.

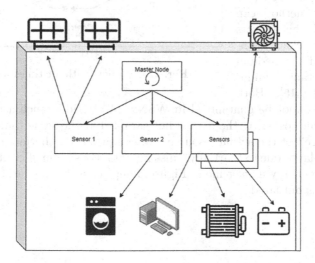

Fig. 1. WSNs to monitor energy consumption in smart buildings

3   Time Synchronization in WSNs

To be able to calculate an accurate image of the current energy consumption in the building, data must flow to the master node with high time precision. Wireless sensors are set up to sample measurements at a fixed frequency, assumed to be the optimal to deliver a real-time picture of the energy consumption while still being able to maximize sensors lifetime on battery. Receiving outdated data can mislead the control loop to actuate the building energy management system [21,22]. To solve the problem of outdated data, two different approaches have been used in the literature to timestamp data: timestamping at destination node and timestamping at source node.

3.1   Timestamping at Receiving Node

This approach relies on sensors sending data to the master node with a known frequency where the master node assumes that the data received is sampled at the same point in time, which can effectively be calculated to be the current time instant minus the communication time [13] (see Fig. 2). This method can only work if the sensors keep a steady clock without drift and if the medium ensure a constant communication time [15]. Both

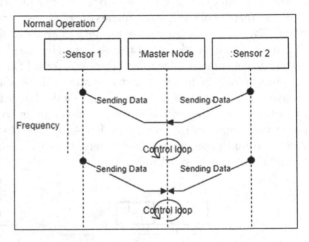

Fig. 2. Data flow without timestamping

requirements cannot be guaranteed in WSNs [14]. Besides, such a method can experience scenarios where the data is not sampled at the same time and therefore does not reflect the actual resources consumption. Furthermore the control loop can be delayed due to (partially) missing data, causing inefficient actuations of the building energy management. Figure 3 depicts such a scenario where data from Sensor2 is outdated.

3.2   Timestamping at Source Node

The solution for the outdated data problem illustrated earlier is to let the sensor nodes time stamp data upon sampling. This requires the sensors to be able to know the system time, however sensors are not equipped clocks to reduce the energy consumption from battery, rather they have a timer hardware to measure the time elapsed from a given relative time point. Thus, the master node needs to send time synchronization packets to sensors regularly so that each

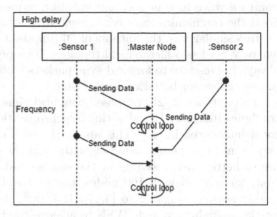

Fig. 3. Outdated data example

sensor can calibrate its own timer [25, 27]. The drawback of this approach is the higher accuracy needed for the timestamp, the more often the master node should send out new synchronization timestamps. Thus, a tradeoff between the scheduling of synchronization packets and battery efficiency must be established [12]. This approach is depicted in Fig. 4.

4   Related Work

This section cites the most relevant energy-aware time synchronization protocols for WSNs [3, 24–27]. The authors of [3, 26] proposed a broadcast-based time synchronization protocol to synchronize sensors within energy-constrained WSNs with an accuracy of 3 microseconds, i.e. the maximum drifting of sensor timers from the master node clock is 3 microseconds. The protocol mainly differs from the state of the art WSN synchronization protocols by letting the sensor itself requesting the synchronization packet instead of having the master node broadcasting the synchronization to all sensors in the WSN. However, such an accuracy is achieved on

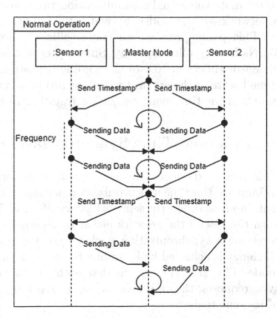

Fig. 4. Flow of timestamped data

the expense of sensors energy given that each sensor needs to calculate the time point for when to issue a synchronization request. Moreover, this approach may flood the communication environment with a large number of sync packets.

In a similar way, the authors of [3] proposed a time synchronization protocol where WSN has a hierarchical topology. The protocol assumes that sensors are always in On-state to forward sync packets to the lower hierarchy levels, which drains the sensor batteries much faster.

The authors of [25] proposed a hybrid time synchronization approach that combines Reference Broadcasting Synchronization [3] and the Timing-Sync protocol introduced in [27]. This approach relies on calculating the optimal time synchronization points, using algorithms of the aforementioned protocols, leading to better energy savings at the sensors end. The experimental results show that, for a WSN with 100 nodes, the protocol proposed in [25] achieves 40% energy saving compared to [3,27]. However, such heavy calculations can be a barrier in highly dynamic WSN to achieve the real-time synchronization.

The authors of [1] proposed a networked control to identify sensors synchronization and estimate potential drifting errors. This might lead to much accurate synchronization result but on the expense of energy given that a drifting of a sensor would require a synchronization of the entire network. The larger the network is, the more frequent synchronization packets are issued.

In [27], Ali et al. introduced a time synchronization protocol based on averaging consensus algorithm. The protocol relies on updating the sensors local time following the expected communication time. This improves time synchronization accuracy but with an increase in the needed number of communication instances to estimate the actual communication time, around 250 package to synchronize a network with 15 nodes, by which the energy consumption increases.

This paper proposes an energy-efficient time synchronization protocol for WSNs having a flat topology. Such a protocol is able to achieve 0-delay drifting of sensor timers in 70% of the sample timestamps. Compared to the aforementioned state of the art protocols, our protocol requires less number of packets to maintain the time synchronization resulting in higher energy efficiency.

5   Proposed Time Synchronization Protocol

This section describes the new synchronization protocol which have the goal to increase the time synchronization accuracy, by minimizing the sensor timers drift, and maximize the sensors battery lifetime. Essentially, each sensor interacts with the rest of the network either by sending a data sample, a sync request of receiving a synchronization packet from the master node. Namely, the energy efficiency is achieved by bounding the time duration a sensor can be in receiving mode. This is obvious given that each sensor is responsible for issuing its own sync requests, thus a sensor can be in receiving mode only right after the issue of its sync request.

The stay duration at receiving mode lasts for the round-trip communication time[1] plus the time for the master node to process the sync request. To be realistic, the duration stay includes also a minor delay to simulate potential delays from the master node processing. The proposed behavior pattern of sensors is depicted in Fig. 5.

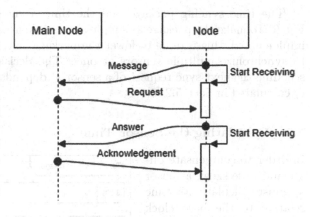

Fig. 5. Synchronization mechanism

5.1 Time Synchronization Mechanism

To convey time information between the master node and sensors, sensors need to know how good their timestamps are, i.e. alignment with the master node clock. In order for sensors to get knowledge about potential drifting, they rely on the master node measurement of the general time accuracy.

Our protocol enables a dynamic sliding mode where the time interval between synchronization requests of sensor is driven by the actual time drifting of such a sensor with respect to the master node clock. Initially, the sensor sends a sync request each time unit. When the underlying drifting gets smaller, the sensor issues sync requests every 2 time units. Finally, when the drifting delay converges towards *zero*, a sensor issues a sync request every 5 time units. If the sensor does not receive a timestamp withing the desired time span it issues another request to the master node again.

Structurally, a sensor s can be described by the variables shown in structure 1, where ID is the sensor number, t denotes the current timer value of s while E denotes the current drifting. One may wonder why drifting is captured in E rather then comparing the value of t before and after synchronization. This is in fact to enable sensors to calculate the time interval to the next request issue, in particular when the synchronization package sent my master node is lost or delayed. A sensor network S can be denoted as a set of sensors $\langle s_1, s_2, s_3, ..., s_n \rangle$ and a master node $M = \langle C, E \rangle$ where C is a clock to track time and E is the energy consumption rate of the master node per time unit.

$$s_i = \{ID_i, t_i, E_i\} \tag{1}$$

$$S = \{M, s_1, s_2, s_3, ..., s_n\} \tag{2}$$

---

[1] Round-trip communication is the journey time for a packet to travel from sensor to master node and come back. This in fact is dependent on the communication throughput and bandwidth.

The time syncing package and the time acknowledgment can be seen on Fig. 6. To make the package as simple as possible no source or destination ID are implemented, this is done to lower the package size, while providing the ability to synchronize multiple sensors at once. The decision making about when to schedule the next sync request of a sensor s_i depends on its actual drifting error e_i calculated in Sect. 5.2 [9].

5.2   Calculating the Sensor Time

In order to compensate off-set and time skew, a sensor s_i must calculate its time relative to the base clock of the master node C. This is done by calculating the error of the current timestamp and correct it. This calculation of sensor drift e_i^t at time t is done as depicted in Eq. 3, whereas the calibration of sensor time is done as shown in Eq. 4. Note here that $C[t]$ is the master clock value at time point t and $t_i[t]$ is the sensor timer at the time point

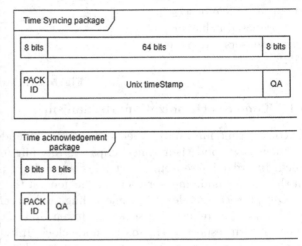

Fig. 6. Time synchronization packet

t. We omit the conversion of sensor timer value (relative time) to the absolute time $| t_i[t] |$ as it trivial and simply obtained by dividing the timer value by the its frequency.

$$e_i^t = C[t] - | t_i[t] | \tag{3}$$

$$t_i[t] = t_i[t] + e_i^t \tag{4}$$

To limit the amount of packages needed to send, a simple quality coefficient is calculated. This coefficient is used to determine how often the sensor should engage in communication with the master node. To not change the sending time that often a simple low pass structure is applied to the error. This coefficient Q can be seen in Eq. 5. The higher the Q value is, the sooner the sensor should ask again for a sync package [11].

$$Q_i^t = 0.5 \cdot Q_i^{old} + 0.5 \cdot e_i^t \tag{5}$$

Accordingly, the next sync request R_i of sensor s_i will be issued at time point t' where:

$$t' = \begin{cases} t+5 & \text{if} \quad Q_i^t = 0 \\ t+2 & \text{if} \quad 0 < Q_i^t \leq 1 \\ t+1 & \text{Otherwise} \end{cases} \qquad (6)$$

5.3 Calculating the Sensor Energy Consumption

The energy consumption $E_i^{[d,d+\delta]}$ of a sensor s_i for a time interval $d, d + \delta$ is the accumulation of energy consumption to sample/communicate measurement data, issue sync requests, being in active receiving mode to acquire sync packets and the energy consumed during idling mode. In similar way to [10], $E_i^{[d,d+\delta]}$ is formally calculated as follows:

$$E_i^{[d,d+\delta]} = I_m \cdot \frac{\delta}{1/F_i} + R_i^\delta \cdot I_i^s \cdot R_i^{cv} + I_i^i \cdot (\delta - (A.R_i^\delta) - (\frac{\delta}{1/F_i} \cdot x_i)) \qquad (7)$$

Where I_m is the consumption rate per sample, F_i is the sensor frequency, R_i^δ is the number of sync requests during δ and I_i^s is the consumption rate per sync request. $R_i^{cv} = I_i^r.A$ is the energy consumption for each receiving mode where I_i^r is the unit receive rate and A is the receiving activation duration. I_i^i is the consumption rate per idling time unit, whereas $\delta - (A.R_i^\delta) - (\frac{\delta}{1/F_i}.x_i)$ calculates the idling time duration during δ with x_i to be the effective time for one sample. In fact, the idling time during δ is the time not spent in sampling, sending a sync request or being in receiving mode.

6 Implementation and Experimental Results

This section sketches the protocol implementation and discusses the analysis results.

6.1 Protocol Implementation

The proposed protocol has been implemented in python and test on actual setup. A sensor class is used to keep track of the timing, offset and the skew. Sensors communicate to the master node through a queue with a communication delay, mirroring therefore a real world application. A sketch of the sensor code is depicted in Listing 1.1.

```
requestTimePKG = pkg()
msg = pack("BIB",timeREQPKG, self.getID(), self.getTimeQA())
requestTimePKG.write(msg)
self.outgoing.put(requestTimePKG)
#Dropping 5\% of the package
if random.randint(0,100) <= 5:
    self.ingoing.get(block=True, timeout=5)
```

```
    #Waiting 5 time units
    self.sleepTime.append(5)
    continue
#Assume the master answers between 1 and 4 time units
self.sleepTime.append(random.randint(1,4))
try:
    recMsg = self.ingoing.get(block=True, timeout=5)
except Empty:
    clockthread.join()
    break
pkgId,id,timestamp,timeQA = unpack("BIQB", recMsg.read())
self.updatetimestamp(timestamp)
if self.QA == 0:
    self.sleep(30)
elif self.QA < 5:
    self.sleep(15)
else:
    self.sleep(5)
```

Listing 1.1. Sensor code

The protocol is implemented with limited data loss (5% of the total communication packets) to simulate an actual wireless communication medium. The calculation of the time drifting can be seen in Listing 1.2.

```
def updatetimestamp(self,newTime):
    oldTime = self.timestamp
    error = newTime-oldTime
    self.timestamp = self.timestamp+error
    self.errorhistory.append(error)
    self.QA =
    int(0.5 * self.QA + 0.5 * abs(error))
```

Listing 1.2. Updating sensors timestamp

To run simulations and analysis both time accuracy and energy consumption, we have created a WSN of 100 sensors connected to the same master node queue. The experiments are run for 3 millions time unit length simulating the lifespan of an actual sensor.

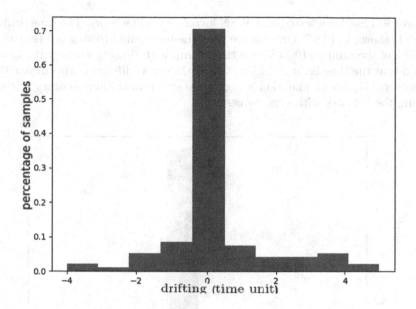

Fig. 7. Sensors time drifting (without packet loss)

6.2 Results and Discussion

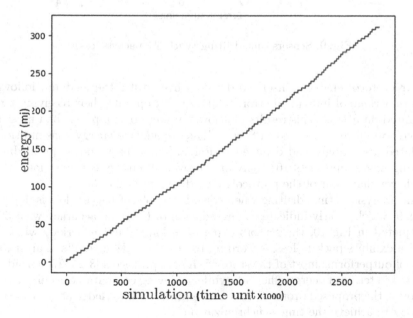

Fig. 8. Cumulative sum of the sensors energy consumption

The protocol has been tested on a WSN formed by 100 sensors. The time drifting (error) is shown in Fig. 7. One can see that the maximum drifting is 5 time units and 70% of the samples (0.7) have a timestamp with *0-delay drifting*. It can also be seen that the time error is ±1 for 90% of the sensor lifespan. This means that our protocol is able to maintain a high time synchronization accuracy without flooding the network with sync requests.

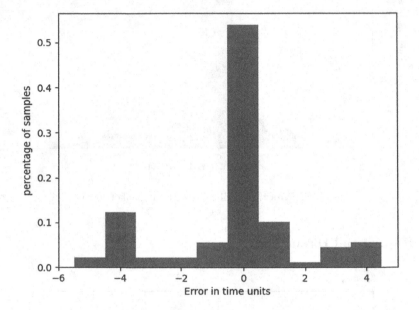

Fig. 9. Sensors time drifting (with 5% packets loss)

Our protocol enables sensors to decide when to use the medium, following the actual value of individual errors, thus sensors operate their receiving mode for limited durations. This results in a lower power consumption than most the protocols we have considered in Sect. 4. The cumulative energy consumption is calculated accordingly and depicted in Fig. 8. The energy consumption during receiving mode represents 10% only of the over all energy consumption, which is far lower than that of the protocols introduced in [3,25,26].

The analysis of time drifting when considering 5% of packets loss is depicted in Fig. 9, which clearly indicates a degradation of the time accuracy with 30%. As depicted in Fig. 10, the sensors experience longer active periods when the network exhibits packets loss. According to the simulation results analysis, our protocol outperforms most of the state of the art protocols [3,25–27] considered in Sect. 4 in terms of energy efficiency while achieving comparable accuracy level. Moreover, the proposed protocol does not require any knowledge about the WSN topology to achieve the time synchronization.

A drawback of our new protocol is that it assumes the master node to be always in receiving mode to respond the sync requests promptly as potential

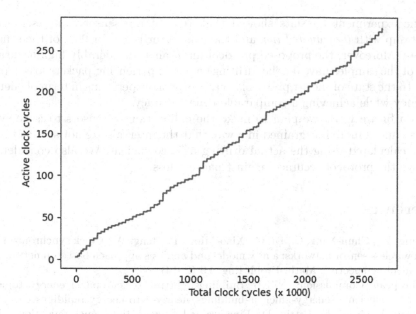

Fig. 10. Cumulative sum of active sensor durations (with 5% packets loss)

delays from the master node lead to deliver the sync packet to the sensor outside its currently active receiving time window. This causes the sensor to waste its energy and issue another sync request. However, this drawback should not be challenging as master nodes (gateways) usually operate with from a grid energy source.

Another important observation is that when the percentage of packets loss increases, the sensors time accuracy decreases by which the number of sync requests to issue increases. This leads usually to higher energy consumption proportional to the frequency of issuing sync requests. As seen in Fig. 9, the percentage (19%) of errors having value -4 and 4 is far higher than that of the protocol without loss (7.5%).

7 Conclusions

This paper proposed an energy-efficient real time calibration protocol to maintain time synchronization between sensors within WSNs. Such a protocol is able to secure a tradeoff between high time accuracy and low energy consumption of the sensors. The frequency of sensors to issue sync requests to the master node depends on their individual time drifting in comparison to the master node clock. This has considerably reduced the traffic related to synchronization. Meanwhile, our protocol does not request sensors to be in receiving mode for long durations. The protocol improves further the energy efficiency by reducing the size of data packets to communicate.

The experimental results showed that 70% of the sensor samples have a timestamp with *0-delay drifting*, and the time error is ± 1 for 90% of the sensor lifespan. Moreover, the proposed protocol maintains considerably high accuracy (55% of the samples have 0-delay drifting) when experiencing packets loss. Compared to the state of the art protocols, our protocol outperforms in term of energy efficiency while achieving a comparable time accuracy.

As a future work, we plan to make the calibration of sensors to issue sync requests much more fine grained in a way that the intervals are not static (1,2,5) rather calculated using the actual drifting as a coefficient. We also consider to improve the protocol accuracy against packets loss.

References

1. Ting, W., Chun-Yang, C., Di, G., Xiao-Ming, T., Heng, W.: Clock synchronization in wireless sensor networks: a new model and analysis approach based on networked control perspective. Math. Probl. Eng. **19** (2014)
2. European Commission: NZEB Buildings. https://ec.europa.eu/energy/topics/energy-efficiency/energy-efficient-buildings/nearly-zero-energy-buildings_en
3. Elson, J., Girod, L., Estrin, D.: Fine-grained network time synchronization using reference broadcasts. ACM SIGOPS Oper. Syst. Rev. **36**, 147–163 (2002)
4. Xiong, N., Fei, M., Yang, T., Tian, Y.-C.: Randomized and efficient time synchronization in dynamic wireless sensor networks: a gossip-consensus-based approach. Complex. J. (2018)
5. Prakash, R., Nygard, K.: Time synchronization in wireless sensor networks: a survey. Int. J. UbiComp **1**(2), 92–102 (2010)
6. Li, F., He, G., Wang, X.: An improved hybrid time synchronization approach in wireless sensor networks for smart grid application. In HPCC conference (2015)
7. Al-Shaikhi, A.: Accuracy-enhanced time synchronization method for WSNs using average consensus control. In: Proceedings of International Multi-Conference on Systems, Signals and Devices 2018 (2018)
8. Magrini, A., Lentini, G., Cuman, S., Bodrato, A., Marenco, L.: From nearly zero energy buildings (NZEB) to positive energy buildings (PEB): the next challenge - the most recent European trends with some notes on the energy analysis. In: Developments in the Built Environment, vol. 3 (2020)
9. Boudjadar, A., et al.: Widening the schedulability of hierarchical scheduling systems. In: Lanese, I., Madelaine, E. (eds.) FACS 2014. LNCS, vol. 8997, pp. 209–227. Springer, Cham (2015). https://doi.org/10.1007/978-3-319-15317-9_14
10. Bouguera, T., Diouris, J.-F., Chaillout, J.-J., Jaouadi, R., Andrieux, G.: Energy consumption model for sensor nodes based on LoRa and LoRaWAN. Sensors **18**, 2104 (2018)
11. Boudjadar, J., Beck, M.M.: Intelligent time synchronization protocol for energy efficient sensor systems. In: Arai, K. (ed.) IntelliSys 2021. LNNS, vol. 295, pp. 609–623. Springer, Cham (2022). https://doi.org/10.1007/978-3-030-82196-8_45
12. Boudjadar, J., David, A., Kim, J.H., Larsen, K.G., Nyman, U., Skou, A.: Schedulability and energy efficiency for multi-core hierarchical scheduling systems. In: International Conference on Embedded Real Time Systems and Software ERTS 2014 (2014)

13. Lundqvist E. Timing and synchronization over ethernet. Thesis Dissertation, Linkøping University 2015. http://urn.kb.se/resolve?urn=urn:nbn:se:liu:diva-115882

14. Zhang, D., Yuan, Y., Bi, Y.: A design of a time synchronization protocol based on dynamic route and forwarding certification. Sensors (Basel) **20**(18), 5061 (2020)

15. Xiong, N., Fei, M., Yang, T., Tian, Y.-C.: Randomized and efficient time synchronization in dynamic wireless sensor networks: a gossip-consensus-based approach. Complexity **2018**, Article ID 4283087, 16 p. (2018)

16. Ding, C., Xu, S., Chen, X., Zhou, G., Zheng, P., Li, Y.: A delay and load-balancing based hierarchical route planning method for transmission line IoT sensing and monitoring applications. In: 2019 IFIP/IEEE Symposium on Integrated Network and Service Management (IM), Arlington, VA, USA, 2019, pp. 207–215 (2019)

17. Liang, G., Weller, S.R., Zhao, J., Luo, F., Dong, Z.Y.: The 2015 Ukraine blackout: implications for false data injection attacks. IEEE Trans. Power Syst. **32**(4), 3317–3318 (2017)

18. ReMoni.: Clamp-on IoT Sensors. https://www.remoni.com/products2/product-overview/

19. Gao, S., Dai, X., Hang, Y., Guo, Y., Ji, Q.: Airborne wireless sensor networks for airplane monitoring system. Wireless Commun. Mobile Comput. **2018**, Article ID 6025825, 18 p. (2018)

20. Dong, Q., Yu, L., Lu, H., Hong, Z., Chen, Y.: Design of building monitoring systems based on wireless sensor networks. Wirel. Sens. Netw. **2**, 703–709 (2010)

21. Gheisarnejad, M., Karimaghaee, P., Boudjadar, J., Khooban, M.H.: Real-time cellular wireless sensor testbed for frequency regulation in smart grids. IEEE Sens. J. **19**(23), 11656–11665 (2019)

22. Gheisarnejad, M., Boudjadar, J., Khooban, M.: A new adaptive type-II fuzzy-based deep reinforcement learning control: fuel cell air-feed sensors control. IEEE Sen. J. **19**(20), 9081–9089 (2019)

23. Carminati, M., Kanoun, O., Ullo, S.L., Marcuccio, S.: Prospects of distributed wireless sensor networks for urban environmental monitoring. IEEE Aerosp. Electron. Syst. Mag. **34**(6), 44–52 (2019)

24. Ganeriwal, S., Kumar, R., Srivastava, M.: Timing-sync protocol for sensor networks. In: SenSys'03: Proceedings of the First International Conference on Embedded Networked Sensor Systems (2004). https://doi.org/10.1145/958491.958508

25. Li, F., He, G., Wang, X.: An improved hybrid time synchronization approach in wireless sensor networks for smart grid application, pp. 798–801 (2015). https://doi.org/10.1109/HPCC-CSS-ICESS.2015.117

26. Lin, X., Lijuan, C., Fubao, W.: A low cost time synchronization algorithm for wireless sensor networks. J. Comput. Res. Dev. **1**, 015 (2008)

27. Al-Shaikhi, A.: Accuracy-enhanced time synchronization method for WSNs using average consensus control, pp. 23–27. https://doi.org/10.1109/SSD.2018.8570599

28. Ruiqiong, C., Ya, L., Xiaohui, L., Duosheng, F., Ying, Y.: High-precision time synchronization based on common performance clock source. In: 2019 IEEE International Conference on Electronic Measurement and Instruments (ICEMI), pp. 1363–1368 (2019)

29. Upadhyay, D., Dubey, A.K., Santhi Thilagam, P.: Time synchronization problem of wireless sensor network using maximum probability theory. Int. J. Syst. Assur. Eng. Manage. **9**, 517–524 (2018)

Edge-to-Fog Collaborative Computing in a Swarm of Drones

Dadmehr Rahbari[1,2]([⊠]), Muhammad Mahtab Alam[1], Yannick Le Moullec[1], and Maksim Jenihhin[2]

[1] Thomas Johann Seebeck Department of Electronics, Tallinn University of Technology, Ehitajate tee 5, 19086 Tallinn, Estonia
[2] Department of Computer Systems, Tallinn University of Technologies, Akadeemia tee 15A, 12618 Tallinn, Estonia
{dadmehr.rahbari,muhammad.alam,yannick.lemoullec, maksim.jenihhin}@taltech.ee

Abstract. Recently, drones technology started unleashing numerous novel applications and services and became one of the killer applications for the Mobile Edge Computing (MEC) paradigm. The main challenge for real-time applications is, however, transferring data between data processing servers and drones, which yields considerable latency and energy consumption and reduces the autonomy and dynamics of operations. In this paper, we consider a swarm of heterogeneous and autonomous drones deployed to detect objects in run-time video streaming. Each drone can execute data-processing related computation tasks locally, or offload them to other nodes in the swarm. For efficient cooperation at the swarm level, forming a system of systems, drones need to cooperate in using each other's resources and managing the communication and offloading operations. To overcome the mentioned challenges and also data privacy, we propose a novel edge-to-fog collaborative computing framework employing federated learning (FL)-based offloading strategy with a rating method. The proposed method also aims to offload the computation tasks between drones in a fair and efficient manner.

Keywords: Collaborative computing · Edge computing · Computation offloading · Federated learning · Drone · UAV swarm · Intelligent and autonomous systems

1 Introduction

Swarms of heterogeneous and autonomous drones or Unmanned Aerial Vehicles (UAVs) increasingly attract the attention in different applications. The collaboration between drones in computations has many advantages over a single drone. Ultimately, the swarm intelligence decreases the energy consumption and cost, and increases the throughput and quality of services [1]. This approach has many applications in monitoring, detection [2], and operations in the 3-D, i.e. dirty, dull and dangerous, environments.

© Springer Nature Switzerland AG 2021
L. Bellatreche et al. (Eds.): MEDI 2021 Workshops, CCIS 1481, pp. 78–87, 2021.
https://doi.org/10.1007/978-3-030-87657-9_6

Drones are constrained in terms of their battery capacity, computing resource capability, etc. They can execute tasks locally if their resources are sufficient to fulfill the local (node-level) and swarm-level requirements, or else they can offload those tasks to other devices. The literature shows that a centralized approach considering the *cloud* can not always be a suitable option for offloading considering the latency, quality of service (QoS), and energy consumption constraints [3]. As an alternative for computation-intensive data processing, it is possible to employ a *fog computing approach* relying on using *edge servers* instead of the cloud [4], but several disadvantages remain. Although edge servers are closer to drones and the communication is faster than with the cloud [5], one has to consider that the swarm of drones can move to some locations far away from the edge servers to perform its mission. Hence, placing edge servers in a fixed and trusted position may imply challenges and restrictions. To overcome these problems, *collaborative edge-to-fog computing* is deemed to be a promising alternative [6]. In such an architecture, drones themselves can be nodes on the edge for processing the local and offloaded data in run-time. This type of network also faces some challenges, e.g. with resource allocation [7]. As a result, we need an efficient solution for orchestrating a group of drones in the field working together for objectives of a specific target mission.

Thus, the main task of an orchestration approach is decreasing the latency and power consumption in the swarm of drones. Federated Learning (FL) as a Machine Learning (ML) algorithm is a distributed strategy that has been used for MEC architecture [8]. Deep Reinforcement Learning (DRL) has been used in drone (or unmanned aerial vehicles) applications [9]. Federated Deep Reinforcement Learning (FDRL) is a distributed version of DRL that can be used in MEC. FDRL significantly reduces network overhead, bandwidth consumption, and latency in a swarm of drones by avoiding to send data to a central entity [10].

Let's assume several drones are monitoring an environment. It is possible that some of them have insufficient resources, a wrong position or an unsuitable angle of the camera. The above-mentioned FL-based methods aggregate all the learning models in the system of systems [11]. In the object detection application, for evaluating the learning method, the accuracy of the detected object can be analyzed. For this purpose, we can rate the drones with their mentioned properties, then we can update the model based on their rating values. This method also has an advantage that drones can update their position based on received ratings from neighbors.

To address the above issues, this paper investigates an edge-to-fog framework employing a novel FDRL method based on a rating mechanism of drones as FLR in a MEC architecture. We also present a fair offloading technique by considering the transmission, computation, and moving energy consumption and also transmission and computation latency of drones.

This paper is organized as follows. Section 2 presents a framework for edge-to-fog collaborative computing. In Sect. 3, we explain the proposed approach for module offloading in a swarm of drones. The experimental results are provided in Sect. 4. Finally, in Sect. 5, a conclusion and suggestions for future work are provided.

2   Framework for Edge-to-Fog Collaborative Computing

As shown in Fig. 1, we consider a swarm of autonomous heterogeneous drones capturing video streams and detecting objects in real time. Some drones with high capacity and good quality can execute the process locally, while others have to offload some of their tasks to other drones. The offloading process between neighbors within each cluster yields lower latency, energy consumption, and higher privacy. The objective is to identify the best destination for executing the computation tasks that the drones need to offload.

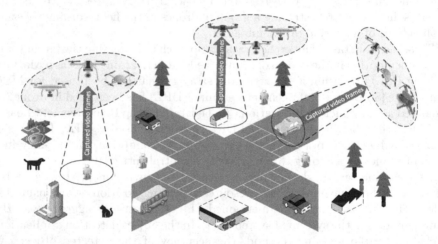

Fig. 1. Architecture of collaborative edge-to-fog computing in a swarm of drones

We propose a new collaborative edge-to-fog computing framework using offloading of application software modules (the computing tasks) that employs Federated Learning methods for both the target swarm-level application (object detection) and real-time orchestration of the collaboration. In this framework, the multiple heterogeneous drones are denoted by i ($i = 1, \ldots, i, \ldots, I$). The properties of each drone may include position (X, Y, Z), CPU frequency, memory allocation, data transmission bandwidth, idle power, and busy power, etc.

The considered object detection application includes some modules. The *sensing* module sends camera video streams to the *client* module. The *client* module executes pre-processing of the sensor-generated data and transfers it to the *processing* module. The *processing* module provides two types of data, i.e.

processed and action commands that can be transferred to *storage* and *client* modules, respectively. The *storage* module is used for saving the output of *processing* modules for location-independent and scalable distribution.

2.1 Latency

Slow and unstable communication may imply serious issues to the swarm-level collaboration efficiency. If the drones send their computations to far-away drones in the network, latency will increase [12]. However, clustering of drones helps them to perform offloading to closer neighbor drones. As some drones temporarily become offline, only the weights are less trained or updated later on, but task execution or offloading is performed continuously.

Each drone, based on its resource status can execute the modules locally or offload that to other neighbor drones. In the case of the local execution by a drone i (D_i), the latency is given by

$$L_i^{Local} = \frac{\rho \alpha_i D_i}{f_i} \tag{1}$$

Where ρ, α_i, and f_i are the offloading coefficient, the module complexity, and the CPU frequency of D_i, respectively. In the case of the offloading, there are two different components for the latency, i.e. the transmission latency and the computation latency; the total latency of a task is given by

$$L_i^{Total} = Max\{L_i^{Local}, (L_i^{Computation} + L_i^{Transmission})\} \tag{2}$$

Computation Latency. The execution of a module in each drone has a latency [13] given as

$$L_i^{Computation} = \frac{\alpha_i \lambda_j (1 - \rho) D_i}{f_j} \tag{3}$$

Where f_j is the CPU frequency of D_j.

Transmission Latency. The transmission latency of that module [13] between D_i and D_j is given by

$$L_i^{Transmission} = \frac{\beta \lambda_j (1 - \rho) D_i}{R^{UL}(i, j)} \tag{4}$$

Where β is a rate of transmission, λ is the path loss exponent, $R^{UL}(i, j)$ is the uplink rate from D_i to D_j.

2.2 Energy Consumption

Transferring data between drones increases energy consumption. In FL, the drone data is not sent to other drones, and only the weights of the learning models are transferred; thus, less energy is consumed. Another energy challenge is that switching off a drone may affect the learning performance. This can be solved by collecting neighbors drones' properties and rating them based on their capabilities.

We consider the total energy consumption model as the sum of the computation, transmission, and moving energy consumptions of drones, as described in what follows.

Computation Energy Consumption. In the local execution in each drone, the computation energy consumption [13] can be given by

$$E_i^{Local} = \frac{uf_i^\delta \rho \alpha_i D_i}{f_i} \tag{5}$$

Moreover, the computation energy consumption in offloading is given as

$$E_i^{Computation} = \frac{\sum_{j=1}^N uf_j^\delta \alpha_i \lambda_j (1-\rho) D_i}{f_j} \tag{6}$$

Where uf_i^δ and uf_j^δ are the computation powers of D_i and D_j, respectively, and N is the number of modules. The total computational energy consumption of a drones' swarm is the sum of them in the local and offloading modes.

Transmission Energy Consumption. We calculate the transmission energy consumption based on the transmitting and receiving of modules between drones, and the total value is their sum, as follows. The transmitting energy consumption [13] is given by

$$E_i^{Transmitting} = \frac{\sum_{j=1}^N P_{Tx} \beta \lambda_j (1-\rho) D_i}{R^{UL}(i,j)} \tag{7}$$

The receiving energy consumption is equal by

$$E_i^{Receiving} = \frac{\sum_{j=1}^N P_{Rx} \beta \lambda_j (1-\rho) D_i}{R^{UL}(i,j)} \tag{8}$$

Where P_{Tx} and P_{Rx} are the transmitting and receiving power of D_i and D_j, respectively.

Moving Energy Consumption. There are many parameters of a drone's energy model such as time of idle, armed, hovering, and horizontal flying, take-off speed, the distance of vertical upwards and downwards flying, the altitude of hovering, and payload. In this work, we assume drones are in the air and their energy is calculated according to [3].

2.3 Fairness of Offloading

The fairness equivalent helps us to evaluate the distribution of offloading in all available drones in the neighborhood of each drone. To calculate this parameter, we propose this fairness parameter based on the energy consumption and latency as follows. The fairness of D_i is given by

$$Fairness_i = \frac{(\sum_{j=1}^{K} f(E, L))^2}{K \sum_{j=1}^{K} f(E, L)^2} \tag{9}$$

Where K is the number of neighbor devices contributed in the offloading, and $f(E, L)$ is the energy consumption with latency that is mentioned based on transmission and computation and moving of drones. The fairness value is the range $[1/K, 1]$. Higher fairness values mean higher performance.

3 Federated Learning-Based Offloading in Swarm of Drones

This section presents the FLR strategy based on cooperation between drones. All the steps are shown in Fig. 2. We explain this strategy in four steps, i.e., initialization of drones and application, finding the best learning model in each drone with a rating strategy and offloading, updating learning model by neighbors of drones, and setting the new position of drones.

3.1 Step 1. Initialization of Drones and Application

All drones are placed in the scenario area with random positions considering the minimum distance to avoid a collision. Since we consider heterogeneous drones, their configurations are different. After that, all the mentioned application modules are mapped to drones.

3.2 Step 2. Finding the Best Drone for Offloading with a Rating Strategy

All drones D_j with distance

$$Distance_{ij} = [(D_i^x - D_j^x)^2 + (D_i^y - D_j^y)^2 + (D_i^z - D_j^z)^2]^{0.5} \leq 100 \tag{10}$$

are considered as neighbors of D_i. Each drone calculates energy consumption, latency, and fairness. If a drone can execute the module locally, it will execute it; otherwise, the offloading process will start.

The DRL steps are as follows. First, it is initializing the primary network Q_1, target network Q_2, and reply buffer D by 0. For all environment steps, 1) Observe state s_t and select action a_t. 2) Execute a_t and observe next state s_{t+1} and $r_t = R(s_t, a_t)=$ average of drone's power and execution time. 3) Store (s_t, a_t, r_t, s_{t+1}) in the reply buffer D. Moreover, for each update step,

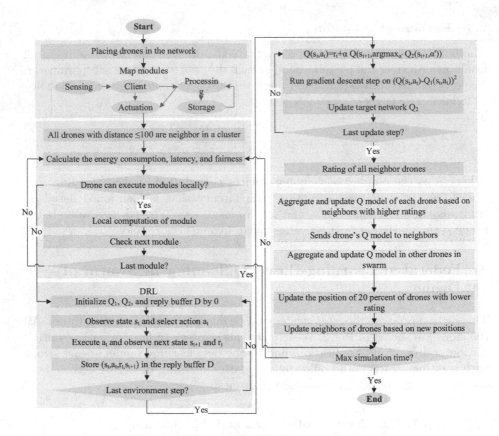

Fig. 2. FL-based offloading between drones

1) Updating the Q value by

$$Q(s_t, a_t) = r_t + \alpha Q(s_{t+1}, argMax_{\alpha'} Q_2(s_{t+1}, \alpha')) \tag{11}$$

2) Executing gradient descent step on

$$(Q(s_t, a_t) - Q_1(s_t, a_t))^2 \tag{12}$$

3) Updating target network by

$$Q_2(s_t, a_t) = \alpha Q_1(s_t, a_t) + (1 - \alpha) Q_2(s_t, a_t) \tag{13}$$

Each drone can rate all its neighbor drones. The rating value is given by

$$Rating_j = \frac{w_1 B_j + w_2 F_j + w_3 J_j}{w_4 L_j} \tag{14}$$

where B_j is the bandwidth between D_i and D_j, and F_j and J_j are the CPU frequency and the fairness of D_j, respectively. All w_i are weighted coefficients for the normalization of parameters. The activity scheme of rating is shown in Fig. 3.

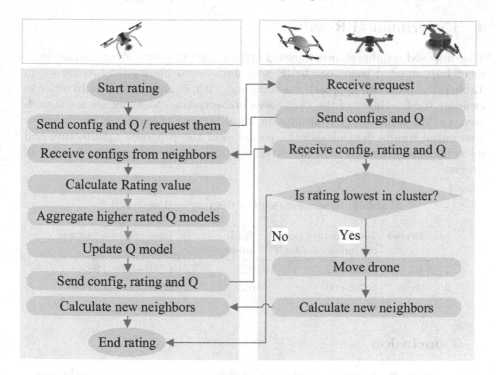

Fig. 3. Activity scheme of rating

3.3 Step 3. Updating Learning Model by Neighbors of Drones

Each drone updates its Q model based on the aggregating (average of weights learning models' weights) of neighbor drones' Q model with a higher rating and send its Q model to the neighbors. Moreover, other drones update their Q models with the same way. Each drone can evaluate the neighbor Q model as soon as receiving it, and update its model based on the higher rating value. After updating the Q model of each drone, it knows the destination of modules for offloading.

3.4 Step 4. Placing Drones in a New Position

To improve the individual contribution of drone's QoS, we move the drones that have low performance. This performance is calculated based on their ratings. We update the position of a few percent of drones with lower ratings. It should be noted that depending on the rating, different drones may change position each time. After moving drones, they update their neighbors based on their new position. To calculate the total energy consumption, we consider the moving energy consumption of drones too. Finally, the process repeats from finding the best drone for offloading to placing drones in the new position, until the maximum simulation time.

4   Experimental Results

The proposed collaborative computing architecture was simulated in an environment implemented based on the iFogsim Java-based library [14]. As shown in Table 1, the proposed approach was analyzed with 10 and 25 drones. In order to evaluate the feasibility of the FLR-based orchestration, four metrics are considered, i.e. the total energy consumption, total latency, throughput, and fairness. The initial results demonstrate the potential of the proposed architecture and its applicability for practical industrial applications of autonomous swarms of drones.

Table 1. Simulation result of the proposed approach

No.	Drones	Total energy consumption (Joule)	Total latency (ms)	Throughput (MB/s)	Fairness
1	10	1.58E+09	0.26	8.53E+03	98%
2	25	5.78E+09	0.28	1.86E+04	97%

5   Conclusion

In this paper, we proposed an edge-to-fog collaborative computing architecture employing FLR-based offloading approach based on a rating technique in a swarm of drones. First, the architecture and a system model of the collaborative computing was provided. Second, the framework of the module offloading strategy was presented. Finally, we evaluate the proposed approach with some metrics as energy consumption, latency, throughput, and fairness. This strategy can be executed on different applications with a swarm of drones. Future research topics include data fusion, placing of drones, reliability, and trust management in the scope of this work.

Acknowledgment. This work in the project "ICT programme" was supported by the European Union through European Social Fund. This project was also partly funded by the European Union's Horizon 2020 Research and Innovation Program under Grant 668995 and Grant 951867.

References

1. Pakrooh, R., Bohlooli, A.: A survey on unmanned aerial vehicles-assisted internet of things: a service-oriented classification. Wirel. Pers. Commun. **119**(2), 1541–1575 (2021). https://doi.org/10.1007/s11277-021-08294-6
2. Zheng, J., et al.: Accurate detection and localization of UAV swarms-enabled MEC system. IEEE Trans. Ind. Inf. (2020). https://doi.org/10.1109/TII.2020.3015730
3. Abeywickrama, H.V., et al.: Comprehensive energy consumption model for unmanned aerial vehicles, based on empirical studies of battery performance. IEEE Access **6**, 58383–58394 (2018). https://doi.org/10.1109/ACCESS.2018.2875040

4. Zhang, Q., et al.: Response delay optimization in mobile edge computing enabled UAV swarm. IEEE Trans. Veh. Technol. **69**(3), 3280–3295 (2020). https://doi.org/10.1109/TVT.2020.2964821
5. Liu, B., et al.: Online computation offloading and traffic routing for UAV swarms in edge-cloud computing. IEEE Trans. Veh. Technol. **69**(8), 8777–8791 (2020). https://doi.org/10.1109/TVT.2020.2994541
6. Chen, W., et al.: When UAV swarm meets edge-cloud computing: the QoS perspective. IEEE Netw. **33**(2), 36–43 (2019). https://doi.org/10.1109/MNET.2019.1800222
7. Sun, L., Wan, L., Wang, X.: Learning-based resource allocation strategy for industrial IoT in UAV-enabled MEC systems. IEEE Trans. Ind. Inf. (2020). https://doi.org/10.1109/TII.2020.3024170
8. Lim, W.Y.B., et al.: Federated learning in mobile edge networks: a comprehensive survey. IEEE Commun. Surv. Tutorials **22**(3), 2031–2063 (2020). https://doi.org/10.1109/COMST.2020.2986024
9. Lu, X., et al.: UAV-aided cellular communications with deep reinforcement learning against jamming. IEEE Wirel. Commun. **27**(4), 48–53 (2020). https://doi.org/10.1109/MWC.001.1900207
10. Brik, B., Ksentini, A., Bouaziz, M.: Federated learning for UAVs-enabled wireless networks: use cases, challenges, and open problems. IEEE Access **8**, 53841–53849 (2020). https://doi.org/10.1109/ACCESS.2020.2981430
11. Zhang, H., Hanzo, L.: Federated learning assisted multi-UAV networks. IEEE Trans. Veh. Technol. **69**(11), 14104–14109 (2020). https://doi.org/10.1109/TVT.2020.3028011
12. Pham, Q.V., et al.: UAV communications for sustainable federated learning. IEEE Trans. Veh. Technol. (2021). https://doi.org/10.1109/TVT.2021.3065084
13. Hou, X., et al.: Distributed fog computing for latency and reliability guaranteed swarm of drones. IEEE Access **8**, 7117–7130 (2020). https://doi.org/10.1109/ACCESS.2020.2964073
14. Gupta, H., et al.: iFogSim: a toolkit for modeling and simulation of resource management techniques in the internet of things, edge and fog computing environments. Softw. Pract. Exp. **47**(9), 1275–1296 (2017). https://doi.org/10.1002/spe.2509

Coverage Maximization in WSN Deployment Using Particle Swarm Optimization with Voronoi Diagram

Khaoula Zaimen[1,2(✉)], Mohamed-el-Amine Brahmia[1],
Jean-François Dollinger[1], Laurent Moalic[2], Abdelhafid Abouaissa[2],
and Lhassane Idoumghar[2]

[1] LINEACT CESI, CESI Engineering School, Strasbourg, France
{kzaimen,abrahmia,jfdollinger}@cesi.fr
[2] IRIMAS UR 7499, University of Haute Alsace, Mulhouse, France
{khaoula.zaimen,laurent.moalic,abdelhafid.abouaissa,
lhassane.idoumghar}@uha.fr

Abstract. Coverage area maximization is a crucial issue that must be considered in Wireless sensor network (WSN) deployment as long as it impacts the sensor network efficiency. In this paper, a novel approach based on particle swarm optimization (PSO) and voronoi diagram is developed to solve WSN deployment problem. The objective of the proposed solution is to reduce both of the coverage hole and coverage overlapping in the region of interest (RoI). In order to achieve it, the PSO fitness function is designed using voronoi diagram for the purpose of efficiently assessing the coverage hole of a particle solution and therefore, compute the improved deployment of the sensor nodes within the target area. The simulation results demonstrate that the proposed algorithm provides a noteworthy initial coverage enhancement.

Keywords: Wireless Sensor Network · Optimal deployment · Coverage optimization · Particle swarm optimization · Voronoi diagram

1 Introduction

In the last years, the important development of the Internet of things (IoT) has allowed Wireless Sensor Networks (WSNs) to become a fundamental research subject in communication technology [1]. This trend has been reinforced by its integration on a wide variety of emergent applications, such as: military, industry, medical and living environment [2]. Furthermore, these applications usually require a massive installation of wireless sensor nodes and thus, the use of automatic deployment techniques. Providing en efficient deployment schemes mainly relies on better area of interest coverage to ensure a high quality of service (QoS) for a given network [3].

Coverage maximization of a region of interest with sensors having limited sensing range is a critical issue considered as a NP-hard optimization problem

© Springer Nature Switzerland AG 2021
L. Bellatreche et al. (Eds.): MEDI 2021 Workshops, CCIS 1481, pp. 88–100, 2021.
https://doi.org/10.1007/978-3-030-87657-9_7

[4]. Indeed, a perfect deployment process should take into consideration a variety of factors and parameters, such as: RoI sector and environment, sensor type and characteristics, obstacles, etc. Many solution have been proposed in literature to solve the problem of WSN deployment while enhancing the coverage. Most of them implement Genetic Algorithms, Computational Geometry, Artificial Potential Fields and Particle Swarm Optimization [5].

In this paper, particle swarm optimization algorithm is adapted to efficiently optimize WSN deployment. Our main focus is to improve the network performance by minimizing the total coverage holes and the overlapped covered area within the region of interest. As one of the global optimization algorithms, PSO has been successfully applied in many applications especially in the area of substation locating and sizing [6]. In our scheme, PSO algorithm is applied to find the improved locations of sensors according to an objective function that minimizes both of the sensor nodes coverage hole and the overlapped covered area.

The rest of the article is organized as follows. Section 2 surveys the related works to the coverage problem in WSNs. Section 3 introduces PSO algorithm and Voronoi diagram. The problem formulation and the proposed solution are presented in Sect. 3 while Sect. 4 contains simulation results. Finally, Sect. 5 concludes the paper and discusses the near future works.

2   Related Work

Several approaches have been proposed in literature to solve WSN deployment problem. Metiaf et al. [7], have proposed a variant of particle swarm optimization algorithm based on voronoi diagram in order to provide the efficient positions of mobile sensor nodes within an obstacle-constrained area. The proposed solution considers minimizing the energy consumption for the mobile sensors for the purpose of increasing the network lifetime. Another work that combines the PSO algorithm with Voronoi diagram with the aim to minimize coverage holes is presented in [8], the proposed solution was compared to a grid based PSO algorithm in attempt to assess the performance of the two approaches. Simulation results show that Voronoi diagram based method provides an improved coverage results within a reasonable execution time compared with the grid based method. Abo-Zahhad et al. [9] have also combined the multi-objective immune algorithm with voronoi diagram to calculate the efficient placement for each mobile sensor node after an initial deployment. The proposed method runs on two phases, the first one aims to maximise the coverage by finding new sensors positions and adjusting the sensing ranges by using voronoi diagram, whereas for the second phase, it increases the network lifetime by adapting the number of active mobile sensors.

Wang et al. [10] have proposed three strategies to tackle mobile sensor deployment which are: VEC, VOR and Minimax. VEC strategy uses the concept of attraction and repulsion forces that may occur between two objects, VOR method is similar to the strategy presented in the work of Argany et al. [11] where the moving distance is equal to the maximum communication radius. The last approach Minimax tries to minimize the important fluctuations between two VOR iterations.

The work of Anurag et al. [12], has introduced another variant of PSO to solve the problem of WSN deployment. The proposed approach seeks to simultaneously minimize the energy consumption by reducing the total distance between the initial position and final position for each sensor node and maximize the coverage ratio. The contribution of this method lies on the use of a negative velocity to escape the local optima.

3   PSO Based Algorithm for WSN Deployment

Before we tackle the proposed solution, we briefly introduce the two related methods used in our approach for WSN deployment which are voronoi diagram and Particle swarm optimization algorithm.

Voronoi Diagram. In order to provide efficient deployment schemes, the *influence area* and the *sensing area* of a sensor node are considered. On the one hand, the sensing area is defined as the zone inside which an environmental parameter variation can be captured by a given sensor. On the other hand, the influence area denotes the portion of the area of interest in the immediate vicinity of a sensor. For this purpose segmenting space with voronoi diagram seems promising. The latter represents a practical mechanism used by researchers in order to detect coverage holes by splitting the RoI according to the sensor nodes positions within it. Its mathematical formulation is defined as follows: Assuming that we have a finite set of distributed points called sites $s_1...s_n$ in n-dimensional Euclidean space E_n $(n \geq 1)$ where a site s_i has the coordinates (x_i, y_i), voronoi diagram is the partition of this space into several regions called voronoi cells where each of them contains only one site. Points inside a given cell are closer to the site inside this cell that any other sites. The mathematical formula of a classical voronoi diagram is expressed as follows [13]:

$$Vor(E_n) = \{x \in E_n | d(x, s_i) \leq d(x, s_j), j \neq i, i, j \in \{1, ...n\}\} \tag{1}$$

where d(x,y) represents the euclidean distance between the point x and the point y.

Particle swarm optimization algorithm (PSO) is a nature-inspired algorithm based on the swarm intelligence [1]. It simulates the collective and social behavior of bird flock in exploring the search space to provide the optimal solution. The population of PSO consists of a set of particles representing candidate solution of a given problem, each Particle has a velocity and a position which are updated at each iteration according to a specific mathematical formula (see (2) and (3)). The particle has a fitness value which helps assessing its performance regarding other particles, the particle having the best fitness value shares its experience with the swarm through the global best position.

Our proposed solution for the deployment problem is designed using a combination of the particle swarm optimization algorithm and voronoi diagram. It aims to find sensor node positions which help minimizing the coverage holes within the area of interest.

In this section, we will present the problem formulation and the proposed methodology to solve it.

3.1   Problem Formulation

The region of interest is depicted as a 2D rectangle shape area, and the objective of our solution is to find the adequate position for each sensor node within it in order to enhance its coverage. We assume that the WSN comprises a set of homogeneous sensor nodes that have the same characteristics. The problem is to find the coordinate (x_i, y_i) within an area of a dimension $H \times W$, for each sensor node s_i in $S = \{s_0, s_1, ...s_{N-1}\}$ where N refers to the number of sensor nodes.

3.2   Proposed Solution

Our global approach to tackle the problem of WSN deployment in an indoor environment can be depicted in Fig. 1. It lies on the use of the Building information modeling (BIM) tool which allows modeling all building characteristics via its computable representation and ease the exchange of building related information. This global approach consists of three main steps [14]: Extract input data from reliable data source (BIM database), Optimise WSN deployment with appropriate method and finally visualise the deployment in BIM model.

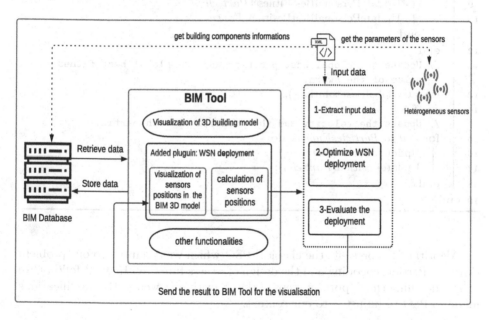

Fig. 1. Global architecture of the proposed approach [14].

In the scope of this paper, we will be focusing on the second step of our global approach which is the WSN deployment optimization. Our deployment method relies on particle swarm optimization Algorithm where each particle represents a potential solution. This algorithm is chosen for its ability to solve geometric optimisation problems by finding the best solutions fitting problem requirements[15]. Algorithm 1 depicts the pseudocode of our method.

Algorithm 1: PSO Algorithm for WSN deployment

---

1 **Input** Number of particles, Number of sensors, PSO parameters values, Target
  area dimensions;
2 **Output** improved sensor nodes positions;

  // Initialize population by generating random deployment for each
     particle, each sensor node position in the random deployment must
     be within the target area.
3 InitializePopulation();
4 int $j = 0$;
5 **while** $j < maxNumberIterations$ **do**
6   **for** $i=0$ **to** $ParticlesNumber$ **do**
          // Assess the fitness value for each particle.
7   ComputeFitness($Particle_i$);
          // For each particle, update the personal best position and
     the personal best fitness value in case where this latter
     is greater than the current fitness value.
8   **if** $Particle_i.getCurrentFitness() < Particle_i.getPersonalBestFitness()$
          then
9   UpdatePersonalBestFitness($Particle_i$);
10   UpdatePersonalBestPosition($Particle_i$);
11   **end**
12   **end**
      // Update the global best position and the global best fitness
     value of the swarm.
13   UpdateGlobalBestSolution();
14     $j = j + 1$;
      // Update the velocity and the position of each particle.
15   **for** $i=0$ **to** $ParticlesNumber$ **do**
16   UpdateVelocity($Particle_i$);
17   UpdatePosition($Particle_i$);
18   **end**
19 **end**

Algorithm 1 represents the classical PSO which was adapted to our problem through: Particle encoding and the design of fitness function. In what follows, we will be detailing the important steps of the algorithm as well as the modifications made to PSO to adjust it to our context.

Particle Encoding: A particle represents a candidate solution in PSO algorithm. In our case, it represents a potential deployment of sensor nodes in the RoI and it is encoded as follows:

Given a set of N sensor nodes, we have: $Particle = \{(x_0, y_0), (x_1, y_1), \cdots, (x_N - 1, y_N - 1)\}$ where (x_i, y_i) describes the coordinates of sensor node s_i.

In addition to the sensor nodes positions, the particle keeps track, at each iteration, of the vertices coordinates of the new voronoi cells generated by the fitness function after updating sensors positions.

Fitness Function: The fitness of a particle is a value that estimates the performance of its potential solution. In our proposed approach, the fitness function measures the total coverage hole generated by a given sensor nodes deployment encoded in a particle. The best solution in the swarm has the smallest fitness value since our objective is to minimize the total uncovered area.

To be able to estimate the coverage hole for a given deployment, we proceed as follows: We start by partitioning the area of interest using the voronoi diagram and we consider the sensor nodes as sites. By the end of this step, each sensor node will have a voronoi cell where its vertices represent the most distant points from the sensor node. The next step aims to close all the cells generated by voronoi diagram so each sensor node will be within a simple polygon P_1. Algorithm (2) is the pseudo code to compute fitness function.

Algorithm 2: Fitness function algorithm

---

1 **Input** particle ;
2 **Output** fitness value for the given particle;

  // Generate voronoi diagram for the sensor nodes deployment encoded
      in the particle solution (sensor nodes represent the sites)
3 ComputeVoronoiDiagram(ParticleSolution);
4 **while** *there is an open voronoi cell for a sensor node s_k in the particle solution*
   do
5 | CloseOpenCell(s_k);
6 **end**
7 int $i = 0$;
8 double *fitness* $= 0$;
9 **while** $i < Number of sensor nodes$ **do**
      // Generate the new virtual polygon representing the real area
          covered by the sensor node s_i
10 | Var *polygon$_i$*= GenerateNewPolygon(s_i);
11 | Var *coverageHoleOfSensor* =
      CalculatePolygonArea(s_i.getClosedVoronoiCell()) -
      CalculatePolygonArea(*polygon$_i$*);
12 | $i = i + 1$;
13 | *fitness*=*fitness*+ *coverageHoleOfSensor*;
14 **end**
   // After calculating the coverage hole of all the sensor nodes
      within the particle solution, we assess the penalty value of the
      Overlapped sensing zones to add it to the fitness value
15 *fitness*=*fitness*+CalculateOverlappingCoveragePenalty(ParticleSolution);

For each sensor node, we generate a new virtual polygon P_2 which represents the effective area it covers within its closed voronoi cell (polygon P_1).

To generate this polygon, we compute the distance between each vertex of the closed voronoi cell and the sensor node, if the distance is less or equal to the sensing range R_s of the sensor node than the cell vertex will be also a vertex for the new polygon, otherwise we compute its new position. Figure 2 illustrates the process of estimating the uncovered area by a sensor node within its voronoi cell.

The fitness function considers also the overlapped sensing zones penalty in order to prevent sensor nodes from moving closer to each other. Figure 3 depicts overlapping sensing zones for a set of sensor nodes. Therefore, the optimal solution must minimise both coverage hole and overlapped area.

Updating Personal Best and Global Best Position: The fitness value for a particle is updated after each iteration and compared to the personal best fitness $Fitness_{pbesti}$: If the current uncovered area is less than the one produced by the personal best solution $Position_{pbesti}$, than $Fitness_{pbesti}$ as well as $Position_{pbesti}$ are updated.

If the best fitness value $Fitness_{pbesti}$, $i = 1,...N$ is better than the global best solution, than $Fitness_{gbest}$ and $Position_{gbest}$ are also updated.

Updating Velocity and Position: Velocity is the particle feature that controls the evolving of its position[16], in our context, it allows computing the movement of sensor nodes within the target area in order to reach their new positions. Velocity is computed according to the Eq. 2:

$$v_i(t+1) = w*v_i(t)+c_1*rand_1*(P_{pbest_i} - P_i(t))+c_2*rand_2*(P_{gbest} - P_i(t)). \quad (2)$$

where w, c_1 and c_2 represent inertia weight, cognitive acceleration and social acceleration respectively, and their values in our algorithm are set to the experiment parameters values shown in [17]. The difference between the current position and the personal best position is the cognitive component, whereas the social component is the difference between the current position and the global best position.

The particle incorporates the updated velocity to compute its new position according the the following equation:

$$P_i(t + 1) = P_i(t) + v_i(t + 1). \quad (3)$$

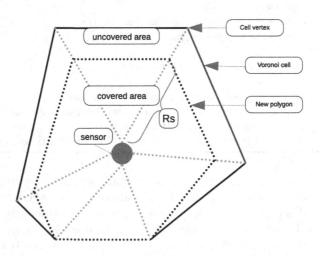

Fig. 2. Coverage hole of a sensor node.

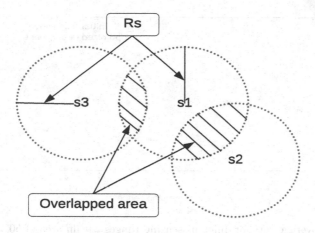

Fig. 3. Overlapped sensing zones of sensor nodes.

4 Results and Discussion

In this section, we will investigate the performance of our algorithm through simulation experiments and study the impact of parameters: RoI area size and sensing range of sensor nodes on the final deployment. The needed sensor node numbers with $R_s = 6$ to reach an ideal coverage of 100% for area of 50×50 m^2, area of 60×60 m^2 and area of 70×70 m^2 is equal to 27, 39 and 53 respectively. For these experiments, the number of sensor nodes is set to 20 in order to assess the performance of the proposed algorithm with a low number of sensor nodes and the fixed values of simulation parameters used for PSO algorithm are shown in Table 1.

Table 1. Parameters of PSO Algorithm

Parameter	Value
Number of iterations	400
Number of particles	20
Inertia weight	0.9
Cognitive acceleration c_1	2
Social acceleration c_2	2

In the first scenario, we considered a square area of 50×50 m^2 with different sensing range values: 6 m, 7 m and 8 m. The Fig. 4 shows that the optimized solution have improved the total coverage of initial solution from 42,2% to 50,5% for $R_s = 6$ and from 49% to 70% for $R_s = 8$ with an average increase of coverage equal to 14,65%

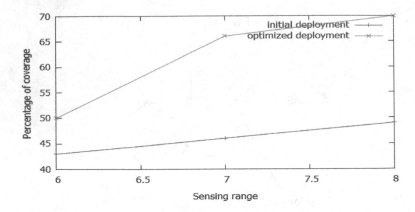

Fig. 4. Coverage rate for different sensing ranges within area of 50×50 m^2

The Fig. 5 illustrates the initial deployment and optimized deployment of sensor nodes within a square of 50×50 m^2.

As shown in the figure, our algorithm tries to minimize both the total coverage hole and the overlapping area by pushing sensor nodes away from each other.

Similar to the first scenario, the second and third tests represent the deployment of sensor nodes within area of 60×60 m^2 and 70×70 m^2 respectively. It is observed in Fig. 8 and Fig. 9 that in both scenarios, the proposed algorithm tries to minimize the coverage hole and reduce the overlapping area. As depicted in Fig. 6 and Fig. 7, the total coverage rate was improved from 35% to 54,5% in the case of 60×60 m^2 area with $R_s = 8$ and from 30,5% to 44,3% in case of 70×70 m^2 area with $R_s = 8$.

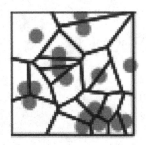
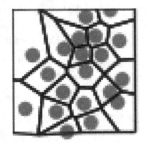

(a) Initial sensor nodes deployment   (b) Optimized sensor nodes deployment

Fig. 5. Sensor nodes deployment in 50×50 m^2 area with $Rs = 6$

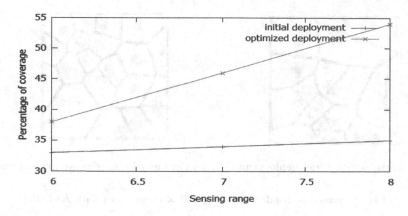

Fig. 6. Coverage rate for different sensing ranges within area of 60×60 m^2

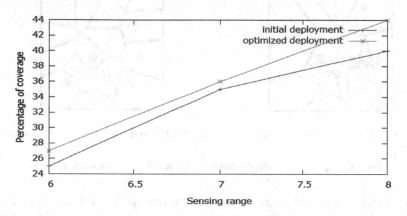

Fig. 7. Coverage rate for different sensing ranges within area of 70×70 m^2

The three scenarios illustrate the impact of sensing range on the final deployment. The proposed algorithm tries to decrease the overlapped area when the sensing radius gets lengthened and simultaneously reduce the uncovered area (see Fig. 8 and Fig. 9).

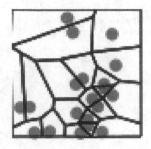
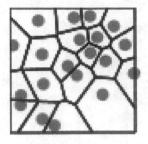

(a) Initial sensor nodes deployment   (b) Optimized sensor nodes deployment

Fig. 8. Sensor nodes deployment in 60×60 m^2 area with $Rs = 6$

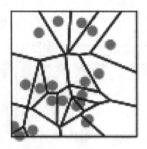
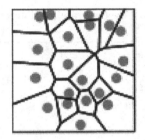

(a) Initial sensor nodes deployment   (b) Optimized sensor nodes deployment

Fig. 9. Sensor nodes deployment in 70×70 m^2 area with $Rs = 6$

The Fig. 10 shows the decrease of coverage rate as the RoI area is increased, this is due to the fact that the maximum area that can be covered by the WSN remains constant since the number of sensor nodes and their sensing range are fixed whereas the RoI area is widened. Thereby we can conclude the significant impact of RoI size on the algorithm performance.

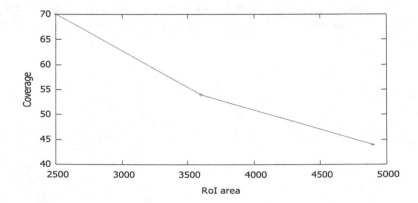

Fig. 10. Coverage rate evolution with the increase of R_s

5   Conclusion

In this paper, we have presented a PSO based algorithm for optimizing WSN deployment within 2D target area. The optimised deployment seeks to enhance the WSN coverage with the objective of increasing the efficiency of the network. In order to reach this objective, our algorithm implements an new fitness function based on Voronoi diagram that aims to minimize both the coverage hole and the overlapping coverage area of the WSN. The experimental results show that the proposed solution is influenced by the RoI size and the sensing range, and it has succeeded in improving the initial coverage rate with average of 20% in case of 50×50 m^2 with $R_s = 8$.

In the near future, we target to enhance the efficiency of our algorithm by considering heterogeneous sensor nodes with the presence of different types of obstacles in RoI. Furthermore, we aim to ensure a full network connectivity while increasing the network lifetime.

References

1. Fei, Z., Li, B., Yang, S., Xing, C., Chen, H., Hanzo, L.: A survey of multi-objective optimization in wireless sensor networks: metrics, algorithms, and open problems. IEEE Commun. Surv. Tutor. **19**(1), 550–586 (2016)
2. Majid, A.S., Joelianto, E.: Optimal sensor deployment in non-convex region using discrete particle swarm optimization algorithm. In: 2012 IEEE Conference on Control, Systems Industrial Informatics, pp. 109–113 (2012)
3. Dahmane, W.-M., Brahmia, M.-E.-A., Dollinger, J.-F., Ouchani, S.: A BIM-based framework for an optimal WSN deployment in smart building. In: 11th International Conference on Networks of the Future, NoF 2020, Bordeaux, France, 12–14 October. IEEE (2020)
4. Zivkovic, M., Bacanin, N., Tuba, E., Strumberger, I., Bezdan, T., Tuba, M.: Wireless sensor networks life time optimization based on the improved firefly algorithm. In: 2020 International Wireless Communications and Mobile Computing (IWCMC), pp. 1176–1181 (2020)
5. Deif, D.S., Gadallah, Y.: Classification of wireless sensor networks deployment techniques. IEEE Commun. Surv. Tutor. **16**(2), 834–855 (2014)
6. Ma, R.-J., Yu, N.Y. and Hu, J.Y.: Application of particle swarm optimization algorithm in the heating system planning problem. Sci. World J. **2013** (2013)
7. Metiaf, A., Wu, Q.: Particle swarm optimization based deployment for WSN with the existence of obstacles. In: 2019 5th International Conference on Control, Automation and Robotics (ICCAR), pp. 614–618. IEEE (2019)
8. Ab Aziz, N.A.B., Mohemmed, A.W., Alias, M.Y.: A wireless sensor network coverage optimization algorithm based on particle swarm optimization and Voronoi diagram. In: 2009 International Conference on Networking, Sensing and Control, pp. 602–607 (2009)
9. Abo-Zahhad, M., Sabor, N., Sasaki, S., Ahmed, S.M.: A centralized immune-Voronoi deployment algorithm for coverage maximization and energy conservation in mobile wireless sensor networks. Inf. Fusion **30**, 36–51 (2016)
10. Wang, G., Cao, G., La Porta, T.F.: Movement-assisted sensor deployment. IEEE Trans. Mob. Comput. **5**(6), 640–652 (2006)

11. Argany, M., Mostafavi, M.A., Gagné, C.: Context-aware local optimization of sensor network deployment. J. Sens. Actuator Netw. **4**(3), 160 (2015)
12. Anurag, A., Priyadarshi, R., Goel, A. and Gupta, B.: 2-D coverage optimization in WSN using a novel variant of particle swarm optimisation. In 2020 7th International Conference on Signal Processing and Integrated Networks (SPIN), pp. 663–668. IEEE (2020)
13. Kiseleva, E.M., Koriashkina, L.S.: Theory of continuous optimal set partitioning problems as a universal mathematical formalism for constructing Voronoi diagrams and their generalizations. I. Theoretical foundations. Cybern. Syst. Anal. **51**(3), 325–335 (2015)
14. Zaimen, K., et al.: A overview on WSN deployment and a novel conceptual BIM-based approach in smart buildings. In: 2020 7th International Conference on Internet of Things: Systems, Management and Security (IOTSMS), pp. 1–6. IEEE (2020)
15. de Almeida, B.S.G., Leite, V.C.: Particle swarm optimization: a powerful technique for solving engineering problems. In: Swarm Intelligence-Recent Advances, New Perspectives and Applications. IntechOpen (2019)
16. Barrera, J., Álvarez-Bajo, O., Flores, J.J., Coello, C.A.C.: Limiting the velocity in the particle swarm optimization algorithm. Computación y Sistemas **20**(4), 635–645 (2016)
17. Qi, W., Yu, H., Fan, G., Chen, L., Wen, X.: WSN coverage optimization based on two-stage PSO. In: Gao, H., Wang, X., Iqbal, M., Yin, Y., Yin, J., Gu, N. (eds.) CollaborateCom 2020. LNICST, vol. 349, pp. 19–35. Springer, Cham (2021). https://doi.org/10.1007/978-3-030-67537-0_2

EPSAAV: An Extensible Platform for Safety Analysis of Autonomous Vehicles

Joelle Abou Faysal[1](✉), Nour Zalmai[2], Ankica Barisic[3], and Frederic Mallet[3]

[1] Renault Software Labs (RSL), Université Cote d'Azur, Cnrs, Inria, I3S,
Sophia Antipolis, France
joelle.abou-faysal@etu.univ-cotedazur.fr
[2] Renault Software Labs (RSL), Sophia Antipolis, France
nour.zalmai@renault.com
[3] Université Cote d'Azur, Cnrs, Inria, I3S, Sophia Antipolis, France
{ankica.barisic,frederic.mallet}@univ-cotedazur.fr

Abstract. In this paper, a novel model related to the safety of autonomous vehicles (AVs) is presented. A simulation platform is designed to analyze the environment and the trajectory of AVs within a given Operational Design Domain (ODD). This platform relies on model-based systems and includes the environment model, safety rules and their priorities, and execution scenarios. The goal is to create a simulation environment that enables safety experts to detect rule breaches by analyzing problems at run-time using generated monitors. Therefore, this platform will help to reevaluate the existing rules in two ways: either by reconsidering rule priorities or by proposing new rules to be integrated into the existing safety model. The validation and verification of the generated rules will follow a process based on the history of the executed scenarios. All the aforementioned work is carried out by using the GEMOC initiative tool to coordinate models using logical time.

Keywords: Autonomous cars · Safety · Model development and verification · Testing and simulating · Formal methods · Rule-Based Planner

1 Introduction

With the advent of autonomous vehicles (AVs), engineers have witnessed several deaths and accidents that raise troubling questions about the safety of such vehicles and the current limitations of the technology. Automobile manufacturers are facing an increasing demand for reliable handling of these autonomous vehicles. It is, therefore, crucial to provide concrete evidence to measure how safe AVs are. Safety is associated with guarantees that some conditions must be met when contingencies arise. If not, the behavior must be adjusted accordingly. In dynamic environments, real-time safety checks of the planned trajectories and the driver

© Springer Nature Switzerland AG 2021
L. Bellatreche et al. (Eds.): MEDI 2021 Workshops, CCIS 1481, pp. 101–111, 2021.
https://doi.org/10.1007/978-3-030-87657-9_8

are sometimes lacking to ensure that the trajectories obtained from trip planning are safe. Nowadays, 90% of car accidents are caused by human errors, such as poor judgment due to a failure of human perception or the driver's lack of attention [1].

It is important to show that the autonomous vehicle makes better decisions than a human driver under all circumstances. One proposal to assess operational safety is to test-drive AVs in real traffic and observe their behavior. As logical as this may sound, it is not efficient because it poses significant risks to the environment. We can look at the Uber accident [2] where the driver was doing mileage tests in Arizona. Several things went wrong while the driver was not paying attention to the road: there was no real-time driver safety check, and Uber did not have the resources in the vehicle to assess the driver's attention.

Mileage testing requires a lot of time and testing to ensure safety, and that doesn't make them scalable [3]. The dilemma of "How many miles autonomous vehicles would need to be driven to demonstrate safety" leads to an answer of 8 billion miles in 400 years with a fleet of 100 vehicles driving all the time [3]. This is somehow unachievable as several works argue that AVs cannot express safety capabilities based on road tests alone [4,5]. Therefore, simulation testing becomes a promising alternative [6]. Moreover, since AVs are currently only tested in limited Operational Design Domains (ODDs), they are not exposed to the wide variety of driving conditions and road user behaviors. Thus, we need rigorous and exhaustive approaches to ensure operational safety.

In the typical software development lifecycle, we try to translate needs into natural language requirements and produce code that meets them. However, it is only after the code has been produced and tested that we discover errors between what was intended and what was built. The same problems occur when testing scenarios. To avoid these problems, Model-Based System Engineering (MBSE) approaches offer a promising alternative by enabling domain models as a communication medium between engineers instead of text documents and supporting automatic code generation. Many researchers now agree that MBSE approaches are a solution for security verification and are seen as an answer to these challenges [7]. MBSE helps to deal with the increasing size and complexity of systems [8], and allows to reason on the model before deployment. Formal modeling and verification in automotive systems are essential to provide sufficient guarantees, especially in the case of dangerous and unforeseen situations.

In this paper, an MBSE approach is proposed based on a simulation environment where a safety rule monitor is specified and generated. It helps us to define types of breaches on an AV trajectory. The main goal is to develop a resilient and safe driver monitoring system that continues to operate safely as long as the assumptions about the environment are satisfied. To sum up, the proposed approach brings a light overview of the **four goals** pursued: (1) formal modeling of safety rules with their priorities alongside the assumptions and the environment on which they rely, (2) monitoring the behavior of the AV at run-time according to these rules and assumptions, (3) triggering alarms to the driver or safety engineer when the behavior of the AV violates some of the safety rules or some of the assumptions and (4) checking and verifying incoherences between the rules and producing the output of the functionality blocs in the planned trajectory.

This paper is organized as follows. Section 2 discusses related work. Section 3 presents the technologies used by the approach, the illustrative real-life use case, and the Extensible Platform for Safety Analysis of Autonomous Vehicles (EPSAAV) approach to specifying the environment and the prioritized rules. It also details the approach to generate an execution policy from the behavior specification. Finally, Sect. 4 draws conclusions and details some possible future work.

2   Related Work

Due to the drawbacks of not having safety verifications, many existing solutions have been proposed. Formal verification approaches are considered as candidates to reduce the intractability of empirical validation [9–11]. One of these approaches is called Responsibility Sensitive Safety (RSS) [5] and has largely inspired our proposal. The authors have developed a white-box verification approach for interpreting safety requirements. They have developed redundant sensing systems with a complex environment. Their interpretable, mathematical model does not guarantee that a vehicle will not be involved in an accident. The limitation of the model also lies in the fact that assumptions and driving policies are taken explicitly to guarantee the safety of the vehicle. They assume that the data is reliable and independent of environmental conditions. The reality is different since there are many scenarios which clearly depend on the weather, sensor reliability, and many other parameters. Our EPSAAV framework allows to circumvent this difficulty by providing the possibility to add measures for safety and environmental conditions. Conceptually, we consider our framework as a complementary safety assessment to [5]. The modularity of our simulation framework easily allows us to include more sophisticated notions of safety, such as temporal-logical specifications or implementations of RSS distances mathematical formulas.

In [12], the authors proposed a modeling and simulation environment called STIMULUS in which they developed and tested requirements in real-time, revealing inconsistencies and ambiguities. Even though textual requirements look simple and reasonable, they contain inconsistencies and ambiguities that lead to undesirable behavior and contradictions. Our framework will help detect these inconsistencies and help the experts to improve the system. Moreover, the tool used in [12] is proprietary and requires a license. However, what the community of autonomous driving needs is an accessible, open-source standard with formal semantics. On the other hand, Measurable Scenario Description Language (M-SDL), created by Foretellix [13], is an open-source solution that unfortunately does not include support for scenario description. Despite the open release, the modeling and simulation tools are proprietary solutions, and there is no way to specify the environmental properties (sampling rate, accuracy) to be captured.

3   Monitoring Platform Specification

Our approach provides a simulation platform that analyzes the environment and trajectory of autonomous vehicles within an operational domain design (ODD). It also aims to help safety designers and experts to verify safety breaches and problems. The proposed Extensible Platform for Safety Analysis of Autonomous Vehicles (EPSAAV) is considered as a testing and verification tool to identify fault types and trigger alerts to the user. It is divided into **three parts**: (1) abstract description of EPSAAV (Fig. 4), (2) the autonomous vehicle environment and formal rules with priorities, and (3) generation of monitors to analyze rule violations and inconsistencies.

3.1   Technologies Used by the Approach

Limited expressiveness makes it harder to express wrong things and facilitates comprehension. Domain-Specific Languages (DSL) can solve some of these problems by raising the level of abstraction closer to the problem domain, rather than code [14]. Our framework uses GEMOC, an open-source tool based on Eclipse. This modeling environment focuses on design and validation problems in complex systems. One of them is enabling the evolution or creation of languages and models. It also integrates heterogeneous parts for different applications that work together to deliver a global service. Specification and simulation techniques aim to model and validate system design and architecture. They are combined with formal verification tools, in particular model checkers, to describe and simulate what a system should do.

The use case of this paper is intended to illustrate this. To implement our DSL, we chose GEMOC Studio [15] to combine several heterogeneous technologies. It covers all aspects of a DSL, from abstract and concrete syntax to semantic operations, as shown in Fig. 1. We started with the definition of the abstract syntax and the metamodel, as shown in Fig. 4. It is based on Eclipse Modeling Framework (EMF), which supports Ecore metamodel implementation. It is also interesting to note that the GEMOC framework generates an IDE with syntax checking. Once we have the final libraries, this generative approach allows us to generate various concrete syntaxes by using Xtext artifacts [16]. Once the concrete syntax was processed, we needed the operational semantics to assign behavior to each of the declarations in our DSL. To do this, we use Xtend, a programming language used to implement the execution semantics of Ecore metamodels. We are generating two types of documents: one for the integration with the internal system, and the other one which is human-readable and which describes rules specification. This technology allows us to add methods and verify the defined properties. The next step will be combining the generated code from Xtend with CCSL that helps to study temporal inconsistencies and concurrent behavior. To visualize the behavior, Sirius is also available for the graphical display implementation. Interestingly, the GEMOC framework is open source and easily integrates with other tools. It features easy code generation and adapts when settings are changed so that it works properly as development

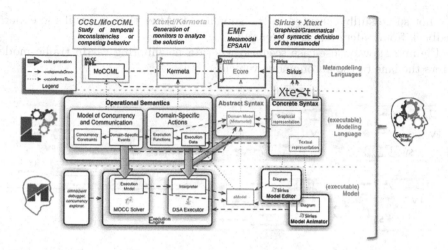

Fig. 1. Overview of the GEMOC execution framework with the used technologies in our approach.

continues. In other words, the language allows us to express the Operational Design Domain (ODD) in a common, non-ambiguous language in which we can express the scenarios that need to be handled safely by a vehicle to achieve "certification" as discussed by [17]. To create this type of system, which is too complicated to do by hand, we use these technologies to shorten the development cycles and have an effective method of reasoning on these rules. The interesting thing about this approach is that we can adopt new requirements that we meet or change the existing ones without changing the language, so it is scalable.

3.2 Illustrative Real-Life Use Case

To apply operational safety to the trajectories of autonomous cars, we will need elementary data necessary for the system that is perception. We also need to know the rules that need to be defined with their types. Therefore, our use case relies on Renault's unsafe scenarios document, which describes the raw data of the abstract scenarios, their risks, and the actions to be taken. Renault's safety requirements are based on the Safety Of The Intended Functionality standard (SOTIF ISO/PAS 21448) [18]. This document aims to determine most of the different use cases for the system based on the verification process. The objective is to verify that Renault can handle all the identified scenarios. We then need to manage each use case in the most different conditions that help us estimate that the other use cases are managed and validate all the other conditions regarding the scenario. Tests will be performed to verify and validate the use cases in each scenario handled by the ego vehicle; the autonomous car on which we are studying safety, while we will focus on specific environmental conditions to show that the perceptual sensors can avoid any hazard, and to verify any scenario that was not successfully executed in the simulation. After that, we will use expert feedback from Safety teams in Renault.

Figure 2 shows a use-case scenario where a neighboring car in traffic mode enters the lane of the autonomous vehicle.

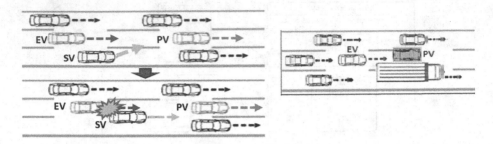

Fig. 2. Straddling Vehicle (SV) swerving over the Go Vehicle (EV) to take over Preceding Vehicle's (PV) place.

There is a risk of collision with this adjacent vehicle. The conditions to be taken are a regulation of the safe distance, i.e. a stable control, and if this lasts longer than a certain time, we perform an emergency maneuver, as we called it *emergency_operation* in our library (Fig. 5a). Based on Renault's document, we could describe these unsafe scenarios more concretely in a specification document, in terms of rules and priorities, warnings and actions, as seen below in Fig. 3:

```
BEGIN GOALS
when
        traffic_jam is yes
then
    BEGIN GOALS
      when
            stable_control is stable AND
          (
              straddling_car_tracking is straddling_more_than_t7

          )
        then goal:
            executing  emergency_operation
```

Fig. 3. Formal rules specification based on the swerving case.

The notion of priority consideration in the model will allow us to determine if the rules are complete, that is if they cover all situations or not. What will also be good is to see the gaps that are missing in this document when examining inconsistencies and rule violations.

3.3 Abstract Description of the Extensible Platform for Autonomous Vehicle Safety Analysis (EPSAAV)

Our metamodel in Fig. 4 is composed of three levels. The first level contains the Rule-Based Planner RBP, which refers to a described scene and is composed of goals. The RBP is responsible for formalizing and specifying rules. Each driving task requires object and Event Detection and Response (OEDR). It helps to identify objects around the ego car, detect events that occur nearby, and then react to them. There are three crucial parts of perception: (1) Static Objects (e.g.: road structure, traffic lights, and signs), (2) Dynamic Objects (e.g.: vehicles and pedestrians), (3) Ego Module that correponds to internal properties of the Autonomous Vehicle (AV).

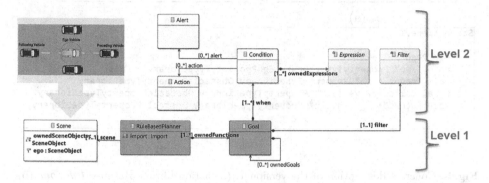

Fig. 4. Abstract description of EPSAAV metamodel using EMF technology.

For this reason, we created a scene specification, which is very important to describe the maximum number of perceived objects around the autonomous vehicle. The scene specifies the roles of these objects and their types. The goals consist of the conditions we want to apply, which relate to actions we can associate with the motion planner, and alarms we want to trigger for the user. This is at the second level of the metamodel. These conditions are described by logical expressions. The metamodel can also filter the rules either by library type or by role or even by expression. The third level defines the libraries in which we want to describe the properties for the ego and the obstacles. Creating this metamodel gives us the right to a more concrete description of the environment and the rules described in Sect. 3.4.

3.4 Concrete Description of the Autonomous Vehicle's Environment

In this part, a concrete description of the environment is presented. The main feature of EPSAAV is to allow the user or safety expert to create multiple libraries to specify the properties. In our use case, the main goal was to have one library for the ego and another one for the obstacles. For future work, we can create properties related to pedestrians, for example, but for now, let us consider them as obstacles. This use case is edited to be able to insert everything that is shown in the Renault specification document. In the scene, as we said before, we specify the roles of the obstacles and their types with reference to the libraries created. We also created a library for actions and one for alarms in Fig. 5.

```
ActionLibrary Actionsv1

Action "brake_moderate"
Action "brake_strong"
Action "emergency_operation"
Action "emergency_maneuver"
Action "no_action_needed"
Action "acceleration_moderate"
```

(a)

```
AlertLibrary Alertsv1

Alert "longitudinal_report"
Alert "lateral_report"
Alert "emergency_operation"
Alert "violation_safety_distance"
```

(b)

```
Scene scenev1
{
    ego ^ego
    role "ego" PropertyTypeLibrary EgoPropertyTypeLibrary
    role "pedestrian" PropertyTypeLibrary ObstaclePropertyTypeLibrary
    role "following_vehicle" PropertyTypeLibrary ObstaclePropertyTypeLibrary
    role "straddling_vehicle" PropertyTypeLibrary ObstaclePropertyTypeLibrary
}
```

(c)

Fig. 5. Concrete description of the version 1: (a) action library *Actionsv1.actions* (b) alert library *Alertsv1.alerts* (c) scene *scenev1.scene*.

Xtext files were also needed to create semantic forms for rules with priorities. Rules without priorities just do not make sense. Take the case of these two rules: one that applies a slight acceleration to maintain a safe distance with the rear vehicle, and one that says you have to brake because a pedestrian is crossing the road. Hence the notion of priority must be included in the syntactic part. Our model gives us the option to prioritize rules in an easy concrete way as shown in Fig. 6.

The user can add new versions of his work and follow this helpful expressive formal specification to write the rules. If something goes wrong, the Rule-based Planner is responsible for informing the driver of the detected problem. It analyzes the event of a subsystem failure, then triggers the alert to the user. The description of the violation's type gives the user a hint when a takeover is requested. There is a possibility to link this description to the trajectory planner if we take it at a higher level in the taxonomy [19]. The verification of the expressiveness of all the rules retrieved from the unsafe scenarios in Renault's documents is done by creating generators as described in the following part.

```
RuleBasedPlanner RBP{
    scene "scenev1"
    GOAL pedestrian_priority{
        filter SelectByRole ego
        WHEN{
            propertyType "EgoPropertyTypeLibrary.front_pedestrian_tracking" is "EgoPropertyTypeLibrary.front_pedestrian_tracking.exist"
            action "Actionsv1.brake_strong"
            alert "Alertsv1.violation_safety_distance"
        }
        GOAL rear_vehicle_safedistance{
            filter SelectByRole ego
            WHEN{
                propertyType "EgoPropertyTypeLibrary.rear_car_distance" is "EgoPropertyTypeLibrary.rear_car_distance.acc_distance"
                action "Actionsv1.acceleration_moderate"
                alert "Alertsv1.longitudinal_report"
            }
        }
    }
}
```

Fig. 6. Prioritizing rules in the RuleBasedPlanner *RBP.rbp.*

3.5   Generation of Monitors to Analyze the Solution

We want to generate behaviors in the Autonomous Vehicle's environment. Using Xtend technology, we created a document generator that describes all the resources and predefined libraries used, as well as the prioritized rules. This text generation has a documentary goal for a good description of our environment and the rules with their priorities. It will help safety experts to save their work whenever a change is made. We also created a code generator that will be used to check violations in an unsafe case and to test for inconsistencies between the priority of these rules and with the block functionalities for Renault. To do this, it is necessary to include in the code generator a function that adapts to the driving data and the rules, and that can access all the driving data from sensors or the simulators. This is an ongoing work while retrieving structures of data in Renault's perception algorithms. Our safety checker module adapts the rules and the input data and then returns the warnings and actions that were triggered in the Rule-Based Planner. It is also important to note that we will be generating C code because the tools in Renault are based on this programming language, but the facility of our tool can generate any code with small modifications. Our modeling-driven engineering tool enables us to verify the properties before generation.

The next phase consists of examining the consistency of the rules. As seen in Fig. 7, we need to compare the output of our safety checker module with the output of a feature block, e.g. the Autonomous Emergency Braking (AEB) block, to see whether or not there is consistency with our actions in an unsafe case in the event of braking.

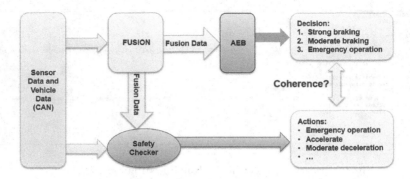

Fig. 7. Study of the consistency between the outputs of the AEB functionality block and the rules described in the safety checker module.

4 Conclusion and Future Work

In this paper, we propose an MBSE approach based on a simulation environment in which we specify and generate libraries and a set of safety rules. These rules have different priorities that help us define the types of violations along a trajectory. We also generated a human-readable document and a code for the internal system integration. The main contribution of this approach is to develop a resilient and safe driver monitoring system that continues to operate safely as long as the assumptions about the environment are met. This is a general approach that could be used in several domains. It is a checker that triggers alerts when rules are violated and detects inconsistencies between these rules. It facilitates the description of formal safety rules for experts and gives them the power to version any modification of the environment. The approach can also modify/replace decision-making in trajectory planning. This approach will also be used to find new scenarios to complete the verification of the operational safety on the databases. This is an ongoing work where we provided concrete syntax, completed our abstract metamodel, and developed the first generator.

For future work, studying inconsistencies by scheduling analysis with CCSL based on priorities of the objectives, and adding a graphical interface using Sirius are the two following steps, along with the integration of other public simulators. Carla and Webots for automobiles show great promise as they are widely used by the community. The use of simulation and display tools at Renault is also possible.

References

1. Vanbever, L.: Self-driving networks: breaking new ground in network automation (2019). http://univ-cotedazur.fr/en/eur/ds4h/research/forum-numerica/forum-numerica/past-sessions/laurent-vanbever. Accessed 05 May 2020
2. Drazkowski, J.F., et al.: Seizure-related motor vehicle crashes in Arizona before and after reducing the driving restriction from 12 to 3 months. Mayo Clin. Proc. **78**(7), 819–825 (2003)

3. Kalra, N., Paddock, S.M.: Driving to safety: how many miles of driving would it take to demonstrate autonomous vehicle reliability? Trans. Res. Part A Policy Pract. **94**, 182–193 (2016)
4. Koopman, P., Wagner, M.: Challenges in autonomous vehicle testing and validation. SAE Int. J. Trans. Saf. **4**(1), 15–24 (2016)
5. Shalev-Shwartz, S., Shammah, S., Shashua, A.: On a formal model of safe and scalable self-driving cars arXiv preprint arXiv:1708.06374 (2017)
6. Yan, X., Feng, S., Sun, H., Liu, H.X.: Distributionally consistent simulation of naturalistic driving environment for autonomous vehicle testing arXiv preprint arXiv:2101.02828 (2021)
7. D'Ambrosio, J., Soremekun, G.: Systems engineering challenges and MBSE opportunities for automotive system design. In: 2017 IEEE International Conference on Systems, Man, and Cybernetics (SMC), pp. 2075–2080. IEEE (2017)
8. Duprez, J.: An MBSE modeling approach to efficiently address complex systems and scalability. In: INCOSE International Symposium, vol. 28, no. 1, pp. 940–954. Wiley Online Library (2018)
9. Seshia, S.A., Sadigh, D., Sastry, S.S.: Formal methods for semi-autonomous driving. In: 52nd ACM/EDAC/IEEE Design Automation Conference (DAC), pp. 1–5. IEEE (2015)
10. O'Kelly, M., Abbas, H., Gao, S., Shiraishi, S., Kato, S., Mangharam, R.: APEX: autonomous vehicle plan verification and execution. In: SAE World Congress, vol. 1 (2016)
11. Althoff, M., Dolan, J.M.: Online verification of automated road vehicles using reachability analysis. IEEE Trans. Robot. **30**(4), 903–918 (2014)
12. Jeannet, B., Gaucher, F.: Debugging embedded systems requirements with stimulus: an automotive case-study. In: 8th European Congress on Embedded Real Time Software and Systems, ERTS 2016 (2016)
13. Foretellix: Open measurable scenario description language (M-SDL) (2020). https://www.foretellix.com/open-language/. Accessed 30 Apr 2021
14. Gray, J., Neema, S., Tolvanen, J.-P., Gokhale, A.S., Kelly, S., Sprinkle, J.: Domain-specific modeling. Handb. Dyn. Syst. Model. **7**, 1–7 (2007)
15. Combemale, B., Barais, O., Wortmann, A.: Language engineering with the GEMOC studio. In: 2017 IEEE International Conference on Software Architecture Workshops (ICSAW), pp. 189–191. IEEE (2017)
16. Bettini, L.: Implementing Domain-Specific Languages with Xtext and Xtend. Packt Publishing Ltd., Birmingham (2016)
17. Koopman, P., et al.: Certification of Highly Automated Vehicles for Use on UK Roads: Creating an Industry-Wide Framework for Safety. White Rose Research Online, Sheffield (2019)
18. Koopman, P., Ferrell, U., Fratrik, F., Wagner, M.: A safety standard approach for fully autonomous vehicles. In: Romanovsky, A., Troubitsyna, E., Gashi, I., Schoitsch, E., Bitsch, F. (eds.) SAFECOMP 2019. LNCS, vol. 11699, pp. 326–332. Springer, Cham (2019). https://doi.org/10.1007/978-3-030-26250-1_26
19. SAE Mobilus: Taxonomy and definitions for terms related to driving automation systems for on-road motor vehicles (2018). https://www.sae.org/standards/. Accessed 30 Apr 2021

Bridging Trust in Runtime Open Evaluation Scenarios

Emilia Cioroaica[1(✉)], Barbora Buhnova[2], Eda Marchetti[3], Daniel Schneider[1], and Thomas Kuhn[1]

[1] Fraunhofer IESE, Kaiserslautern, Germany
{emilia.cioroaica,daniel.schneider,thomas.kuhn}@iese.fraunhofer.de
[2] Masaryk University, Brno, Czech Republic
buhnova@mail.muni.cz
[3] ISTI-CNR, Pisa, Italy
eda.marchettii@isti.cnr.it

Abstract. Solutions to specific challenges within software engineering activities can greatly benefit from human creativity. For example, evidence of trust derived from creative virtual evaluation scenarios can support the trust assurance of fast-paced runtime adaptation of intelligent behavior. Following this vision, in this paper, we introduce a methodological and architectural concept that interplays creative and social aspects of gaming into software engineering activities, more precisely into a virtual evaluation of system behavior. A particular trait of the introduced concept is that it reinforces cooperation between technological and social intelligence.

Keywords: Trust · Virtual evaluation · Gaming

The systematic adoption of AI solutions is envisioned to uplift the human responsibilities in the emergent *feeling economy* [12] with an increased assignment of repetitive and analytical human cognitive processes to AI components, i.e. smart agents. Such a transition leaves human workers a free space for addressing more interpersonal, empathetic and ethical tasks.

However, from an engineering perspective there are ongoing challenges that hinder ssfigthe trust into AI performance during operation. Particularly challenging from a trustworthiness perspective are intelligent systems that learn continuously during operation. While a different set of outputs provided for the same set of inputs may be an evidence of improved behaviour (due to continuous learning), it can also be a sign of sporadic malicious behavior that only activates in specific situations when a catastrophic impact is foreseeable. In our previous work [11] we have proposed a solution for ensuring a trusted execution of software smart agents based on runtime behavior prediction within a safe environment. The prediction is performed without executing the software that can potentially contain malicious behavior, but by executing its digital twins in a trusted real-time environment. In this paper we bring forward the idea of trust

© Springer Nature Switzerland AG 2021
L. Bellatreche et al. (Eds.): MEDI 2021 Workshops, CCIS 1481, pp. 112–120, 2021.
https://doi.org/10.1007/978-3-030-87657-9_9

assurance of intelligent (and continuously evolving) behavior, by addressing the decision challenge of runtime behavioral control of a system. When a behavior or system component cannot be activated due to doubts regarding its trustworthiness, a decision needs to be taken whether or not to activate alternative trusted behaviors or components in the spirit of a fail operational scheme.

Although general to any system under the control of software smart agents, we'll exemplify our concept for the domain of safety critical systems, allowing us to be more specific in the explanations. For example, when an autonomous vehicle, which is a safety critical system, is faced with evidence of possible untrusted intentions of a software smart agent, it needs to decide very fast on a trusted course of action. If the vehicle driving around a school area relies on the intelligent activation of speed limits and the responsible behaviour is deceived by a malicious attack, the vehicle needs to detect this to trigger a fail-over behavior early enough in order to avoid accidents. Key to the envisioned scheme is the dynamic acquisition of trust evidence. Such evidence can be provided by humans that exercise system behaviors in creative settings within a design and runtime co-engineering framework. Based on evidence of challenging operational contexts collected from the field, creative explorations of behavioral variants of systems can be performed upfront. Such evidence, can support runtime activation of intelligent behavior. Crowd intelligence is in our opinion an immediate and scalable resource that enables a creative evaluation of intelligent behavior. To support this transition, in the current paper we propose an architectural and methodological concept that supports the outsourcing of behavioral evaluation in open scenarios to crowd intelligence through gaming.

In what follows, Sect. 1 presents an overview of the emerging transitions and trends on the roles of humans in the creative process of virtual evaluation. Section 2 introduces our methodological approach for using gaming as a resource to create trust during runtime with an architectural concept of platform presented in Sect. 3. Section 4 presents discussions and conclusions together with ongoing work and future research directions.

1   Emerging Transitions

1.1   Crowd Intelligence and AI Intelligence

Basing system intelligence on crowdsourcing, crowd intelligence [18] can through motivational schemes engage the large population into performing intelligent tasks, such as image recognition [16]. Engagement of population in supporting AI evolution is traditionally enforced through monetary rewards which build on extrinsic human motivation.

An emerging trend of gaining human engagement is further on brought through gamification schemes [19] which builds on the intrinsic motivation of a human being. Through an advanced level of commitment used in competition-based crowd-sourcing platforms, unidirectional technological solutions are developed.

We believe that an uplift of the traditional crowd-sourcing concept can further on construct a sustainable AI-socio-technical evolution through integration of social and psychological human aspects shaped by social experts.

1.2   From Machine to Human Readable Specification Scenarios

The advancements of autonomous vehicles rely on development of intelligent control trained on huge datasets. Large scale training is expected to improve reactions of autonomous systems to certain situations. But despite large data sets, accidents still occur when the training data does not cover all situations [17]. In order to fix this, development of corner case detection aim at identifying untypical situations [8], with an emerging trend of exploring human creativity in this direction. For example, frameworks such as [3] enable derivation of as many test scenarios as possible for autonomous driving, by closing the gap between machine-readable representations and human understanding.

On top of this, languages such as M-SDL (Measurable Scenario Description Language) [4] allow a simplified capture and reuse of scenarios, enabling specification of a mixture of conditions with the scope of identifying unknown hazards and edge cases for which an autonomous behavior can be safeguarded at runtime. Specifications that result from test scenarios then become requirements that guide the development of intelligent behavior.

Elevating from the idea of human understandable description of virtual evaluation scenarios, our approach also envisions the availability and readiness of solutions in a gaming setting at the convenience of the crowd.

1.3   Enriching the Input Domain

The dynamic acquisition of human-generated evidence of trust in open runtime environments can still be time consuming. Therefore, we propose enriching the variety of valid and invalid input through usage of techniques capable to manipulate available data sets in order to generate new inputs for valid solution. Usually applied for assessing the effectiveness of a testing approach, mutation analysis [13] is a commonly adopted approach for input transformations. In mutation testing, a mutant is a slightly modified version of the program under test, differing from it by a small, syntactic change. The underlying assumption of mutation testing and the coupling effect, is that, by looking for simple syntactic modifications, more complex, but real, faults can be found.

Creating new inputs by applying semantic information-preserving transformations is a challenge in different software research areas. As analyzed in [15] different approaches can be adopted such as: the metamorphic transformations focused on input alterations that mimic the environment conditions or real-world phenomena; the application of search-based approaches for eliciting collision scenarios; the exploitation of the boundaries of the input space so as to maximize the transitions in the behavior; or the investigation of the adversarial inputs able to trigger misbehaviors often very unlikely or impossible to occur in reality.

In our concept we envision the adoption of mutation approaches to enrich the dynamic acquisition of trust evidence.

2   Gaming for Trust

During the design of autonomous processes, such as autonomous driving, different types of AI components are envisioned to either automate parts of the vehicle control or provide increased awareness of the runtime operational context. Typically, AI components are trained on data sets at design time. Then, during operation, the degree of matching between new situations and previously trained situations provides a level of trust into planned actions. Particularly challenging however are those situations, for which a trusted action that was initially decided needs to be modified due to an unforeseen event, e.g. the sudden detection of an obstacle. These situations stress the reactions speed of an autonomous vehicle and moreover has the potential to reduce the vehicles ability to keep an operational state. For example, a vehicle making a right turn at an intersection might need to react quickly to a sudden overtaking of another vehicle that is approaching from the opposite direction. Stopping the vehicle as a result of an immediate fail-over behavior will not only decrease the human trust into the autonomous driving capabilities but in this risky situation, it might not avoid an immediate crash. Instead, the vehicle should e.g. drive to the far right side of the street, which implies activation of another trusted behavior. Trust can be supported by evidence from previous similar evaluation scenarios in which the system did prove correct decisions and behavior.

A high degree of variations for the scenario configurations can be derived during design time by applying specific mutation operators to scenarios objects and data. Specifically, equivalence classes can be defined for context awareness or for related game objects that represent AI. These can be further used for deriving new equivalent scenarios for assessing the established level of trust and derivation of additional unexpected scenarios for behavioral evaluation. For example, considering a scenario in which a vehicle reacts quickly to sudden overtaking of a vehicle: i) different equivalent scenarios can be derived either by changing the type of weather condition or the type of road surface. In both cases the vehicle reaction should not be largely conditioned by the applied mutations, i.e., the vehicle should in any case drive to the far-right side of the street, but with a slight adaptation of speed. Alternatively, additional unexpected scenarios could be derived by mutating the overall situation. For instance substituting the *overtaking of a vehicle* with *approaching of blind curve* or ongoing earthquake. In both cases the vehicle reaction should not be the same as before. In this situations, the vehicle should not only keep the right side of the street but should also drastically reduce the speed in order to avoid possible hazards. In both cases, previous evaluation of complex scenes can be opportunely mutated for providing evidences trusted behavior.

Figure 1 presents a high level view of our proposed approach. Efficiency of behavior evaluation is achieved through creative gaming while its effectiveness

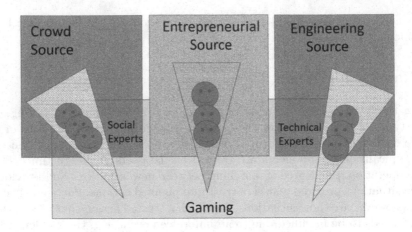

Fig. 1. High level view of the methodological approach

is supported by a systematic mapping between the engineering world and the gaming world. The engineering world can be represented by real devices within a lab or virtual entities such as simulation models, and diagrams within a virtual testing environment. Psychological benefits for the population are assured through an interplay of social experts with the role of framing gaming scenes for the psychological needs of the crowd and at the same time leverage gamification schemes for engagement. We based this decision on recent developments within the gaming industry [7]. Even though until recently the scope of systematic triggering of emotions has been directed towards achieving business gains, recently, the gaming industry has been approved to produce games for the psychological benefits of humans.

Figure 2 depicts the main components of a framework that enables the mapping between the engineering and gaming world. The virtual evaluation within an engineering setting needs to be framed into game scenes. Each scene contains multiple gaming objects which are mappings of systems, system components and technologies, such as AI components. This mapping is performed by engineers and technical experts, and can be blinded if the player is not aware of the representation of the game object in the real world, or unblinded if the game object represents concrete systems. Blinded mapping enables exploration of concepts in a creative manner and relies on logical mapping only, not structural mapping. For example, different types of wireless technologies can be mapped to different types of strings that connect two objects.

Unblinded mapping enables explorations with new concepts through an accurate representation of real world objects. Configurations from explorations within gaming scenes are then passed to a co-simulation framework which executes simulation models of systems and system components in various scenarios.

Evidence that supports trusted deviations of behavior within specific technical situations are then shipped on the real system as blueprints. The blueprints can describe trusted reconfiguration in a set of scenarios. The degree of trust

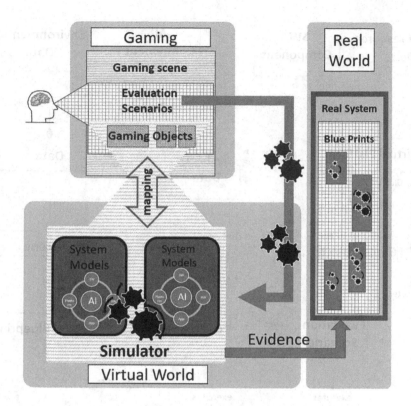

Fig. 2. Interplay of virtual and technical world

results from evidence within virtual evaluation scenarios and guide the real-time decision process. Based on sufficient evidence of scenario evaluation in the simulated environment, during runtime, the blueprints assign according levels of trust on the planned course of action.

3 Prototype Platform

In this section, we exemplify the components of a platform that enables implementation of our methodological approach.

Figure 3 outlines the architecture of such a platform in which *Game scenes* aggregate both *Data* and *Game Objects*. *Environmental Data* can be provided by simulators specialized in driving maneuvers and simulation of weather conditions, such as the LGSVL [5] which is Unity3D-based and Carla [1], an Unreal-based automotive simulator plugin. *Game objects* either represent only a logical mapping of engineering and technical concepts or accurately represent real-world objects. *Environmental Data* represents the inputs that a specific technology or system component is processing in a given scenarios, whereas *System Data* is provided by simulation models of *Virtual Platforms*. System data can consist of

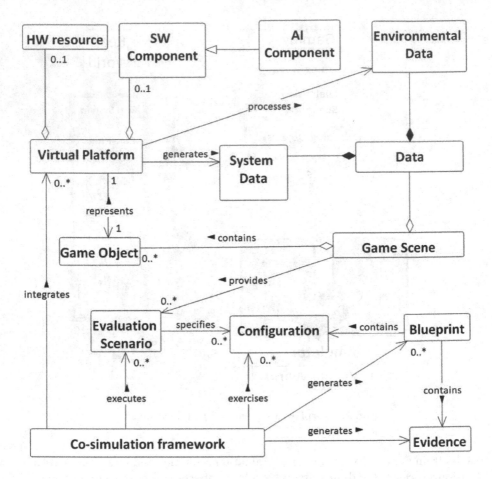

Fig. 3. Logical view of the platform

continuous or discrete values generated from the execution of simulation models. These values specify functional and non-functional properties of a system component, subject of virtual evaluation. The simulation models can be high level specifications models, detailed models defined in Simulink [6] or concrete implementations, including software implementation of *AI components*. In this way, within a game setting a deep learning algorithm, which is an AI component responsible for image recognition of an autonomous vehicle can be evaluated on a variety of input stimuli and provide a higher level of confidence in the intelligent reaction of the vehicle.

Each *Virtual Platform* is represented in the gaming world by a *Game Object* exercised within a *Game Scene*. The creative experimentation with game objects within a game scene creates a variety of virtual *Evaluation Scenarios*. These scenarios are executed by a *Co-simulation framework* which integrates virtual platforms represented by simulation models. For enabling simulator interoperability, the integration of different simulation models within the co-simulation framework needs to be in conformance to standard interfaces, such as the FMI (Functional Mockup Interface) [2].

The evaluation scenarios within games specify *Configurations* that are further on exercised by the co-simulation framework. These configurations together with evidence of trust are integrated within *Blueprints* ready to be downloaded on systems.

4   Discussion and Conclusions

Elevating from the idea of human-understandable description of scenarios, the approach we have introduced, enables, through gaming availability and readiness of solutions a creative virtual evaluation of intelligent system behavior. Further on, with the support of a runtime simulation framework that we have introduced in [11], blueprints of trusted scenarios can increase the level of confidence into fast decisions with a direct support for agile adaptations to unforeseen runtime situations.

4.1   State of Work and Preliminary Results

Our platform is based on FERAL simulator [14] and builds on the integration between virtual and real world, introduced in [10]. Additional research and engineering aspects that enable a runtime and design time co-engineering of trusted behavior have been introduced in [9].

4.2   Future and Ongoing Work

The scope of the entire concept encompasses many interesting research questions for further investigation, such as (a) definition of structural description of blue prints that support real-time decision control, (b) definition of blueprints for use cases within different domains, and (c) specification of evidence that supports the time criticality of runtime control activation.

Acknowledgment. This work is co-funded from the European Union's Horizon 2020 research and innovation programme under grant agreement No. 952702 (BIECO) and by ERDF "CyberSecurity, CyberCrime and Critical Information Infrastructures Center of Excellence" (No. CZ.02.1.01/0.0/0.0/16_019/0000822).

References

1. Carla Simulator. https://carla.org/. Accessed 04 Dec 2020
2. FMI. https://fmi-standard.org/. Accessed 06 Dec 2020
3. Foretellix. https://www.foretellix.com/open-language/. Accessed 12 Dec 2020

4. Foretellix M-SDL. https://www.foretellix.com/category/m-sdl/. Accessed 12 Dec 2020
5. LGSVL simulator. https://www.lgsvlsimulator.com/. Accessed 12 Dec 2020
6. Simulink. https://www.mathworks.com/products/simulink.html. Accessed 02 Dec 2020
7. Anderson, M.: Prescription-strength gaming: ADHD treatment now comes in the form of a first-person racing game-[News]. IEEE Spectr. **57**(8), 9–10 (2020)
8. Bolte, J., Bar, A., Lipinski, D., Fingscheidt, T.: Towards corner case detection for autonomous driving. In: 2019 IEEE Intelligent Vehicles Symposium (IV), pp. 438–445 (2019). https://doi.org/10.1109/IVS.2019.8813817
9. Cioroaica, E., et al.: Towards creation of automated prediction systems for trust and dependability evaluation. In: 2020 International Conference on Software, Telecommunications and Computer Networks (SoftCOM), pp. 1–6. IEEE (2020)
10. Cioroaica, E., Kuhn, T., Bauer, T.: Prototyping automotive smart ecosystems. In: 2018 48th Annual IEEE/IFIP International Conference on Dependable Systems and Networks Workshops (DSN-W). IEEE (2018)
11. Cioroaica, E., Kuhn, T., Buhnova, B.: (Do not) trust in ecosystems. In: Proceedings of the 41st International Conference on Software Engineering: New Ideas and Emerging Results, pp. 9–12. IEEE Press (2019)
12. Huang, M.H., Rust, R., Maksimovic, V.: The feeling economy: managing in the next generation of artificial intelligence (AI). Calif. Manag. Rev. **61**(4), 43–65 (2019)
13. Jia, Y., Harman, M.: An analysis and survey of the development of mutation testing. IEEE Trans. Softw. Eng. **37**(5), 649–678 (2011). https://doi.org/10.1109/TSE.2010.62. Sept
14. Kuhn, T., Forster, T., Braun, T., Gotzhein, R.: FERAL-framework for simulator coupling on requirements and architecture level. In: 2013 Eleventh IEEE/ACM International Conference on Formal Methods and Models for Codesign (MEMOCODE), pp. 11–22. IEEE (2013)
15. Riccio, V., Jahangirova, G., Stocco, A., Humbatova, N., Weiss, M., Tonella, P.: Testing machine learning based systems: a systematic mapping. Empir. Softw. Eng. **25**(6), 5193–5254 (2020). https://doi.org/10.1007/s10664-020-09881-0
16. Sullivan, D.P., et al.: Deep learning is combined with massive-scale citizen science to improve large-scale image classification. Nat. Biotechnol. **36**(9), 820–828 (2018)
17. Tian, Y., Pei, K., Jana, S., Ray, B.: DeepTest: automated testing of deep-neural-network-driven autonomous cars. In: Proceedings of the 40th International Conference on Software Engineering, pp. 303–314 (2018)
18. Xin, K., Zhang, S., Wu, X., Cai, W.: Reciprocal crowdsourcing: building cooperative game worlds on blockchain. In: 2020 IEEE International Conference on Consumer Electronics (ICCE), pp. 1–6. IEEE (2020)
19. Yang, C., Ye, H.J., Feng, Y.: Using gamification elements for competitive crowdsourcing: exploring the underlying mechanism. Behav. Inf. Technol. **40**(9), 837–854 (2021)

A Generation and Recovery Framework for Silicon PUFs Based Cryptographic Key

Fahem Zerrouki[1]([✉]) [ID], Samir Ouchani[2] [ID], and Hafida Bouarfa[1] [ID]

[1] University of Blida, Blida, Algeria
[2] Lineact CESI, Aix-en-Provence, France
souchani@cesi.fr

Abstract. Integrated Circuits (ICs) and electronic devices became the main part of human daily life (mobile, home, car, etc.). However, for the safety of the transported information to and from these devices, some specifics security measures should be taken. In general, ICs are a source of high randomness due to the manufacturing variation process which elects them to be potential physically unclonable functions (PUFs) and known as Silicon PUFs (SPUFs). Many propositions have shown that SPUFs could guarantee the three pillars of security: confidentiality, authenticity, and privacy of the user information by these devices. More importantly, extracting strong cryptographic keys from them, error correction, and hashing code techniques should be considered. Unfortunately concerning Silicon PUFs, generating many time the same response for the same input is not possible due to many factors especially environmental variables such as noise, supply voltage, temperature and aging. To overcome this issue and recover the original response from the noisy one, a secure sketch based approach is recommended. This paper proposes a framework that generates easily the cryptographic keys and efficiently recovers them for a Silicon PUF. The experiments have been validated on an Arbiter PUF under different temperatures.

Keywords: Physical unclonable function · Arbiter PUF · Fuzzy extractor · Secure sketch · Key generation · Syndrome · Error correction codes

1 Introduction

Conventional cryptography schemes mainly rely on uniform distribution and random string of the generated key such as random passwords and tokens. Indeed, random strings must have enough high entropy. Further, they should have been able to securely generate, store and recover keys. Hence, the minimal needed requirements are: 1) a *randomness source* to generate a unique and unpredictable key, and 2) a *secure memory* that reliably stores the key's information whereas totally protecting it from unauthorized parties and allows the recovering of a

© Springer Nature Switzerland AG 2021
L. Bellatreche et al. (Eds.): MEDI 2021 Workshops, CCIS 1481, pp. 121–137, 2021.
https://doi.org/10.1007/978-3-030-87657-9_10

given key several times. However, for a given system, it is not easy to create and memorize a random string of high entropy. In addition, it is difficult to secure and store the key information on non-volatile storage, as it is generally vulnerable to physical attacks [18,19].

In practice, numerous high entropy randomness sources exist, such as biometrics and human-generated data, quantum information, and physical unclonable functions (PUFs) [1]. Exploiting them avoids the need for a pseudo-random generator since the randomness is already intrinsically present on them. In addition, a protected secure memory is dispensable, since the used randomness is generally considered static over the lifetime of the source. So, it can be measured several times to regenerate the same key. Unfortunately, reusing many times the source may introduce errors and not identical values at repeated readings. For example, a random person's fingerprint or iris scan is clearly not a uniformly random string, nor does it get reproduced precisely each time it is measured. Turning similar readings into identical values is known as information reconciliation [16]. Further, converting those values into uniformly random secret strings is known as privacy amplification [16].

This focuses mainly on exploiting the randomness of PUFs. The latter is a one-way function defining the identity of a physical object through its behavior that is represented by a set of challenge-response pairs (CRPs). When a challenge is presented as input to a PUF, a corresponding response will be generated as output. CRPs are impossible to be duplicated because they have uncontrollable physical parameter variations that occur during hardware device manufacture [13]. Two PUFs categories exist, weak and strong, the first has a limited number of CRPs and physically they are impossible to be duplicated. Whereas, strong PUFs are defined by the security properties, the impossibility of duplication [17]. Also, they are characterized by a large set of CRPs as well as they are resilient to model-building attacks (an adversary cannot predict the response). This work targets mainly silicon PUFs (SPUFs) that are considered as a subclass of electronic PUF implemented on a silicon chip. Due to the silicon chip randomness caused by the manufacturing process variations, they use the chip components to drive a unique device response without any additional circuits [12]. Unfortunately, the generation process of SPUFs responses is affected by the device environment variables such as temperature and supply voltage, which means, SPUF responses are generally not perfectly reproducible (noisy) for the same challenge.

Guarantying information reconciliation and privacy amplification of noisy sources to derive uniform and reproducible keys for cryptographic applications can be carried by Fuzzy Extractors (FE) [16]. This work relies on fuzzy extractors, secure sketch, and strong random extractors (Sect. 3) for the aim to extract, generate, recover, then reproduce cryptographic keys (Sect. 5) from Silicon PUFs. To ensure the recovery of the initial key from noise or errors when reuse, the proposed solution develops techniques related to error correction codes, mainly binary linear block code (Sect. 4). Indeed, the implementation of the proposed framework shown a full recovery of keys generated from an Arbiter PUF (Sect. 6).

2   Related Work

There exists a wide body of previous work that surveys PUF based key generation constructions such as [2,4,7]. Hiller *et al.* [7] discuss several schemes using
to correct errors that appeared in PUF's outputs such as fuzzy commitment,
fuzzy extractor, syndrome construction, parity construction, and systematic low
leakage coding. Fuzzy extractors [5] are widely used to extract secure keys from
noisy and not fully random silicon PUF responses [6,9,20]. FE has two major
steps: correcting possible bit errors (noise elimination) and extracting uniform
random string from the non-noisy PUF output or the corrected one. For the latter step, a universal hash function is generally used [15]. And for the first step,
is based on error-correcting codes like syndrome construction, code-offset construction, index-based syndrome coding, complementary index-based syndrome,
and differential sequence coding [3]. Code offset and syndrome construction are
two prevalent constructions used with silicon PUF, and they are classified as
linear schema, due to the process of generation of the helper data and the secret
key that is based on linear between the PUF response and codewords of the
error correction code. The code-offset approach: to create the public helper data
s, Dodis *et al.* [5] XOR a sequence m of n bits of the PUF response with a
random codeword c of an ECC (n,k,t) ($s = m \oplus c$). For ECC, van der Leest *et al.*
[10] use Bose-Chaudhuri- Hocquenghem (BCH) with relatively short block sizes
to implement code offset construction and soft-decision decoding. Maes *et al.*
[11] presented a soft-decision approach, and they implemented it using Reed–
Muller codes. In the syndrome-based approach, the syndrome is calculated by
multiplying a sequence m of n bits of the PUF response with the transposed
parity-check-matrix H^T of the ECC (n,k,t) [5] ($s = m.H^T$), and the syndrome
is stored as helper data. Mase et al. [12], implemented a PUF key generator with
Ring-Oscillator PUFs and a BCH code on an FPGA.

3   Preliminaries

In this section, we briefly recall the needed definitions in our work.

Statistical Distance. Also known as variation distance, it is the difference
between the distributions of two random variables X and Y from the same set
given by: $SD(X,Y) \triangleq \frac{1}{2} \sum_v |Pr(X = v) - Pr(Y = v)|$. Here, the probability of
a random variable X is written as $Pr(X)$.

Min-entropy. The entropy specifies the amount of information contained in
data. But when discussing security, one is often interested in the probability
that the adversary predicts a random value. Thus, the best strategy is to guess
the most probable value. However, the predictability of a random variable X is
$max_x Pr[X = x]$, and correspondingly, the min-entropy $H_\infty(X)$ of a random
variable X is: $H_\infty(X) = -log(max_x Pr[X = x])$

For two random variables X and Y, the average min-entropy of X given Y is:
$H_\infty(X|Y) = -log(E_{y \leftarrow Y}[max_x Pr[X = x|Y = y]]) = -log(E_{y \leftarrow Y}[2^{H_\infty(X|Y=y)}])$.

Secure Sketching. Secure Sketch (SS) [5] is a primitive performing error correction on a noisy data w' by eliminating noises and reconstructing the original one w, clean from noise. SS takes w as input and produces a public sketch or a public helper data s, without revealing enough information about w. Rec uses s to recover w from w' by cleaning noise while $w' \approx w$.

Definition 1. *A $\langle M, m, m\prime, t \rangle$-secure sketch for the metric space $\{M\}$ is a pair of randomized procedures, sketching procedure (SS) and recovery procedure (Rec), defined as follows.*

- *The sketching procedure (SS) takes $w \in M$ as input and returns a public helper data $s \in \{0,1\}^*$.*
- *The recovery procedure (Rec) takes $w' \in M$ and s as input and outputs w.*

Secure sketch have to satisfy the following properties:

- ***Correctness or error tolerance***: $\forall w \in M$, $s \leftarrow$ SS(w): Rec$(w', s) = w$ if $dis(w, w') \leq t$.
- ***Security***: It requires that s does not leak too much information about w. Specifically, for any random variable W over M with min-entropy m, the secure sketch must ensure that average conditional min-entropy of W given $SS(W)$ is at least m'. $\forall W \in M$, i.e. $H_\infty(W|SS(W)) \geq m'$.

Randomness Extraction. A randomness extractor (RE) [14] is a method to drive a key from an available non-uniform randomness source. It is used to derive near-uniform or 'perfect' randomness from non-uniform or 'imperfect' randomness sources. So, this perfect randomness can be used to generate uniform keys that can be used in cryptographic applications. Randomness extractor can be constructed from cryptographic hash functions.66perfect99

Definition 2. *Let Ext: $\{0,1\}^n \rightarrow \{0,1\}^\ell$ be a polynomial time probabilistic function which uses r bits of randomness. We say that Ext is an efficient (n, m, ℓ, ϵ)-strong extractor if for all random variables $Y \leftarrow \{\{0,1\}\}^n$ with $H_\infty(Y) \geq m$, it holds that: $SD((Ext(Y; R), R); (U_\ell, R)) \leq \epsilon$, where R and U_ℓ are uniform on $\{0,1\}^r$ and $\{0,1\}^\ell$, respectively.*

Fuzzy Extractor. Fuzzy Extractor (FE) [5] extracts uniformly random string from noisy non-uniform random data. This string can be used as a secure key in cryptographic applications. Definition 3 formally defines a fuzzy extractor.

Definition 3. *An $\langle M, m, \ell, t, \epsilon \rangle$-fuzzy extractor is a pair of randomized procedures, Generate (Gen) and Reproduce (Rep), satisfying the following properties.*

- *Gen generates, for a given input $w \in M$, an extracted string $k \in \{0,1\}^\ell$ and a helper data string $p \in \{0,1\}^*$, i.e.: Gen$(w) \rightarrow (k, P)$.*
- *Rep takes an element $w' \in W$ and a bit string $p \in \{0,1\}^*$ as inputs and produces an extracted string $k' \in \{0,1\}^\ell$, such that: Rep$(w', P) \rightarrow K$ if $dis(w; w') \leq t$.*

FE satisfies the following properties.

- The correctness property of FE guarantees that if $dis(w, w') \leq t$ and (k, P) were generated by $(k, P) \leftarrow$ Gen(w), then Rep$(w', P) = k$. Otherwise, no guarantee is provided about the output of Rep.
- The security property guarantees that for any distribution W on M of min-entropy m, the string K is nearly uniform even for those who observe P:
  if $(K, P) \leftarrow$ Gen(W), then $SD((K, P), (U_\ell, P)) \leq \epsilon$.

4   Linear Block Codes

Error correction code (ECC) is commonly used to correct errors in data that are transmitted over noisy communication channels. When the sender wants to send a U binary information sequence, first, this latter is segmented into message blocks of fixed length k, denoted by m. Also, for a secure transition, the sender encodes each message block to so-called *codeword* c ($c = encode(m)$) with redundant information in the form of an ECC. The *codeword* is transmitted over a noisy channel to the receiver, and at the reception phase, the receiver checks, if there exist errors in the received *codeword* of data U (error detection). If an error found, ECC is used to reconstruct and recover the original and the true message m (m = decode(c)). The redundancy information allows the receiver to detect a fixed and limited number of errors that may occur in the message during the transition process, and to correct these errors without retransmitting the *codeword*.

Since we deal with only binary code, firstly, we define the finite field GF(2) of two elements as follows.

Definition 4. *Given the binary field $GF(2) = \{0, 1\}$, we have:*

- *A binary word w of length n over $GF(2)$ is an n-tuple $w = \{w_0, \ldots, w_{n-1}\}$ of binary digits $w_i \in GF(2)$, $\forall i = 0, 1, 2, \ldots, n - 1$.*
- *A binary block code of length n over $GF(2)$ is a nonempty set C of binary words w of length n each.*
- *Each element w of C is called a codeword in C.*

A set of 2^k distinct *codewords* w of length n each, over the binary field $GF(2) = \{0, 1\}$, is called a Binary Block Code $C(n, k)$. The latter is linear if for any two *codewords* in (n, k) results in another *codeword* in (n, k). (n, k, t) is a linear Binary Block Code which can correct t errors. A *codeword* $c \in C$ represents an n-bit sequence, formed from the k bit messages $m \in M$ and $(n - k)$ parity bits used to recover the transmitted *codeword* from errors. Linear block codes can detect up to $d - 1$ errors and correct up to $t = (d - 1)/2$ errors in the n-element *codeword*, where, d is the minimum number of bits in which any two distinct *codewords*.

Encoding. In linear block codes, the message m is encoded by multiplication with a generator matrix G to yield a *codeword* c:

$$c = m \cdot G \tag{1}$$

Recall that c is a $(1 \times n)$ row vector and m is a $(1 \times k)$ row vector. G has a dimension of $k \times n$, its rows are linearly independent and form a basis for C. In general, several G matrices generate the same code book, and only the mapping order from m to c changes. Two codes with the same code book are considered equivalent, no matter the order of the rows in C. A linear block code C is referred to as a (n, k) block code. For block codes, we can also define the matrix H, of dimension $(k \times n)$, which is called the parity check matrix of the code, such that c is a valid *codeword* $c \in C$, where:

$$c \cdot H^T = H^T \cdot c = 0 \tag{2}$$

H can therefore be used to validate that received data is indeed a *codeword*. If the received data r is not a valid *codeword*, then:

$$r \cdot H^T \neq 0 \tag{3}$$

Systematic codes are codes that still contain the original, unaltered, message bits. Their codewords can be partitioned into two parts: one containing the message and one containing the redundant parity bits. This makes them easy to decode. To achieve this their generator matrix is presented in the standard systematic form.

$$G = [P; I_k] \tag{4}$$

I_K is the $(k \times k)$ identity matrix, which keeps the k original bits in the *codeword* and P is the $k \times (n-k)$ parity matrix, which is unique to the code and generates the n redundant (parity) bits. Any linear block code can be put into systematic form, *i.e.* G of any linear block code can be written in the standard form. Hence, the parity check matrix can be constructed from their generator matrix as follows:

$$H = [I_{n-k}; P^T] \tag{5}$$

Decoding. For the error correction in a linear block code, we correct invalid received data to the closest valid *codeword*. For this we define s, the syndrome, for a received vector r, where H^T is the transpose of H, by:

$$s = r \cdot H^T \tag{6}$$

It is known that an error has occurred (i.e. $r \notin C$) if $s \neq 0$. The vector e containing the occurred errors is defined as:

$$e = r + c \tag{7}$$

Recall that there is no difference between addition and subtraction in $GF(2)$, therefore also $r = e + c$. This leads to:

$$s = (e + c).H^T = e \cdot H^T + 0 = e \cdot H^T \tag{8}$$

If the syndrome as defined in Eq. 6 is not equal to 0, then a value of e is chosen which satisfies Eq. 8 with the lowest possible $w(e)$. In other words, we assume that the errors which occurred is the difference between r and the closest valid *codeword* c. The valid *codeword* which was transmitted, v, is then given by $v = e + r$. So, the message represented by v is then recovered. This is called minimum distance decoding.

Example 1. To transmit the data U using the code word (n, k), first U needs to be segmented into a set of messages of k information digits. Let $m = (m_0, \ldots, m_{k-1})$ be the message to be encoded, using Eq. 1, the corresponding code word is $c = (c_0, \ldots, c_{n-1}) = (m_0, \ldots, m_{k-1}).G$. To encode the message $m = (110)$, we use $(6, 3)$ which has the following generator matrix and the transposed parity-check-matrix.

$$G = \begin{bmatrix} g_0 \\ g_1 \\ g_2 \\ g_3 \end{bmatrix} = \begin{bmatrix} 1\ 1\ 0\ 1\ 0\ 0 \\ 0\ 1\ 1\ 0\ 1\ 0 \\ 1\ 0\ 1\ 0\ 0\ 1 \end{bmatrix}; H = \begin{bmatrix} 1\ 0\ 0 \\ 0\ 1\ 0 \\ 0\ 0\ 1 \\ 1\ 1\ 0 \\ 0\ 1\ 1 \\ 1\ 0\ 1 \end{bmatrix} \tag{9}$$

$$c = m \cdot G = m_0 \cdot g_0, m_1 \cdot g_1, m_2 \cdot g_2 = 1 \cdot g_0, 0 \cdot g_1, 1 \cdot g_2 = 110100 + 011010 = 101110 \tag{10}$$

The codeword corresponding to the message (110) is (101110) which is divided into two parts, $n - k$ parity-check digits (101) and the message part $m = 110$. At the receiving side, the code word c is received as r. To recover the encoded message m, the decoding procedure is needed. According to Eq. 6, first we calculate the so called syndrome $s = r \cdot H^T$, if $s = 0$ (all-zeros vector), this means that r is a valid codeword and we may conclude that there is no error in r. Or, since $r = c + e$, if $s = r \cdot H^T = 0$ this means e is also a codeword which is known as undetectable error. Otherwise ($s \neq 0$), the received codeword r contains errors.

Locating the Error Pattern. To locate this error, we refer to Eq. 7, where $r = (r_0, r_1, r_2, \ldots, r_{n-1})$ represents a received *codeword* of n elements, and $e = (e_0, e_1, e_2, \ldots, e_{n-1})$ which referred to as the *error pattern*. After assuming that r has errors bits, Eq. 8 is used to locate the error pattern.

Based on (6,3) code, we use Eq. 8 to determine the syndrome corresponding to each correctable error pattern, with computing $e.H^T$, as follows.

$$s = (e_0, e_1, e_2, e_3, e_4, e_5) \cdot H^T$$

Since each of the mentioned error patterns of the results listed in Table 1 has a one-to-one relationship with each syndromes, so solving for a syndrome identifies the specific error pattern that corresponds to that syndrome. As we showed

Table 1. Syndrome lookup table.

Error pattern c	Syndrome s
000000	000
000001	101
000010	011
000100	110
001000	001
010000	010
100000	100
010001	111

by using $(6, 3)$ code, the corespondent *codeword* of $m = 110$ is $c = 101110$, assume that the vector $r = 001110$ is received. From Eq. 7, we compute the syndrome by: $s = (001110) \cdot H^T = 100$. From Table 1, we can verify that the error pattern is $e = 100000$. Then, using Eq. 7, the corrected vector is estimated by $c^* = r + e = 001110 + 100000 = 101110$ where c^* is the actual transmitted code word. The error correction procedure yields $c^* = c$, which means that the output m^* will correspond to the actual message $m^* = m = 110$. The possible codewords for the code $(6,3)$ are: $(000000, 001101, 010110, 011011, 100111, 101010, 110001, 111100)$. For this list of *codewords*, the minimal distance is $d = 3$, so $(6,3)$ can detect up to 2 errors and correct up to $t = 1$ error, and it can be given as $(6,3,1)$.

5   Cryptographic Key Generation from PUFs

To illustrate the use of a source with high randomness on an example, let us consider the task of biometric data authentication. As a user, Alice uses her biometric data (e.g., iris) as a unique identity w when she wants to gain access to her account. A trusted server stores some information $y = f(w)$ about the password. When Alice enters w, the server lets Alice if only if $f(w) = y$. In this naive authentication scheme, we accept that Alice could use w itself as her identity for the verification process. Hence, two issues can be found with this authentication process. First, when Alice reused her biometric information w' at a latter authentication step, the new generated identity w' will differ from the initial one. Unfortunately, it is close to it, but not equal to the initial value w, due to some noise on w'. In fact, she will not be able to recover her original identity by using a standard encryption scheme. Second, w is not uniform, and it cannot be used as a cryptographic key in standard encryption schemes.

5.1   Silicon PUFs

Silicon PUFs [8] refer to PUFs that are based on conventional integrated circuits. By exploiting the inherent manufacturing variations of wires and transistors that differ from an IC to another, SPUF is classified as intrinsic PUF as it does not require any modification in the manufacturing process to be used. According to the different sources of variation, Silicon PUF is mainly divided into three major categories [8]: delay-based PUFs such as Arbiter PUFs, Memory-based PUFs like SRAM-PUF, and Analog electronic PUFs such as Power distribution PUF.

Definition 5 describes the Silicon PUF ($SPUF$) as a parameterized random function denoted by $\Pi_{S \in S}$ ($\Pi_{S \in S} \in \mathcal{P}$) where the structural parameters ($S \in \mathcal{S}$) are random variables describing the $SPUF$ structure.

Definition 5. *An SPUF is a function $\Pi_{S \in S} : \mathcal{C} \to \mathcal{R}$, where:*

- *$\mathcal{S}$: set of parameters that characterize the structure of the physical system.*
- *$\mathcal{C}$: set of challenges.*
- *$\mathcal{R}$: set of responses.*

Definition 6 evaluates the $SPUF$ reliability using the min-entropy, where a less reliability means more changes and instability.

Definition 6 (Reliability). *The reliability of a SPUF p_i is estimated by:*

$$\gamma_i = 1 + \frac{1}{|\mathcal{R}|(|\mathcal{R}| - 1)|\mathcal{C}|} \sum_{i=1}^{|\mathcal{R}|-1} \sum_{j=i+1}^{j=|\mathcal{R}|} \log_2 \max(\vartheta_i, 1 - \vartheta_i)$$

5.2 Framework Overview

Due to the manufacturing process of the integrated circuits, SPUF is classified as a source of randomness and it can be used to generate a cryptography key without storing the key's information for future use. This advantage is guaranteed since the key can be generated on demand. Nevertheless, one of the biggest challenges with SPUF is to guarantee the stability of the key in each regeneration phase, which is caused by the environmental variables. To achieve the stability (zero error rate) of the PUF response, it usually needs to be post-processed. The latter is generally composed of two phases: *enrollment* and *reconstruction* (see Fig. 1).

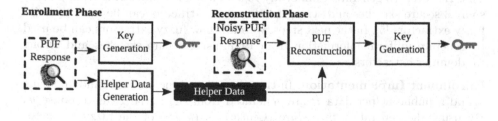

Fig. 1. Enrollment and reconstruction phases.

Enrollment Phase. During this phase, the unique identifier (or the key) is generated from the initial PUF response. At the same time, the public helper data is also generated. Clearly, the key has to be kept secret as it is used in cryptographic applications. On the other hand, if the helper data does not reveal information about the secret, it can be classified as public and stored in non-secure non-volatile memory.

Reconstruction Phase. At this stage, the stored public helper data is used to recover the enrolled key and to correct the bit errors that occurred in the actual PUF response (noisy response). This can be achieved since the helper data content describing the secret key allows a reliable key reconstruction, even under the variations of the environmental conditions.

Several approaches have been used to correct an error in the PUF response and generate a unique reproducible key such as Fuzzy Commitment, fuzzy vault, Code-offset fuzzy extractor, Syndrome construction, Parity construction, and Systematic low leakage coding [7].

Deriving a uniformly random string from non-uniform randomness sources has two major obstacles. The first, called information reconciliation, by tolerating the noise in the sources without leaking any information. The second, converting those values into uniformly random secret strings is known as privacy amplification. Several approaches *like* fuzzy extractors accomplish both information reconciliation using the secure sketch and privacy amplification using randomness extractor [5].

5.3   Constructing Fuzzy Extractor from Secure Sketch

Fuzzy extractors (FE) extract a uniformly random string and a public string from an initial input. The first string can be recovered from another noisy input using the second extracted string. This step can be achieved in the case where both inputs are close to each other.

Secure sketch (SS) allows reconstructing the initial input from noisy input by making use of some helper data. The difference between these two techniques is that fuzzy extractors return a uniform string and a secure sketch returns a non-uniform string but it permits noise's elimination.

Generating cryptographic keys from PUFs go through two phases, enrollment and reconstruction, and both phases can be achieved using fuzzy extractors. However, to generate a uniformly reproducible random string from a noisy source, secure sketches and strong randomness extractors can be used to build fuzzy extractors [5]. In the next steps, we show how fuzzy extractors can be used to generate uniform information from PUF using secure sketches and strong randomness extractors.

Enrollment Implementation. In this phase, a unique uniform random string k and a public helper data P are generated from the initial PUF response w. By using the generation procedure $(\mathsf{Gen}(w) \to (k, P))$ of the fuzzy extractor to generate the pair (K, P), we use the secure sketch and strong randomness extraction as follows.

– For the response w, SS returns the helper data s.
– Use strong randomness extractor (Ext) with a random r for w to obtain a secret string key.
– Store $(s; r)$ as the helper string P.

Reconstruction Implementation. This phase allows recovering the initial response w from a noisy one w' with few bits of errors. Using the Reproduction procedure (Rep) of the fuzzy extractor to reproduce the secret string key. Thus, we use the secure sketch, strong randomness extraction, and the stored public helper string $P(s, r)$ as follows.

– Use the recovery procedure (Rec) with the helper string s for the noisy response w' to return the initial non noisy response w.
– Use strong randomness extractor (Ext) with randomness r for w to get key.

5.4 Secure Sketch Construction

Since the reconstruction procedure of the initial PUF response from the noisy one depends mainly on the distance between both responses. From the three metrics Set difference, Edit and Hamming metric, we focus on the latter one, since it is used in the generation of PUF-based keys. Further, the main building block of fuzzy extractor construction is the secure sketch. In other words, in the PUF-based key generation process, a secure sketch is used to correct errors in the noisy PUF output using the Helper Data. Thus, the use of error-correcting codes (ECC) is one of the solutions. Many possibilities exist to realize a Secure Sketch based on error-correcting codes like syndrome construction, code-offset construction, index-based syndrome coding, complementary index-based syndrome coding, and differential sequence coding. For Hamming distance metric, syndrome construction is the prevalent secure sketch in a PUF-based key generation.

Syndrome Construction. During sketching, compute $s = w.H^T$, where H^T is the transposed parity-check-matrix of the used linear error correction code C. For recovery, compute $s' = w'.H^T$. Determine $e = locate(s' \oplus s)$ by using the error-location algorithm $locate()$ of the code C. Then, $w^* = Rec(w', s) = w' \oplus e$ with $w^* = w$ if $d(w', w) \leq t$. The syndrome construction does not require extra input random $codeword$ c to extract the helper data s.

5.5 Key Reproduction Process

The PUF-based key generation process is achieved through two steps: enrollment and reconstruction (see Sect. 5.2). On another side, extraction of uniform random string from high entropy randomness sources also goes through two steps; information reconciliation and privacy amplification, which are guaranteed by Fuzzy Extractors, using secure sketches and strong randomness extractors respectively.

In this section, we present the needed steps used by the Fuzzy extractor to accomplish PUF-based key generation operation using secure sketches and strong randomness extractors. Here, we use syndrome construction as secure sketch construction and hash function as strong randomness extractors function.

Example 2. Let's consider the initial and reference PUF response from what the key is extracted the first time, $w = 100010010111$ with 12 digits, and for the error correction code lets refer to the used binary linear block code $(6, 3, 1)$ with the flowing transposed parity-check-matrix H^T (Matrix 9).

Enrollment Phase. In this phase, the secret string key and a public helper data s are extracted from the initial PUF response w, using a hash function for the first one as a strong randomness extractor (ext) and the sketching procedure (SS) for the second one.

Example 3. First, let us compute the helper data s where: $s = w.H^T$, with $(6, 3, 1)$. The initial response needs to be segmented in message blocks of length ($n = 6$) which results in four messages $\{m_0 = 100010, m_1 = 010111\}$. To compute s, we calculate s_i correspondent to each message m_i, where $s_i = m_i.H^T$. The syndrome s_0 of the first message m_0 is calculated as follow.

$$s_0 = m_0.H^T = (100010). \begin{bmatrix} 1 & 0 & 0 \\ 0 & 1 & 0 \\ 0 & 0 & 1 \\ 1 & 1 & 0 \\ 0 & 1 & 1 \\ 1 & 0 & 1 \end{bmatrix} = 100 + 011 = 111$$

Hence, $s_0 = 111$ and by following the same steps we found $s_1 = 010$, and finally the helper data will be $s = (111, 010)$.

Second, for the secret key generation from the response w, lets use a universal hash function $sha1$ as a strong randomness extractor (ext), $ext(w) = sha1(w)$.

$$sha1(w) = sha1(100010010111) = fc85f381d98096c60b763230399e4e4c40bfa693$$

At the end of this phase, we have the secret string $key = fc85f381d98096c60b76$ $3230399e4e4c40bfa693$, and the public helper data is $s = (111, 010)$.

Reconstruction Phase. In this phase, we use the stored helper data s to recover the initial response w from a noisy one w', and calculate the secret key key from the recovered response w. Lets consider a noisy response $w' = 110010010101$. First, we compute $s' = w'.H^T$. So, $s'_0 = m'_0.H^T = 110010.H^T = 101$, $s'_1 = 010101.H^T = 001$, and we consider $s' = (101, 001)$. Then, we evaluate $s'_0 \oplus s_0 = 101 \oplus 111 = 010$ to compute $e_0 = locate(010)$. $locate(010)$ uses Table 1 to find the corresponding error pattern e_0 for the syndrome 010, which is $e_0 = 010000$. Then, $m^*_0 = m'_0 \oplus e_0 = 110010 \oplus 010000 = 100010 = m_0$.

By repeating the same steps to calculate m^*_0, $s'_1 \oplus s_1 = 001 \oplus 010 = 011$, and $e_1 = locate(011) = 000010$, then $m^*_1 = m'_1 \oplus e_1 = 010101 \oplus 000010 = 010111 = m_1$.

To reproduce and recover the secret information *key*, we concatenate m_0^* and m_1^* that gives w^* and by using *sha*1 we will have: $sha1(w^*) = sha1(100010010111) = fc85f381d98096c60b763230399e4e4c40bfa693$ Finally, we can show that using the public helper data $s = (111, 010)$, the secret string *key = fc85f381d98096c60b76 3230399e4e4c40bfa693* has been recovered from a noisy response w' = 110010010101.

6   Implementation and Experimental Results

By experimenting with our methodology on an Arbiter PUF, this section presents a real implementation of the fuzzy extractor with a secure sketch based on syndrome construction to extract a unique reproducible secret key from noisy PUF response. The experimental setup uses this latter as a module for cryptographic key generation, in which, the noise of the new response was eliminated and the secret key and the helper data were generated. By exploiting the inherent manufacturing variations of transistors and wires in an integrated circuit, Arbiter PUF (APUF) [18] generates unique secret information for each IC. APUF consists of two paths as chains of switch blocks that are connected to an arbiter block. Based on the common enable signal as input of the first switch blocks and challenge's bit introduced to each switch block, APUF introduces a race condition between the two digital paths on a silicon chip. The arbiter block determines which signal arrived first, and outputs a single bit known as the response bit (Fig. 2).

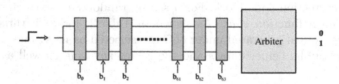

Fig. 2. A structure of an Arbiter PUF.

6.1   Arbiter PUF Evaluation

By evaluating the reliability metrics, we will show how much the output of this APUF is stable. Also, we check the redundancy and the consistency with which the APUF generates the same response for the same challenge across different environmental factors.

APUF Dataset. Our experimented APUF is of 16 switch blocks, which means it needs a 16-bit challenge and outputs a 32-bit response. To check the performance of the used APUF, we evaluate its reliability metric (environmental factors' influence) using 30 different APUF instances. Given the same challenge as input, the responses were generated under three different temperatures: 25 C,

−40 C, and 85 C. Under each temperature condition, each response is measured. The result of the simulation process of this APUF is used as a dataset [1].

Reliability. As shown in Fig. 3, the reliability of the used APUF is between 93% and 100%, where the ideal value is 100%. This means that all 30 APUF instances generate a near stable response at different temperatures 25 C, −40 C, and 85 C. Using the same challenge as an input, this APUF outputs a noisy response that has some error bits, compared to the reference response (initial response).

Bit Error Rate. The unreliability is expressed by the expected bit error rate (BER) between two evaluations w and w' of the same response with $32 - bits$. Let's consider the responses generated under 25 C as reference (initial response w), and the ones generated under −40 C, and 85 C as noisy (w'). Figure 4 shows and compares the BER values for the responses' evaluations for both (25 C, −40 C) (blue color) and (25 C, 85 C) (red color). For the first evaluation, 22 times BER is 0, which means that the output of APUF under −40 C is stable in 22 cases. Also, the 8 other outputs were slightly lower than 3%, which means this helps to recover them more efficiently.

6.2 Cryptography Key Generation

Now, we show how we eliminate these errors and reconstruct again the initial response from the noisy ones by implementing the fuzzy Extractor technique with a secure sketch and strong extractor. For the secure sketch, we implement a *syndrome construction* using the example of the linear binary code block (6,3,1) as an error correction code block. For a strong randomness extractor, we used a universal hash function $sha1$. As shown in Table 2, for each three selected responses (responses generated under 85C are selected as noisy ones). First, we calculate the public helper data s and the secret key key, as well as the error

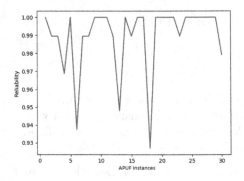

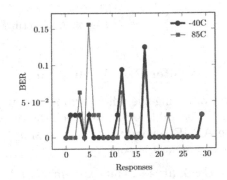

Fig. 3. APUF reliability.

Fig. 4. Bit error rate evaluation. (Color figure online)

---

[1] https://github.com/salaheddinhetalani/PUF.

Table 2. APUF based keys generation and recovery.

APUF#3	w	01010000101001111111110010101111	**BER=0.06** Detection=Yes
	w'	00010000101001111111110010001111	Correction=Yes
	s	(100,010,011,001,011,110)	Recovery=Yes
	r	e29ceebae34de478ef11b79ed6d3a6fa70b96e66	
APUF#5	w	00000000101011111100010000001101	**BER=0.16** Detection=Yes
	w'	01000010101011101101010000101101	Correction=Yes
	s	(000,010,111,110,110,010)	Recovery=Yes
	r	04ca0be3e9caaac06c4ae59bee8447bbb3009145	
APUF#17	w	01010100100000000010101010011010	**BER=0.09** Detection=Yes
	w'	01000000100001000010101010011010	Correction=No
	s	(001,001,000,110,001,100)	Recovery= No
	r	9bb8fa44812f776d031a175bd43513134d3b5ef9	

detection and correction capabilities. Then, all error bits are eliminated in the noisy response w', and the initial response w is recovered and reconstructed, which results in the *key*. The experiments showed that all keys were recovered except the last one due to the error bits distribution where two error bits are presented in the first segmented message 010000. We recall that using the error correction code (6, 3, 1) can correct up to one-bit error and detect two-bit errors in each segmented message. For more than one-bit error in the same segmented message, cyclic codes are required.

7   Conclusion

In this paper, we have detailed and developed the needed steps to implement the fuzzy extractor in the PUF based key generation, using syndrome construction as a secure sketch procedure and a universal hash function *sha*1 as a strong randomness extractor procedure. Further, the effectiveness of the presented framework was presented on a real dataset. The latter has been generated from an Arbiter PUF under three different temperatures (25 C, 85 C, and −40 C). Its performance measures showed good reliability with some error bits. By using a binary linear code block (6.3.1), a unique and reproducible key has been recovered for each PUF instance. In the near future, we intend to deploy the presented framework in an authentication protocol that exploits a PUF based on IoT and smartphones. Further, we look to check the security properties of the stored public helper data.

References

1. Alamélou, Q., et al.: Pseudoentropic isometries: a new framework for fuzzy extractor reusability. In: Proceedings of the 2018 on Asia Conference on Computer and Communications Security, pp. 673–684 (2018)

2. Delvaux, J.: Security analysis of PUF-based key generation and entity authentication. Ph. D. dissertation (2017)
3. Delvaux, J., Gu, D., Schellekens, D., Verbauwhede, I.: Helper data algorithms for PUF-based key generation: overview and analysis. IEEE Trans. Comput. Aided Des. Integr. Circuits Syst. **34**(6), 889–902 (2014)
4. Delvaux, J., Gu, D., Verbauwhede, I., Hiller, M., Yu, M.-D.M.: Efficient fuzzy extraction of PUF-induced secrets: theory and applications. In: Gierlichs, B., Poschmann, A.Y. (eds.) CHES 2016. LNCS, vol. 9813, pp. 412–431. Springer, Heidelberg (2016). https://doi.org/10.1007/978-3-662-53140-2_20
5. Dodis, Y., Reyzin, L., Smith, A.: Fuzzy extractors: how to generate strong keys from biometrics and other noisy data. In: Cachin, C., Camenisch, J.L. (eds.) EUROCRYPT 2004. LNCS, vol. 3027, pp. 523–540. Springer, Heidelberg (2004). https://doi.org/10.1007/978-3-540-24676-3_31
6. Gianfelici, G., Kampermann, H., Bruß, D.: Theoretical framework for physical unclonable functions, including quantum readout. Phys. Rev. A **101**(4), 042337 (2020)
7. Hiller, M., Kürzinger, L., Sigl, G.: Review of error correction for PUFs and evaluation on state-of-the-art FPGAs. J. Cryptogr. Eng. **10**, 229–247 (2020)
8. Huang, Z., Wang, Q.: A PUF-based unified identity verification framework for secure IoT hardware via device authentication. World Wide Web **23**(2), 1057–1088 (2020)
9. Kang, H., Hori, Y., Katashita, T., Hagiwara, M., Iwamura, K.: Performance analysis for PUF data using fuzzy extractor. In: Jeong, Y.-S., Park, Y.-H., Hsu, C.-H.R., Park, J.J.J.H. (eds.) Ubiquitous Information Technologies and Applications. LNEE, vol. 280, pp. 277–284. Springer, Heidelberg (2014). https://doi.org/10.1007/978-3-642-41671-2_36
10. van der Leest, V., Preneel, B., van der Sluis, E.: Soft decision error correction for compact memory-based PUFs using a single enrollment. In: Prouff, E., Schaumont, P. (eds.) CHES 2012. LNCS, vol. 7428, pp. 268–282. Springer, Heidelberg (2012). https://doi.org/10.1007/978-3-642-33027-8_16
11. Maes, R., Tuyls, P., Verbauwhede, I.: A soft decision helper data algorithm for SRAM PUFs. In: 2009 IEEE International Symposium on Information Theory, pp. 2101–2105. IEEE (2009)
12. Maes, R., Van Herrewege, A., Verbauwhede, I.: PUFKY: a fully functional PUF-based cryptographic key generator. In: Prouff, E., Schaumont, P. (eds.) CHES 2012. LNCS, vol. 7428, pp. 302–319. Springer, Heidelberg (2012). https://doi.org/10.1007/978-3-642-33027-8_18
13. Ouchani, S.: Ensuring the functional correctness of IoT through formal modeling and verification. In: Abdelwahed, E.H., Bellatreche, L., Golfarelli, M., Méry, D., Ordonez, C. (eds.) MEDI 2018. LNCS, vol. 11163, pp. 401–417. Springer, Cham (2018). https://doi.org/10.1007/978-3-030-00856-7_27
14. Roel, M.: Physically Unclonable Functions: Constructions, Properties and Applications. Katholieke Universiteit Leuven, Belgium (2012)
15. Wen, Y., Lao, Y.: Efficient fuzzy extractor implementations for PUF based authentication. In: 2017 12th International Conference on Malicious and Unwanted Software, pp. 119–125. IEEE (2017)
16. Wen, Y., Liu, S., Han, S.: Reusable fuzzy extractor from the decisional Diffie-Hellman assumption. Designs Codes Cryptogr. **86**(11), 2495–2512 (2018)
17. Zerrouki, F., Ouchani, S., Bouarfa, H.: Quantifying security and performance of physical unclonable functions. In: 2020 7th International Conference on Internet of Things: Systems, Management and Security (IOTSMS), pp. 1–4 (2020)

18. Zerrouki, F., Ouchani, S., Bouarfa, H.: Towards an automatic evaluation of the performance of physical unclonable functions. In: Hatti, M. (eds.) Artificial Intelligence and Renewables Towards an Energy Transition. International Conference in Artificial Intelligence in Renewable Energetic Systems, pp. 775–781. Springer, Cham (2020). https://doi.org/10.1007/978-3-030-63846-7_74
19. Zerrouki, F., Ouchani, S., Bouarfa, H.: A low-cost authentication protocol using Arbiter-PUF. In: Attiogbé, C., Ben Yahia, S. (eds.) MEDI 2021. LNCS, vol. 12732, pp. 101–116. Springer, Cham (2021). https://doi.org/10.1007/978-3-030-78428-7_9
20. Zhao, B., Zhao, P., Fan, P.: ePUF: a lightweight double identity verification in IoT. Tsinghua Sci. Technol. **25**(5), 625–635 (2020)

Record Linkage for Auto-tuning of High Performance Computing Systems

Sophie Robert[1,2]([✉]), Lionel Vincent[1], Soraya Zertal[2], and Philippe Couvée[1]

[1] Atos BDS R&D Data Management, Échirolles, France
{sophie.robert,lionel.vincent,philippe.couvee}@atos.net
[2] Li-PaRAD, University of Versailles, Versailles, France
{sophie.robert2,soraya.zertal}@uvsq.fr

Abstract. To become auto-adaptive, computer systems should be able to have some knowledge of incoming applications even before launching the application on the system, so that the runtime environment can be customized to the particular needs of this application. In this paper, we propose the architecture of an auto-tuner which relies on record linkage methods to match an incoming application with a database of already known applications. We then present a concrete implementation of this auto-tuner on High Performance Computing (HPC) systems, to submit unknown incoming applications with the best possible parametrization of a smart prefetch strategy by analyzing their metadata. We test this auto-tuner in conditions close to a production environment, and show an improvement of 28% compared to using the default parametrization. The conducted evaluation reveals a negligible overhead of our auto-tuner when running in production and a significant resilience for parallel use on a high-traffic HPC cluster.

Keywords: Record linkage · Auto-tuning · Autonomous system · Performance · High performance computing

1 Introduction

Autonomous distributed and parallel computer systems should be able to provide run-time environments customized for the particular needs of each running application. When applications present regular characteristics and stable behaviors over time, which happens frequently in High Performance Computing (HPC), the system can be configured directly upon the submission of the application, by matching it with previously collected knowledge. This allows to configure the best possible runtime environment and make the most of the system's resources. In this paper, we propose the architecture of an auto-tuner which relies on record linkage methods to match the metadata of an incoming application collected by a workload manager with metadata collected on previously run applications, in order to take some auto-adaptive decisions before the submission of the application in a complete autonomous way. The main application of our auto-tuner that we present here is the development of auto-parametrizable runtime

© Springer Nature Switzerland AG 2021
L. Bellatreche et al. (Eds.): MEDI 2021 Workshops, CCIS 1481, pp. 138–151, 2021.
https://doi.org/10.1007/978-3-030-87657-9_11

environments: once an application has been recognized as previously known, the optimal running environment that had been computed for this application can be applied to the running platform. We will detail in depth the implementation of this auto-tuner for the case of a smart prefetch strategy for HPC systems. Upon the submission of the application, the auto-tuner uses the metadata to find the best possible parametrization for the prefetch strategy, given previously optimized applications. The main contributions of this paper are:

- The definition of the architecture of an auto-tuner to match incoming applications to previously run ones
- The original use of record linkage methods for matching applications through their metadata
- The validation of this auto-tuner in conditions close to production settings

In the remainder of the paper, we discuss in Sect. 2 works that are related to record linkage and its use. Section 3 describes the architecture of the auto-tuner that we propose. In Sect. 4 we describe in depth the methodology used for matching the incoming application with previously known applications. Section 5 describes the validation plan designed to test the performance of the matcher for an adaptive prefetch strategy and Sect. 6 describes the results found through this validation plan. Conclusion and further works are detailed in Sect. 7.

2   Related Works

The automation of the tuning process using Record Linkage is absolutely original as no reference was found of close works in the literature. We can find works on prediction using the application's submission informations and the execution environment for HPC problems as the power-aware scheduling using inference models [16] or backfilling algorithms [5] and execution time using Decision Trees [17]. They exploit different Machine Learning methods but as far as we know, none of them used unsupervised method as we suggest, and especially record linkage techniques. While uncommon in computer science, record linkage is a very popular technique for matching data records across same individuals in the health and bio-statistics field.

Record linkage [2], also known as *data matching*, is a process which goal is to match several records corresponding to the same entity across difference data sources. The first idea of Record Linkage was introduced by Halbert Dunn in 1946 [4] as a book of life for each individual and since the 1950s several research domains explored, developed and applied this technique. The main popular ones are health [6,10,12] to improve the quality of clinical care and statistical studies as population census [7] to target the right development plans governments have to anticipate. This use of Record Linkage to develop many domains, goes with its own continuous optimization and a substantial work is achieved to preserve the record linkage privacy [13], cleaning and adjusting linkage errors [19]. While widely used in biostatistics and the medical field [7,8], record linkage has to our knowledge never been used to match computer records for application re-identification (Fig. 1).

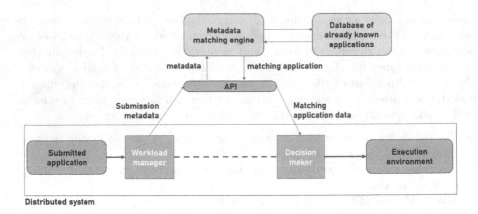

Fig. 1. Schematic representation of the matching pipeline

3   Suggested Pipeline and Practical Implementation

We present in this section the workflow of the auto-tuner, as well as a practical implementation we use in order to quantify its efficiency.

3.1   Tuner Workflow

Upon submission of an application by the user, the metadata of this application is collected, using environment variables in the submission environment such as the name of the user and the name of the program, but also the requested resources, such as the number of nodes. This data is then sent to the interface between the submission systems and the metadata matching engine. When this engine receives the data, it performs the matching using the records of applications that have been previously run on the system. These records contain the metadata as well as some information recorded after the run is finished. The application with the best match is then sent back to the API, which sends it to the module responsible for making decisions using this information. For example, this module could correspond to the scheduler that will adapt itself and select the most promising parametrization of the prefetcher. The application can then be run on the system and its information will be collected to enrich the knowledge base.

In our auto-tunner architecture, the submission of the application hangs until the matching process is over, thus requiring the matching process to be efficient enough to not affect the performance of the user.

3.2   Auto-tuning of HPC Components Using the Tuner

Most modern hardware or software come with many configuration parameters, which have a strong impact on the performance. This is for example the case of hardware components, MPI collectives, I/O accelerators... The impact of these parameters are highly dependent on the characteristics of the running application, and running the system with the best possible configuration is crucial to make the most of the performance of the system. Several methods are available to find the optimal parametrization of a system given the application's input, whether relying on agnostic tuning methods such as black-box optimization or analytical models which predicts the behavior of the system. Once found, this configuration has to be set manually by the user each time the optimized application is run and this is a human error prone process. Furthermore, it did not allow to apply a configuration for new unseen incoming applications, although the knowledge of other applications that have already been evaluated on the system could lead to apply a better configuration than the default one. We adapt the tuner workflow of Sect. 3.1 to use it to automatically set the appropriate configuration of a HPC component given its optimal configuration. As described in Fig. 2, the database of already known applications contains data collected from previously optimized applications: the application metadata, as well as their optimum parametrization, found through black-box optimization. This optimal parametrization is then used by the system to run the application.

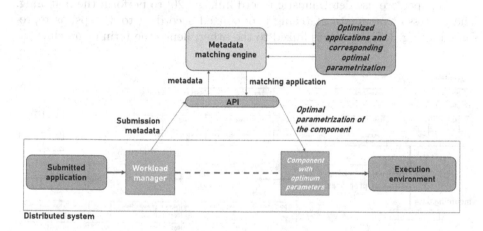

Fig. 2. Particular implementation of the auto-tuner for I/O accelerators

3.3   Practical Implementation and Use-Case

We test the metadata matching system for auto-tuning of an I/O accelerator, called the *Small Read Optimizer* [1] acting as a prefetch strategy. The configuration of this accelerator has both a strong impact on the performance and a strong dependence on the particular profile of the application. Our particular implementation is done on a HPC cluster, using the Slurm workload manager [9]. The metadata collected by this workload manager are described in Table 1. The optimal parametrization is found using a black-box optimization framework called SHAMan [14], used to collect the metadata of the application as well as find the

Table 1. Metadata collected by the workload manager and used for matching

Variable name	Description	Variable type
Username	Name of the user that submitted the application	String
Jobname	Name of the job	String
Program name	Name of the running program	String
Command line	Command line used to submit the program	String
Start time	Time of submission of the application	Date
Node count	Number of nodes the application is running on	Integer

optimal parametrization of the accelerator. More details on this accelerator and its parametrization are available in [15].

4   Matching Methodology

In this paper, we use deterministic record linkage [20] to perform the matching. The process of metadata matching is organized according to 3 steps, as represented in Fig. 3. Each step is linked to the other, hence the term of pipeline.

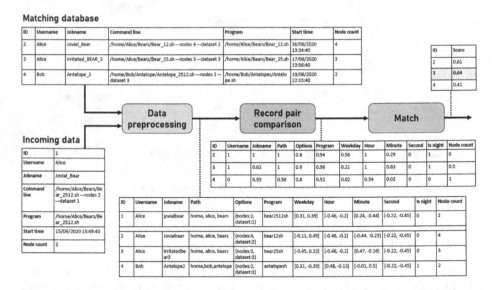

Fig. 3. Schematic representation of the matching pipeline

4.1 Data Preprocessing

The goal of the pre-processing step is to transform the data into a standard format so that it can be optimally compared. In our matching engine, we use 3 distinct steps of data preprocessing before performing the matching:

- **Data cleaning:** it is necessary to remove possible unnecessary characters.
- **Data segmentation:** its goal is to ensure that at the output of the cleaning block, there is no redundancy in the data.
- **Extraction of new data:** it consists in adding a possible new field to the dataset.

The cleaning and extraction process created for each of the metadata variables described in Table 1 are explicited in Table 2. An example of extraction and cleaning are available in Fig. 3.

Table 2. Cleaning and extraction performed on the metadata

Variable name	Applied cleaning	Extracted variables
Username	None	
Jobname	Removal of non-alphanumeric symbols, lowercase	
Program name	Removal of non-alphanumeric symbols, lowercase	
Command line	None	Path to the program options of the program
Start time	Projection in a trigonometric circle (depending on the periodicity of each variable)	Second Minute Hour Day Weekday
Node count	None	

Table 3. Comparison function applied for each of the available fields

Variable name	Comparison function
Username	Exact comparison
Jobname	Levenshtein similarity
Program name	Levenshtein similarity
Path	Soft TFIDF comparison
Options	Default dict comparison
Weekday	Euclidean comparison
IsNight	Exact comparison
Minutes	Euclidean comparison
Hours	Euclidean comparison
Node count	Absolute comparison

4.2 Record Pair Comparison

The comparison step consists in comparing 2 records field by field. As the fields, described in Table 1, are of heterogeneous types, an adapted similarity measure must be used for each field depending on its type, in order to compute the similarity between the 2 records. At the end of this step, we obtain a vector with

a similarity score for each of the already available applications for matching
with the incoming application. Because we do not want a particular field to
weigh more than another, each of the used similarity score gives a value located
between 0 and 1.

Depending on the nature of the field, one of the similarity functions bellow
and summarized in Table 3, will be applied:

- **Exact comparison:** Exact comparison consists in returning a boolean if the
  field is exactly equal for both records, regardless of their data type. The fields
  concerned by this similarity are the username as they are set by the system,
  and the boolean field which indicates if a job is running at night.
- **Single string comparisons:** To perform single string comparisons between
  the two string variables jobname and program name, we use the Levenshtein
  similarity measure [11]. It computes the similarity between two words as the
  minimum number of single-character edits (insertions, deletions or substitutions) required to change one word into the other. The Levenshtein distance
  between two strings a and b is defined as:

$$
sim_{lev} = \begin{cases} |a| \text{ if } |b| = 0 \\ |b| \text{ if } |a| = 0 \\ sim_{lev}(a, b) \text{ if } a[0] = b[0] \\ 1 + min \begin{cases} sim_{lev}(\text{tail}(a), b) \\ sim_{lev}(a, \text{tail}(b)) \\ sim_{lev}(\text{tail}(a), \text{tail}(b)) \end{cases} \end{cases}
$$

  with the function *tail* a function returning the string without its first element.
- **Option comparisons:** To compare the options of the application between
  the two records, we compute for each option the ratio of values in common
  given for this key, and attribute the value of this ratio to the score. When
  two applications have the same option name or key, we add a constant weight
  depending on each value to the score for each key in common in the option
  dictionary.
- **Multiple string comparison:** Soft Tf-Idf [3] consists in considering how
  frequently vario leter combinations appear in the whole dataset, instead of
  just taking into account the values for the two records. It allows to downplay
  strings that are repeated across every record (in our case, the/home/suffix is
  very common among command lines) in order to focus on the less frequent
  ones. The frequency of the terms present in the records are computed and
  then divided by their frequency over the whole dataset.
- **Numerical comparisons:** To locate the similarity score between 0 and 1,
  we can only calculate traditional distance measures on values already located
  between -1 and 1, such as the coordinates extracted from the trigonometric
  projection. For the other numeric measures as the number of nodes, we use
  the *absolute* similarity, which sets the distance to zero if the two elements

are too far away when compared to a threshold d_{max}, and otherwise to the distance between the two data points normalized by the threshold.

$$sim_{abs} = \begin{cases} 1 - \frac{|n_1-n_2|}{d_{max}} & \text{if } |n_1 - n_2| \le d_{max} \\ 0 & \text{else} \end{cases}$$

with:
- n_1: the first number to compare
- n_2: the second number to compare

In our case, we set the threshold to the number of maximum of nodes available in the cluster.

4.3 Matcher

The goal of the matcher is to determine the similarity output during the comparison step. We compute the average value of the similarity score, normalized by the number of extracted field per original fields so that fields like the submission time do not weigh more than others because of their many extracted fields. If no record go above a set threshold, then the application is considered to not have any match and their parametrization is set to the default one. Otherwise, the application with the highest score is set for matching.

In our case, the weighted matcher score is:

$$\begin{aligned} \text{score} = \ &\frac{1}{6}sim_{\text{username}} + \frac{1}{6}sim_{\text{jobname}} + \frac{1}{6}sim_{\text{program}} \\ &+ \frac{1}{12}(sim_{\text{path}} + sim_{\text{options}}) \\ &+ \frac{1}{24}(sim_{\text{second}} + sim_{\text{minutes}} + sim_{\text{hours}} + sim_{\text{weekDay}}) \\ &+ \frac{1}{6}sim_{\text{nodeCount}} \end{aligned}$$

For our experiment, we have decided to put some even weights on every similarity and thus on every collected metadata to avoid any design bias, but in practice, it is advised to perform a careful examination of the behavior of the users on the particular cluster in order to select the weights of each similarity. These weights are chosen empirically and their relevance for each use-case has to be evaluated using performance metrics.

5   Validation Plan

To validate our auto-tuner and appreciate its usefulness in a conditions close to those encountered in production clusters, we built a validation environment based on a small HPC cluster of 5 compute nodes and 1 master node. Three different users are created to represent several user behaviors observed from a real setting: each user launches their needed applications in their particular way.

5.1   Cluster Usage Scenario

We started by creating a pool of possible applications, defined by their I/O characteristics and their names. Each one corresponds to an HPC application which I/O patterns can be altered by a different parametrization or a different input dataset. These applications are generated thanks to a home-made highly configurable I/O generator. It allows to generate any combination of parallel and sequential I/O patterns representing the set of HPC applications that users are allowed to run on the production cluster. In our validation scenario, three different users are using the cluster, each with their own behavioral profile. Each user has access to every application in the defined pool and can run it on the cluster, possibly adding its particular variations (e.g. application options or input dataset) composing a job per variation. The I/O characteristics of the application remain the same regardless of the user who picked it, but the metadata used for the application depends on the user: for example the user can choose the jobname, he can edit the program name or add some options to the command line. The possible variation in the metadata is detailed in Sect. 5.3. The users can choose to run the application once but they can also choose to use a black-box optimization tuning framework. These applications will then be included in the database used to perform the matching and will have their metadata stored as well as the optimal parametrization found by the black-box tuner. This validation scenario allows us to have a set of jobs owned by each different user, as well as a set of optimized job.

5.2   Tested Applications and Environment

In practice, we have designed a set of 9218 different possible applications the users can pick from. The selection of the applications per each user is done according to random distributions described in Table 4, to model different type of user behaviors. In practice, we model the behavior of 3 different users as described in Table 4. Table 5 gives the final number of each application selected by each user as well as the number of optimized ones.

Table 4. Parametrization of the metadata matching experiment

User ID	Number of applications	Number of jobs per application	Number of optimized jobs per application
1	10	$\mathcal{U}(5,10)$	$\mathcal{U}(1,2)$
2	20	$\mathcal{U}(1,5)$	$\mathcal{U}(1,3)$
3	25	$\mathcal{U}(5,15)$	$\mathcal{U}(2,4)$

5.3   Variation in Metadata

As said in the previous section, each user launches an application with a different metadata, called job. The metadata that can be changed by the user are:

Table 5. Applications and experiment numbers per used ID

User ID	Number of applications	Total number of jobs	Total number of optimization
1	10	73	13
2	20	66	40
3	25	227	71

- **Username.** The name of the user is set by the user ID using the application.
- **Jobnames.** The only variation in the metadata performed by the user is the modification of the jobname, which is in practice highly dependent on the user behavior and his choices. We define two possible users' behavior. Each application has a root name, and the users can randomly add a prefix and a suffix containing the selected configuration. This mimics some guidelines that have been observed on systems' running in production. For example, if we have an application called `ant`, in two thirds of the cases, an adjective randomly picked is appended as a prefix to the jobname (becoming for example `angry_ant`) and in one third of the cases, the number of nodes is added at the end of the jobname (running on 2 nodes, `angry_ant_2`).
- **Nodes configuration.** Once the user has selected an application, the topology of the system is randomly drawn from a list of available compute nodes. These nodes have different names and configurations and their choices have a strong impact on the behavior of the application and thus on the impact of the auto-tuner. This configuration is reflected by the number of nodes.

5.4   Evaluation Metrics

We evaluate the usability of our auto-tuner according to two metrics:

1. **Impact of the auto-tuner on execution times:** We compare the time spent by the application when using the parametrization selected by the matcher, against the one using the default parametrization. This quantifies the positive impact of our auto-tuner on users' usage of the cluster.
2. **Matching elapsed time:** We evaluate the time needed to perform the matching between the incoming application and the previously executed applications, as a function of the number of applications in the matching database. We also provide some insights in the load resilience of the suggested architecture, by testing the impact of having several users launching their application in parallel.

Additionally, we provide insight on the relevance of the matches performed by the auto-tuner and discuss how the quality of these matches impacts the performance gain as well as the matching score. We also examine the relationship between the users' behavior and the observed performance gain attributed to the tuning process.

6   Results

6.1   Impact of the Auto-tuner on Execution Times

Over all runs we find a median improvement of 28.39% (26.06% in mean) over the 366 different jobs and 41 applications, compared to using the application with the default parametrization. When removing the 150 jobs who had been directly optimized by the user, we still have a median performance improvement of 27.50% (25.47%) over applications that have never been seen by the optimizer. The accelerability potential of each job has a strong dependence on the used application, but we found that overall, on average, no application was slowed down by using the tuner. When looking at individual runs, we find that only 7 runs out of the 366 were slowed down because of our tuner, compared to the default parametrization, for a median loss of only 3% in execution time. Overall, these results highlight the performance and usefulness of our matcher when running in production.

6.2   Matching Quality

The study of the behavior of the matcher shows that the right application is matched in 92% of the cases and the right number of nodes are matched in 56% of the cases. As described in Table 6, a matching application and a matching number nodes yield a better matching score and bring a better improvement in performance than applications that do not match (from 25% to 29%).

Table 6. Median value of the score and the auto-tuning gain

Matched application	Matched nodecount	Score	Auto-tuning gain (%)	Number of jobs
False	False	0.73	25.61	13
	True	0.74	24.73	15
True	False	0.80	25.93	148
	True	0.93	29.27	190

6.3   Impact of the User's Behavior on the Tuning Process

When designing our experiment, we selected several different users' profile. The distribution of the score and auto-tuning gain per user profile is reported in Table 7. We find that the user with the highest ratio of experiments per number of jobs (user 2) is the one who benefits the most from the auto-tuner. The user with the lowest ratio of experiment is the one with the lowest measured gain.

Table 7. Distribution of score and auto-tuning gain per user profile

User ID	Average score	Avg. auto-tuning gain
1	0.78	23.85
2	0.87	27.40
3	0.88	26.24

6.4   Elapsed Time

Time to Match. The time required for matching a single application to databases of different size are described in Fig. 4. The tests are performed with an API running on a server with 94 GB of RAM, with an Intel(R) Xeon(R) CPU E5-2470 0 @ 2.30 GHz with 16 cores and only 4 nodes dedicated to running the matching API. We find that for a very large database of 2000 job, the submission time goes up to 20 s. While this response time can seem high, it has to be considered in the perspective of the HPC context: upon submission, the application is sent to the workload manager queue and can stay there for several hours until the cluster is available, especially for cluster under high traffic. Also, HPC applications often take hours to days to run.

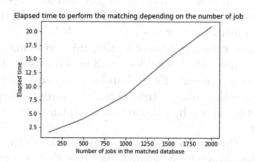

Fig. 4. Time to match applications per database size

Load Tests. To test the resilience of the API to parallel submission by different users, we performed some load testing on the system running the API, for a database of 150 jobs. We perform a series of load tests simulating the behavior of users running applications on the cluster. We test a population of up to 500 users submitting an application every second. The results of the tests are reported in Fig. 5. In the worst case scenario, we find a worst response time of 180 s, when 500 users are submitting one application every second in parallel. While the number of users stays below 200, the response time is inferior to 30 s (submitting a request every second), which makes the use of the auto-tuner transparent to the user even in a very high traffic scenario.

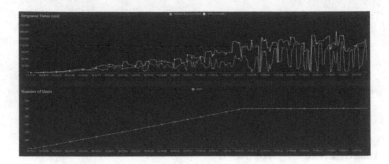

Fig. 5. Load tests on the API

7   Conclusion and Further Works

In conclusion, we present in this paper the architecture of an auto-tuner which relies on record linkage techniques to match an unknown incoming application with a database of previously run applications. We evaluate this matcher by auto-tuning a smart prefetch strategy and show a median performance improvement of 28% compared to using the default parametrization over a dataset representative of conditions found in production. An analysis of required elapsed times show a negligible overhead for a user submitting his job, and load tests show that up to 200 users launching a new job every second do not have an impact on the user's experience when submitting a new job.

In terms of further works, we aim at testing this auto-tuner on a cluster running in production, to have a better understanding of the user's behavior. Another research axis is the development of a probabilistic record linkage rather than the deterministic to reduce the linkage errors [18] and improve the quality of our uto-tuning as the probabilistic method theoretically captures more matches.

Acknowledgments. This work was partially supported by the EU project "ASPIDE: Exascale Programming Models for Extreme Data Processing" under grant 801091. We would also like to acknowledge Thibaut Arnoux for his contributions to this paper.

References

1. Atos: Tools to improve your efficiency (2018)
2. Christen, P.: Data Matching: Concepts and Techniques for Record Linkage, Entity Resolution, and Duplicate Detection. Springer, Heidelberg (2012). https://doi.org/10.1007/978-3-642-31164-2
3. Cohen, W.W., Ravikumar, P., Fienberg, S.E.: A comparison of string distance metrics for name-matching tasks. In: Proceedings of the 2003 International Conference on Information Integration on the Web, IIWEB 2003, pp. 73–78. AAAI Press (2003)
4. Dunn, H.: Record linkage. Am. J. Public Health **66**, 1412–1416 (1946)
5. Dutot, P., Georgiou, Y., Glesser, D., Lefevre, L., Poquet, M., Rais, I.: Towards energy budget control in HPC. In: EEE/ACM International Symposium on Cluster, Cloud and Grid Computing (CCGrid), pp. 381–390 (2017)

6. Haukka, J., et al.: Incidence of cancer and statin usage-record linkage study. Int. J. Cancer **126**, 279–284 (2010)
7. Jaro, M.A.: Advances in record-linkage methodology as applied to matching the 1985 census of Tampa, Florida. J. Am. Stat. Assoc. **84**(406), 414–420 (1989)
8. Jaro, M.A.: Probabilistic linkage of large public health data files. Stat. Med. **14**(5–7), 491–498 (1995)
9. Yoo, A.B., Jette, M.A., Grondona, M.: SLURM: simple Linux utility for resource management. In: Feitelson, D., Rudolph, L., Schwiegelshohn, U. (eds.) JSSPP 2003. LNCS, vol. 2862, pp. 44–60. Springer, Heidelberg (2003). https://doi.org/10.1007/10968987_3
10. Kelman, C.W., Bass, J., Holman, D.: Research use of linked health data - a best practice protocol. Aust. NZ J. Public Health **26**, 251–255 (2002)
11. Miller, F.P., Vandome, A.F., McBrewster, J.: Levenshtein Distance: Information Theory, Computer Science, String (Computer Science), String Metric, Damerau? Levenshtein Distance, Spell Checker, Hamming Distance. Alpha Press (2009)
12. Mitchell, R., Braithwaite, J.: Evidence-informed health care policy and practice: using record linkage to uncover new knowledge. J. Health Serv. Res. Policy **26**, 62–67 (2021)
13. Ranbaduge, T., Christen, P.: A scalable privacy-preserving framework for temporal record linkage. Knowl. Inf. Syst. **62**(1), 45–78 (2019). https://doi.org/10.1007/s10115-019-01370-1
14. Robert, S., Zertal, S., Goret, G.: SHAMan: an intelligent framework for HPC auto-tuning of I/O accelerators (2020)
15. Robert, S., Zertal, S., Vaumourin, G., Couvée, P.: A comparative study of black-box optimization heuristics for online tuning of high performance computing I/O accelerators. Concurr. Comput. Pract. Exp. e6274. https://doi.org/10.1002/cpe.6274. https://onlinelibrary.wiley.com/doi/abs/10.1002/cpe.6274
16. Saillant, T., Weill, J.-C., Mougeot, M.: Predicting job power consumption based on RJMS submission data in HPC systems. In: Sadayappan, P., Chamberlain, B.L., Juckeland, G., Ltaief, H. (eds.) ISC High Performance 2020. LNCS, vol. 12151, pp. 63–82. Springer, Cham (2020). https://doi.org/10.1007/978-3-030-50743-5_4
17. Tanash, M., Dunn, B., Andresen, D., Hsu, W., Yang, H., Okanlawon, A.: Improving HPC system performance by predicting job resources via supervised machine learning. In: Proceedings of the PEARC, pp. 1–8, July 2019
18. Tromp, M., Ravelli, A.C., Bonsel, G.J., Hasman, A., Reitsma, J.B.: Results from simulated data sets: probabilistic record linkage outperforms deterministic record linkage. J. Clin. Epidemiol. **64**, 565–572 (2021)
19. Winkler, W.E.: Cleaning and using administrative lists: enhanced practices and computational algorithms for record linkage and modeling/editing/imputation. In: Administrative Records for Survey Methodology. Wiley Online Library (2021)
20. Zhu, Y., Matsuyama, Y., Ohashi, Y., Setoguchi, S.: When to conduct probabilistic linkage vs. deterministic linkage? A simulation study. J. Biomed. Inform. **56**, 80–86 (2015)

Protecting Sensitive Data in Web of Data

Fethi Imad Benaribi[1]([✉]), Mimoun Malki[2], and Kamel Mohamed Faraoun[1]

[1] EEDIS Laboratory, Djillali Liabes University of Sidi Bel Abbes,
Sidi Bel Abbès, Algeria
`fethi.benaribi@univ-sba.dz`
[2] LabRI-SBA Laboratoy, Ecole Supérieure en Informatique de Sidi Bel-Abbes
(ESI-SBA), Sidi Bel Abbès, Algeria
`m.malki@esi-sba.dz`

Abstract. Over the last few years, the web of data has been increased. It permitted sharing and an interconnection of a large data in several domains and it keeps increasing day by day. However, certain sectors such as health, economic, government, etc., have a limited participation, due to the confidential nature of data. In order to develop the web of data, taking in consideration the confidentiality and the utility of data, we propose in this paper a framework of confidentiality preservation and sharing of the linked data. Our approach provides the means to generate privacy policies that specify the sensitive data to be protected in an Resource Description Framework (RDF) triple. Subsequently the application of the policy on the graph will allow their replacement by their encryption, thus ensuring a balance between confidentiality and utility of data.

Keywords: Linked data · Privacy policy · Access control · Encryption triplet

1 Introduction

The web of data is an extension of the traditional web which is based on hypertext links between documents. It uses the web to create links between data from different sources in order that the elements described in the Resource Description Framework (RDF) can be interpreted by a machine. The linked data is based on four rules defined by Tim Berners-Lee [1]:

- The use of URIs to identify individuals in the Web.
- The use of HTTP URIs to allow access to data, describing resources, and to be identified by HTTP requests.
- The search for URIs is done by providing useful information using RDF and SPARQL Protocol and RDF Query Language (SPARQL) standards.
- Linking of URIs to each other, linking published data sources to existing sources and build a web of linked data in which information can be found by navigating from an input URI.

© Springer Nature Switzerland AG 2021
L. Bellatreche et al. (Eds.): MEDI 2021 Workshops, CCIS 1481, pp. 152–165, 2021.
https://doi.org/10.1007/978-3-030-87657-9_12

The web of data could not be used only to distribute and share public data, but also to selectively share sensitive data (personal, medical or financial data) with specific individuals and organizations. This data richly described and shared on the web, where authentication is not mandatory, are exposed to the risk of malicious use. This leaves businesses and some organizations reluctant to share their data.

The proposal of an access control mechanism applied to linked data will restrict access to sensitive private data by unauthorized users. Extending the web of data by this aspect of security will give producers confidence to publish their data while protecting them from illicit access. This will allow the development of the web of data.

Hence, the interest of our work which is a part of the Privacy Preserving data Publishing (PPDP) [2]. We propose a platform that allows the specification and enforcement of the privacy policy, describing the sensitive data to be protected in an RDF data-set. The application of the policy is carried out using two algorithms, namely Privacy Preserving Sensitive Data (P2SD) algorithm and Disable Privacy Preserving Sensitive Data (D-P2SD) algorithm. The first algorithm allows the encryption of sensitive data and their replacement by the encrypted data into the graph. The second allows the interrogation of the data-set and the return of protected and unprotected data to the different types of users of the system. In the case where a user is authorized the protected data is decrypted. We illustrate our approach with an example as depicted in Fig. 1, where a patient is represented using an RDF based graph.

The remainder of the paper is organized as follows. In Sect. 2, we review the research work on the security and confidentiality of linked data. Section 3 describes the specification of our privacy policy specifying the sensitive data to be protected in the graph. Enforcement is detailed in Sect. 4. In Sect. 5, we propose the architecture of our approach as well as the results of the performance analysis on large RDF graphs containing sensitive data. Section 6 concludes the paper and presents our future work.

2 Related Work

There are several works on access control on RDF documents and linked data. Initially, the researchers focused on the adaptation of existing access control approaches to the semantic web [3,4] as well as the proposed access control vocabulary [5–7].

Authors in [3] addressed the representation of role-based access control and attribute in OWL. In [4], the security model proposed by the authors is inspired by the administration of databases, by creating secure view. The approach is an adaptation of the SQL security model view-based system. The proposed solution is to calculate the SPARQL views from the RDF data then define security rules that govern access to the different views. The approach does not allow a granular access control. In this type of approach the view is calculated before the application of policy without counting the loss of space and time.

Authors in [5] provide an access control solution based on a light vocabulary. The goal is to provide users with the means to express their privacy preferences for restricting access to specific RDF data. Privacy Preference Ontology does not provide a mechanism for conflict management. In other words, there is no tool for checking conflicting preferences. In [6], the author proposes an access control model that allows granular policy specification based on mobile context. Firstly, a description of the mobile context vocabulary named PRISSMA has been established in order to extend the Social Semantic SPARQL Security Access Control (S4AC) vocabulary [7] with the mobile context. S4AC is based on the Web Control Access (WAC) vocabulary. The access conditions are represented by SPARQL 1.1 ASK requests. If the solution exists then the ASK request returns true and we say that the access condition is verified. Specifying a large number of authorizations will decrease the performance side due to ASK request usage to evaluate the access conditions before accessing the data.

On the other hand, in terms of authentication, the authors in [8] demonstrate the actual use of linked data in the student registration process. In order to respond to the security aspect of the system, authors use WebID [9] for authentication and authorization of data access. However, this does not allow a granular access control to the data but just an authentication of the different users by a semantic web protocol.

There are other works on the enforcement of access control policies [10,11]. In the Work [10], the author chose to apply the access control model DAC on RDF graphs. An authorization is specified in the form of a quintuple containing the subject, the sign of the authorization $(+/-)$, the type of access, the resource to be protected which is a pattern graph, the type of authorization (explicit or implicit) and the author of the authorization. In order to allow the delegation operation of the DAC model, an extension of SPARQL with the grant and revoke clauses has been proposed. In [11], the authors aim to define an authorization policy applied to an RDF data set, in order to ensure that the data disclosed cannot be used to infer confidential information. The proposed access control model is based on the SPARQL pattern graphs. The authorization is a triplet effect $(+/-)$, head and body. This specification is based on the structure of a query that has a head and a body starting with the "where" keyword, containing the pattern graph.

There are a few works in the field Privacy preserving publishing linked data, which can be divided into two sub-domains: encryption [12–15] and anonymization [16,17]. There is no much works on RDF graph encryption, the researchers in this field have focused either on the encryption of triplets or on the interrogation of an encrypted graph.

In the paper [12], XML-based encryption techniques are used to protect triplets. The authors of the paper [13] provide a framework for querying encrypted data using triple patterns. In recent works we quote [14,15]. In [14] the authors use the functional encryption method and indexing strategies that focus on triplets. This approach is very expensive and affects the performance of large queries, this solution offers no policy specification model to indicate sensitive data to be encrypted or method of applying privacy policies. In [15], the authors proposed an encryption extension of the RDF HDT graph compression model. The compressed graph is partitioned before encrypted, which decreases performance as partitions of the graph grow. Querying the encrypted compressed graph can be done only after decryption of the data. These works on the encryption of the elements of an RDF graph do not allow the execution of the queries and the realization of complex computation on the encrypted data without forgetting the problems of performance relating to the processing time.

The most popular form of PPDP is graph anonymization where sensitive data is obscured. In this type of approach, it is necessary to create a new graph with anonymous attributes, which implies the loss of utility of the data in the graph. In [16] researchers have tried to apply existing K-anonymity mechanisms to ensure non-disclosure of sensitive data by offering mathematical safeguards. By privileging confidentiality, we lose the utility of the data obtained by interrogating the system. In order to find the right balance between utility and data privacy the authors in [17] provide a declarative platform that allows data providers to specify the privacy and utility policies of data in the form of SPARQL queries. The strong point of this approach is to propose a policy specification using semantic web standards as well as policy specification language. Another interesting point is that this approach allows an anonymization of sensitive data while preserving the utility of the data. Privacy and utility policies are expressed using SPARQL requests to preserve the utility and confidentiality of the data. It seems difficult to strike a balance between privacy and usability policies. Add to that the authors propose a platform which generates a sequence of important choice of operations of anonymization to apply only once on the graph of origin, so the approach is static. After anonymizing the graph, it is impossible to find the original graph. Not to mention the calculation time that increases with the number of policies.

Our approach of protection of the sensitive data which answers to the challenge of the PPDP quoted [2], which is to find a compromise between preserving privacy and the availability of privacy. Unlike the anonymization works [16,17] which favours confidentiality. Added to this in the demarche of anonymization it is imperative to keep the data-set original and duplicate while anonymizing sensitive data. Which implies a significant storage cost. Our method provide control over the selective disclosure of sensitive information while preserving the original data graph as much as possible and not duplicate them. Furthermore, we provide a proactive solution. That works even after updating the data-set with new triples, compared to work [12–15]. Because applying the encryption mechanism again on the data set will make already encrypted data impossible to decrypt.

3   Formalization and Specification of the Privacy Policy

In this Section, we present the formalization of our confidentiality policy, which deals with the triple pattern and more particularly with the sensitive range of certain properties in an RDF graph. Let's take the following example: the triple pattern ?S foaf:name ?O, the evaluation of the variable ?O will return all the values name encountered in the graph, thus causing risks of unauthorized disclosure involving an invasion of privacy of others. For the formalization, we use the formal definitions and notations proposed in [18].

Definition 1. *The triplet $(s, p, o) \in I \cup B \times I \times I \cup B \cup L$, I (IRIS), B (blank node), L (literals). An RDF term is designated by the set $T \in I \cup B \cup L$.*

Definition 2. *Let V be the set of all the variables, V is disjoint with T. A triple pattern is: $I \cup B \cup V \times I \cup V \times I \cup B \cup V$.*

Definition 3. *A policy is defined by a header and a body. The body of the policy is a basic graph pattern (BGP) set of triple pattern policy:*
Let t_{pol} be a triple pattern policy $t_{pol}(s', p', o') \in I \cup B \cup V \times I \times V$.

Definition 4. *Let the mapping function $\mu : V \to T$*
$$[[t_{pol}]]_D = \{\mu / dom(\mu) = dom_s(\mu) \cup dom_o(\mu) = var(t_{pol})\} . \mu(t_{pol}) = \mu(s') \cup \mu(o').$$

Definition 5. *The protection covers all the values obtained by the mapping of the variable o'. The encryption function $\eta : L \to L'$, L' The is the set of encrypted literals $\eta(\mu(o')) \in L'$.*

We used the algebraic expressions of SPARQL as the policy specification language. For the following reasons:

- It is easy to target BGP where evaluation variables contains sensitive data.
- Easier to write for a user unfamiliar with SPARQL because it just needs to indicate the predicate where range is sensitive data.
- It is easy to go from an algebraic expression SPARQL to a SPARQL query.
- The general syntax of a privacy policy:

```
(project (?s ?v1...?v2)              /*Header part of the policy*/
(extend ((?v1(:encryption ?v1))(?vn(:encryption ?vn)))
(group ( ?s ?v1 ?v2 ?v3 ... ?vn)     /* body part of the policy */
            (bgp (triple ?s :Name property1 ?v1)
            (triple ?s :Name property2 ?v2)
            (triple ?s :Name propertyn ?vn) ))))
```

In the example of the graph in Fig. 1, we find that the graph contains private information that should not be shared with anyone. This is an invasion of the privacy of this patient with type 2 diabetes. The predicate ranges foaf:name, foaf:phone, chup:address and cnas:ssn are sensitive data. We describe this through a privacy policy as follows:

```
@prefix drug:  <http://bio2rdf.org/> .
@prefix rdfs:  <http://www.w3.org/2000/01/rdf-schema#> .
@prefix bio:   <http://bioportal.bioontology.org/ontologies/>.
@prefix owl:   <http://www.w3.org/2002/07/owl#> .
@prefix rdf:   <http://www.w3.org/1999/02/22-rdf-syntax-ns#> .
@prefix foaf:  <http://xmlns.com/foaf/0.1/> .
@prefix cnas:  <http://www.cnas.dz/fr/>.
@prefix dc:    <http://purl.org/dc/elements/1.1/> .
@prefix xsd: <http://www.w3.org/2001/XMLSchema#> .
@prefix chures: <http://www.chu.dz/ressources/> .
@prefix chup:  <http://www.chu.dz/property/> .
chures:P01 a          foaf:Person ; foaf:name  "bacha Ahmed";
  chup:adress "10 rue Mouloud Feraoun Oran";
  foaf:phone "+2135578956";
  foaf:age "40"^^xsd:integer;
  foaf:gender "M";
  cnas:ssn "12345678910"^^xsd:integer;
  chup:diagnoses <http://purl.bioontology.org/ontology/ICD9CM/250>;
  chup:doctor_name "benahmed";
  chup:adm_service "endocrinology"  ;
  chup:drug_t    drug:drugbank:DB00030.
```

Fig. 1. Example of an RDF graph of a patient

Policy1

```
(project(?p ?x ?b ?c ?t)
(extend((?x (<http://example/encryption>?N)
(?b (<http://example/encryption> ?A))
(?c (<http://example/encryption> ?S))
 (?t (<http://example/encryption> ?ph)))
(group (?p ?N ?A ?S ?ph)
  (bgp  (triple ?p <http://xmlns.com/foaf/0.1/name> ?N)
  (triple ?p <http://www.chu.dz/property/adress> ?A)
  (triple ?p <http://www.cnas.dz/fr/ssn> ?S)
  (triple ?p <http://xmlns.com/foaf/0.1/phone> ?ph)  ))))
```

4   Enforcement of the Policy

In this Section, we carried out a part responsible for the application of policies, in order to protect confidential data and to allow access to all triplets protected and unprotected by different types of users. For this purpose, we have implemented two modules Privacy Preserving Sensitive Data (P2SD) and Disable Privacy Preserving Sensitive Data (D-P2SD).

4.1   The P2SD Algorithm

Policy1 described in Sect. 3 will be transformed into a SPARQL query by P2SD as follows:

```
Input:  D(dataset), Policy = {pol₁, ⋯ , polₙ}
Output: Trable-Pred, D'
foreach  pol∈ Policy do
    foreach tₚₒₗ ∈ Body(pol)/Body(pol) ∈ Bgp do
        if object(tₚₒₗ)∈ head(pol).extend then
            foreach μᵢ(object(tₚₒₗ)), μᵢ(subject(tₚₒₗ)) ∈ D do
                Mₒ ← μᵢ(object(tₚₒₗ)) ;
                Mₛ ← μᵢ(subject(tₚₒₗ)) ;
                Enc₀ ← Encrypted(Mₒ) ;
                P' ← generate − abstrat − predicate(pred(tₚₒₗ)) ;
                Add (P', pred(tₚₒₗ)) to Trable-Pred ;
                Add the triple {Mₛ, P', Enc₀} to D ;
                Delete {Mₛ, pred(tₚₒₗ), Mₒ} in D ;
            end
        end
    end
end
```

$$\text{Input:}\ D(dataset), Policy = \{pol_1, \cdots , pol_n\}$$
$$\text{Output: Trable-Pred, } D'$$

Algorithm 1: Enforcement Algorithm P2SD

- The creation of encrypted triplets, in this article we opt for stream encryption.
- Replacement of triple pattern properties with abstract predicates. This operation is necessary to avoid providing information on the nature of the encrypted data. In order to restore the original data, it is necessary to save the correspondences between abstract and real properties, e.g. $chup : pred_1$ corresponds to $foaf : name$.

```
insert{ ?p chup:pred_1 ?x; chup:pred_2 ?b ;   chup:pred_3 ?c;
        chup:pred_4 ?t.} where {
        SELECT   ?p  (<http://example/encryption>(?N) AS ?x)
                     (<http://example/encryption>(?A) AS ?b)
                     (<http://example/encryption>(?S) AS ?c)
                     (<http://example/encryption>(?ph) AS ?t)
        WHERE { ?p  foaf:name ?N; chup:adress ?A; cnas:ssn ?S;
            foaf:phone ?ph;} GROUP BY ?p ?N ?A ?S ?ph }
```

- Deletion of sensitive data obtained by evaluating patterns returning confidential data.

```
delete{ ?p foaf:name ?N;
        chup:adress ?A;
        cnas:ssn ?S;
        foaf:phone ?ph.}
        WHERE { ?p  foaf:name ?N;
                chup:adress ?A;
                cnas:ssn ?S; foaf:phone ?ph.}.
```

After applying policy 1 on the patient graph, we obtain the result described in Fig. 2.

```
chures:P01  a          foaf:Person ;
    chup:adm_service  "endocrinology" ;
    chup:diagnoses    <http://purl.bioontology.org/ontology/ICD9CM/250> ;
    chup:doctor_name  "benahmed" ;
    chup:drug_t       <http://bio2rdf.org/drugbank:DB00030> ;
    chup:pred_1       "511112101b1253321b1e161751" ;
    chup:pred_2       "51424353010616533e1c061f1c061753351601121c061d533c01121d51" ;
    chup:pred_3       "424140474645444b4a4243" ;
    chup:pred_4       "51584142404646444b4a464551" ;
    foaf:age         40 ;
    foaf:gender      "M" .
```

Fig. 2. RDF graph of the patient after P2SD application

4.2 The D-P2SD Algorithm

This component will process the interrogation part of protected and unprotected data. Before proceeding, the user of the system must provide authentication information. After checking the profile, the authentication result is returned to the D-P2SD algorithm. In the case where the user is not authorized to consult the real data, his request is sent directly to the SPARQL query engine. The response of the secured view obtained from the graph is returned to the requester. For authorized users, the program extracts the triple pattern of the request and checks whether its property or evaluation is in the correspondence table created by P2SD.

The D-P2SD algorithm rewrites the request with the projection of the triple pattern object by applying the deciphering aggregation function. The new query obtained is subject to evaluation by the SPARQL query engine. Once the view is calculated just replace the abstract properties by their matches in the table. This part of the policy application is described in the algorithm2. If an authenticated user is allowed to view the actual data of the graph and the graph submits the following SPARQL query:

```
Select ?S   ?O
Where {?S chup:pred_1 ?O}
```

The request is transmitted to the query engine by D-P2SD module after rewriting it as follows:

```
Select ?S    ?O1 (<http://example/decryption>(?O) AS ?O1)
                    Where{?S chup:pred_1 ?O}
```

Input: $D'(dataset\ Enc), Policy = \{pol_1, \cdots, pol_n\}$, Trable-Pred., User, Query
Output: $View \subseteq D, View' \subseteq D$
if *user is not authorised* then
$\quad$| $\ View \leftarrow excuteQ(query, D')$;
end
if *user is not authorised* then
$\quad$ foreach $bgp \in Query$ do
$\quad\quad$ foreach $tp \in bgp$ do
$\quad\quad\quad$ if $pred(tp) \in rTable\text{-}Pred$ then
$\quad\quad\quad\quad$ foreach $object(tp)$ do
$\quad\quad\quad\quad\quad$ $M_o \leftarrow \mu_i(object(tp))$;
$\quad\quad\quad\quad\quad$ Project(Decrypted(M_o));
$\quad\quad\quad\quad\quad$ View $\leftarrow$ excuteQ(query,D) ;
$\quad\quad\quad\quad\quad$ View' $\leftarrow$ change-Abstract-pred(view) by real in Trable-pred;
$\quad\quad\quad\quad$ end
$\quad\quad\quad$ end
$\quad\quad$ end
$\quad$ end
end

Algorithm 2: Enforcement Algorithm D-P2SD

5 Architecture and Experimental Results

In this section, we explain our approach and introduce our architecture of access control to sensitive data.

5.1 Architecture

In this paper, we propose a platform that allows the specification of a policy that indicates the sensitive data to be protected in a graph. Once the policies are introduced, the access control platform uses the Privacy Preserving Sensitive Data (P2SD) application sub-module that transforms the policies into a SPARQL request, deletes the triplets containing sensitive data and replaces them in the graph with triplets where objects are encrypted and abstract predicates.

After securing the RDF data set, it becomes accessible to users of the system. After authentication, the user can submit his request. The request is sent to disable privacy preserving Sensitive Data (D-P2SD). In the case where the user is authorized to see the data, the module rewrites the SPARQL request allowing the decryption of the data and the replacement of the abstract predicates by the real properties. Our approach is described in the Fig. 3.

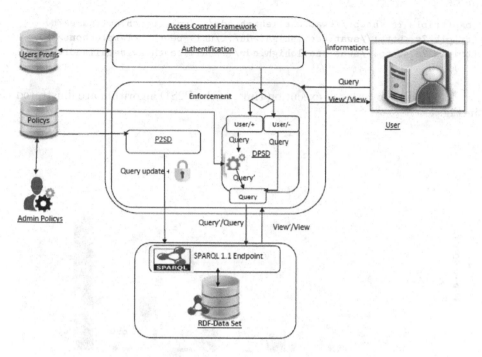

Fig. 3. Architecture of the access control platform

5.2 Experimentation Results

The implementation of our platform was done in java using API JENA[1]. The experiment was performed on a Core Intel (R) Core (TM) i5-8265U CPU @ 1.60 GHz 1.80 GHz 8th generation computer with 16 GB RAM on a 64-bit Windows 10 Professional operating system. We applied our PPDP system on the benchmark Lehigh University Benchmark LUBM [19] on generated data-sets of 100,000 up to 5,000,000 triplets. We have chosen as sensitive properties ub:email, ub:name and ub:telephone on the under graduate Student and Graduate Student person types. this is described by the following policy:

Policy 2

```
(project(?s ?x ?c ?t)
(extend ((?x (<http://example/encryption>?N))
(?c (<http://example/encryption> ?P))
(?t(<http://example/encryption> ?H)))
(group (?s ?N ?P ?S ?H) ( sequence
(union(bgp(triple ?s <http://www.w3.org/.../02-rdf-syntax-ns#type>
<http://swat.cse.lehigh.edu/../univbench.owl#UndergraduateStudent>))
(bgp (triple ?s <http://www.w3.org/../22-rdf-syntax-ns#type>
<http://swat.cse.lehigh.edu/../univ-bench.owl#GraduateStudent>))
```

---

[1] https://jena.apache.org.

```
(bgp(triple ?s <http://swat.cse.lehigh.edu/../univ-bench.owl#name>?N)
(triple ?s <http://swat.cse.lehigh.edu/../univ-bench.owl#telephone>?P)
(triple ?s <http://swat.cse.lehigh.edu/../univ-bench.owl#emailAddress>?H)
   )))))
```

The results, in terms of execution time, of the P2SD algorithm are illustrated in Fig. 4.

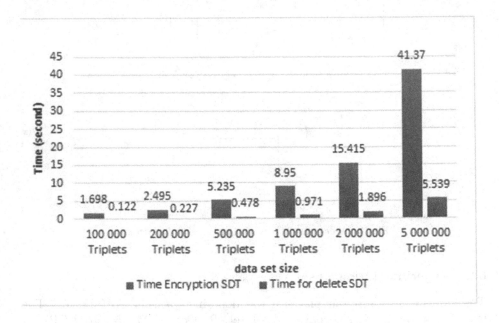

Fig. 4. Execution time of P2SD on the LUBM data-set.

We have opted for the performance evaluation for the most time-consuming request where the triple pattern is ?S ?P ?O. Its execution by D-P2SD for an unauthorized user is done by adding a filter on the prefix sec designates the URI of the abstract properties added in the data-set.

- Query Q1 for public data:

```
PREFIX rdf:<http://www.w3.org/1999/02/22-rdf-syntax-ns#>
PREFIX sec:<http://swat.cse.lehigh.edu/onto/univ-benchsecure.owl#>
PREFIX ub:<http://example.org#>
PREFIX owl:<http://www.w3.org/2002/07/owl#>
PREFIX rdfs:<http://www.w3.org/2000/01/rdf-schema#>
SELECT ?s ?p ?o
WHERE {?s ?p ?o. filter(!(strstarts(str(?p),str(sec:))))}
```

In case of authentication of an authorized user, a second Q2 request is added to Q1 to return the decrypted sensitive data plus the public data.

- Query Q2 for sensitive data:

```
PREFIX rdf:<http://www.w3.org/1999/02/22-rdf-syntax-ns#>
PREFIX sec:<http://swat.cse.lehigh.edu/onto/univ-benchsecure.owl#>
PREFIX ub:<http://example.org#>
PREFIX owl:<http://www.w3.org/2002/07/owl#>
PREFIX rdfs:<http://www.w3.org/2000/01/rdf-schema#>
SELECT ?s ?p (<http://example/dechiffrement>(?N) AS ?o)
WHERE {?s ?p ?N.
filter((strstarts(str(?p),str(sec:))))}GROUP BY ?s ?p ?N;
```

The execution time of the query Q1 and Q2 is reported in Figure Fig. 5.

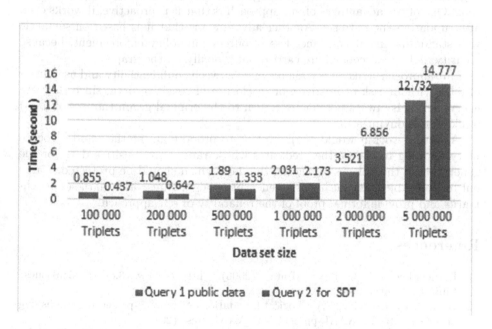

Fig. 5. Query execution time performance by applying D-P2SD to the LUBM data-set.

Our approach does not affect the performance of query execution time on a large graph while ensuring data confidentiality. The performance tests of the D-P2SD algorithm are repeated several times for the execution of the query Q1 and Q2. The execution time remains reasonable which implies that the execution of our approach on a server type machine will be fast. Through this experiment we have shown the feasibility and effectiveness of our application for the protection of sensitive data. Our solution makes it possible to secure the original RDF graph without copying it while ensuring the confidentiality and usefulness of the data as opposed to anonymization. In the case of adding new triples, it suffices to launch the P2SD module which will just secure the new elements added in the RDF graph by applying the confidentiality policy.

6   Conclusion and Perspectives

In this paper we propose the definition of a granulated security policy based on triple patterns whose syntax is an algebraic SPARQL expression. Enforcement is provided by the execution of SPARQL queries which allow the deletion of sensitive data and its replacement by triplets containing the encrypted data. Encryption is achieved with an extension of the aggregation functions of SPARQL that we have developed, which makes encryption easier. Our system allows authorized users to view confidential data by executing queries incorporating a decryption aggregation function. This way of doing things allows for a reasonable execution time. One of the advantages of our approach is that it is proactive, it works even after updating the data-set. Another advantage is that it is based on semantic web standards and it consumes less resources for policy enforcement, because security and access control are carried out globally on the graph.

Our approach strikes a certain balance between confidentiality and usefulness of data without risk of inference or disclosure of sensitive data, since they are encrypted. It is always possible to return to the original graph (no loss of data) unlike the anonymization.

As future work it would be interesting to propose an interface and a vocabulary allowing to choose the predicates whose ranges are sensitive data for the generation of the policies indicating the data which should be protected. Carry out further experiments using other encryption algorithms, other data-set benchmarks and provide formal proof of the reliability of our approach.

References

1. Berners-Lee, T.: Linked Data (2006). http://www.w3.org/DesignIssues/LinkedData.html
2. Grau, B.C., Kostylev, E.V.: Logical foundations of privacy-preserving publishing of linked data. In: AAAI, pp. 943–949. AAAI Press (2016)
3. Finin, T., et al.: ROWLBAC: representing role based access control in OWL. In: 13th ACM Symposium on Access Control Models and Technologies, Estes Park, CO, USA (2008)
4. Gabillon, A., Letouzey, L.: A view based access control model for SPARQL. In: NSS 2010, pp. 105–112, (2010)
5. Sacco, O., Passant, A.: A Privacy Preference Ontology (PPO) for linked data. In: Proceedings of the 4th Workshop about Linked Data on the Web, LDOW 2011 (2011)
6. Costabello, L., Villata, S., Delaforge, N.: Linked data access goes mobile: contextaware authorization for graph stores. In: LDOW - 5th WWW Workshop on Linked Data on the Web (2012)

7. Meersman, R., et al. (eds.): OTM 2011. LNCS, vol. 7045. Springer, Heidelberg (2011). https://doi.org/10.1007/978-3-642-25106-1
8. Mainini, P., Laube, A.: Access control in linked data using WebID: a practical approach validated in a lifelong learning use case. In: 12th International Conference on Semantic Systems - SEMANTiCS2016, Leipzig, Germany, (2016)
9. Sambra, A., Corlosquet, S.: WebID 1.0, Web Identity and Discovery (2015). https://dvcs.w3.org/hg/WebID/raw-file/tip/spec/identity-respec.html
10. Kirrane, S., Abdelrahman, A., Mileo, A., Decker, S.: Secure manipulation of linked data. In: Alani, H., et al. (eds.) ISWC 2013. LNCS, vol. 8218, pp. 248–263. Springer, Heidelberg (2013). https://doi.org/10.1007/978-3-642-41335-3_16
11. Sayah, T., Coquery, E., Thion, R., Hacid, M.-S.: Access control enforcement for selective disclosure of linked data. In: Barthe, G., Markatos, E., Samarati, P. (eds.) Security and Trust Management. STM 2016. LNCS, vol. 9871. Springer, Cham (2016). https://doi.org/10.1007/978-3-319-46598-2_4
12. Giereth, M.: On partial encryption of RDF-Graphs. In: Gil, Y., Motta, E., Benjamins, V.R., Musen, M.A. (eds.) ISWC 2005. LNCS, vol. 3729, pp. 308–322. Springer, Heidelberg (2005). https://doi.org/10.1007/11574620_24
13. Kasten, A., Scherp, A., Armknecht, F., Krause, M.: Towards search on encrypted graph data. In: Proceedings of the International Conference on Society, Privacy and the Semantic Web-Policy and Technology, pp. 46–57 (2013)
14. Fernandez, J. D., Kirrane, S., Polleres, A., Steyskal, S.: Self-enforcing access control for encrypted RDF. In: Blomqvist, E., Maynard, D., Gangemi, A., Hoekstra, R., Hitzler, P., Hartig, O. (eds.) The Semantic Web. ESWC 2017. LNCS, vol. 10249. Springer, Cham. https://doi.org/10.1007/978-3-319-58068-5_37
15. Fernandez, J.D., Kirrane, S., Polleres, A., Steysal, S.: HDTcrypt: compression and encryption of RDF datasets. Semant. Web J. **11**, 337–359 (2018)
16. Heitmann, B., Hermsen, F., Decker, S.: k-RDF-neighbourhood anonymity: combining structural and attribute-based anonymisation for linked data. In: PrivOn@ISWC. CEUR Workshop Proceedings, vol. 1951. CEUR-WS.org (2017)
17. Delanaux, R., Bonifati, A., Rousset, M.-C., Thion, R.: Query-based linked data anonymization. In: The 17th International Semantic Web Conference (ISWC 2018), Monterey, USA (2018)
18. Pérez, J., Arenas, M., Gutierrez, C.: Semantics and complexity of SPARQL. ACM Trans. Database Syst. **34**, 1–45 (2009)
19. Guo, Y., Pan, Z., Heflin, J.: LUBM: a benchmark for owl knowledge base systems. J. Web Semant. (2005). http://swat.cse.lehigh.edu/projects/lubm/

COVID-DETECT: A Deep Learning Based Approach to Accelerate COVID-19 Detection

Nicolas Dimeglio$^{(\boxtimes)}$, Sébastien Romano, Alexandre Vesseron, Vincent Pelegrin, and Samir Ouchani

CESI Engineering School, Aix-en-Provence, France
nicolas.dimeglio@viacesi.fr

Abstract. After two years of COVID-19 first infection and its speedy propagation, death and infection cases are till exponentially increasing. Unfortunately, during this a non-fully controlled situation, we noticed that the existing solutions for COVID-19 detection based on chest X-ray were not reliable enough in relation to the number of infected patients and the severity of the outbreak. To handle this issue by increasing the reliability and the efficiency of COVID-19 detection, we therefore deploy and compare the results of a set of reconfigurable classification approaches and deep learning techniques. Indeed, we have achieved a score of up to 99% accuracy with a dataset of 15,000 X-ray images, which makes the selected detection technique, *deep learning*, more reliable and effective.

Keywords: COVID-19 detection · Deep learning · Machine learning

1 Introduction

In less than a year, COVID-19 outbreak rose up to a critical standpoint for hospitals around the planet. One of the challenges of the pandemic was to rapidly identify people affected by the virus. Being a respiratory disease affecting the lungs, chest X-ray was used as a reliable way to diagnosis patients. CT chest scans can be used as an alternative to a reverse-transcriptase polymerase chain reaction (RT-PCR). RT-PCR is still the principal method of detection used for the COVID-19, but the emergence of accurate diagnosis based on already existing tools such as CT scans or chest X-ray is a field worth exploring for detecting future diseases and possibly help control an outbreak. To help detecting COVID-19 on chest CT Scan, deep learning and other classification methods are used to make diagnosis [7,9]. Those techniques imply the creation of tools using imagery analysis to identify an infected person. In the hope to generalize this tool on other imagery analysis and classification problems, our objective is to have an agile tool capable of identifying through different X-ray images datasets, the important impacted characteristics and classify them to give an acceptable answer to different COVID-19 problems.

Supported by CESI Engineering School.

In fact, medical imaging is often perceived to designate the set of techniques that non-invasively produce images of the internal aspect of the body. It is the set of techniques and processes used to create images of the human body for clinical purposes such as seeking to reveal, diagnose or examine injury, dysfunction or pathology. As a discipline and in its widest applications, it incorporates radiology, tomography, endoscopy, thermography, medical imagery, and microscopy. However, the most characteristic CT abnormalities in COVID-19 pneumonia are multi-focal, bilateral, asymmetric ground glass areas (about 80% of cases) [6,13].

In practice, artificial intelligence (**AI**) is helping, reducing the physician's workload in regions with the outbreak, and improves the diagnosis accuracy for physicians before they could acquire enough experience with the new disease. Deep learning [9], in particular, is a sub-part of machine learning in **AI** domain that mimics the functionalities of the human brain in data processing as well as creating patterns to make a decision. It contains networks capable of learning unattended with unstructured datasets. We can improve the performance of the neural models by changing the pre-processing of the images at the input of the model (CNN) for example reducing the noise to extract the image's features more finely. We can also play on the used features at the output of the CNN to keep only the most relevant ones in order to reduce the noise before passing them into a classifier. We can also play with the classifier model to increase the classification accuracy.

In real world, the existing solutions could be limited by their datasets (maybe too small or not very clear) or, by choosing less efficient algorithms. However, accessible datasets of lung images are growing every day and cleaning methods concerning images too. This paper targets to increase the reliability and the accuracy of the existing COVID-19 detection solutions. After collecting a large data set of X-ray images, we developed a CNN to extract X-ray features. Based on them, we build a *Random Forest algorithm* to identify the weight of each feature and select the most potential ones. After that, we have implemented different algorithms to classify the selected potential data, so we can compare their efficiency on predicting Covid-19 cases. At this stage, we have used different classifiers, especially: Decision tree, RandomForest classifier, Logistic Regression, Perceptron, GradientBoosting classifier, and MultiLayer Perceptron Classifier.

In the next section, we survey the research initiatives that deal with anomaly detection. Then, in Sect. 3, we detail our framework about accelerating COVID-19 and validate it through experiments on real datasets in Sect. 4. Finally, Sect. 5 concludes this paper and gives hints about our future works.

2 Related Work

In this section, we survey and compare the existing work related to COVID detection with our work.

Galbusera *et al.* [2] presented the various AI and ML techniques used in localization and labeling of spinal structures. Recently ANNs and deep learning were also employed for the localization of spinal structures. Chen *et al.* [12]

used a hybrid method involving a random forest classifier which performs a first coarse localization used to drive a deep CNN63, 64. For the segmentation, CNNs are designed to subdivide the image in regions at a pixel level so that each pixel belongs to a specific region. Also, ML and DL techniques were used to achieve images recognition, image segmentation, prediction of clinical outcomes and complications, and decision support systems.

Upadhyay *et al.* [1] presented the analysis of images by **DL** for medical applications in order to detect an epidemic as soon as possible and to be able to give the right treatment. **DL** is used to enable visual perception, recognition and decision-making. It is composed of different layers. First, the **ML**, is used to identify patterns and makes decisions with less human intervention. Then, **DL** is contained in the Machine Leaning and based on cancer data representation. Nguyen *et al.* [5] highlighted the importance of using AI and blockchains to monitor and control an epidemic situation. They proposed a conceptual architecture that support AI in a blockchain for the case of COVID-19. Then, they identified the use of blockchains as a key to track, protect users' information, and assuring the management operations between different services. Thus, they surveyed the deployed tools and the tested use cases on COVID-19. They identified deep learning as a potential technique for detecting, diagnosing, and treating COVID-19.

Raju Vaishya *et al.* [11] concluded that healthcare organizations should adopt AI technologies to help them during the outbreak in their decision-making process. The use of AI in the medical field could improve screening, analyzing and overall improve the understanding of the disease while helping keep track of every patient and detect patterns that could help the development of a vaccine for COVID-19. This observation encourages us to develop an AI-based system to detect the disease quicker. In our case, we are interested in early prognosis particularly in medical image analysis. However, deep Learning algorithms can categorize, identify and list disease characteristics from medical images.

Jin *et al.* [12] presented on AI-assisted CT imaging. Their goal is to solve two key challenges in COVID-19 screening: the sudden outbreak of COVID-19 overwhelming healthcare facilities in the Wuhan area, and training physicians for COVID-19 screening. In a broad country like China, it is nearly impossible to train such a large number of experienced physicians in time to screen this new disease, especially in regions without an outbreak yet. AI systems could be a good solution to both. So, they focused on helping screen COVID-19 pneumonia using chest CT imaging. By taking advantage of the end-to-end deep neural network models for the training data, they developed a three-stage annotation and quality control pipeline, allowing inexperienced data annotators to work with senior radiologists. Indeed, they got reasonable training result to make the diagnosis more intuitive to the radiologists and physicians.

Different studies use other models to detect COVID-19, Aras M. Ismael *et al.* [3] show the highest result of 94,7% accuracy score using a ResNet50 model and SVM classifier. This study concludes that a deep approaches yield to better results, and deep learning confirms their conclusion. Also, J. Zhang *et al.* [13]

achieved a score of 96% sensitivity which is a good score considering their low inputs (only 100 images from COVID-19 subjects). One of the main concerns of their score is the high rate of false positive, almost 30% which can be caused by the size of the dataset. Compared to them, we include almost 15000 chest X-ray including 3600 COVID-19 images. Other studies, like the one from Rodolfo M. Pereira *et al.* [8] use a more realistic scenario trying to identify pneumonia from different pathogens resulting in a multi-class output which result to F1-Score of 89% for COVID-19. The use of hierarchical classification proved to be efficient in the detection of COVID-19. Such results could lead us to change our model to detect different pathologies using hierarchical classification.

Particularly, CNN model [4] has been proposed to detect COVID-19 from thoracic radiographic images. The network is trained to make the following predictions: normal (no infection), COVID-19, Viral Infection (no-COVID-19) and bacterial infection. The training of the neural network is based on 1341 normal radiographic images with 111 cases of COVID-19. The evaluation carried out on the CNN allows a visualization of the regions on the radiographic images used by the CNNs to obtain their final prediction scores. Also, Rahman *et al.* [10] discussed some of the existing challenges and methods of COVID-19 detection from radiography images along with a description of the existing datasets. Their finding suggest that a primary challenge in COVID-19 detection is the imbalance of the different datasets due to the scarcity of COVID-19 images data. The main problem is the lack of properly annotated dataset from reliable source to benchmark the different deep learning models used for the diagnosis of COVID-19.

3 COVID-DETECT Framework

Based on a set of lungs images, our proposed framework as depicted in Fig. 1 accelerates and efficiently improves COVID-19 detection by setting the following steps.

1. The input layer takes image data as an input represented by a three-dimensional matrix.
2. Data step removes the corrupted images, cleans and normalizes them to be prepared for the CNN training phase.
3. CNN phase models a neural network using convolution by taking into consideration i as parameters defining the NN structure.
4. Features identify all possible criteria that can pertinent in the detection/classification process using Gini importance
5. Features selection extracts the best features in order to optimize the results and accelerates the training phases. We use a CNN (ResNet 152) to extract our features.
6. Classification step assigns images to a positive/negative class.
7. Output part matches our classification results to our label list (reporting).

In the following, we will detail each part of the framework.

Input. The framework considers a set of heterogeneous X-rays lungs images as presented in Fig. 2 that shows clear abnormalities. The image formats are of different sizes and types (png, jpg, jpeg, etc.). Since we deal with X-rays images, we avoid the filtering process. In fact, the experiments with different segmentation filters did not show a different result. This part also identifies two classes of images, either with abnormality or not.

Since the used datasets are lung scanners, so they are in black and white and already processed by the scanner. We do not need to do any other processing on the images. But then if, we use color images, we will have to use filters to make the image black and white, but also superimposed another filter to accentuate the contours. Or train our algorithm with color images so that it can process black and white and color images simultaneously.

Data. For a better processing of images, we resize and normalize all images that help construct a complete and homogeneous dataset. Figure 2 shows the images non-normalized.

Convolutional Neural Network. It is a neural network initially designed to process input images. Its architecture, as depicted in Fig. 3, is composed of two main blocks.

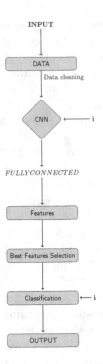

Fig. 1. COVID-DETECT framework: an overview architecture.

– The first block makes the particularity of this type of neural network since it functions is feature extractors. It performs as a template matching by applying convolution filtering operations. The first layer filters the image with

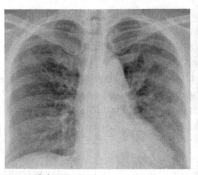

(a) With abnormalities.

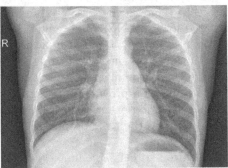

(b) Without abnormalities.

Fig. 2. Non-normalized X-rays lungs images.

several convolution kernels and returns "feature maps", which are then normalized (with an activation function) and/or resized.
- The second block is not a real characteristic of a CNN, it is in fact at the end a type of all the neural network used for classification. The input vector values are transformed (with several linear combinations and activation functions) to return a new vector to the output. The framework generates automatically different NN structures to perform and compare experiments by taking the following parameters as input: layer size, layers number, activation function, weight initialization techniques.

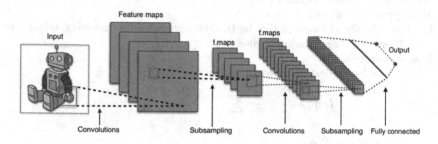

Fig. 3. A convolutional neural network structure.

Features Selection. To identity the best features of our images that are characterized by almost 2048 different features, we deploy a RandomForest algorithm. The feature importance is calculated using the mean and standard deviation accumulated on each tree. So, we easily identify the best features and parameters that we need to perform the prediction. To do that, The RandomForest is a meta estimator that fits a number of decision tree classifiers on various subsamples of the dataset and uses averaging to improve the prediction and control overfitting. The Random Forest classifier can be managed with the number of trees in the forest with "n_estimator". We can modify the "criterion" value, to change the function to measure the quality of a split, and changing the number of features to consider when looking for the best split with "max_features". Algorithm 3 shows the main steps of constructing a random forest pondered with pertinent features.

Algorithm 1. Random Forest for Classification (RFC)

1: Inputs : Array of 2048 features
2: **for** $b \leftarrow 1, B$ **do**
3:     (a) Draw a bootstrap sample $\mathbb{Z}^*$ of size N from the training data.
4:     (b) Grow a random forest tree T_b to the bootstrapped data, by recursively repeating the following steps for each terminal node of the tree, until the minimum node size $n_{\min}$ is reached.
5:             (I)   Select m variables at random from the p variables.
6:             (II)   Pick the best variable/split-point among the m.
7:             (III) Split the node into two daughter nodes.
8: **end for**
9: Output the ensemble of trees $\{T_b\}_1^B$
10: Make prediction at new point x:
11: Let $\hat{C}_b(x)$ be the class prediction be the class prediction of the bth random forest tree. Then $\hat{C}_r f^B(x) = $ majority vote $\{\hat{C}_b(x)_1^B\}$.
12: Feature selection :
13: Finding the list of best features using Gini importance:

$$Imp(X_m) = \frac{1}{N_T} \sum_{T} \sum_{t \in T : v(s_t) = X_m} p(t) \Delta i(s_t, t)$$

14: **for** $Imp(X_m) = 0, F$ **do**
15:     Throw feature
16: **end for**
17: Output : List of best features

Classification. To compare the efficiency of different binary classifiers, the framework develops and supports different images classifiers, mainly:

- Decision tree: A decision tree is a flexible model that can output a categorical prediction or numerical prediction, they are composed of two elements, branches and nodes. At each node our data is evaluated.
- RandomForest: Random Forests train each tree independently, using a random sample of the data. This randomness helps to make the model more robust than a single decision tree, and less likely to overfit on the training data. There are typically two parameters in RF - number of trees and the number of features to be selected at each node.
- Logistic regression: The logistic model (or logit model) is used to model the probability of a certain class or event existing such as pass/fail, win/lose, alive/dead or healthy/sick.
- Perceptron: The perceptron is a supervised learning algorithm for binary classifiers (separating two classes). It is then a type of linear classifier, and the simplest type of artificial neural network. It has several inputs and a single output. It consists of an input layer, a hidden layer and an output layer.
- Gradient-boosting: Gradient boosting is a machine learning technique for regression and classification problems, which produces a prediction model in the form of an ensemble of weak prediction models, typically decision trees.

When a decision tree is the weak learner, the resulting algorithm is called gradient boosted trees, which usually outperforms random forest.

– Multi-level perceptron: A multi-layer perceptron is composed of many perceptron. By assembling several perceptrons, we obtain a multi-layer perceptron, which generally composed of n input, n hidden layer and n output.

[height=4]   [count=3, bias=true, title=Input layer, text=x[count=4, bias=false, title=Hidden layer 1, text=$h^{(1)}$[count=3, bias=false, title=Hidden layer 2, text=$h^{(2)}$[count=2, title=Output layer, text=$\hat{y}$

Fig. 4. Neural network architecture

Output. Our algorithm returns an int, which will determine the class of the input image. We get the class that has the index of our output int of the algorithm.

4 Experiments

To perform our tests, we follow the solution's steps developed in the previous section.

Data. First, we have merged several datasets to get a wider one. The first dataset is called COVID-19_Radiography_Dataset[1] that contains 3616 chest-X-ray of patients with COVID-19 and 10192 normal chest-X-ray. The second is COVID-19 Chest X-ray Image Dataset[2] with 69 chest X-ray images of patients with COVID-19 and 25 of normal cases. The last one is Chest X-Ray Images (Pneumonia)[3] that contains 1583 normal chest-X-ray.

As we have different images coming from different datasets, we need to normalize them. First, we resize them to 224×224 pixels, so they will correspond to the smallest size of images in our dataset. Afterwards, we use a RandomHorizontalFlip to randomly turn the image of a random degree thus improving detection. Then, we tensor those images and decrease their value to reduce the gap between the different values.

For a better data analysis management, we dynamically separate data into three parts: 'train' to train the classifiers and the CNN, 'val' for the evaluation, and 'test' to check the prediction accuracy. We used a random_split from pytorch to separate them at the ratio of 70% train, 20% val and 10% test which means we conserve in every folder the same ratio of COVID-19 and non COVID-19 images.

---

[1] https://www.kaggle.com/tawsifurrahman/covid19-radiography-database.
[2] https://www.kaggle.com/alifrahman/covid19-chest-xray-image-dataset.
[3] https://www.kaggle.com/paultimothymooney/chest-xray-pneumonia.

CNN Construction. For this part, we use ResNet 152[4] as CNN. It is a short for Residual Networks which is a classic neural network. Resnet 152 trained on ImageNet competition data to identify the main objects in an image. ResNet-152 introduced the concept of residual learning in which the subtraction of feature is learned from the input of that layer by using shortcut connections (directly connecting input of (n)th layer to some (n+x)th layer, which is shown as curved arrows). It has proven that the residual learning can improve the performance of model training, especially when the model has deep network with more than 20 layers, and also revolve the problem of degrading accuracy in deep networks.

Feature Extraction. At the output of the Resnet network, we get a tensor, which is reverted to an array including 2048 features. To increase the performance of our classification we want to fine-tune our result by reducing the number of features. To do that, we use a Gini importance included in a RandomForestRegressor to select the most important features. On average, we reduce the number of features to 300 which help the different binary classifier to perform better, reducing the noise, and improving the classification. Figure 5 shows the weight distribution over the selected features.

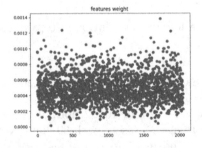

Fig. 5. Weight of features selections

Classification. In this part, we experience the following approaches: Decision tree, Random Forest, Logistic regression, Perceptron, Gradient Boosting, Multi Level Perceptron. Then, we compare them in terms of: recall_mean, recall_std, accuracy_mean, accuracy_std, roc_auc_mean, and roc_auc_std. Figure 6 depicts the obtained classification results with respect to the classifiers and the metrics.

---

[4] https://pytorch.org/hub/pytorch_vision_resnet/.

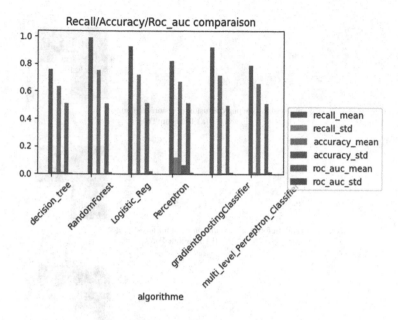

Fig. 6. Classifiers comparison

Note that the accuracy does not fit perfectly with our experiment since the absolute number of the used non COVID-19 images is very important. Hence, we look more on recall scoring instead of accuracy while false positive cases are less important than false negative ones for our case. It means that, people identified positive with our solution should be confirmed with a clinical test. Indeed, the recall score is more representative and gives us more information about the efficiency of the solution. To show the performance for each model, we construct their confusing matrices. (Figure 7) to present the distributed data in terms of false positive/negative.

We recall that, with a feature selection, it is clear that the random forest classifier has scored the best value with 97%. However, without feature selection, the implemented multi-level perceptron classifier using Pytorch gave a score of 99%.

Discussions. From the results, we observe an interesting conclusion showing that the machine learning is more accurate in terms of COVID-19 case detection as well as with a lower error rate. The best scored algorithms are : Random Forest, Logistic regression, and Gradient Boosting Classifier. The prediction time also is interesting and it is around 0.03 s per image (Fig. 8). Thanks to the confusion matrix, we can observe that deep learning technique is more efficiently and rapidly trained with few errors compared to the experimented algorithms.

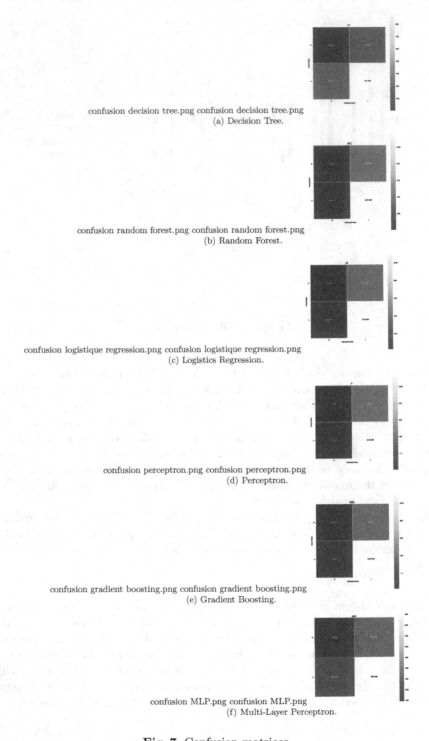

confusion decision tree.png confusion decision tree.png
(a) Decision Tree.

confusion random forest.png confusion random forest.png
(b) Random Forest.

confusion logistique regression.png confusion logistique regression.png
(c) Logistics Regression.

confusion perceptron.png confusion perceptron.png
(d) Perceptron.

confusion gradient boosting.png confusion gradient boosting.png
(e) Gradient Boosting.

confusion MLP.png confusion MLP.png
(f) Multi-Layer Perceptron.

Fig. 7. Confusion matrices.

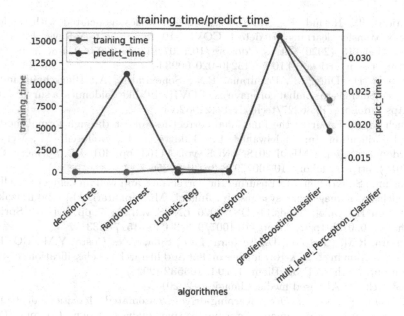

Fig. 8. Execution time

5 Conclusion

Currently, the use of machine learning to detect COVID-19 is exponential. This manuscript develops a framework, called COVID-DETECT, that efficiently advances detecting COVID-19. COVID-DETECT implements several machine and deep learning for the classification and the features selections. Based on a dataset of 15000 images where 14550 are correctly identified, the results showed that Random Forest detects 97%, whereas the proposed Deep Learning scored the best accuracy ratio of 99% (i.e. 14,850 images that have been correctly processed). This model proved itself effective to detect COVID-19 and could be used to decrease the rate of error detection for COVID-19, which results on helping medical staff management and the society safety.

As a next step, we will integrate different techniques of normalization for the image to get better results. In addition, we target introducing other techniques for the feature extraction. Also, we will make our solution online to produce a more robust and normalized datasets.

References

1. Upadhyay, D., Jain, S. and Jain, A.: A fuzzy clustering algorithm for high dimensional streaming data. J. Inf. Eng. Appl. 3, 1–9 (2020)
2. Galbusera, F., Casaroli, G., Bassani, T.: JOR Spine **2**(1), e1044 (2019)
3. Ismael, A.M., Şengür, A.: Deep learning approaches for COVID-19 detection based on chest X-Ray images. Exp. Syst. Appl. **164**, 114054 (2021)

4. Majeed, T., Rashid, R., Ali, D., Asaad, A.: Issues associated with deploying CNN transfer learning to detect COVID-19 from chest X-Rays. Phys. Eng. Sci. Med. **43** (2020). https://doi.org/10.1007/s13246-020-00934-8, https://link.springer.com/article/10.1007/s13246-020-00934-8

5. Nguyen, D., Ding, M., Pathirana, P.N., Seneviratne, A.: Blockchain and AI-based solutions to combat coronavirus (COVID-19)-like epidemics: a survey (2020). https://doi.org/10.36227/techrxiv.12121962.v1

6. Ouchani, S.: Ensuring the functional correctness of iot through formal modeling and verification. In: Abdelwahed, E., Bellatreche, L., Golfarelli, M., Méry, D., Ordonez, C. (eds.) MEDI 2018. LNCS, vol. 11163, pp. 401–417. Springer, Cham (2018). https://doi.org/10.1007/978-3-030-00856-7_27

7. Ouchani, S., Krichen, M.: Ensuring the correctness and well modeling of intelligent healthcare management systems. In: Jmaiel, M., Mokhtari, M., Abdulrazak, B., Aloulou, H., Kallel, S. (eds.) ICOST 2020. LNCS, vol. 12157, pp. 364–372. Springer, Cham (2020). https://doi.org/10.1007/978-3-030-51517-1_33

8. Pereira, R.M., Bertolini, D., Teixeira, L.O., Silla, C.N., Costa, Y.M.: COVID-19 identification in chest X-Ray images on flat and hierarchical classification scenarios. Comput. Methods Prog. Biomed. **194**, 105532 (2020)

9. Research, P.: AI based medical imaging (2020)

10. Rahman, S., et al.: Deep learning-driven automated detection of COVID-19 from radiography images: a comparative analysis. Cogn. Comput. (2021) (2021). https://doi.org/10.1007/s12559-020-09779-5, https://link.springer.com/article/10.1007/s12559-020-09779-5

11. Vaishya, R., Javaid, M., Khan, I.H., Haleem, A.: Artificial intelligence (AI) applications for COVID-19 pandemic. Diabetes Metab. Syndr.: Clin. Res. Rev. **14**(4), 337–339 (2020)

12. Wang, B., et al.: AI-assisted CT imaging analysis for COVID-19 screening: building and deploying a medical AI system. Appl. Soft Comput. **98** (2021). https://doi.org/10.1016/j.asoc.2020.106897

13. Zhang, J., Xie, Y., Li, Y., Shen, C., Xia, Y.: COVID-19 screening on chest X-Ray images using deep learning based anomaly detection. arXiv abs/2003.12338 (2020)

Control Software: Methods, Models, and Languages (CSMML)

Time Insertion Functions

Damas P. Gruska[✉]

Institute of Informatics, Comenius University, Mlynska dolina,
842 48 Bratislava, Slovakia
gruska@fmph.uniba.sk

Abstract. Time insertion functions as a tool to guarantee security of
processes with respect to timing attacks are discussed and studied. We
work with a security property called opacity and we investigate how
it can be enforced by such functions. The time insertion function can
alter time behaviour of original system by inserting some time delays
to guarantee its security. We investigate conditions under which such
functions do exist and also some of their properties.

Keywords: Security · Opacity · Process algebras · Information flow ·
Insertion function · Timing attack

1 Introduction

Suppose that we are able to show, by means of formal methods, that a system
is not secure. Then there are a couple of options what to do. We can either redesign its behavior, what might be costly, difficult or even impossible, in the case
that it is already part of a hardware solution, proprietary firmware and so on, or
we can use supervisory control (see [14]) to restrict system's behaviour in such
a way that the system becomes secure. A supervisor can see (some) system's
actions and can control (disable or enable) some set of system's action. In this
way it restricts system's behaviour to guarantee its security (see also [8]). This is
a trade-off between security and functionality. Situation is in the case of timing
attacks. They, as side channel attacks, represent serious threat for many systems.
To protect systems against timing attacks we propose application of inserting
functions (see [10–12,15]). Such functions can add some idling between actions
to enforce process's security. In this paper we investigate conditions under which
such functions do exist and also their properties.

As regards formalism, we will work with a timed process algebra and opacity,
which is the security property based on an absence of information flow. This
formalism enables us to formalize timing attacks. In [7] we have introduced time
insertion functions and showed some of their properties. In this (research in
progress) paper we study conditions under which there exists a timed insertion

This work was supported by the Slovak Research and Development Agency under the
Contract no. APVV-19-0220 (ORBIS) and by the Slovak VEGA agency under Contract
no. 1/0778/18 (KATO).

function for a given process and security property. Moreover, we present some decidability and undecidability results.

The paper is organized as follows. In Sect. 2 we describe the timed process algebra TPA which will be used as a basic formalism. In Sect. 3 two information flow-based security properties are introduced. The next section is devoted to time insertion functions. In Sect. 5 an existence of such functions is investigated.

2 Timed Process Algebra

In this section we briefly recall Timed Process Algebra, TPA for short (for more details see [9]). TPA is based on Milner's Calculus of Communicating Systems (for short, CCS, see [13]) but the special time action t which expresses elapsing of (discrete) time is added and hence the set of actions is extended from Act to $Actt$. The presented language is a slight simplification of Timed Security Process Algebra introduced in [3]. We omit an explicit idling operator ι used in tSPA and instead of this we allow implicit idling of processes. Hence processes can perform either "enforced idling" by performing t actions which are explicitly expressed in their descriptions or "voluntary idling" (i.e. for example, the process $a.Nil$ can perform t action despite the fact that this action is not formally expressed in the process specification). But in both cases internal communications have priority to action t in the parallel composition. Moreover we do not divide actions into private and public ones as it is in tSPA. TPA differs also from the tCryptoSPA (see [4]). TPA does not use value passing and strictly preserves *time determinancy* in case of choice operator $+$ what is not the case of tCryptoSPA (see [9]).

To define the language TPA, we first assume a set of atomic action symbols A not containing symbols τ and t, and such that for every $a \in A$ there exists $\bar{a} \in A$ and $\bar{\bar{a}} = a$. We define $Act = A \cup \{\tau\}, At = A \cup \{t\}, Actt = Act \cup \{t\}$. We assume that $a, b, \ldots$ range over A, $u, v, \ldots$ range over Act, and $x, y \ldots$ range over $Actt$.

We give a structural operational semantics of terms by means of labeled transition systems. We define the transition relation as the least relation satisfying the inference rules for CCS plus the following inference rules:

$$\frac{}{Nil \xrightarrow{t} Nil} \; A1 \qquad \frac{}{u.P \xrightarrow{t} u.P} \; A2$$

$$\frac{P \xrightarrow{t} P', Q \xrightarrow{t} Q', P|Q \xrightarrow{\tau}}{P|Q \xrightarrow{t} P'|Q'} \; Pa \qquad \frac{P \xrightarrow{t} P', Q \xrightarrow{t} Q'}{P+Q \xrightarrow{t} P'+Q'} \; S$$

Axioms $A1, A2$ allow arbitrary idling. Concurrent processes can idle only if there is no possibility of an internal communication (Pa). A run of time is deterministic (S) i.e. performing of t action does not lead to the choice between summands of $+$. In the definition of the labeled transition system we have used negative premises (see Pa).

For $s = x_1.x_2.\ldots.x_n, x_i \in Actt$ we write $P \xrightarrow{s}$ instead of $P \xrightarrow{x_1}\xrightarrow{x_2} \cdots \xrightarrow{x_n}$ and we say that s is a trace of P. The set of all traces of P will be denoted by $Tr(P)$. By ϵ we will denote the empty sequence of actions. Let $s \in Actt^*$. By $s|_B$ we will denote the sequence obtained from s by removing all actions not belonging to B.

3   Opacity

To formalize process security based on an absence of information flow we do not divide actions into public and private ones at the system description level, as it is done for example in [4], but we use a more general concept of observation and opacity. This concept was exploited in [1] and [2] in a framework of Petri Nets and transition systems, respectively. First we define observation function on sequences from $Actt^*$.

Definition 1 (Observation). *Let Θ be a set of elements called observables. Any function $\mathcal{O} : Actt^* \to \Theta^*$ is an observation function. It is called static/ dynamic/orwellian/m-orwellian $(m \geq 1)$ if the following conditions hold respectively (below we assume $w = x_1 \ldots x_n$):*

- *static if there is a mapping $\mathcal{O}' : Actt \to \Theta \cup \{\epsilon\}$ such that for every $w \in Act^*$ it holds $\mathcal{O}(w) = \mathcal{O}'(x_1) \ldots \mathcal{O}'(x_n)$,*
- *dynamic if there is a mapping $\mathcal{O}' : Actt^* \to \Theta \cup \{\epsilon\}$ such that for every $w \in Actt^*$ it holds $\mathcal{O}(w) = \mathcal{O}'(x_1).\mathcal{O}'(x_1.x_2) \ldots \mathcal{O}'(x_1 \ldots x_n)$,*
- *orwellian if there is a mapping $\mathcal{O}' : Actt \times Actt^* \to \Theta \cup \{\epsilon\}$ such that for every $w \in Actt^*$ it holds $\mathcal{O}(w) = \mathcal{O}'(x_1, w).\mathcal{O}'(x_2, w) \ldots \mathcal{O}'(x_n, w)$,*
- *m-orwellian if there is a mapping $\mathcal{O}' : Actt \times Actt^* \to \Theta \cup \{\epsilon\}$ such that for every $w \in Actt^*$ it holds $\mathcal{O}(w) = \mathcal{O}'(x_1, w_1).\mathcal{O}'(x_2, w_2) \ldots \mathcal{O}'(x_n, w_n)$ where $w_i = x_{max\{1,i-m+1\}}.x_{max\{1,i-m+1\}+1} \ldots x_{min\{n,i+m-1\}}$.*

In the case of the static observation function each action is observed independently from its context. In the case of the dynamic observation function an observation of an action depends on the previous ones, in the case of the orwellian and m-orwellian observation function an observation of an action depends on the all and on m neighboring actions in the sequence, respectively. The static observation function is the special case of m-orwellian one for $m = 1$. Note that from the practical point of view the m-orwellian observation functions are the most interesting ones. An observation expresses what an observer - eavesdropper can see from a system behavior and we will alternatively use both the terms (observation - observer) with the same meaning. Note that the same action can be seen differently during an observation (except static observation function) and this express a possibility to accumulate some knowledge by intruder. For example, an action not visible at the beginning could become somehow observable. In this paper we will assume that $\Theta \subseteq Actt$.

Now suppose that we have some security property. This might be an execution of one or more classified actions, an execution of actions in a particular classified order which should be kept hidden, etc. Suppose that this property is expressed by predicate ϕ over process traces. We would like to know whether an observer can deduce the validity of the property ϕ just by observing sequences of actions from $Actt^\star$ performed by given process. The observer cannot deduce the validity of ϕ if there are two traces $w, w' \in Actt^\star$ such that $\phi(w), \neg\phi(w')$ and the traces cannot be distinguished by the observer i.e. $\mathcal{O}(w) = \mathcal{O}(w')$. We formalize this concept by opacity.

Definition 2 (Opacity). *Given process P, a predicate ϕ over $Actt^\star$ is opaque w.r.t. the observation function $\mathcal{O}$ if for every sequence w, $w \in Tr(P)$ such that $\phi(w)$ holds and $\mathcal{O}(w) \neq \epsilon$, there exists a sequence $w', w' \in Tr(P)$ such that $\neg\phi(w')$ holds and $\mathcal{O}(w) = \mathcal{O}(w')$. The set of processes for which the predicate ϕ is opaque with respect to $\mathcal{O}$ will be denoted by $Op_{\mathcal{O}}^{\phi}$.*

A predicate is opaque if for any trace of a system for which it holds, there exists another trace for which it does not hold and both traces are indistinguishable for an observer (which is expressed by an observation function). This means that the observer (intruder) cannot say whether a trace for which the predicate holds has been performed or not.

Suppose that all actions are divided into two groups, namely public (low level) actions L and private (high level) actions H. It is assumed that $L \cup H = A$. Strong Nondeterministic Non-Interference (SNNI, for short, see [3]) property assumes an intruder who tries to learn whether a private action was performed by a given process while (s)he can observe only public ones. If this cannot be done, then the process has SNNI property. Note that SNNI property is the special case of opacity for static observation function $\mathcal{O}(x) = x$ iff $x \notin H$ and $\mathcal{O}(x) = \epsilon$ otherwise, and $\phi(w)$ is such that it is true iff w contains an action from H.

4   Insertion Functions

Timing attacks belong to powerful tools for attackers who can observe or interfere with systems in real time. On the other side these techniques is useless for off-line systems and hence they could be consider safe with respect to attackers who cannot observe (real) time behaviour. By the presented formalism we have a way how to distinguish these two cases. First we define untimed version of an observation function, i.e. a function which does not take into account time information. From now on we will consider observation functions $\mathcal{O} : Actt^\star \rightarrow Actt^\star$ for which there exists untimed variants $\mathcal{O}_t$. Function $\mathcal{O}_t$ is untimed variant of $\mathcal{O}$ iff $\mathcal{O}(w) = \mathcal{O}_t(w|_{Act})$, i.e. untimed variant represents an observer who does not see elapsing of time since both traces, with and without actions t, are seen equally. Now we can formally describe situation when a process could be jeopardized by a timing attack i.e. is secure only if an observer cannot see elapsing of time.

Definition 3 (Timinig Attacks). *We say that process P is prone to timing attacks with respect to ϕ and $\mathcal{O}$ iff $P \notin Op_{\mathcal{O}}^{\phi}$ but $P \in Op_{\mathcal{O}_t}^{\phi}$.*

Example 1. Let us assume an intruder who tries to learn whether a private action h was performed by a given process while (s)he can observe only public action l but not h itself. Then process $P = t.t.t.l.Nil + t.h.t.Nil$ is not opaque for static observation function $\mathcal{O}(x) = x$ iff $x \in \{l, t\}$, $\mathcal{O}(h) = \epsilon$ and $\phi(w)$ is such that it is true iff w contains an action h, i.e. $P \notin Op_{\mathcal{O}}^{\phi}$. But if an observer cannot see elapsing of time this process is opaque, i.e. $P \in Op_{\mathcal{O}_t}^{\phi}$.

There are basically three ways how to solve vulnerability to timing attacks except putting a system off-line. First, redesign the system, put some monitor or supervisor which prevents dangerous behavior which could leak some classified information (see, for example, [8]) or hide this leakage by inserting some time delays between system's action (see [11,15] for general insertion functions for non-deterministic finite automata). Now we will define and study this possibility. First we need some notation. For $w, w' \in Actt^*$ and $w = x_1.x_2 \ldots x_n$ we will write $w \ll_S w'$ for $S \subset Actt$ iff $w' = x_1.i_1.x_2 \ldots x_n.i_n$ where $i_k \in S^*$ for every $k, 1 \leq k \leq n$. In general, an insertion function inserts additional actions between original process's actions (given by trace w) such that for the resulting trace w' we have $w \ll_S w'$. and w' is still a possible trace of the process. In our case we would consider insertion functions (called time insertion functions) which insert only time actions i.e. such functions that $w \ll_{\{t\}} w'$. Results of an insertion function depends on previous process behaviour. We can define this dependency similarly as it is defined for observation functions.

Definition 4 (Time Insertion function). *Any function $\mathcal{F} : Actt^* \to Actt^*$ is an insertion function iff for every $w \in Actt^*$ we have $w \ll_{\{t\}} \mathcal{F}(w)$. It is called static/dynamic/orwellian/m-orwellian ($m \geq 1$) if the following conditions hold respectively (below we assume $w = x_1 \ldots x_n$):*

- *static if there is a mapping $f : Actt \to \{t\}^*$ such that for every $w \in Actt^*$ it holds $\mathcal{F}(w) = x_1.f(x_1).x_2.f(x_2) \ldots x_n.f(x_n)$,*
- *dynamic if there is a mapping $f : Actt \to \{t\}^*$ such that for every $w \in Act^*$ it holds $\mathcal{F}(w) = x_1.f(x_1).x_2.f(x_1.x_2) \ldots x_n.f(x_1. \ldots .x_n)$,*
- *orwellian if there is a mapping $f' : Actt \times Actt^* \to \{t\}^*$ such that for every $w \in Actt^*$ it holds $\mathcal{F}(w) = x_1.f(x_1, w).x_2.f(x_2, w) \ldots x_n.f(x_n, w)$,*
- *m-orwellian if there is a mapping $f' : Actt \times Actt^* \to \{t\}^*$ such that for every $w \in Actt^*$ it holds $\mathcal{F}(w) = x_1.f(x_1, w_1).x_2.f(x_2, w_2) \ldots x_n.f(x_n, w_n)$, $w_i = x_{max\{1, i-m+1\}}.x_{max\{1, i-m+1\}+1} \cdots x_{min\{n, i+m-1\}}$.*

Note that contrary to general insertion function (see [11,15]) inserting time actions is much simpler due to transition rules $A1, A2, S$. The purpose of time insertion function is to guaranty process security with respect to opacity (timing attacks). Let $P \notin Op_{\mathcal{O}}^{\phi}$ but $P \in Op_{\mathcal{O}_t}^{\phi}$, i.e. the process P is prone to timing attack. Now we define what it means that process can be immunized by a time insertion function.

Definition 5. *We say that process P can be immunized for opacity with respect to a predicate ϕ over $Actt^*$ and the observation function $\mathcal{O}$ if for every sequence w, $w \in Tr(P)$ such that $\phi(w)$ holds and $\mathcal{O}(w) \neq \epsilon$, and there does not exist a sequence $w', w' \in Tr(P)$ such that $\neg\phi(w')$ holds and $\mathcal{O}(w) = \mathcal{O}(w')$ there exist*

$w_t, w_t \in Tr(P)$ such that $w \ll_{\{t\}} w_t$ and $\phi(w_t)$ either does not hold or holds and in this case $\mathcal{O}(w_t) \neq \epsilon$, and there exists a sequence $w'_t, w'_t \in Tr(P)$ such that $\neg\phi(w'_t)$ holds and $\mathcal{O}(w_t) = \mathcal{O}(w'_t)$.

If $\mathcal{O}$ and ϕ are clear from the context we say just that process P can be immunized.

5   Existence of Time Insertion Functions

In this section we will study an existence of time insertion functions. From now on we will consider only processes which are prone to timing attacks (see Definition 5) and moreover we will assume that predicate ϕ is decidable. First we need some notations. We begin with observational functions which do not see τ actions.

Definition 6. We say that observational function $\mathcal{O}$ is not sensitive to τ action iff $\mathcal{O}(w) = \mathcal{O}(w|_{At})$ for every $w \in Act^*$. Otherwise we say that $\mathcal{O}$ is sensitive to τ action.

Example 2. Process $P, P = h.\tau.t.\tau.Nil + (a.b.Nil|\bar{a}.\bar{b}.Nil) \setminus \{a, b\}$, cannot be immunized if $\mathcal{O}$ is sensitive to τ action and $\phi(w)$ is such that it is true iff w contains action h. An immunization should put a time delay into the trace performed by the right part of the process P but this subprocess cannot perform t action due to the inference rule Pa.

Another problem, which causes that processes cannot be immunized, is related to observation of time, namely, if this observation is context sensitive, as it is stated by the following example.

Example 3. Process $P, P = h.l.Nil + t.l.Nil$ cannot be immunized for dynamic $\mathcal{O}$ such that $\mathcal{O}(w.h.t^*.w') = \mathcal{O}(w.w')$, $\mathcal{O}(w.l.w') = \mathcal{O}(w).l.\mathcal{O}(w')$, and if w does not end with action h we have $\mathcal{O}(w.t.w') = \mathcal{O}(w).t.\mathcal{O}(w')$, and $\phi(w)$ is such that it is true whenever w contains action h.

Definition 7. Let $w = t^{i_1}.s_1 \ldots s_n.t^{i_{n+1}}$ where $i_j \geq 0$ for $0 \leq j \leq n+1$ and $s_i \in Act^*$ for for $0 \leq i \leq n$. We say that observational function $\mathcal{O}$ is time non-contextual if $\mathcal{O}(w) = t^{i_1}.p_1 \ldots p_n.t^{i_{n+1}}$ where $p_i \in Act^*$.

Proposition 1. Let process P is prone to timing attacks with respect to ϕ and time non-contextual observation function $\mathcal{O}$ which does not see τ. Then P can be immunized for opacity with respect to timing attacks.

Proof. The main idea. Let $P \notin Op_{\mathcal{O}}^\phi$ but $P \in Op_{\mathcal{O}_t}^\phi$. This means that there exists a sequence $w, w \in Tr(P)$ such that $\phi(w)$ holds and $\mathcal{O}(w) \neq \epsilon$ such that there does not exist a sequence $w', w' \in Tr(P)$ such that $\neg\phi(w')$ holds and $\mathcal{O}(w) = \mathcal{O}(w')$. Since $P \in Op_{\mathcal{O}_t}^\phi$ then there exists $w'', w'' \in Tr(P)$ such that $\mathcal{O}_t(w) = \mathcal{O}_t(w'')$. Since according the assumption $\mathcal{O}$ is time non-contextual observation function we can add time actions (by an insertion function) between actions in w and w'' such that for resulting sequences w_i and w''_i we have $\mathcal{O}(w_i) = \mathcal{O}(w''_i)$. Moreover, due to transition rules for TPA (A1, A2, S) we can arbitrary insert t actions and still have $w_i, w_i'' \in Tr(P)$. The only problem could be the rule Pa, which states that before τ action resulting from an internal communication t action cannot be inserted. But it can be inserted after such communication(s) since $\mathcal{O}$ does not see, according to the assumption, τ action.

Corollary 1. Let $\mathcal{O}$ is a static observation function such that $\mathcal{O}(\tau) = \epsilon$ and $\mathcal{O}(t) = t$. Then process P which is prone to timing attacks with respect to ϕ and observation function $\mathcal{O}$ can be immunized for opacity with respect to timing attacks.

Proposition 2. *Let process P is prone to timing attacks with respect to ϕ and time non-contextual observation function $\mathcal{O}$ which does not see τ. Then P can be immunized for opacity with respect to timing attacks by a m-orwellian insertion function, moreover such one, which can be emulated by finite state process.*

Proof. The prove follows from Proposition 1 and Theorem 4.10 and Lemma 4.5. in [7], where insertion functions are modeled by processes run in parallel with P.

In general, we cannot decide whether process can be immunized as it is stated by the following proposition. Fortunately, it is decidable for the most important static and m-orwellian observation functions.

Proposition 3. *Immunizability is undecidable i.e. it cannot be decided whether P can be immunized for opacity with respect to timing attacks.*

Proof. Sketch. Let T_i represents i-th Turing machine under some numeration of all Turing machines. We start with generalized process from Example 3. Let $P = h.l.Nil + \sum_{i \in N} t^i.l.Nil$. Let $\mathcal{O}(w.h.t^i.w') = \mathcal{O}(w.w')$ whenever T_i halts with the empty tape and $\mathcal{O}(w.h.t^i.w') = \mathcal{O}(w).t^i.\mathcal{O}(w')$ otherwise. It is easy to check that immunization of P is undecidable.

Proposition 4. *Immunizability is decidable for static and m-orwellian observation function $\mathcal{O}$.*

Proof. According to Proposition 1 it is enough to show that observation function $\mathcal{O}$ is time non-contextual observation function and it does not see τ. Clearly both these properties are decidable for static and m-orwellian observation functions.

6   Conclusions

We have investigated time insertion functions for timed process algebra which enforce the security with respect to timing attacks. Time insertion functions add some delays to system's behaviour to prevent a timing attack. We study an existence of an insertion function for a given process, given observational function and a predicate on process's traces. In future work we plan to investigate minimal insertion functions, i.e. such functions which add as little as possible time delays to guarantee process's security with respect to timing attacks. The presented approach allows us to exploit also process algebras enriched by operators expressing other "parameters" (space, distribution, networking architecture, power consumption and so on). Hence we could obtain security properties which have not only theoretical but also practical value. Moreover, we can use similar techniques as in [16] to minimize time, as well as other resources, added to process's behaviour.

References

1. Bryans, J.W., Koutny, M., Mazaré, L., Ryan, P.Y.A.: Modelling non-deducibility using Petri Nets. In: Proceedings of the 2nd International Workshop on Security Issues with Petri Nets and other Computational Models (2004)
2. Dimitrakos, T., Martinelli, F., Ryan, P.Y.A., Schneider, S. (eds.): FAST 2005. LNCS, vol. 3866. Springer, Heidelberg (2006). https://doi.org/10.1007/11679219
3. Focardi, R., Gorrieri, R., Martinelli, F.: Information flow analysis in a discrete-time process algebra. In: Proceedings of 13th Computer Security Foundation Workshop. IEEE Computer Society Press (2000)
4. Gorrieri, R., Martinelli, F.: A simple framework for real-time cryptographic protocol analysis with compositional proof rules. Sci. Comput. Program. **50**(1–3), 23–49 (2004)
5. Goguen, J., Meseguer, J.: Security policies and security models. In: Proceedings of IEEE Symposium on Security and Privacy (1982)
6. Gruska D.P., Ruiz M.C.: Security testing for multi-agent systems. In: Rojas, I., Joya, G., Catala, A. (eds.) Advances in Computational Intelligence. IWANN 2019. Lecture Notes in Computer Science, vol 11506, pp. 703–715. Springer, Cham (2019). https://doi.org/10.1007/978-3-030-20521-8_58
7. Gruska, D.P.: Security and time insertion. In: PCI 2019. ACM (2019)
8. Gruska, D.P., Ruiz, M.C.: Opacity-enforcing for Process Algebras. In: CS&P 2018 (2018)
9. Voronkov, A., Virbitskaite, I. (eds.): PSI 2014. LNCS, vol. 8974. Springer, Heidelberg (2015). https://doi.org/10.1007/978-3-662-46823-4
10. Jacob, R., Lesage, J.-J., Faure, J.-M.: Overview of discrete event systems opacity: models, validation, and quantification. Ann. Rev. Control **41**, 135–146 (2016)
11. Keroglou, C., Ricker, L., Lafortune, S.: Insertion functions with memory for opacity enforcement. IFAC-PapersOnLine **51**(7), 394–399 (2018)
12. Keroglou, C., Lafortune, S.: Embedded insertion functions for opacity enforcement. IEEE Trans. Autom. Control. **66**(9), 4184–4191 (2021). https://doi.org/10.1109/TAC.2020.3037891
13. Milner, R.: Communication and Concurrency. Prentice-Hall International, New York (1989)
14. Ramadge, P.J.G., Wonham, W.M.: The control of discrete event systems. Proc. IEEE **77**(1), 81–98 (1989)
15. Wu, Y.-C., Lafortune, S.: Enforcement of opacity properties using insertion functions. In: Proceedings of 51st IEEE Conference on Decision and Control (CDC) (2012)
16. Ji, Y., Yin, X., Lafortune, S.: Enforcing opacity by insertion functions under multiple energy constraints. Automatica **108**, 108476 (2019)

Static Checking Consistency of Temporal Requirements for Control Software

Natalia Garanina[1](✉) and Dmitry Koznov[2]

[1] A.P. Ershov Institute of Informatics Systems, Institute of Automation and Electrometry, Novosibirsk, Russia
garanina@iis.nsk.su
[2] St. Petersburg University, Saint Petersburg, Russia
d.koznov@spbu.ru

Abstract. In this paper, we propose an approach to checking consistency of control software requirements described using pattern-based notation. This approach can be used at the beginning of control software verification to effectively identify contradicting and incompatible requirements. In this framework, we use pattern-based Event-Driven Temporal Logic (EDTL) to formalize the requirements. A set of requirements is represented as a set of EDTL-patterns which formal semantics defined by formulas of linear-time temporal logic LTL. Based on this semantics, we define the notion of requirement inconsistency and describe restrictions on the values of pattern attributes which make requirements inconsistent. Checking algorithm takes as an input pairs of requirements and compare their attributes. Its output is sets of consistent, inconsistent and incomparable requirements.

Keywords: Requirement engineering · Requirement consistency · Formal semantics · Linear temporal logic

1 Introduction

The long-term goal of our work is formal verification of control software (CS), specified in the process-oriented paradigm, in particular, written using the Domain-Specific Language (DSL) Reflex and poST [1,3,9].

In [16], for control software requirements, we propose a pattern-based specification formalism EDTL (Event-Driven Temporal Logic). EDTL-specifications has the following features: (1) a pattern form includes CS-specific concepts (such as trigger, reaction, etc.) which allow engineers to easily define requirements; (2) formal semantics provides possibility to apply formal verification methods. In particular, we can use model checking methods if EDTL-semantics is LTL-formulas [4].

Pattern-based systems for the development of requirements and their formal verification are an active topic of research for a long time [2,5,6,10,11,13–15]. Patterns are parameterized natural language expressions that describe typical

© Springer Nature Switzerland AG 2021
L. Bellatreche et al. (Eds.): MEDI 2021 Workshops, CCIS 1481, pp. 189–203, 2021.
https://doi.org/10.1007/978-3-030-87657-9_15

requirements for a system behavior. Typically, parameters of patterns are system events or their combinations (for example, in the pattern "Event *Device_enabled* will occur", *Device_enabled* is a parameter). Patterns usually have strict formal semantics. Patterns make it easy for requirement engineers to specify and verify typical system requirements.

Usually, control software systems have to meet a large number of requirements. Therefore, before applying formal verification methods, it is reasonable to check this list for consistency of the requirements in order to avoid unnecessary use of expensive formal methods. In this paper, we propose a method for checking the consistency of a requirements set based on pairwise comparing requirements with LTL-semantics. This pairwise consistency checking is propositional in the sense that it uses only the pattern representation of requirements and does not use a description of the control system. While this method only gives an exact answer for requirements that satisfy certain constraints, it can significantly reduce the time and cost of full consistency checking a set of requirements.

Checking consistency of requirements is rather necessary process in concurrent system development. A semi-automatic method presented in [12] helps to write use-case scenarios in a natural language iteratively and to verify temporal consistency of the behavior encoded in them. This method is used to check consistency of the textual specification of the use-case scenarios taking into account specific annotations written by user. These annotations are converted into temporal logic formulas and verified within the framework of a formal behavior model. A commercial requirement engineering tool for embedded systems Argosim [17] allows software engineers to test the systems and perform inconsistency checking for requirements. Ontology based checking is suggested in [7].

The rest of the paper is orgaised as follows. In Sect. 2, we give a brief description of syntax and semantics for EDTL-requirements. Section 3 describes the method of checking inconsistency for two requirements which patterns have non-constant attributes only. Section 4 uses results of the previous section to define a function that verify inconsistency of two requirements. In Sect. 5, we describe the algorithms that implement our method. Section 6 is conclusion.

2   Event-Driven Temporal Logic Pattern

Let us define EDTL-requirements. Informally, a EDTL-requirement is a combination of system events bounded by specified temporal interrelations. These events are attributes of the EDTL-requirement.

Definition 1. *(EDTL-requirements)*
An EDTL-requirement R is a tuple of the following EDTL-attributes:

$$R = (\textbf{trigger}, \textbf{invariant}, \textbf{final}, \textbf{delay}, \textbf{reaction}, \textbf{release}).$$

We give the informal meaning of the attributes and interrelations:

trigger an event after which the invariant must be true until a release event or a reaction takes place; this event is also the starting point for timeouts to produce final/release events (if any);

invarian a statement that must be true from the moment the trigger event occurs until the moment of a release or reaction event;

final an event, after which a reaction must occur within the allowable delay; this event always follows the trigger event;

delay a time limit after the final event, during which a reaction must appear;

reaction this statement must become true within the allowable delay from the final event;

release upon this event, the requirement is considered satisfied.

The following natural language description of EDTL-requirement semantics corresponds to this informal description:

Following each trigger event, the invariant must hold true until either a release event or a final event. The invariant must also hold true after final event till either the release event or a reaction, and besides the reaction must take place within the specified allowable delay from the final event.

The values of EDTL-attributes are EDTL-formulas. The EDTL-formulas are divided into two classes: state formulas and event formulas. Informally, the state formulas assert about system variables' values in a given time moment, but the event formulas assert about events that just happen or not happen, i.e. changing/keeping variables' values since the previous time moment. In this paper, we focus on LTL semantics of EDTL-requirements, hence we consider EDTL-formulas are constructed from propositions as follows:

Definition 2. *(EDTL-formulas)*
Let p be a proposition, φ and ψ be EDTL-formulas. Then:

- state formulas:
  - *true*, *false*, and p are an atomic EDTL-formulas;
  - $\varphi \wedge \psi$ is the conjunction of φ and ψ;
  - $\varphi \vee \psi$ is the disjunction of φ and ψ;
  - $\neg\varphi$ is the negation of φ;
- event formulas with proposition[1] p:
  - $\backslash p$ is the falling edge: the value of p changes from *false* to *true*;
  - $/p$ is the rising edge: the value of p changes from *true* to *false*;
  - $\_p$ is low steady-state: the value of p remains equal to *false*;
  - $\sim p$ is high steady-state: the value of p remains equal to *true*.

The detailed semantics of these formulas is given in [16]. Informally, the semantics of the state formulas is standard semantics for LTL-formulas without temporal operators, but the semantics of the event formulas uses satisfiability of the proposition in the previous system state. This semantics can be modelled

---

[1] In general, event formulas can take all EDTL-formulas, but for simplicity, we restrict them by propositions only. The results of this paper can easily be generalised for all EDTL-formulas.

by temporal operator $\mathbf{X}^{-1}$ of PLTL [8] or by introducing into the model special ghost variable $prev(p)$ which keep the previous value of proposition p. In the latter case, the semantics of the event formulas is reduced to semantics of the state EDTL-formulas as follows:

Definition 3. *(Semantics of event EDTL-formulas)*

- $/p \equiv \neg prev(p) \wedge p$;
- $\backslash p \equiv prev(p) \wedge \neg p$;
- $\sim p \equiv prev(p) \wedge p$;
- $\_p \equiv \neg prev(p) \wedge \neg p$.

Further in the paper, we assume that all EDTL-formulas are state formulas.

Let us define the LTL-semantics for EDTL-requirements. In this paper, we consider control systems which have model as a Kripke structure. Let P be set of propositions.

Definition 4. *(Kripke structures)*
A Kripke structure is a tuple $M = (S, I, R, L)$, where

- S is a set of states, and
- $I \subseteq S$ is a finite set of initial states, and
- $R \subseteq S \times S$ is a total transition relation, and
- $L : P \rightarrow 2^S$ is a mapping function.

A path $\pi = s_0, s_1, \ldots$ is an infinite sequence of states $s_i \in S$ such that $\forall j > 0 : (s_j, s_{j+1}) \in R$, and let $\pi(i) = s_i$. An initial path π^0 is a path starting from initial state, i.e. $\pi^0(0) \in I$.

Let for control system C its Kripke structure be M_C. Let *trigger, invariant, final, delay, reaction,* and *release* be EDTL-formulas which are the values of the EDTL-attributes of a requirement *req*.

Definition 5. *(Semantics of EDTL-requirements)*
EDTL-requirement req is satisfied in a control system C iff the following LTL-formula Φ_{req} is satisfied in M_C for every initial path:
$$\Phi_{req} = \mathbf{G}(trigger \rightarrow ((invariant \wedge \neg final \mathbf{W} release) \vee$$
$$(invariant \mathbf{U}(final \wedge (invariant \wedge delay \mathbf{U}(release \vee reaction)))))).$$

We use this semantics in model checking control systems w.r.t. the EDTL-requirements and for checking consistency of the EDTL-requirements.

Definition 6. *(Satisfiability of EDTL-requirements)*
Requirement r is *satisfiable* iff there exists a Kripke structure M_r that for every initial path π: $M_r, \pi \models \Phi_r$. This M_r is a *model* for r.

3   Consistency of EDTL-Requirements

In this section, we give the method of checking consistency for two requirements which patterns have non-constant attributes only.

Definition 7. *(The checking inconsistency problem for EDTL-requirements)*
Requirement r_2 is *inconsistent* with satisfiable requirement r_1 iff every Kripke structure M_{r_1} is not a model for r_2, or, equivalent, the conjunction of their semantics is unsatisfiable formula in every model M_{r_1} there exists an initial path π of M_{r_1}: $M_{r_1}, \pi \nvDash \Phi_{r_1} \wedge \Phi_{r_2}$.

The *checking inconsistency problem* for EDTL-requirements is to check if two EDTL-requirements are inconsistent.

We use the second form of the inconsistency definition in our checking method because we compare only the requirements' attributes without addressing the models of the requirements and paths in these models. Moreover, due to this independence from the requirement model, we can deduce that $M_{r_1}, \pi \nvDash \Phi_{r_1} \wedge \Phi_{r_2}$ for *every* initial path π of M_{r_1} if r_2 is inconsistent with r_1.

From Definition 5, the requirement semantics is $\Phi_{req} = \mathbf{G}(trigger \rightarrow \Psi_{req})$. Let we be given two EDTL-requirements r_1 and r_2 with corresponding patterns $R_1 = (trig_1, inv_1, fin_1, del_1, rea_1, rel_1)$ and $R_2 = (trig_2, inv_2, fin_2, del_2, rea_2, rel_2)$. Hence, for every initial path of every Kripke structure M: $M, \pi \nvDash \Phi_{r_1} \wedge \Phi_{r_2}$ iff $M, \pi \models \neg(\Phi_{r_1} \wedge \Phi_{r_2})$. Here $\neg(\Phi_{r_1} \wedge \Phi_{r_2}) = \neg(\mathbf{G}(trig_1 \rightarrow \Psi_1) \wedge \mathbf{G}(trig_2 \rightarrow \Psi_2)) = \neg\mathbf{G}((trig_1 \rightarrow \Psi_1) \wedge (trig_2 \rightarrow \Psi_2))$. Our consistency checking procedure *Compare* is based on assumption that $trig_1 \rightarrow trig_2$. This assumptions gives us possibility to reason about simultaneous satisfiability of EDTL-attributes at some point of a model path in many cases described below because the last formula implies $\neg\mathbf{G}(trig_1 \rightarrow (\Psi_1 \wedge \Psi_2))$. Definitely, with this weakening inconsistency condition, the results of our algorithm are partial, i.e. there exists inconsistent req_1 and req_2 for which procedure *Compare* gives the output "unknown". For checking such requirements, an explicit description of a control software model or an automata-based satisfiability checking method is required.

The following reasoning is based on assumptions that (1) $trig_1 \rightarrow trig_2$ and (2) Φ_{r_1} is satisfiable in some model M_{r_1}, i.e. for every initial path π of M_{r_1}, $M_{r_1}, \pi \models \Phi_{r_1}$. By Definition 7 with the weak inconsistency condition $M_{r_1}, \pi \models \neg\mathbf{G}(trig_1 \rightarrow (\Psi_1 \wedge \Psi_2))$ and assumption (2), r_2 is inconsistent with r_1 iff there exist initial path π' of M_{r_1} such that $M_{r_1}, \pi' \models \mathbf{F}\neg(trig_1 \rightarrow \Psi_2)$, i.e. there is some point s' on π' where $\neg(trig_1 \rightarrow \Psi_2)$ holds on suffix $\pi'_{s'}$ of π'. We can use this fact to describe inconsistency restrictions for r_2. We also know that $M_{r_1}, \pi'_{s'} \models trig_1 \rightarrow \Psi_1$ due to assumption (2), hence, $M_{r_1}, \pi'_{s'} \models \Psi_1 \rightarrow \neg\Psi_2$. Therefore, we consider two cases to describe some inconsistency restrictions for r_2 which do not require knowledge about model M_{r_1}: (1) $\neg(trig_1 \rightarrow \Psi_2)$ in Subsect. 3.1 and (2) $\Psi_1 \rightarrow \neg\Psi_2$ in Subsect. 3.2.

Let φ_1 and φ_2 be EDTL-attributes which conjunction is false. We call φ_1 and φ_2 *inconsistent EDTL-formulas* and use the following notation: $\varphi_1 \bullet \varphi_2$ iff $\varphi_1 \wedge \varphi_2 \equiv false$, and $\varphi_1 \circ \varphi_2$ in other case. For any pair of EDTL-formulas we can check their inconsistency using standard boolean rules and Definition 3. Obviously, this checking can be reduced to NP-complete SAT problem. But due to the small size of EDTL-formulas, check their inconsistency takes reasonable time. In the description of inconsistency restrictions, for every attributes a_1 and a_2, we suppose that if not $a_1 \bullet a_2$ then $a_1 \circ a_2$.

The values of EDTL-attributes of requirements can be constant $false/true$ or mutable var. In this section, we consider the most general case when every attribute of R_1 and R_2 has non-constant value.

3.1   Inconsistency Restrictions with Attribute *trigger*

In this subsection, we describe inconsistency restriction for r_2 which provide $\neg(trig_1 \rightarrow \Psi_2) = \neg(trig_1 \wedge \Psi_2)$ on path $\pi'_{s'}$. By assumption (2), $trig_1$ holds at s'. From Definition 5, $\Psi_2 = (inv_2 \wedge \neg fin_2 \mathbf{W} rel_2) \vee (inv_2 \mathbf{U}(fin_2 \wedge (inv_2 \wedge del_2 \mathbf{U}(rel_2 \vee rea_2))))$. The following restriction on EDTL-attributes of r_1 and r_2 implies $\neg(trig_1 \wedge \Psi_2)$:

1. $trig_1 \bullet inv_2$ and $C_2 = \neg((trig_1 \vee inv_1 \vee trig_2) \rightarrow (rel_2 \vee (fin_2 \wedge rea_2)))$;
2. other restrictions are unknown.

Because Ψ_2 includes temporal operators and $trig_1$ do not include them, we can reason only about first point s' of the path where $trig_1$ definitely holds and Ψ_2 does not. The negation of C_2 cancels necessity of satisfiability of inv_2. Hence, in this case, its inconsistency with $trig_1$ does not matter for inconsistency of r_2.

3.2   Inconsistency Restrictions with Other Attributes

In this subsection, we describe inconsistency restrictions for r_2 which provide $\Psi_1 \rightarrow \neg\Psi_2$ at $\pi'_{s'}$. From Definition 5, $\Psi_1 = A_1 \vee B_1$ and $\Psi_2 = A_2 \vee B_2$. Hence, $\Psi_1 \rightarrow \neg\Psi_2 = \neg(A_1 \vee B_1) \vee \neg(A_2 \vee B_2)$. Due to satisfiability of Φ_{r_1}, $A_1 \vee B_1$ is satisfiable. Hence, we consider the cases $A_1 \rightarrow \neg(A_2 \vee B_2)$ and $B_1 \rightarrow \neg(A_2 \vee B_2)$. These cases are also divided to subcases: (AA) $A_1 \rightarrow \neg A_2$, (AB) $A_1 \rightarrow \neg B_2$, (BA) $B_1 \rightarrow \neg A_2$, and (BB) $B_1 \rightarrow \neg B_2$. We formulate inconsistency restrictions for all these cases. Again, from Definition 5:

- $A_1 = (inv_1 \wedge \neg fin_1 \mathbf{W} rel_1)$,
- $B_1 = (inv_1 \mathbf{U}(fin_1 \wedge (inv_1 \wedge del_1 \mathbf{U}(rel_1 \vee rea_1))))$,
- $A_2 = (inv_2 \wedge \neg fin_2 \mathbf{W} rel_2)$,
- $B_2 = (inv_2 \mathbf{U}(fin_2 \wedge (inv_2 \wedge del_2 \mathbf{U}(rel_2 \vee rea_2))))$.

(AA) $A_1 \rightarrow \neg A_2$. A_1 is satisfiable on path $\pi'_{s'}$. The following restrictions on EDTL-attributes of r_1 and r_2 imply $\Psi_1 \rightarrow \neg\Psi_2$:

1. $inv_1 \bullet inv_2$, $C_1 = \neg((trig_1 \vee inv_1 \vee \neg fin_1 \vee trig_2) \rightarrow rel_1)$, and $C_2 = \neg((trig_1 \vee inv_1 \vee \neg fin_1 \vee trig_2) \rightarrow rel_2)$;
2. $\neg fin_1 \bullet inv_2$, and $C_1 \wedge C_2$;
3. $inv_1 \bullet \neg fin_2$, and $C_1 \wedge C_2$;

4. $\neg fin_1 \bullet \neg fin_2$, and $C_1 \wedge C_2$;
5. $rel_1 \bullet inv_2$, and $\neg C_1 \wedge C_2$;
6. $rel_1 \bullet \neg fin_2$, and $\neg C_1 \wedge C_2$;
7. $rel_1 \bullet rel_2$, and $\neg C_1 \wedge \neg C_2$;
8. other restrictions are unknown.

In all cases, $trig_1$ and $trig_2$ hold at s', inv_1 and $\neg fin_1$ also hold at s', if only rel_1 does not happen at this point. Let all restrictions of every case hold at s' separately. Formulas C_1 and C_2 provides that, respectively, releases rel_1 or rel_2 do not happen at s', because their appearing makes senseless inconsistency of the corresponding attributes. From now on, formulas C_1 and C_2 specify cancelling conditions respective to considering cases of restrictions.

(1–2) Obviously, in these cases, $A_1 \rightarrow \neg inv_2$ holds, which implies unsatisfiability of A_2 at s'.

(3–4) In these cases, the reasoning is the same.

(5–7) Restrictions of these cases specify appearing rel_1 at s' and its inconsistency with attributes of r_2. Definitely, in these cases, $A_1 \rightarrow \neg(inv_2 \vee \neg fin_2 \vee rel_2)$ holds which implies unsatisfiability of A_2 at s'.

(8) Our inconsistency checking algorithm checks EDTL-attributes and their Boolean combinations which are state formulas. Hence, this algorithm can detect inconsistency of EDTL-requirements in model states only. In case (AA), there is only one state s' at which we know about satisfiability of r_1-attributes and can define inconsistency restrictions for r_2-attributes. Hence, all possibilities for defining static inconsistency restrictions are considered in cases 1–7, and for defining other inconsistency restrictions, the description of model M_{r_1} is required.

(AB) $A_1 \rightarrow \neg B_2$. A_1 is satisfiable on path $\pi'_{s'}$. The following restrictions on EDTL-attributes of r_1 and r_2 imply $\Psi_1 \rightarrow \neg\Psi_2$:

1. $inv_1 \bullet inv_2$, $C_1 = \neg((trig_1 \vee inv_1 \vee \neg fin_1 \vee trig_2) \rightarrow rel_1)$, and $C_2 = \neg((trig_1 \vee inv_1 \vee \neg fin_1 \vee trig_2) \rightarrow (rel_2 \vee (fin_2 \wedge rea_2)))$;
2. $\neg fin_1 \bullet inv_2$, and $C_1 \wedge C_2$;
3. $inv_1 \rightarrow fin_2$, $\neg fin_1 \bullet del_2$, $(inv_1 \vee \neg fin_1) \bullet rel_2$, $(inv_1 \vee \neg fin_1) \bullet rea_2$, and C_1;
4. $\neg fin_1 \rightarrow fin_2$, $inv_1 \bullet del_2$, $(inv_1 \vee \neg fin_1) \bullet rel_2$, $(inv_1 \vee \neg fin_1) \bullet rea_2$, and C_1;
5. $rel_1 \bullet inv_2$, and $\neg C_1 \wedge C_2$;
6. other restrictions are unknown.

In all cases, $trig_1$ and $trig_2$ hold at s', inv_1 and $\neg fin_1$ also hold at s', if only rel_1 does not happen at this point. Let all restrictions of every case hold at s' separately.

(1–2) In these cases, $A_1 \rightarrow \neg inv_2$, hence $A_1 \rightarrow \neg B_2$.

(3–4) Here, inv_1 (or $\neg fin_1$) causes fin_2, and inconsistency $\neg fin_1$ (or inv_1) with del_2 requires immediate release rel_2 or reaction rea_2, but they are also inconsistent with inv_1 or $\neg fin_1$. Hence, $A_1 \rightarrow \neg(fin_2 \wedge (inv_2 \wedge del_2 \mathbf{U}(rel_2 \vee rea_2)))$, which implies unsatisfiability of B_2 at s'. Note, that an event which causes some final event cannot be inconsistent with the corresponding delay because this delay starts from this final event which implies that *delay* must hold at the state where *final* happens after the corresponding *trigger*.

(5) Restrictions of these cases specify appearing rel_1 at s' and its inconsistency with attributes of r_2 similarly to cases 1–4.

(6) As for the case (AA), there is only one state s' at which we know about satisfiability of r_1-attributes. Hence, for defining inconsistency restrictions different from 1–5, the description of model M_{r_1} is required.

(BA) $B_1 \rightarrow \neg A_2$. B_1 is satisfiable on path $\pi'_{s'}$. The following restrictions on EDTL-attributes of r_1 and r_2 imply $\Psi_1 \rightarrow \neg \Psi_2$:

1. $inv_1 \bullet inv_2$, and $C_1 = \neg(C_1^1 \vee C_1^2)$, and $C_2 = \neg((trig_1 \vee inv_1 \vee trig_2) \rightarrow rel_2)$, where $C_1^1 = \neg((trig_1 \vee inv_1 \vee trig_2) \rightarrow rel_1)$ and $C_1^2 = \neg((trig_1 \vee inv_1 \vee trig_2) \rightarrow (fin_1 \wedge rea_1))$;
2. $inv_1 \bullet \neg fin_2$, and $C_1 \wedge C_2$;
3. $rel_1 \bullet inv_2$, and $\neg C_1^1 \wedge C_2$;
4. $rel_1 \bullet \neg fin_2$, and $\neg C_1^1 \wedge C_2$;
5. $(fin_1 \wedge rea_1) \bullet inv_2$, and $\neg C_1^2 \wedge C_2$;
6. $(fin_1 \wedge rea_1) \bullet \neg fin_2$, and $\neg C_1^2 \wedge C_2$;
7. other restrictions are unknown.

In all cases, $trig_1$ and $trig_2$ hold at s', and inv_1 also hold at s', if only rel_1 or fin_1 with rea_1 do not happen at this point, and there exists states s'_1 and s'_2 on path π' after s' at which $fin_1 \wedge inv_1$ and $rel_1 \vee rea_1$ hold respectively. Let all restrictions of every case hold at s' separately.

(1–2) In both restriction cases, $B_1 \rightarrow \neg inv_2$, hence $B_1 \rightarrow \neg A_2$.

(3–6) These cases describes inconsistency restrictions when release rel_1 or final fin_1 with immediate reaction rea_1 cancel invariant inv_1 and contradict r_2-attributes. All these restrictions obviously imply $B_1 \rightarrow \neg A_2$.

(7) Surprisingly, although we know that there exists states s'_1 and s'_2, we cannot decide about inconsistency of rel_1, fin_1, and rea_1 respective to neither inv_2, nor $\neg fin_2$ because appearing rel_2 may happen at any π'-path state between s' and s'_1/s'_2. Formula that specify this appearance is $\neg(\mathbf{F}(rel_1 \vee (fin_1 \wedge rea_1)) \wedge (\neg rel_2 \mathbf{U}(rel_1 \vee (fin_1 \wedge rea_1))))$. The negation of this formula could be the sufficient condition for inconsistency restrictions combining rel_1, fin_1, rea_1 with inv_2 and $\neg fin_2$, but it is not static EDTL-formula and its checking requires the description of model M_{r_1}.

(BB) $B_1 \rightarrow \neg B_2$. B_1 is satisfiable on path $\pi'_{s'}$. The following restrictions on EDTL-attributes of r_1 and r_2 imply $\Psi_1 \rightarrow \neg \Psi_2$:

1. $inv_1 \bullet inv_2$, and $C_1 = \neg(C_1^1 \vee C_1^2)$, and $C_2 = \neg((trig_1 \vee inv_1 \vee trig_2) \rightarrow (rel_2 \vee (fin_2 \wedge rea_2)))$, where $C_1^1 = \neg((trig_1 \vee inv_1 \vee trig_2) \rightarrow rel_1)$ and $C_1^2 = \neg((trig_1 \vee inv_1 \vee trig_2) \rightarrow (fin_1 \wedge rea_1))$;
2. $rel_1 \bullet inv_2$, and $\neg C_1^1 \wedge C_2$;
3. $(fin_1 \wedge rea_1) \bullet inv_2$, and $\neg C_1^2 \wedge C_2$;
4. $rel_1 \rightarrow fin_2$, $rel_1 \bullet inv_2$, and $\neg((rel_1 \vee fin_2) \rightarrow (rel_2 \vee rea_2))$;
5. $rea_1 \rightarrow fin_2$, $rea_1 \bullet inv_2$, and $\neg((rea_1 \vee fin_2) \rightarrow (rel_2 \vee rea_2))$;

6. $fin_1 \rightarrow fin_2$, $fin_1 \bullet inv_2$, and $\neg((fin_1 \vee fin_2) \rightarrow (rel_2 \vee rea_2))$;
7. $fin_1 \rightarrow fin_2$, $inv_1 \bullet del_2$, $(inv_1 \vee fin_1) \bullet rel_2$, and $(inv_1 \vee fin_1) \bullet rea_2$;
8. other restrictions are unknown.

In all cases, $trig_1$ and $trig_2$ hold at state s', and inv_1 also hold at state s', if only rel_1 or fin_1 with rea_1 do not happen at this point, and there exists states s'_1 and s'_2 on path π' after state s' at which $fin_1 \wedge inv_1$ and $rel_1 \vee rea_1$ hold respectively. Let (a) all restrictions of cases 1–3 hold at s', (b) all restrictions of cases 4–5 hold at s'_2, and (c) all restrictions of cases 6–7 hold at s'_1.

(1–3) These cases are similar to the case (BA).

(4–6) These cases exploit the fact that inv_2 must hold at the state where fin_2 holds if only there is no release rel_2 or reaction rea_2. In cases 4 and 5, this state is s'_2, and in case 6, it is s'_1.

(7) In this case, similarly to case (AB-3), fin_1 causes fin_2 at state s'_1, and inconsistency of inv_1 with del_2 requires immediate release rel_2 or reaction rea_2, but they are also inconsistent with $inv_1 \vee fin_1$.

(8) We consider all possible restrictive combinations for attributes of requirements r_1 and r_2 which allow static inconsistency checking. Other restrictions require the description of model M_{r_1}.

The restrictions on EDTL-attributes of r_1 and r_2 formulated above implies unsatisfiability of $\Phi_{r_1} \wedge \Phi_{r_2}$ in model M_{r_1}. Hence, if the requirements satisfy these restrictions, our algorithm yields definite result of inconsistency checking, otherwise it says "unknown". We summarise these restrictions in the next section.

4   Procedure *Compare*

Our goal is to describe a function which solves if two EDTL-requirements (in)-consistent using the attribute values of their patterns only. Let $Compare(R_1, R_2)$ be a function which input is two patterns and output is answer from the set {*consistent, inconsistent, unknown*}. To compare the requirements, we use the following method. First, using the results of the previous section, we define answers and their conditions of function *Compare* for the most general case when every attribute of R_1 and R_2 has non-constant value. For attribute constant values, we substitute them into the general form of the restriction to get the answers and their conditions for these particular cases.

In the following definition of the outputs of $Compare(R_1, R_2)$, we summarise the restrictions on the attributes of requirement r_2 which cause its inconsistency with requirement r_1. In this definition, conjunction of all cases of each output marked by letters gives its necessary condition.

1. $Compare(R_1, R_2) = inconsistent$, if
   (a) $inv_1 \bullet inv_2$;
   (b) $\neg((trig_1 \vee inv_1 \vee \neg fin_1 \vee trig_2) \rightarrow (rel_1 \vee (fin_1 \wedge rea_1)))$;
   (c) $\neg((trig_1 \vee inv_1 \vee \neg fin_1 \vee trig_2) \rightarrow (rel_2 \vee (fin_2 \wedge rea_2)))$.
2. $Compare(R_1, R_2) = inconsistent$, if

(a) $\neg fin_1 \bullet inv_2$;

(b) $\neg((trig_1 \lor inv_1 \lor \neg fin_1 \lor trig_2) \to rel_1)$;

(c) $\neg((trig_1 \lor inv_1 \lor \neg fin_1 \lor trig_2) \to (rel_2 \lor (fin_2 \land rea_2)))$.

3. $Compare(R_1, R_2) = inconsistent$, if

(a) $inv_1 \bullet \neg fin_2$;

(b) $\neg((trig_1 \lor inv_1 \lor \neg fin_1 \lor trig_2) \to (rel_1 \lor (fin_1 \land rea_1)))$;

(c) $\neg((trig_1 \lor inv_1 \lor \neg fin_1 \lor trig_2) \to rel_2)$.

4. $Compare(R_1, R_2) = inconsistent$, if

(a) $\neg fin_1 \bullet \neg fin_2$;

(b) $\neg((trig_1 \lor inv_1 \lor \neg fin_1 \lor trig_2) \to rel_1)$;

(c) $\neg((trig_1 \lor inv_1 \lor \neg fin_1 \lor trig_2) \to rel_2)$.

5. $Compare(R_1, R_2) = inconsistent$, if

(a) $rel_1 \bullet inv_2$;

(b) $(trig_1 \lor inv_1 \lor \neg fin_1 \lor trig_2) \to rel_1$;

(c) $\neg((trig_1 \lor inv_1 \lor \neg fin_1 \lor trig_2) \to (rel_2 \lor (fin_2 \land rea_2)))$.

6. $Compare(R_1, R_2) = inconsistent$, if

(a) $rel_1 \bullet \neg fin_2$;

(b) $(trig_1 \lor inv_1 \lor \neg fin_1 \lor trig_2) \to rel_1$;

(c) $\neg((trig_1 \lor inv_1 \lor \neg fin_1 \lor trig_2) \to rel_2)$.

7. $Compare(R_1, R_2) = inconsistent$, if

(a) $rel_1 \bullet rel_2$;

(b) $(trig_1 \lor inv_1 \lor \neg fin_1 \lor trig_2) \to rel_1$;

(c) $(trig_1 \lor inv_1 \lor \neg fin_1 \lor trig_2) \to rel_2$.

8. $Compare(R_1, R_2) = inconsistent$, if

(a) $inv_1 \to fin_2$;

(b) $\neg fin_1 \bullet del_2$;

(c) $(inv_1 \lor \neg fin_1) \bullet rel_2$;

(d) $(inv_1 \lor \neg fin_1) \bullet rea_2$;

(e) $\neg((trig_1 \lor inv_1 \lor \neg fin_1 \lor trig_2) \to rel_1)$.

9. $Compare(R_1, R_2) = inconsistent$, if

(a) $\neg fin_1 \to fin_2$;

(a) $inv_1 \bullet del_2$;

(b) $(inv_1 \lor \neg fin_1) \bullet rel_2$;

(c) $(inv_1 \lor \neg fin_1) \bullet rea_2$;

(d) $\neg((trig_1 \lor inv_1 \lor \neg fin_1 \lor trig_2) \to rel_1)$.

10. $Compare(R_1, R_2) = inconsistent$, if

(a) $(fin_1 \land rea_1) \bullet inv_2$;

(b) $(trig_1 \lor inv_1 \lor trig_2) \to (fin_1 \land rea_1)$;

(c) $\neg((trig_1 \lor inv_1 \lor trig_2) \to (rel_2 \lor (fin_2 \land rea_2)))$.

11. $Compare(R_1, R_2) = inconsistent$, if

(a) $(fin_1 \land rea_1) \bullet \neg fin_2$;

(b) $(trig_1 \lor inv_1 \lor trig_2) \to (fin_1 \land rea_1)$;

(c) $\neg((trig_1 \lor inv_1 \lor trig_2) \to rel_2)$.

12. $Compare(R_1, R_2) = inconsistent$, if

(a) $rel_1 \to fin_2$;

(b) $rel_1 \bullet inv_2$;

   (c) $\neg((rel_1 \lor fin_2) \to (rel_2 \lor rea_2))$.
13. $Compare(R_1, R_2) = inconsistent$, if
   (a) $rea_1 \to fin_2$;
   (b) $rea_1 \bullet inv_2$;
   (c) $\neg((rea_1 \lor fin_2) \to (rel_2 \lor rea_2))$.
14. $Compare(R_1, R_2) = inconsistent$, if
   (a) $fin_1 \to fin_2$;
   (b) $fin_1 \bullet inv_2$;
   (c) $\neg((fin_1 \lor fin_2) \to (rel_2 \lor rea_2))$.
15. $Compare(R_1, R_2) = inconsistent$, if
   (a) $fin_1 \to fin_2$;
   (b) $inv_1 \bullet del_2$;
   (c) $(inv_1 \lor fin_1) \bullet rel_2$;
   (d) $(inv_1 \lor fin_1) \bullet rea_2$.
16. $Compare(R_1, R_2) = consistent$, if
   (a) $inv_1 \to inv_2$;
   (b) $fin_1 \to fin_2$;
   (c) $del_1 \to del_2$;
   (d) $rea_1 \to rea_2$;
   (e) $rel_1 \to rel_2$;
17. $Compare(R_1, R_2) = unknown$, other cases.

All outputs above are based on results of Sect. 3 except case 16. In this case, weakening every attribute of R_1 in R_2 implies satisfiability of r_2 in every model where r_1 is satisfiable.

Outputs of $Compare$ for the other combinations of attribute values of R_1 and mutable attribute values of R_2 can be found in [18].

5   Algorithm for Checking Consistency of EDTL-Patterns

Let a given set of requirements be presented as EDTL-patterns. The checking consistency algorithm $Consistency\_Checker$ compares the requirements in pairs using the function $Compare$. For each requirement the algorithm generates a list of inconsistent, consistent and undefined requirements. Note that the inconsistency relation is not transitive. Using these lists, we can compile sets of consistent requirements, as well as lists of requirements, whose consistency should be further verified by stronger methods. The complexity of this algorithm is quadratic with respect to the size of the set of requirements.

```
type Req :
    struct {
        pattern : array [6] of EDTL_formula; // 0-trig, ..., 5-rel
        inconsistent : list of Req;
        consistent : list of Req;
        unknown : list of Req;
}
```

```
Consistency_Checker (reqs : array [n] of req){
for i = 1 .. n-2
    for j = i+1 .. n
        res = Decide( reqs[i], reqs[j]);
        case (res) {
                inconsistent : reqs[i].inconsistent.add(reqs[j]);
                               reqs[j].inconsistent.add(reqs[i]);
                consistent : reqs[i].consistent.add(reqs[j]);
                             reqs[j].consistent.add(reqs[i]);
                unknown : reqs[i].unknown.add(reqs[j]);
                          reqs[j].unknown.add(reqs[i]);
        }
}
```

First, the function *Decide* checks comparability of requirements ($trig_1 \rightarrow trig_2$ or $trig_2 \rightarrow trig_1$), which takes exponential time with respect to the size of the triggers. Then it tries if the semantics of incoming requirements is *true* or *false* with partial function *Compute_semantics* which substitute the attribute values to LTL semantic formula, and returns 'true'/'false' iff the result of the substitution is identically true or false, and 'unknown' in other cases. The time complexity of this function is linear with respect to the size of the requirements. Its definition is trivial and out of the scope of this paper. If there are the cases 'true' or 'false', it returns values to *Consistency_Checker* immediately. If not, it calls function *Compare* which compute if the requirements inconsistent.

```
Decide (pat1, pat2){
  if !imply(pat1[0], pat2[0]) && !imply(pat2[0], pat1[0]) &&
                                  !pat1[0] && !pat2[0]
                                              then return unknown;
  res = Compute_semantics( pat1 );
  if res = 'true' then return unknown;
  if res = 'false' then return inconsistent;
  res = Compute_semantics( pat2 );
  if res = 'true' then return unknown;
  if res = 'false' then return inconsistent;
  if imply(pat1[0], pat2[0]) then return Compare( pat1, pat2 );
  if imply(pat2[0], pat1[0]) then return Compare( pat2, pat1 );
}
```

The function *Compare* implements the definition given the previous section. For example, the following part of the code of *Compare* models case (13) of this definition. The function *Compute(frm)* returns *true* iff *frm* is identically true formula. The definition of this function is based on standard Boolean rules and Definition 3. The complexity of this function is exponential with respect to the size of the attributes of requirements because it solves the SAT problem.

```
Compare (pat1, pat2){
        ...
        // case 13
        if Compute(((pat1[4] -> pat2[2]) &&
                !(pat1[4] && pat2[1]) &&
                !((pat2[2]||pat1[4])->(pat2[4]||pat2[5])))
                                        then return inconsistent;
        ...
        return unknown;
}
```

Using the mentioned above time complexities of the algorithm and its functions, we state the following

Theorem 1. *There exists the algorithm partially solving the checking inconsistency problem for EDTL-requirements which takes quadratic time with respect to the size of the set of requirements and exponential time with respect to the size of the requirements' attributes.*

Standard automata-based satisfiability checking algorithms for LTL-formula φ take exponential time $T_s(\varphi)$ with respect to the size of the checking formula. Roughly, if the size of every EDTL-attribute of each EDTL-requirement is a then $T_s(\Phi_{r_1} \wedge \Phi_{r_2}) \geq 2^{20a}$. The time complexity $T_d(r_1, r_2)$ of the most expensive function *Decide* is the sum of complexities of the first line checking and the *Compare* function: $T_d(r_1, r_2) \leq 2^{8a}$. Definitely, T_s is always exponentially greater than T_d for a pair of EDTL-requirements independently their size. Hence, our simple checking algorithm can be used before more powerful and complex automata-based checking inconsistency.

6   Conclusion

In this paper, we propose the method and algorithm for checking the consistency of requirements presented as EDTL-patterns. This method uses LTL semantics of requirements. It analyses key cases for combinations of pattern attribute values. We present an exhaustive description of these cases to determine that two requirements are not consistent if the attribute values of their patterns are not Boolean constants. For other attribute values, the method suggests substituting them into the described inconsistency conditions to obtain the conditions corresponding to these values. We describe the pseudocodes of algorithms that implement the proposed method. The results of the algorithm can be used to compile sets of (in)consistent requirements, as well as lists of requirements for consistency checking by stronger methods. The complexity of the main algorithm is quadratic with respect to the size of the set of requirements. The complexity of the comparison function used in the algorithm is exponential with respect to the size of the attributes. Nevertheless, we show that the overall complexity of our algorithm is exponentially better than the complexity of automata-based satisfiability checking algorithms for LTL-formulas. Hence, incompleteness of results of our algorithm is balanced by its relatively low complexity.

This study is a part of theoretical and practical research on the development and verification of process-oriented control software [1,9,16]. The results of the paper will be used in a general approach to checking the consistency of EDTL-requirements. For this approach, we currently develop methods that explicitly use the temporal semantics of requirements. One of them is the construction of equivalent finite automata for semantics of EDTL-requirements and checking their consistency.

References

1. Anureev, I.S.: Operational semantics of annotated reflex programs. Autom. Control Comput. Sci. **54**(7), 719–727 (2020). https://doi.org/10.3103/S0146411620070032
2. Autili, M., Grunske, L., Lumpe, M., Pelliccione, P., Tang, A.: Aligning qualitative, real-time, and probabilistic property specification patterns using a structured English grammar. IEEE Trans. Softw. Eng. **41**(7), 620–638 (2015)
3. Bashev, V., Anureev, I., Zyubin, V.: The post language: process-oriented extension for IEC 61131-3 structured text. In: International Russian Automation Conference (RusAutoCon), Sochi, Russia, 2020, pp. 994–999 (2020). https://doi.org/10.1109/RusAutoCon49822.2020.9208049
4. Clarke, E.M., Henzinger, Th.A., Veith, H., Bloem, R. (Eds.): Handbook of Model Checking. Springer, Cham (2018). https://doi.org/10.1007/978-3-319-10575-8
5. Dwyer, M.B., Avrunin, G.S., Corbett, J.C.: Patterns in property specifications for finite-state verification. In: Proceedings of the 21st International Conference on Software Engineering, pp. 411–420. IEEE Computer Society Press (1999)
6. Garanina, N., Anureev, I., Sidorova, E., Koznov, D., Zyubin, V., Gorlatch, S.: An ontology-based approach to support formal verification of concurrent systems. In: Sekerinski, E., et al. (eds.) FM 2019. LNCS, vol. 12232, pp. 114–130. Springer, Cham (2020). https://doi.org/10.1007/978-3-030-54994-7_9
7. Garanina, N., Borovikova, O.: Ontological approach to checking event consistency for a set of temporal requirements. In: 2019 International Multi-Conference on Engineering, Computer and Information Sciences (SIBIRCON), Novosibirsk, Russia, pp. 0922–0927 (2019). https://doi.org/10.1109/SIBIRCON48586.2019.8958119
8. Heljanko, K., Junttila, T., Latvala, T.: Incremental and complete bounded model checking for full PLTL. In: Etessami, K., Rajamani, S.K. (eds.) CAV 2005. LNCS, vol. 3576, pp. 98–111. Springer, Heidelberg (2005). https://doi.org/10.1007/11513988_10
9. Liakh, T.V., Rozov, A.S., Zyubin, V.E.: Reflex language: a practical notation for cyber-physical systems. Syst. Inform. **12**, 85–104 (2018)
10. Mondragon, O., Gates, A.Q., Roach, S.: Prospec: support for elicitation and formal specification of software properties. In: Proceedings of Runtime Verification Workshop of Electronic Notes in Theoretical Computer Science, vol. 89, pp. 67–88 (2014)
11. Salamah, S., Gates, A.Q., Kreinovich, V.: Validated patterns for specification of complex LTL formulas. J. Syst. Softw. **85**(8), 1915–1929 (2012)

12. Simko, V., Hauzar, D., Bures, T., Hnetynka, P., Plasil, F.: Verifying temporal properties of use-cases in natural language. In: Arbab, F., Ölveczky, P.C. (eds.) FACS 2011. LNCS, vol. 7253, pp. 350–367. Springer, Heidelberg (2012). https:// doi.org/10.1007/978-3-642-35743-5_21
13. Smith, M., Holzmann, G., Etessami, K.: Events and constraints: a graphical editor for capturing logic requirements of programs. In: Proceedings of the 5 IEEE International Symposium on Requirements Engineering, 27–31 August, pp. 14–22 (2001)
14. Wong, P.Y.H., Gibbons, J.: Property specifications for workflow modelling. In: Leuschel, M., Wehrheim, H. (eds.) IFM 2009. LNCS, vol. 5423, pp. 56–71. Springer, Heidelberg (2009). https://doi.org/10.1007/978-3-642-00255-7_5
15. Yu, J., Manh, T.P., Han, J., Jin, Y., Han, Y., Wang, J.: Pattern based property specification and verification for service composition. In: Aberer, K., Peng, Z., Rundensteiner, E.A., Zhang, Y., Li, X. (eds.) WISE 2006. LNCS, vol. 4255, pp. 156–168. Springer, Heidelberg (2006). https://doi.org/10.1007/11912873_18
16. Zyubin, V., Anureev, I., Garanina, N., Staroletov, S., Rozov, A., Liakh, T.: Event driven temporal logic for control software requirements. In: Fundamentals of Software Engineering. 9th International Conference, FSEN 2021, Virtual Event, 19–21 May 2021, Revised Selected Papers. Due: 25 November 2021. https://www.springer.com/gp/book/9783030892463
17. Argosim. www.argosim.com. Accessed 20 Apr 2021
18. Garanina, N.: EDTL: Checking consistency tables (2021). https://github.com/GaraninaN/CheckEDTL. Accessed 20 Apr 2021

Visual Language for Device Management in Telecommunication Product Line

Eugeny Semenov[1], Sheng Kai[1], Chen Gen[1], Dmitry Luciv[2,3],
and Dmitry Koznov[2(✉)]

[1] Huawei Technologies Co., Ltd., Shenzhen, China
{semyonov.eugeny,kaisky.sheng,chengen}@huawei.com
[2] Saint-Petersburg State University, Saint Petersburg, Russia
{d.lutsiv,d.koznov}@spbu.ru
[3] Alferov University RAS, Saint Petersburg, Russia
dluciv@spbau.ru

Abstract. In the present paper, we consider the task of creating hardware specifications for telecommunication devices that close the communication gap between hardware engineers and software developers. This task has arisen during the development of a family of telecommunication systems at Huawei. The specifications need to describe hardware from the viewpoint of driver development (i.e., device management), omitting many hardware details and including information for automatic generation of driver data structures and signatures. Furthermore, they need to be comprehensive and illustrative for both engineering groups. To meet this challenge, we propose a visual language supporting five views (representations): Structured view (all structural elements of a device), Composite view (all connections of a device), Datapath view (device parts that process the data flow), Control view (device parts that control the data flow processing), and Service view (device parts that provide additional functionality). We present an implementation of the visual language built with the Eclipse Modeling Tools Xtext/EMF/Sirius and integrated into a development environment for device management. We have received positive feedback from the device management software engineers.

Keywords: Telecommunication systems · Control systems · Model-based approach · Product lines · Domain specific modeling · Domain specific programming

1 Introduction

Development of various telecommunication devices such as routers, firewalls, etc. is a very laborious task for a multitude of reasons. First, the final product includes very different, complex components, ranging from special hardware to control software. Second, companies that release such systems, usually, instead of a single product, create entire product lines [7] which encompass a variety of analogs, as

L. Bellatreche et al. (Eds.): MEDI 2021 Workshops, CCIS 1481, pp. 204–216, 2021.
https://doi.org/10.1007/978-3-030-87657-9_16

well as the new versions of already existing devices. Therefore, the development process includes a product line and concurrent work on several products, and can involve up to several hundred developers.

The complexity of the systems and their mass production produce large volumes of information. Therefore, establishing effective communication between teams is of utmost importance. A team should share information with other teams carefully: i.e., provide them with exactly what they require. At the same time, such "informational junctions" should support illustrative and convenient methods of specification representation to enable collaborative work between teams.

This problem has arisen in a project at Huawei that was developing network routers. During the interactions between hardware and software developers, a need was identified for hardware models of products that could be used in developing hardware drivers. This model needed to include high-level hardware descriptions, free from various hardware details. At the same time, it could contain additional information necessary for developing control software, which is a part of the final product. The model also needed to be complete, i.e., allowing automatic generation of essential parts of code for hardware drivers, as well as illustrative and easy to comprehend, discuss and develop.

We have decided to employ the domain-specific model driven approach [20, 32] and create a special visual language for this purpose. This language supports the multiple view point concept [25], allowing to model different aspects of the target products, and based on Domain Specific Modeling (DSM) approach [20]. We present an implementation of the language built with the Eclipse Modeling Tools Xtext/EMF/Sirius [13,31], and integrated into a device management development environment, specifically developed for this product line. We have received positive feedback from the device management software engineers.

2   Approach Context

In our work, we consider a particular product line of network routers. This product line consists of a set of systems (routers) that include both hardware and software components. In the current paper, we concentrate on a single task concerning the product line—device management. In short, device management refers to the development of drivers for the hardware included in the system.

The visual language that we present is a part of the device management development environment. The problem is that driver programmers need a large volume of information about hardware devices, but a still considerably smaller one than hardware engineers possess. Obtaining this information is a labor-intensive task, as hardware engineers are not able to easily extract information that is essential for software development from their body of knowledge. Moreover, it is important to formalize this extracted information in order to use it for automatic generation of software data structures, function signatures (parameters and their types), event sequence processing, etc. Generated code is an essential part of target code, although driver code can not be completely generated due to various peculiarities and specifics of particular systems.

To specify the hardware information used for driver development, we have developed a special textual device management domain specific language (DSL). The language allows to define not only the hardware structure of the system, but also a large number of its properties. Additionally, it provides facilities for specifying connections between hardware elements, which can be rather complicated due to a possibility of hardware structure changing dynamically: a system administrator can insert a special card into an existing router to increase the number of its network connections, and router drivers must obtain access to the new hardware elements on the card.

The visual language that we present is a part of the environment for driver development for the router product line. It is intended for graphical representation of the hardware structure and connections from the programming point of view, omitting secondary details. As it has turned out, the device management DSL is not enough for the product line needs. Our experiments have shown that quite often, software developers and hardware engineers need to discuss the structure of the system. Consequently, they need to use high level tools. Moreover, software developers are also needed to renew the information concerning the structure of a particular board or card due to the target system including decades of various. It should be noted that people operate with the visual presentation of the complex system structure much more efficiently than using other representations. However, it is more appropriate to perform everyday work using textual programming language [23].

3   Metamodel

To describe the proposed visual language, we use the metamodel approach [4,31]. This approach provides a formal method for language specification, and it can be used for graphical editor development. We used the Ecore notation [31]. Apart from some technical details, we present the simplified metamodel in the current paper (see Fig. 1).

Our visual language includes the main entities of the problem domain which are hardware elements **Module**, **Chip**, **Element**, **Port** and their connections. Hardware drivers can access these hardware entities and enable upper level software to influence their behavior (launch, re-launch, re-configure, etc.).

Let us describe in more detail the constructions of the language following Fig. 1.

HardwareElement is the root entity, denoting a hardware element that could contain ports. Its properties are *name*, *type*, and *multiplicity*, where the latter denotes the number of instances of this hardware element in a system. Instances can not be created dynamically and thus are statically presented in the system model. **HardwareElement** is virtual entity, and is introduced only for gathering properties of real life hardware elements.

Module represents a hardware part of the target router. There are two kinds of modules: *board* and *card*. Board is the main part of the router holding hardware elements which support the main functions of a router. Furthermore, a board enables communication between all of the hardware elements placed on it. Card is used to extend the capabilities of a board or another card to be inserted into a target module. In our visual language, we provide the module types, but not the target configuration of the system, which can be modified dynamically.

Chip addresses the next layer of hardware decomposition: a module consists of a number of chips. Chips perform various module functions, e.g. coding/decoding an optical signal, board temperature control, etc. There are four kinds of chips: *core*, *slot*, *to_slot*, *to_bus*. Core chips are used to express main functionality of the module they belong to. Other chip kinds are used to express the mechanism of card insertion. Any module (*board* or *card*) could have a number of chips marked as a slot for various cards to be inserted in. If a module is a card, it must have a special chip marked as *to_slot* for insertion of the parent card into any suitable slot of another module (see chip `PicSlot` in Fig. 2). At last, a card could have special chips marked as *to_bus* for connecting to the board bus directly (see chip `CanBus` in Fig. 2).

Element is the last decomposition layer of the hardware device. Elements are parts of a chip that provide more detailed functionality. In particular, they are carriers of the ports of the chip. Every chip port provides special functionality for processing input/output, and, precisely, this functionality is encapsulated into the elements. A single element can implement a number of ports.

Hardware elements communicate with each other and the environment via ports. A single hardware element can have several groups of ports of the same type. To represent these groups, we use the **PortGroup** entity. **PortGroup**'s properties are *kind*, *type*, and *multiplicity*. There are two kinds of ports: *internal* (for internal communication of the hardware elements inside of the module), and *panel* (for external communication of the module). The **PortGroup**'s *type* addresses the control of connections for ports that belong to the group. There are special rules for types which can be connected. These roles are expressed in the textual device management DSL. **PortGroup**'s *multiplicity* refers to the number of ports in the particular **PortGroup**. All ports from a **PortGroup** have the same type and kind. Ports of various chips/elements may have the same type. Additionally, the ports of a **PortGroup** are enumerated. The **Port**'s *number* is a significant property, as ports of the same type are often numbered sequentially throughout the entire module.

Essentially, a **PortGroup** is a collection of multiple entry/exit points (ports) of a hardware element with sharing properties. It could be said that **PortGroup**'s properties are a very simple interface of such a point. We do not need explicit interfaces for **PortGroup/Port**, as signals and data that are passed through the ports are out of scope of device management. On the other hand, we need not only port groups, but separate ports as well to control port to port connections in our specification: drivers need access to this information to provide network management functions. That is why using layer connections, similarly to ROOM [8], is not suitable in our case.

Some chips could be connected to each other without ports, e.g., voltage sensors `VltPT` are linked like that to the `CanBus` chip (see Fig. 6).

We have omitted a considerable number of parameters of hardware elements, in particular, the complex name/type hierarchy and some additional entities describing it via the means of the device management DSL. The first version of our visual language included all of this information (at the time we did not properly understand the role of a programming domain specific language). We had created a really complicated visual language, and implemented a lot of property sheets for each language construction in a graphical editor. This elicited negative feedback from the users due to the reluctance of the product line developers to use the modeling tool for everyday work, which required them to specify a lot of details in the property sheets.

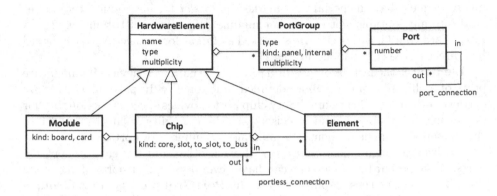

Fig. 1. Language metamodel

4 View Types

Our visual language is intended to provide the ability to browse the specifications on device management DSL to simplify discussing the system structure, renew knowledge about the selected system part (the specification usually has a lot of details, and developers can forget them very quickly), as well as make the introduction of a new employee to the project easier. No new entities can be added using the visual modeling tool, and no editing facilities are provided. We are following the ideas of the visualization toolkit for the Cobol reengineering system described in [6]: visualization of existing software-related entities and their relations using numerous views.

Multiple well-elaborated views are required to enable suitable browsing of a complicated textual specification or program. The multiple view point concept [25] is well-known in the model-based approach: it is used everywhere, from structure analysis approaches to object-oriented notations and UML. However, in our situation, we need to concentrate on this issue due to the following fact. Various views are easy to create because they are not manually constructed, but generated on developer request based on the existing specification. Therefore, we provide a large number of view types so the developers will not need to spend their efforts on creating them manually. Furthermore, view type variety helps to understand, discuss and analyze the system better.

The visual language we present supports the following view types:

- *Structured view* presents all structural hardware elements of a system to be developed (see Fig. 2); since this is a large volume of information, no connections and elements of chips are depicted. However, chip ports are depicted directly on chips.
- *Composite view* is similar to structured view, but it is augmented with multiplicity indicators in order to depict the instances of chips, elements, and ports (see Fig. 3). This is the reason why this view is not as large as the previous one. To ensure this, in contrast with the previous view type, the elements are shown inside of chips. Furthermore, port connections are depicted as well. However, using multiplicity augmentations does not allow to depict port to port connections because the view presents grouped ports only.
- *Datapath view* presents the data flow process which indicates the main functionality of the module (see Fig. 4). In this view, all other details are omitted.
- *Control view* presents chips, ports, and connections of the module which control the main functionality (see Fig. 5). In short, chips and elements from the previous view perform tasks, and hardware elements from this view control them.
- *Service view* presents the service functionality of the module, e.g., control of temperature or voltage sensors, fan controllers (see Fig. 6).

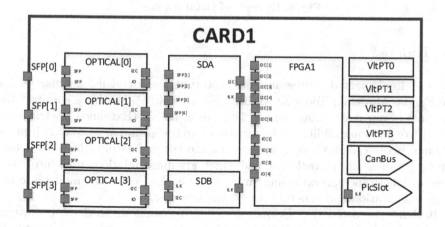

Fig. 2. Example of Structured view

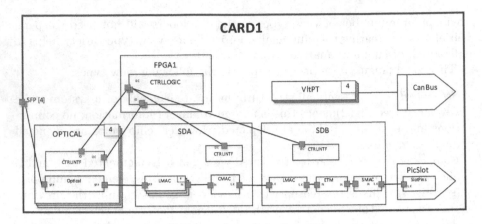

Fig. 3. Example of Composite view

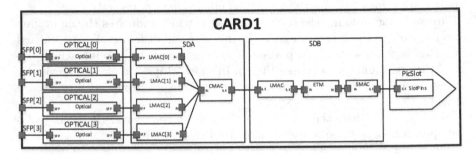

Fig. 4. Example of Datapath view

5 Tool

We have implemented a programming prototype for our visual language using the Eclipse Modeling Tools Xtext/EMF/Sirius [13,31]. We have specified the grammar of our device management DSL using EBNF (Extended Backus-Naur Form). We put some additional information into the grammar to convert it properly into Ecore (i.e., a visual language metamodel), indicating which constructs can be grouped into metaclasses, and which grammar relations map into references or inheritances. Next, using Sirius, we map the Ecore metamodel into the graphical notation and generate the graphical editor.

It should be noted that Eclipse Modeling Tools allows to develop a target visual tool and an environment for textual DSL that are seamlessly connected to each other. In our case, seamlessness refers to the automatic synchronization of constructions on diagrams and in the textual editor. Moreover, Eclipse Modeling Tools provides rapid development process, which is very important taking into account the iterative process of development based on regular user feedback. However, implementing non-standard features using Sirius can be problematic.

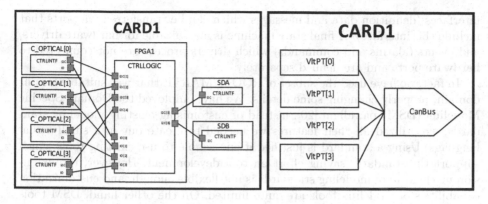

Fig. 5. Example of Control view   **Fig. 6.** Example of Service view

In fact, there is a wide variety of aspects that should be kept in mind while choosing a development technology for an industrial solution.

To validate our target tool, we have implemented 15 modules and demonstrated results and tool features to the product line developers. They have given us positive feedback, but insisted on *Structured view* being able to show all of important structural elements of a module on a single diagram, ignoring the big size of such a diagram for real life modules. Following [21], we would like to not ignore the use process, even if we imagined it in a different way (i.e., we thought that the *Composite view* would be enough for a high-level view). However, we will have more feedback after a full introduction of our tool into the development process.

6   Related Work

Hierarchical component models are widely used for modeling real-time systems starting from SDL (70's–90's) [1]. In ROOM [8], the concept of components with ports and interfaces was thoroughly elaborated on, including various kinds of ports, layer connections, and deep integration ports/interfaces with an extended final state machine. Furthermore, this model was used in UML in composite structured diagrams [3], in the real-time UML profile MARTE [2], and SysML [5]. In avionics the special modeling language AADL is used, including features for modeling hardware elements [15].

We have used components and ports from ROOM/MARTE in our visual language, allowing three decomposition levels (module, chip, element). However, in contrast to ROOM, our components are not black boxes: elements placed on one chip can be connected directly to other elements in another chip via element ports. We also allow to create simple relations between chips without ports (in Service view). At last, we do not use a final state machine and port interfaces (definition data and messages which can be transferred via ports that include this interface). A final state machine is not suitable for hardware drivers, and events (alarms and commands) which drivers process are not connected to hardware ports and are defined separately.

In fact, we have used the subset of ROOM/MARTE that was suitable for our domain, properly changing some details. We have employed the Domain Specific Modeling (DSM) paradigm [20]: instead of customising existing modeling standards, we utilized all their features we needed to create our own small visual language. Using a standard is justified if one is able to use existing tools which support the standard, saving effort on tool development. However, the extension mechanism of modeling standards is not flexible enough, and customization capabilities of modeling tools are quite limited. On the other hand, DSM tools (especially Eclipse Modeling Tools) are mature nowadays. Moreover, it was necessary for us to integrate visual language support with the DSL programming toolset. Consequently, the DSM approach is more efficient in our case than using standard visual modeling languages/tools.

The concept of a product line was actively researched and introduced to the software industry in 1990–2000 [7]. The idea behind it is developing and promoting a set of products together for a specific market segment, and, at the same time, building the products from common (reusable) assets. The significant number of methods and tools were created to support software product lines. Below some recent reviews can be found. In [10], a systematic literature review of the empirical studies on software product lines is presented (reviewed studies were published between 2000 and 2018). In [14], variability metrics for software product lines are collected and analyzed. Approaches to product line evolution are reviewed in [27]. A survey of software product line management tools is presented in [29]. Actually, the topic is a matter of practice rather than intensive research nowadays.

Domain specific programming languages and model-based approach are used in product line development. In [17], the product line is considered as a software factory based on development by assembly, i.e. a significant part of the target applications is supplied from ready-built and built-to order components. However, it is more of a conceptual framework than a set of real development assets (tools, languages, models, etc.). It should be also stressed that it does not support any telecommunication specifics.

The model-driven approach is actively being employed in the context of variability management in product lines [9,18,33,35]. There is a special branch of this approach that focuses on feature modeling [19,34,36], including development of various artifacts, e.g., documentation [24]. The problem of these approaches is the high complexity of variability languages and procedures. Additionally, it requires a formal specification of the reusable artifacts.

A lot of research is dedicated to generation of applications in a product line based on model-based specifications [12,17,22]. The problem of these approaches is creating a labor-intensive and inflexible development infrastructure, which becomes problematic in case of market changes [23].

It should be noted that a large number of model-based approaches has already been created. However, there is a problem with its wide adoption in the industry [30]. Product lines appear to be a suitable context for model-based development combined with domain-specific modeling and programming languages [17,20]. Thus, both research and industrial communities need reports on successful large-scale applications of the model-based approach in order to exchange their successful and unsuccessful experiences.

Finally, let us note that software/hardware telecommunication product lines have become more and more labor-intensive, involving hundreds and even thousands of developers. Meanwhile, there is a lack of research for telecommunication product lines: we have found [11] concerning performance variability, and [28] that considers the problem of defining a product line's scope. In particular, we were not able to find research on the device management problem.

7   Conclusion

In this paper, we have proposed a domain specific visual language for device management in a telecommunication product line. The language addresses the need for browsing hardware specifications using the multiview concept. The implementation of the language in Eclipse Modeling Tools is presented.

The visual language proposed in the paper, could be extended, providing view on modules (boards and cards) of product line. The most obvious relationship between board and card is "a card could be inserted into a board". However, we plan to move ahead basing on feedback and demands of device management engineers. It means we will develop features, which are most required.

As a further research direction, we plan to apply the concept of view-to-view transformation [23] to produce more views demanded by the various needs of the developers. One of the main tasks to solve in order to achieve this goal is the layout problem: the generated views should be arranged properly. One of the partial solutions of this problem is allowing manual layouting. In any case, if the automatic layouting is not good enough, the tool will not be accepted by users.

Another potential research direction is the support of planned reuse and variability management of device management specifications. We could extend the visual language by feature modeling formalism [19,36] for visual variability management. It would be the next step after visualization of hardware structure for device management.

Finally, using knowledge graphs and ontology engineering [16,26] as an alternative approach to gather and access information required for device management appears to be promising. This approach may be efficient due to the significant heterogeneity of the device management information, although we have not highlighted this issue in the paper.

References

1. ITU Recommendation Z.100: Specification and Description Language. ITU-T (2002)
2. A UML Profile for MARTE: Modeling and Analysis of Real-Time Embedded systems. OMG, June 2008
3. Unified Modeling Language (UML). OMG (2013)
4. Meta Object Facility (MOF) Core Specification. OMG (2015)
5. OMG Systems Modeling Language. OMG, November 2019
6. Baburin, D.E., Bulyonkov, M.A., Emelianov, P.G., Filatkina, N.N.: Visualization facilities in program reengineering. Program. Comput. Softw. **27**(2), 69–77 (2001)
7. Böckle, G., van der Linden, F.J.: Software Product Line Engineering: Foundations, Principles and Techniques. Springer, Heidelberg (2010). https://doi.org/10.1007/3-540-28901-1
8. Selic, B., Gullekson, G., Ward, P.T.: Real-Time Object-Oriented Modeling. Wiley, New York (1994)
9. Buchmann, T., Greiner, S.: Managing variability in models and derived artefacts in model-driven software product lines. In: Proceedings of the 6th International Conference on Model-Driven Engineering and Software Development, MODELSWARD 2018, Funchal, Madeira, Portugal, 22–24 January 2018, pp. 326–335. SciTePress (2018)
10. Chacón-Luna, A.E., Gutiérrez, A.M., Galindo, J.A., Benavides, D.: Empirical software product line engineering: a systematic literature review. Inf. Softw. Technol. **128**, 106389 (2020)
11. Cvetković, R., Nešković, S.: An approach to defining scope in software product lines for the telecommunication domain. In: Catania, B., Ivanović, M., Thalheim, B. (eds.) ADBIS 2010. LNCS, vol. 6295, pp. 555–558. Springer, Heidelberg (2010). https://doi.org/10.1007/978-3-642-15576-5_44
12. Dageförde, J.C., Reischmann, T., Majchrzak, T.A., Ernsting, J.: Generating app product lines in a model-driven cross-platform development approach. In: 49th Hawaii International Conference on System Sciences, HICSS 2016, Koloa, HI, USA, 5–8 January 2016, pp. 5803–5812. IEEE Computer Society (2016)
13. Eclipse Project: Eclipse Sirius. https://www.eclipse.org/sirius/
14. El-Sharkawy, S., Yamagishi-Eichler, N., Schmid, K.: Metrics for analyzing variability and its implementation in software product lines: a systematic literature review. In: Berger, T., et al. (eds.) Proceedings of the 23rd International Systems and Software Product Line Conference, SPLC 2019, vol. A, p. 33:1. ACM (2019)
15. Feiler, P.H., Gluch, D.P.: Model-Based Engineering with AADL - An Introduction to the SAE Architecture Analysis and Design Language. SEI Series in Software Engineering, Addison-Wesley, Boston (2012)
16. Gavrilova, T.: Ontological engineering for practical knowledge work. In: Apolloni, B., Howlett, R.J., Jain, L. (eds.) KES 2007. LNCS (LNAI), vol. 4693, pp. 1154–1161. Springer, Heidelberg (2007). https://doi.org/10.1007/978-3-540-74827-4_144
17. Greenfield, J., Short, K., Cook, S., Kent, S., Crupi, J.: Software Factories: Assembling Applications with Patterns, Models, Frameworks, and Tools. Wiley, Chichester (2004)
18. He, X., Fu, Y., Sun, C., Ma, Z., Shao, W.: Towards model-driven variability-based flexible service compositions. In: 39th IEEE Annual Computer Software and Applications Conference, COMPSAC 2015, Taichung, Taiwan, 1–5 July 2015, vol. 2, pp. 298–303. IEEE Computer Society (2015)

19. Kang, K.C., Lee, J., Donohoe, P.: Feature-oriented product line engineering. IEEE Softw. **19**(4), 58–65 (2002)
20. Kelly, S., Tolvanen, J.P.: Domain-Specific Modeling: Enabling Full Code Generation. Wiley, New York (2008)
21. Kelly, S., Pohjonen, R.: Worst practices for domain-specific modeling. IEEE Softw. **26**(4), 22–29 (2009)
22. Kim, S.D., Min, H.G., Her, J.S., Chang, S.H.: DREAM: a practical product line engineering using model driven architecture. In: Third International Conference on Information Technology and Applications (ICITA 2005), 4–7 July 2005, Sydney, Australia, pp. 70–75. IEEE Computer Society (2005)
23. Koznov, D.V.: Process model of DSM solution development and evolution for small and medium-sized software companies. In: Workshops Proceedings of the 15th IEEE International Enterprise Distributed Object Computing Conference, EDOCW 2011, Helsinki, Finland, 29 August–2 September 2011, pp. 85–92. IEEE Computer Society (2011)
24. Koznov, D.V., Romanovsky, K.Y.: DocLine: a method for software product lines documentation development. Program. Comput. Softw. **34**(4), 216–224 (2008)
25. Kruchten, P.: The 4+1 view model of architecture. IEEE Softw. **12**(6), 42–50 (1995)
26. Kudryavtsev, D., Gavrilova, T.: Diagrammatic knowledge modeling for managers - ontology-based approach. In: KEOD 2011 - Proceedings of the International Conference on Knowledge Engineering and Ontology Development, Paris, France, 26–29 October 2011, pp. 386–389. SciTePress (2011)
27. Marques, M., Simmonds, J., Rossel, P.O., Bastarrica, M.C.: Software product line evolution: a systematic literature review. Inf. Softw. Technol. **105**, 190–208 (2019)
28. Myllärniemi, V., Savolainen, J., Männistö, T.: Performance variability in software product lines: a case study in the telecommunication domain. In: 17th International Software Product Line Conference, SPLC 2013, Tokyo, Japan, 26–30 August 2013, pp. 32–41. ACM (2013)
29. Pereira, J.A., Constantino, K., Figueiredo, E.: A systematic literature review of software product line management tools. In: Schaefer, I., Stamelos, I. (eds.) ICSR 2015. LNCS, vol. 8919, pp. 73–89. Springer, Cham (2014). https://doi.org/10.1007/978-3-319-14130-5_6
30. Petre, M.: UML in practice. In: 35th International Conference on Software Engineering, ICSE 2013, San Francisco, CA, USA, 18–26 May 2013, pp. 722–731. IEEE Computer Society (2013)
31. Steinberg, D., Budinsky, F., Paternostro, M., Merks, E.: EMF: Eclipse Modeling Framework. Addison-Wesley Professional, Boston (2008)
32. Tolvanen, J., Kelly, S.: Applying domain-specific languages in evolving product lines. In: Proceedings of the 23rd International Systems and Software Product Line Conference, SPLC 2019, vol. B, Paris, France, 9–13 September 2019, pp. 65:1–65:2. ACM (2019)
33. Tolvanen, J., Kelly, S.: How domain-specific modeling languages address variability in product line development: investigation of 23 cases. In: Proceedings of the 23rd International Systems and Software Product Line Conference, SPLC 2019, vol. A, Paris, France, 9–13 September 2019, pp. 24:1–24:9. ACM (2019)
34. Usman, M., Iqbal, M.Z., Khan, M.U.: A product-line model-driven engineering approach for generating feature-based mobile applications. J. Syst. Softw. **123**, 1–32 (2017)

35. Verdier, F., Seriai, A.-D., Tiam, R.T.: Combining model-driven architecture and software product line engineering: reuse of platform-specific assets. In: Hammoudi, S., Pires, L.F., Selic, B. (eds.) MODELSWARD 2018. CCIS, vol. 991, pp. 430–454. Springer, Cham (2019). https://doi.org/10.1007/978-3-030-11030-7_19
36. Yang, G., Zhang, Y.: A feature-oriented modeling approach for embedded product line engineering. In: 12th International Conference on Fuzzy Systems and Knowledge Discovery, FSKD 2015, Zhangjiajie, China, 15–17 August 2015, pp. 1607–1612. IEEE (2015)

Using Process-Oriented Structured Text for IEC 61499 Function Block Specification

Vladimir Zyubin[✉] and Andrei Rozov

Institute of Automation and Electrometry, Acad. Koptyuga prosp. 1,
630090 Novosibirsk, Russia
{zyubin,rozov}@iae.nsk.su

Abstract. This paper deals with leveraging the IEC 61499 Function Blocks with the poST language. The poST language is a process-oriented extension of the IEC 61131-3 Structured Text (ST) language. The language targets specifying stateful behavior of PLC-based control software. The main purpose of our contribution is to provide coherence of the PLC source code with technological description of the plant operating procedure. The language combines the advantages of FSM-based programming with conventional syntax of the ST language and can be easily adopted by the community. The poST language assumes that a poST-program is a set of weakly connected concurrent processes. Each process is specified by a sequential set of states. The states are specified by a set of the ST constructs, extended by TIMEOUT operation, SET STATE operation, and START/STOP/check state operations to communicate with other processes. The paper describes the basics of the poST language, design constructs, and demonstrates usage of the poST language by developing control software for a wheel-chair elevator, and discusses the poST language over the control software implementation in Execution Control Chart.

Keywords: PLC languages · IEC 61499 · IEC 61131-3 · Control software development · Process-oriented programming · ECC

1 Introduction and Motivation

The ongoing transition to Industry 4.0 means a dramatic increase in complexity and use of embedded and cyber-physical systems in our lives. This demands a reassessment of the tools used for design and development of such systems. Behavior of a cyber-physical system is determined by the control system, and behaviour of control system is specified by software. Thus the models, methods and languages employed in development of control software need to be revised.

The majority of automation professionals predict that the tooling for Industry 4.0 software will be based on IEC 61131-3 and its evolution to IEC 61499.

This work was supported by the Russian Ministry of Education and Science, project no. AAAA-A19-119120290056-0.

© Springer Nature Switzerland AG 2021
L. Bellatreche et al. (Eds.): MEDI 2021 Workshops, CCIS 1481, pp. 217–227, 2021.
https://doi.org/10.1007/978-3-030-87657-9_17

There is a heated debate on the pros and cons of these standards in research papers. On the one hand, it is stated that IEC 61131-3 [1], developed in the early 90s and having known shortcomings, needs serious refactoring [2]. On the other hand, there are active attempts to modernize IEC 61131-3 by the IEC 61499 standard [3]. A third side argues that the proposed changes are not fundamental and are rather cosmetic in nature [4]. Additionally, it should be noted that possibility of reconfiguring and porting systems to distributed platforms of various topologies is initially declared in IEC 61499, and it is undoubtedly an essential attribute of the Industry 4.0 concept. IEC 61499 defines a program as a collection of interconnected and communicating function blocks. The external interface for the blocks is set up in data connections and event connections sections. A function block encapsulates the desired functionality which is specified by algorithms implemented in IEC 61131-3 languages. These algorithms are activated depending on the incoming events.

IEC 61499 therefore allows an automata-based description of system behavior. This is directly stated by the standard authors.

The effectiveness of automata-based approaches has long been recognized by the time IEC 61131-3 was submitted. Nevertheless, such mechanisms were not adopted until IEC 61499.

This evokes mixed thoughts. No doubt, it is a significant event for the mainstream practice of industrial automation. And yet it only happened decades after the adoption of IEC 61131-3. Besides, there is a perception that the standard does not fully take account of the common practices in automaton programming.

At implementation level, the behavior of function blocks is specified in the Execution Control Charts section with the Execution Control Chart (ECC) language. An ECC is roughly equivalent to a Moore-type state machine [5]. It monitors the input events and, based on the current state it executes a certain part of the encapsulated functionality. ECC is a graphical notation which leads to a possibility of ambiguous interpretation.

The order of ECC transitions' evaluation follows their order in textual XML-based representation of the FB. However, in graphical representation no hints provided to determine the order. This can result in two ECCs looking identically, but producing completely different reactions [5]. Also [4] lists such examples and argues that one of the most important reasons the industry has not yet adopted this standard is confusion over the execution semantics of the IEC61499 FB model.

The rest of the paper has the following structure: in Sect. 2, we give a basics of poST languages; in Sect. 3, we present a wheelchair lift as an example for control software specification; in Sect. 4, we describe control software structure; in Sect. 5, we illustrate using poST for FB specification; and in Sect. 6, we discuss the result.

2   Introduction to PoST

To address the restrictions and challenges in development of present-day complex control software, the process-oriented programming (POP) has been suggested in [6]. Process-oriented programming (POP) involves specifying control software with a set of concurrently running processes. Internally the processes have a state-machine-like structure and are equipped with operations for managing time intervals and inter-process communication. Concurrent behavior of the system is arranged via consequent execution of active process states on each program cycle. Compared to other known state-machine-based approaches, such as CSP [7], Input/Output Automata [8], Harels State-charts [9], Hybrid Automata [10], Esterel [11], Calculus of Communicating Systems [12], and their extensions [13,14], the POP approach combines system concurrency on the global scale with local linearity of behavior within each process. POP provides a conceptual basis for multiple domain-specific programming languages (DSLs) that are intended for natural control software specification.

Within this paradigm new C-like languages Reflex and IndustrialC [15,16] have been developed. The Reflex language targets PC-based control software for large-scale industrial applications, while IndustrialC is tailored for microcontroller-based embedded systems.

As practice shows, the Reflex language can be successfully used in industrial applications and offers a number of significant advantages in control software programming [17–19]. However, its widespread use in practice is hindered by the conservative nature of the domain. The developer community tends to be wary of introducing any new emerging technology to the process. Historically, the majority of control software is still implemented within the so called PLC-approach, that is based on the IEC 61131-3 languages IEC 61131-3 [1], and PLC manufacturers are reluctant to deviate from this standard.

In order to face this challenge we proposed to adapt the process-oriented approach for the ST procedural programming language in the same way as it was done for the C language in case of Reflex. The process-oriented extension of ST was called the poST language [20].

The poST language can therefore be of particular interest to the PLC community as it extends the Structured Text language from IEC 61131-3. The additional attractiveness of the poST language is due to the wide popularity of the ST language. According to the CoDeSys GmbH (former 3S-SmartSoftware Solutions GmbH), the ST language is regularly used by up to 70 % of users, and the number is constantly growing [21].

The poST language combines advantages of the process-oriented paradigm with conventional syntax of the ST language and can be easily adopted by the PLC community. The poST language assumes that a poST-program is a set of weakly connected concurrent processes, structurally and functionally corresponding to the technological description of the plant. Each process is specified by a set of states. The states are specified by a sequence of the ST constructs, extended by TIMEOUT operation, SET STATE operation, and START/STOP/check state operations to communicate with other processes. Apart from these operators, the poST language follows the syntax and semantics of ST.

For the poST language we have already developed an Eclipse-based IDE [22], including a parser and syntax-directed editor. Code generation modules for the

C and ST languages have been implemented. The generated ST-code can be automatically converted in the PLCopen XML Exchange format [23], which makes integration with the IEC 61131-3 tools easier. The approach assumes that the generated code will be translated to executable form and uploaded to the target platform with an existing C or IEC 61131-3 toolchain.

3   Wheelchair Lift Example

To demonstrate the approach, we choose the task of automating a lifting platform for low-mobility users (Fig. 1).

The lift is an alternative to a ramp and it is intended to overcome vertical barriers.

The *cyber-physical diagram* (Fig. 2) considers the system as three interacting components. The lift user acts as *Environment*. The lift acts as *Plant*. *Controller* defines the behavior of the system in accordance with the Reflex program. The user can press the external and internal call buttons as well as open and close the doors. The call buttons (*up_call*, *down_call*, *up_call*, *down_call*) and lift doors (*top_door_closed*, *bot_door_closed*) are used as *Controls*. LED indicators (*up_call_led*, *down_call_led*, *up_call_led*, *down_call_led*) are used to signal unhandled calls. The controller monitors the states of the controls and floor sensors (*on_top_floor* and *on_bot_floor*). Using the values of these inputs, the controller generates control signals (*up* and *down*) to the lift movement motor and controls the LED indicators. Turning on the motor causes the lifting platform to move between floors.

Fig. 1. Wheelchair lift for users with limited mobility

The control program includes the states of pressing each of the buttons, platform movement in both directions, and waiting for the end of a movement or a new command.

The requirements we use to design poST-program are formulated in natural language:

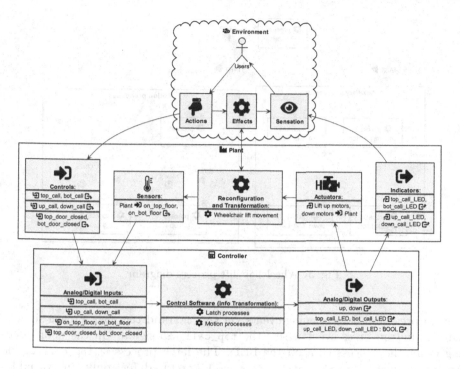

Fig. 2. Wheelchair lift cyber-physical diagram

- The simultaneous appearance of *up* and *down* signals is prohibited.
- Platform movement is only possible with closed doors.
- The movement begins after pressing one of the call buttons.
- In the absence of control commands for 20 s, the lift should be automatically moved to the lower floor.

4   Software Design and Implementation in PoST

The process diagram (Fig. 3) depicts the poST-program structure. Initially, the *Initialization process* deploys the control algorithm. It starts the *Auxiliary processes* and the *Motion process*. Then it stops itself. The Auxiliary processes (the *xxx_call_Latch* processes) light up the LEDs when the user releases the corresponding call buttons and turns them off when the lift arrives at the corresponding floor. In accordance with the requests and the state of the sensors, the *Motion* process starts the *go_up* or *go_down* processes. After starting a process, the *Motion* process controls its completion (transition to the inactive state).

Each latch process has two local variables and two states. The local variables store previous values of the `top_call` and `top_door_closed` signals and are used to detect the rising and falling edges. In the initial state the process sets the starting values of its local variables. In its second and main state the process monitors the

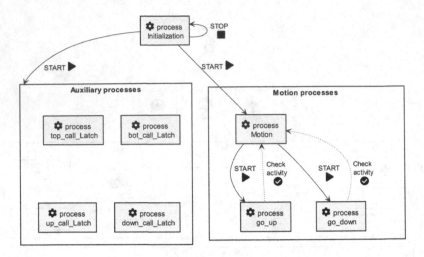

Fig. 3. Wheelchair lift process diagram

button press and door opening events via `top_call` and `top_door_closed` signals. On the button press event it sets the `top_call_LED` signal. On the door opening event the process turn off the LED. The latch processes (`top_call_Latch`, `bot_call_Latch`, `up_call_Latch`, `down_call_Latch`) differ only in variables (Listing 1).

```
PROCESS top_call_Latch
    VAR
        prev_in : BOOL;
        prev_out : BOOL;
    END_VAR
    STATE init
        prev_in := NOT top_call;
        prev_out := top_door_closed;
        SET NEXT;
    END_STATE
    STATE check_ON_OFF LOOPED
        IF top_call AND NOT prev_in THEN
            top_call_LED := TRUE;
        END_IF
        IF NOT top_door_closed AND prev_out THEN
            top_call_LED := FALSE;
        END_IF
        prev_in := call0;
        prev_out := open0;
    END_STATE
END_PROCESS
```

Listing 1. Latch process

The flowchart (Fig. 4) shows operation of the `Motion` process. Listing 2 represents the `Motion` process in poST.

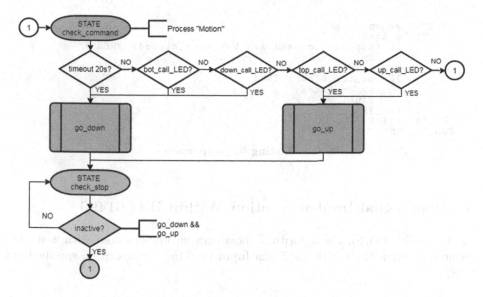

Fig. 4. Motion process flowchart

```
PROCESS Motion (* motion *)
    STATE check_command
        IF  (bot_call_LED) THEN
            START PROCESS go_down;
            SET STATE check_stop;
        ELSIF (down_call_LED) THEN
            START PROCESS go_down;
            SET STATE check_stop;
        ELSIF (top_call_LED) THEN
            START PROCESS go_up;
            SET STATE check_stop;
        ELSIF (up_call_LED) THEN
            START PROCESS go_up;
            SET STATE check_stop;
        END_IF
        TIMEOUT (#T20s) THEN
            START PROCESS go_down;
            SET STATE check_stop;
        END_TIMEOUT
    STATE check_stop
        IF ((PROCESS go_down IN STATE INACTIVE)
            AND (PROCESS go_up IN STATE INACTIVE)) THEN
            RESTART; // set the initial state
        END_IF
    END_STATE
END_PROCESS
```

Listing 2. Motion process

Code in Listing 3 defines the behavior of the `go_up` process. The process waits for both top and bottom doors to be closed, before setting for upward motion. The process stops once the lift reaches the top floor.

```
PROCESS go_up
    STATE motion
        IF (top_door_closed AND bot_door_closed) THEN
            up := TRUE;
        END_IF
        IF (on_top_floor) THEN
            up := FALSE;
            STOP;
        END_IF
    END_STATE
END_PROCESS
```

Listing 3. go_up process

5   Conceptual Implementation Within IEC 61499

Conceptually (Fig. 5), the algorithm above can be implemented with a single reduced function block with one Event Input invoking the algorithm specified in poST.

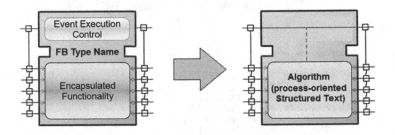

Fig. 5. Process-oriented function block

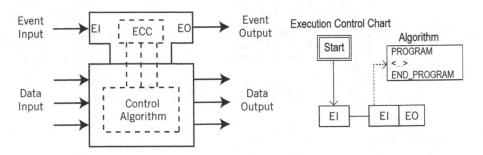

Fig. 6. ECC of process-oriented function block

Figure 6 depicts the internal structure of such a reduced function block.

This approach to implementation allows for the poST algorithm to be split into multiple function blocks. These can then be mapped unto multiple computing platforms thus enabling distributed control. Communication between the parts of the algorithm executing on separate PLCs can be organized using the IEC 61499 Virtual Bus concept, as seen on Fig. 7 and would primarily be presented by interaction between processes.

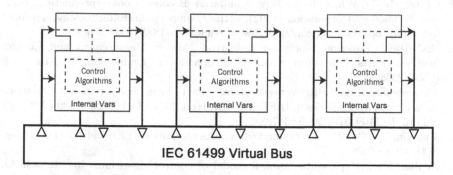

Fig. 7. Distributed implementation with IEC 61499 Virtual Bus

6   Discussion and Conclusion

The industrial systems market within the framework of the Industry 4.0 concept needs open solutions that can be implemented on distributed platforms. Currently, these are an open question for which a simple and effective answer needs to be worked out. IEC 61499 offers some solutions primarily attractive due to their ability for creating distributed control systems. However, this standard is highly dependent on the 30 year old standard IEC 61131-3. The 61131-3 standard is based on a device-centric paradigm and can only be successfully modified using existing process-oriented programming techniques. This shift to the application-centric paradigm can lead to a very steep learning curve. We propose to smooth the learning curve by using the poST language – a process-oriented extension of ST. Preliminary studies show that poST is compatible with the FB concept; moreover, when poST and the IEC 61499 are used, a synergistic effect appears. This synergy manifests in that specifying IEC 61499 function blocks in poST provides an application-centric paradigm for control software development with distributed architectures.

As a further direction of this research, we plan to formalize a new operational semantics of the poST language to align it with the IEC 61499 virtual bus features. An operational semantics would allow to adapt existing approaches in formal verification of process-oriented programs to the distributed case.

Acknowledgments. We thank the JetBrains Foundation for the charitable support of our research activity.

References

1. IEC 61131-3: Programmable Controllers Part 3: Programming Languages. International Electrotechnical Commission Std., Rev. 2.0 (2003)
2. Crater, K.C.: When Technology Standards Become Counterproductive. Control Technology Corporation (1992). https://support.controltechnologycorp.com/index.php?option=com_content&view=article&id=188&Itemid=null
3. IEC 61499: Function Blocks for Industrial Process Measurement and Control Systems, Parts 1–4. International Electrotechnical Commission Std., Rev. 1.0 (2004/2005)
4. Thramboulidis, K.: Different perspectives [face to face; "IEC 61499 function block model: facts and fallacies"]. IEEE Ind. Electron. Mag. **3**(4), 7–26 (2009). https://doi.org/10.1109/MIE.2009.934788
5. Vyatkin, V.: The IEC 61499 standard and its semantics. IEEE Ind. Electron. Mag. **3**(4), 40–48 (2009)
6. Zyubin, V.E.: Hyper-automaton: a model of control algorithms. In: Stukach, O. (ed.) Proceedings of the IEEE International Siberian Conference on Control and Communications, Tomsk, Russia, pp. 51–57. IEEE (2007). https://doi.org/10.1109/SIBCON.2007.371297
7. Hoare, C.A.R.: Communicating Sequential Processes. Prentice-Hall Inc. (1985)
8. Lynch, N., Tuttle, M.: An introduction to input/output automata. CWI Q. **2**, 219–246 (1989)
9. Harel, D.: Statecharts a visual formalism for complex systems. Sci. Comput. Program. **8**, 231–274 (1987)
10. Milner, R.: Communication and Concurrency. Series in Computer Science, Prentice Hall, Englewood Cliffs (1989)
11. Berry, G.: The foundations of Esterel. In: Plotkin, G., Stirling, C., Tofte, M. (eds.) Proof, Language and Interaction: Essays in Honour of Robin Milner. Foundations of Computing Series, pp. 425–454. MIT Press (2000)
12. Kaynar, D.K., Lynch, N., Segala, R., Vaandrager, F.: Timed I/O automata: a mathematical framework for modeling and analyzing real-time systems. In: Proceedings of the IEEE 24th International Real-Time Systems Symposium (RTSS 2003), Cancun, Mexico, pp. 166–177. IEEE Computer Society (2003)
13. Kof, L., Schätz, B.: Combining aspects of reactive systems. In: Broy, M., Zamulin, A.V. (eds.) PSI 2003. LNCS, vol. 2890, pp. 344–349. Springer, Heidelberg (2004). https://doi.org/10.1007/978-3-540-39866-0_34
14. Henzinger, T.A.: The theory of hybrid automata. In: Inan, M.K., Kurshan, R.P. (eds.) Verification of Digital and Hybrid Systems. NATO ASI Series (Series F: Computer and Systems Sciences), vol. 170, pp. 265–292. Springer, Heidelberg (2000). https://doi.org/10.1007/978-3-642-59615-5_13
15. Anureev, I., Garanina, N., Liakh, T., Rozov, A., Schulte, H., Zyubin, V.: Towards safe cyber-physical systems: the reflex language and its transformational semantics. In: International Siberian Conference on Control and Communications (SIBCON), Tomsk, Russia, pp. 1–6 (2019). https://doi.org/10.1109/SIBCON.2019.8729633
16. Rozov, A.S., Zyubin, V.E.: Adaptation of the process-oriented approach to the development of embedded microcontroller systems. Optoelectron. Instrum. Data Process. **55**(2), 198–204 (2019). https://doi.org/10.3103/S8756699019020122
17. Liakh, T.V., Rozov, A.S., Zyubin, V.E.: Reflex language: a practical notation for cyber-physical systems. Syst. Inform. (12), 85–104 (2018)

18. Kovadlo, P.G., et al.: Automation system for the large solar vacuum telescope. Optoelectron. Instrum. Data Process. **52**(2), 187–195 (2016). https://doi.org/10.3103/S8756699016020126

19. Liah, T.V., Zyubin, V.E.: The Reflex language usage to automate the large solar vacuum telescope. In: 2016 17th International Conference of Young Specialists on Micro/Nanotechnologies and Electron Devices (EDM), Erlagol, Russia, pp. 137–139 (2016). https://doi.org/10.1109/EDM.2016.7538711

20. Bashev, V., Anureev, I., Zyubin, V.: The post language: process-oriented extension for IEC 61131-3 structured text. In: 2020 International Russian Automation Conference (RusAutoCon), Sochi, Russia, pp. 994–999 (2020). https://doi.org/10.1109/RusAutoCon49822.2020.9208049

21. Petrov, I., Wagner, R.: Debugging applied PLC software in CoDeSys (part 3). In: Industrial Automatic Control Systems and Controllers, vol. 4, pp. 34–36. Nauchtekhlitizdat (2006)

22. Wiegand, J.: Eclipse: a platform for integrating development tools. IBM Syst. J. **43**(2), 371–383 (2004). https://doi.org/10.1147/sj.432.0371

23. Marcos, M., Estevez, E., Perez, F., Der Wal, E.V.: XML exchange of control programs. IEEE Ind. Electron. Mag. **3**(4), 32–35 (2009). https://doi.org/10.1109/MIE.2009.934794

Blockchain for Inter-organizational Collaboration (BIOC)

The DibiChain Protocol: Privacy-Preserving Discovery and Exchange of Supply Chain Information

Elias Strehle[1]([✉])([iD]) and Martin Maurer[2]

[1] Blockchain Research Lab, Max-Brauer-Allee 46, 22765 Hamburg, Germany
elias@strehle.de
[2] CHAINSTEP, Max-Brauer-Allee 46, 22765 Hamburg, Germany

Abstract. Connecting and exchanging information across organizations becomes increasingly important as supply chains become more complex and expectations with regard to sustainability, transparency and resilience increase. At the same time, organizations are adamant about protecting any competitive advantage which derives from private information about, for example, supplier networks, available inventory or production processes. Technology aimed at enabling information exchange within and across supply chains must therefore ensure high degrees of privacy and control over private information. In light of this, we specify the DibiChain protocol for the discovery and exchange of supply chain information. The protocol prioritizes data minimization in shared data stores, avoidance of persistent user identifiers and anonymous communication with minimal intermediation. We further outline how the DibiChain protocol can serve as the foundation for privacy-preserving supply chain applications, including an anonymous discovery service for GS1 EPCIS event data.

Keywords: Privacy · Anonymity · Supply chain · Distributed ledger technology · Blockchain

1 Introduction

Supply chain relationships are characterized by the paradox of coopetition: Actors try to reap the benefits of cooperation and coordination without jeopardizing their competitive advantage [53]. The fear of leaking valuable private information may cause actors to refuse to cooperate even if cooperation would benefit everyone [33,56]. Addressing this source of inefficiency seems especially worthwhile in the context of transitioning to a more sustainable, circular economy [26] as lack of information sharing in supply chains and the resulting risks,

The authors gratefully acknowledge funding through the joint research project DIBICHAIN within the framework of the ReziProK program, which is funded by Germany's Federal Ministry of Education (funding reference number: 033R241). Apart from the provision of funding, the funding source had no involvement in this study.

L. Bellatreche et al. (Eds.): MEDI 2021 Workshops, CCIS 1481, pp. 231–247, 2021.
https://doi.org/10.1007/978-3-030-87657-9_18

e.g., when refurbishing or recycling products with unknown material composition, can be an obstacle to circular policies and business models [54].

We propose the DibiChain protocol as a potential solution for situations in which organizations (or humans) want to connect, discover and exchange information while preserving a high degree of anonymity and unlinkability. The protocol builds on a shared data store, for example a distributed ledger, and a public or private Tor network [17]. The shared data store lets users publish anonymous pointers, called addresses, to reference private information without leaking it. It further lets users connect these address via links to allow other users to discover addresses connected to their own through a chain of links. Users can then send anonymous queries via the Tor network to request the private information referenced by an address. In this way, a direct information exchange becomes possible without giving up anonymity or channeling queries through a trusted third party; an implementation of the DibiChain protocol can provide the "missing links" between data silos within and across supply chains while ensuring a high degree of privacy.

The remainder of the paper is structured as follows. In Sect. 2 we discuss existing work dealing with the standardization and exchange of supply chain information. In Sect. 3 we describe the DibiChain protocol and some extensions. In Sect. 4 we outline an ecosystem for the discovery and exchange of supply chain information based on the DibiChain protocol. We further illustrate the practical implications by sketching a DibiChain-based discovery service for EPCIS visibility event data. In Sect. 5 we discuss the advantages and disadvantages of the DibiChain protocol in relation to alternative approaches. Section 6 concludes.

2   Related Work

The non-profit organization GS1 publishes standards to promote the collection and exchange of information within and across supply chains, including a specification of standardized object identifiers [31], a core business vocabulary [29], the EPCIS standard for visibility event data [27] and a global traceability standard [30]. Together, these standards can serve as the foundation for instance-level traceability of the "what, when, where and why" of supply chain events such the manufacturing, packaging, shipping and receiving of goods [28, Section 2.2]. Traceability has many potential applications, including curbing illegal practices, improving sustainability performance, increasing operational efficiency, enhancing supply chain management and sensing market forces and trends [34, Figure 1].

A key challenge for traceability is how to connect information across companies. The pragmatic approach of "one up, one down" tracing may not yield sufficient transparency and leave supply chains vulnerable to fraud and low quality of ingredients [44]. More comprehensive approaches, however, face the "data discovery problem" of finding out which companies are connected by a chain of events, establishing trust between companies without a direct business relationship and transferring data once connection and trust have been established [30, p. 36].

In recent years, blockchain technology or—more generally—distributed ledger technology (DLT) has been discussed as a promising foundation to solve the data discovery problem within supply chains [35]. DLT is an umbrella term for technologies that enable a network of independent parties to operate an ordered, persistent and tamper-evident ledger of cryptographically-validated records [46].

[52] propose a blockchain-based discovery.service for EPCIS visibility event data. The proposed solution lets companies store sanitized EPCIS event data and access policies pertaining to these data on a service provider's distributed ledger. During the sanitization process, the data are shortened and sensitive values are replaced with salted hashes. Connections between the sanitized event data on the ledger are stored by a discovery service provider in a graph database.

Among the various other blockchain-based solutions for exchanging supply chain information, many store business information in shared data stores (often the ledger itself) to create transparency and harness the power of consensus-based validity checks and smart contracts [1, 5–7, 10, 11, 13, 16, 39]. In a proposal for food safety monitoring, [51] tackles privacy requirements by only storing "key information" on the distributed ledger and relegating storage of detailed information to trusted third parties. [22] propose a distributed ledger for cattle supply chains. Their approach ensures pseudonymity but remains susceptible to correlation through persistent user IDs and a one-to-one mapping of business processes to publicly visible transactions.

3   The DibiChain Protocol

In this section we describe the abstract DibiChain protocol. It allows users to reference and connect private information in a shared data store, which in turn allows other users to discover these references and request the corresponding information from its owner. While our focus is on supply chain applications, the protocol itself is generic and makes no assumptions on the format or content of the referenced private information.

We presuppose a persistent data store that can be accessed by all users. This could be a shared database, a private and permisioned distributed ledger or a public blockchain. We further presuppose a Tor network [17] which is used for anonymous communication both from user to data store and from user to user. Note that this need not be the public Tor network.[1] Instead, one can choose to deploy a dedicated, non-public Tor network which is only accessible to the DibiChain users—similar to non-public deployments of public blockchain technologies like Ethereum [8]. Using a dedicated network ensures that nodes do not handle Tor traffic unrelated to the DibiChain application.

The DibiChain data store knows two types of data objects: addresses and links. An address is identified by a public key and provides information on how users can anonymously contact the address owner. A link connects addresses on

---

[1] https://www.torproject.org.

the DibiChain, providing context and allowing users to represent relationships between addresses.

A DibiChain *address* is a hidden service descriptor as specified in the Tor protocol.[2] It has an ID which is derived from a public key and contains a list of introduction points. The introduction points reference Tor nodes through which users can establish an anonymous communication channel with the address owner. A user creates a DibiChain address in the following way:

1. Create a public/private key pair.
2. Set up introduction points for the corresponding address ID according to the Tor protocol.
3. Create the hidden service descriptor and sign it with the private key.
4. Publish the signed hidden service descriptor as an address on the DibiChain data store.

A DibiChain *link* connects addresses. The link data object contains the following fields:

- `fromAddressIds`: A list of address IDs.
- `toAddressIds`: A list of address IDs.
- `toTags`: A list of strings, each representing a (hash of a) topic or keyword.
- `linkId`: The hash of all fields above.
- `signatures`: A collection of cryptographic signatures of all fields above. Each signature corresponds to one address in `fromAddressIds` or `toAddressIds`. For example, a complete signature set for a link with two addresses in `fromAddressIds` and three addresses in `toAddressIds` contains five signatures.

A user creates a DibiChain link in the following way:

1. Create a partial link object with fields `fromAddressIds`, `toAddressIds` and `toTags`.
2. Compute the link ID by hashing the partial link object.
3. Add the link ID to the partial link object and sign it with the private keys corresponding to the referenced addresses.
4. Publish the signed link object on the DibiChain data store.

The purpose of `toAddressIds` and `toTags` is similar. Both represent a relationship with the addresses in `fromAddressIds`, allowing users to discover connected addresses by following a chain of links. The main difference is that the owner of an address in `toAddressIds` approves the link by signing it whereas tags have no concept of ownership and thus require no signature.

Figure 1 illustrates how addresses are connected on the DibiChain. We speak of a direct connection from address A to address B if there is a link where

---

[2] For an illustration of how hidden services work, see https://community.torproject. org/onion-services/overview. For the full technical specification, see https://github. com/torproject/torspec/blob/master/rend-spec-v3.txt.

A is contained in `fromAddressIds` and B is contained in `toAddressIds`. We speak of an indirect connection between address A and address B if there is a tag T for which there are (1) a link where T is contained in `toTags` and A is contained in `fromAddressIds` and (2) a link where T is contained in `toTags` and B is contained in `fromAddressIds`. In Fig. 1, for example, the addresses with IDs `a13f..` and `ba58..` have a direct connection and the addresses with IDs `a13f..` and `e9a9..` have an indirect connection. Direct references require coordination as every involved user must contribute one or more addresses and signatures to the link object prior to publication. Indirect references are easier to negotiate since users can pre-agree on a tag and then publish links independently from each other. At the same time, direct connections can foster additional trust by documenting the common intent of involved users. We discuss direct and indirect connections in the context of supply chain tracing in Sect. 4.1.

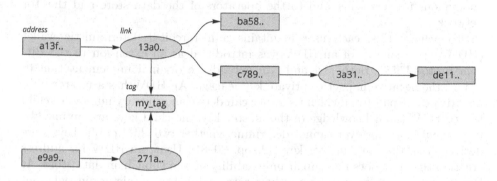

Fig. 1. Illustration of connections on the DibiChain.

A downside of anonymity is lack of accountability, which can encourage misbehavior such as spamming or violation of use-case-specific rules. In Sect. 3.1 we describe how a trusted third party can provide accountability for activity on the DibiChain data store without sacrificing anonymity and unlinkability among users and between users and data store operators.

While a DibiChain data store could be operated by a single service provider, some use cases may benefit from more sophisticated implementations with multiple operators and advanced security and trust guarantees, such as those provided by distributed ledger technology. In Sect. 3.2 we discuss how the DibiChain can benefit from the desirable features of distributed ledgers by adding capabilities for timestamping and notarization.

3.1 Achieving Accountability

Anonymity can encourage misbehavior [20]. Malicious DibiChain users could spam addresses and links or even mount denial-of-service (DoS) attacks without the risk of being caught. Some user activity on the DibiChain may also violate contracts or laws. For example, a user could write personally identifying information into a link tag without the person's consent. For these reasons, it can be advantageous or even necessary to have a way of holding users accountable for undesired behavior. But how to establish accountability without giving up anonymity?

Balancing accountability and anonymity is especially challenging for networks which can be used without authorization, also called permissionless networks [25]. Solutions suggested and pursued for permissionless networks include proof of work [4,19,36,41], native tokens for transaction fees [8,41] and accountability delegates [38,40,43]. How those or other measures could be employed to secure a permissionless DibiChain implementation remains an open question. In this section, we propose instead an extension to the DibiChain protocol for a permissioned setting in which users register with a trusted third party called the *administrator*. Users can be held accountable by the administrator but remain anonymous to each other and to the operators of the data store and the Tor network.

To achieve this, each user maintains a hierarchical deterministic wallet (HDW). The concept of an HDW was introduced as an extension to the Bitcoin protocol [55]. Both [32] and [15] extend the original implementation to reduce the negative impact of private key leakage. An HDW has a master public/private key pair from which its owner can derive an arbitrary number of child key pairs. Without knowledge of the master key, the child keys are unlinkable; in particular, an observer cannot determine whether two child public keys were derived from the same master key [42, pp. 80–81]. Using an HDW for address creation therefore does not impair unlinkability on the DibiChain data store. At the same time, anyone who knows the master public key can determine whether a given public key was derived from it.

Accountability against the administrator is therefore achieved in the following way:

- At initialization, each user sets up an HDW by creating a master public/private key pair.
- The user shares the master public key and some identifying information (depending on the use case: a self-chosen user name, an e-mail address, a means of legal identification, etc.) with the administrator. The master private key is never shared.
- The user creates new addresses based on child key pairs derived via the HDW.
- When a data store operator receives a new address for publication, she sends the corresponding public key to the administrator. The administrator checks whether the public key has been derived from a known master public key and responds with an "OK" or "not OK." In the latter case, the operator refuses to publish the address on the data store.

In this way, addresses on the DibiChain remain anonymous and unlinkable to all participants except the administrator. In case of undesired behavior, the administrator can take action on his own (e.g., by blacklisting the misbehaving user) or reveal the identifying information (e.g., to law enforcement in case of illegal activity).

It may be interesting to note that this extension also enables anonymous pay-per-use schemes for the DibiChain data store. The administrator can keep track of how many addresses and links are published by each user and either bill the users directly or forward the aggregated information to the data store operators. In this way, operators can offer usage-based payment models without learning which addresses belong to whom.

3.2   Adding Capabilities for Timestamping and Notarization

The desirable features of DLT make it suitable for the implementation of timestamping and notarization services [12]. Publishing (a hash of) data on an immutable ledger creates a timestamped and tamper-proof copy which can lend external validity to claims about the data and assist in conflict resolution. We can extend the DibiChain protocol to offer trustworthy timestamping and notarization if the DibiChain data store is operated on a distributed ledger or the data store operators are trusted to provide and persist correct timestamps.

Timestamping capabilities are implemented by adding a `timestamp` field to the link object. In the interest of external validity and incentive alignment, the timestamp is not created by the user who publishes the link. Instead, it is added by the data store operators during publication. The timestamp field is *not* incorporated by the user when computing the link ID and the signatures as it is unknown before publication.

Notarization capabilities are implemented by adding a `dataHash` field to the link object. The field can contain arbitrary strings but should be a (salted) hash to ensure confidentiality. The content of the `dataHash` field is determined by the users who create the link and, unlike the timestamp, is incorporated when computing the link ID and the signatures. The data hash therefore inherits the following properties from the link object: It is (1) public among those who can access the data store, (2) timestamped by the data store operators, (3) confirmed by all involved users through cryptographic signatures and (4) tamper-proof (because changing it would invalidate the link ID and the signatures). These properties give data hashes on the DibiChain a high degree of trustworthiness.

4   Exchanging Supply Chain Information with the DibiChain Protocol

In this section we describe an implementation in which the DibiChain protocol powers an ecosystem for the secure and trustworthy exchange of supply chain information. To ensure privacy and data control, data storage is federated: Users store their own business-relevant data (or rely on a trusted third party to store the data for them). On top of the user-operated data stores, an implementation of the DibiChain protocol on a distributed ledger acts as a "discovery service" [30, Section 4.3.3]. The DibiChain data store is accessible to all users, allowing them to register business information via anonymous DibiChain addresses and connect information within or across local data stores via DibiChain links. It is run by a small number of operators who coordinate through the DLT's consensus mechanism. In addition, an administrator as described in Sect. 3.1 acts as a gatekeeper to the ecosystem. Figure 2 shows a sketch of the system architecture.

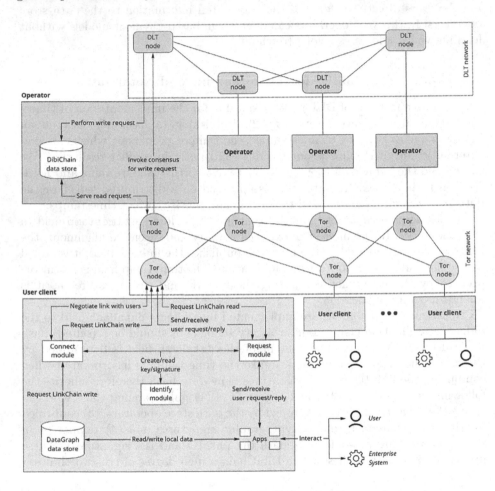

Fig. 2. Ecosystem architecture. The DibiChain administrator is not shown.

The DibiChain data store is implemented as a distributed ledger. Every operator maintains a full copy of the ledger and uses it to answer read requests from users. A fault-tolerant consensus algorithm ensures that operator copies of the ledger stay in sync and that the ledger tolerates errors or misbehavior from a minority of operators. Our prototype simulates four data store operators and implements the distributed ledger with crash fault tolerance (CFT) on Hyperledger Fabric [3]. Stronger fault tolerance could be achieved by implementing a Byzantine fault tolerant (BFT) consensus algorithm [9,14,37].

To foster user acceptance and trust, ensure scalability and allow data store operators to monetize their services, the ecosystem is permissioned. To be able to publish information on the DibiChain data store and use the system's Tor network, users must register with an administrator as described in Sect. 3.1. The system's Tor nodes are operated by the users. This ensures that the network is large enough to provide sufficient anonymity.

Users access the ecosystem through a local user client. In addition to the Tor node, the user client consists of three core modules (Identify, Connect, Request), a graph data store (DataGraph) and a collection of so-called apps.

The Identify core module maintains the user's HDW (see Sect. 3.1), derives and stores key pairs and creates and checks cryptographic signatures. The Connect core module manages the publication of addresses and links in the DibiChain data store and provides tools to negotiate multi-party links with other user clients. The Request module allows users to send and receive requests and responses. Requests can be sent to DibiChain addresses through the Tor network and include a reply address to which the receiver can send a response, again through the Tor network. This allows users to request and exchange business-relevant information in a privacy-preserving way.[3]

The DataGraph is the user's local data store. In the interest of flexibility and extensibility, the data store is a graph database. Users can store business information in the DataGraph and make it discoverable by publishing corresponding addresses and links on the DibiChain data store. In addition, the DataGraph provides support for connecting user enterprise systems to minimize the need for data duplication or migration. Figure 3 illustrates the three data layers—enterprise systems, DataGraph, DibiChain data store—of the supply chain ecosystem.

Specific use cases are implemented within the ecosystem via apps. An app provides a user interface, connects to enterprise systems, defines and enforces data models and business logic, stores information in the DataGraph and interacts with other user clients and the DibiChain data store through the user client's core components. In this way, apps enable the implementation of a wide range of supply chain use cases (tracing, exchange of compliance documents, collection of sustainability data, etc.) within a single ecosystem.

4.1   A Discovery Service for EPCIS Event Data

To illustrate the practical implications of the ecosystem, we sketch how it can serve as a discovery service for EPCIS event data. In line with the federated approach to data storage, no event data are stored in shared databases—neither in full nor in sanitized form. Instead, every company stores its data locally in

---

[3] An important implementation detail is to ensure that users do not overutilize their own Tor node as an introduction point for their addresses, as this would allow observers to correlate them. The prototype implementation of the Connect core module randomly chooses introduction points from a regularly updated list of available Tor nodes.

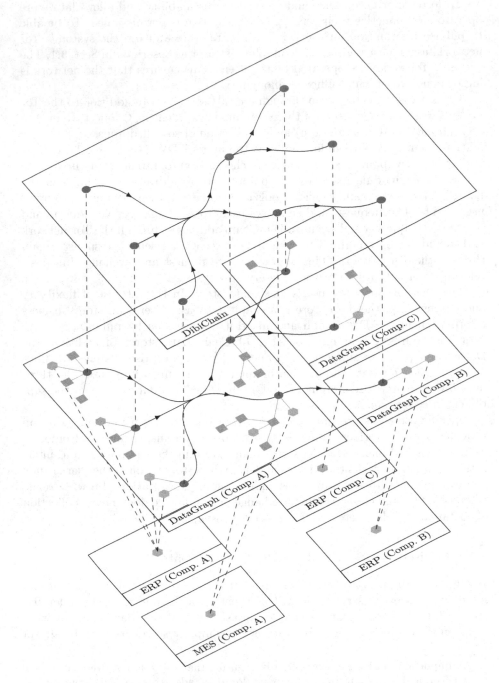

Fig. 3. Data layers of the ecosystem for supply chain information.

its own DataGraph. For each data object, the company publishes a corresponding address on the DibiChain data store. Connections between event data are published as DibiChain links.

As discussed in Sect. 3, addresses can be connected indirectly through multiple links with the same tag or directly through a single link. For product tracing, the (hash of the) product's unique identifier is a natural candidate for an indirect connection tag. A direct connection would require companies to collect addresses and signatures at the time of link publication. While this requires more coordination, it can also provide increased trust by documenting that all involved companies agree that a direct connection between the two events exists. In particular, a direct connection attests that there is no "hole" in the chain of custody and can therefore help prevent the introduction of counterfeits into the supply chain.

Once the links are established, a company can determine which addresses are (directly or indirectly) connected to its own events on the DibiChain data store. The company can then send queries from its user client to the address IDs via Tor and request the corresponding EPCIS data. The address owner and the data itself remain unknown to the sender until the owner chooses to answer. Furthermore, the request itself and any subsequent communication are only visible to the sender and the receiver and cannot be observed by any third party, including the data store operators and the administrator.

Figure 4 illustrates how EPCIS event data are registered and connected on the DibiChain. In addition to the chain of events, we show how the DibiChain can also represent the chain of custody. Maintaining a separate chain of custody makes it possible to define access rights based on the distance in the supply chain. For example, Farmer A could prove to Distributor C that he is a direct supplier of their common business contact (Processor B) by signing a request with the private key corresponding to his address in the chain of custody.

5   Discussion

The DibiChain protocol combines ideas and approaches from various internet technologies. It builds on the Tor protocol for anonymous communication. Indeed, the DibiChain data store can be viewed as a "Tor lookup service with links." Tamper-resistance by means of cryptographic hashes and signatures is achieved in a similar way as in the Bitcoin protocol. In comparison to protocols for blockchain-based cryptocurrency, the DibiChain protocol is more generic. Whereas cryptocurrency protocols implement validity checks to prevent double-spending and the uncontrolled creation of new currency, the DibiChain protocol employs a lower degree of "algorithmic self-policing" [50, p. vii] as all well-formed addresses and links are considered valid. This makes the DibiChain more flexible but less strict.

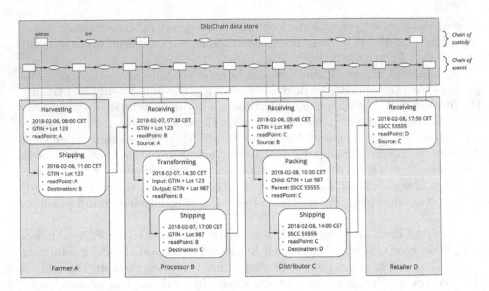

Fig. 4. Illustration of how a chain of EPCIS event data are registered and connected on the DibiChain data store. The example EPCIS events are taken from Fig. 2 in [52]. For simplicity, we show all connections as direct connections. Supply chain members can request EPCIS data by sending queries to the corresponding address IDs via the Tor network.

DibiChain addresses and links also share similarities with concepts of self-sovereign identity (SSI) [2], such as the W3C's specifications for decentralized identifiers (DIDs) [47] and verifiable credentials (VCs) [48]. These specifications, too, deal with the publication of anonymous identifiers on a public data store and achieve non-repudiability and tamper-resistance by cryptographic means. In the same way that DibiChain links make claims about DibiChain addresses, VCs make claims about DIDs. DibiChain links, however, differ from VCs in three important respects: (1) They are visible to anyone who can access the DibiChain data store, (2) they are self-signed by the affected address owners and (3) they make generic claims ("address A is connected to address B") as opposed to specific claims ("this DID belongs to a person who is at least 18 years old").

Many aspects of the DibiChain specification were chosen to ensure a high level of privacy. By using Tor, users remain anonymous on the communication level. (A user can nonetheless provide identifying information via message payloads, particularly as part of user-to-user communication.) Furthermore, address and link identifiers are single-use. There are no persistent user identifiers which would make it easy to correlate addresses and analyze usage patterns or user relationships.

Adding timestamps and data hashes as described in Sect. 3.2, however, could potentially jeopardize privacy. Analysis of timestamps may allow observers to correlate addresses, for example when links are published at regular time intervals [18]. Data hashes of structured data (e.g., JSON objects with known field names and data ranges) are prone to brute-force and dictionary attacks [21]. For each use case, the benefits and potential privacy risks of timestamping and notarization capabilities should be weighed carefully.

Some supply chain blockchains which store business information in shared data stores address privacy concerns by restricting the visibility of data to a pre-defined group of users in a "channel" or "stream" (see, e.g., [7]). This, however, requires a priori knowledge of who should be part of which channel, which can be problematic in supply chains where upstream producers do not know where their products end up. In addition, fine-grained access control in large applications can require a staggering number of channels. While not a supply chain use case, this is illustrated by the banking cooperative SWIFT[4], which estimated that a DLT implementation of its international money transfer system would require more than 100,000 channels to address all privacy requirements [23]. While channels could be added to the DibiChain data store if required, the protocol's focus is on data minimization to ensure that the information value of shared data is as small as possible.

The high degree of privacy in the DibiChain-based discovery service comes at the cost of efficiency and availability. A company may only be interested in a single event in a highly complex supply chain (e.g., the provenance of the tin contained in one component of an airplane). Without out-of-band information, the company must send a query to every connected DibiChain address. Furthermore, if a company's DibiChain client is unavailable, the query cannot be delivered and thus not answered. Efficiency can be increased by publishing additional information, e.g., by extending the DibiChain address object to include additional use case specific information. But this also increases the information content within the DibiChain data store, thus increasing the risk of correlation. Availability can be increased by making user clients highly available or by delegating the task of storing data and answering queries to a service provider who guarantees high availability.

In addition to ensuring privacy, the DibiChain protocol is designed to provide favorable security and trust properties. For addresses, deriving the ID from a public key and attaching a cryptographic signature ensures that users can only control addresses for which they know the corresponding private key. For links, the signatures document that the affected address owners have seen and approved the link. These measures provide non-repudiation against address owners. They also provide tamper-resistance against the DibiChain operators: All users can check the link ID as well as address and link signatures to convince themselves that the data object has not been modified by an operator, e.g., by switching out the introduction points or adding tags.

Link signatures document approval from address owners at the cost of increased communication effort during link creation. For some use cases, requiring a full signature set may in fact be unnecessary. As an example, consider a cryptocurrency like Bitcoin [41]. Bitcoin transactions only require a proof of ownership from the senders of Bitcoin, not the receivers. This one-sided approval is

---

[4] https://www.swift.com.

sufficient because presumably nobody would object to receiving Bitcoins. On the DibiChain, the Bitcoin example corresponds to a link which only contains signatures for the addresses in `fromAddressIds`, not the addresses in `toAddressIds`. Other use cases, however, are likely to require a full signature set to be considered valid, especially when a DibiChain link represents a transaction which incurs liabilities for all involved users.

With regard to security and trust, it is also important to note that the capabilities of the administrator as described in Sect. 3.1 are clearly staked out. A malicious administrator could leak identifying information or censor a user's new addresses (assuming the data store operators follow his verdict), but he could *not* publish addresses or links in the name of another user, tamper with DibiChain data or access locally stored data unnoticed or unauthorized. The administrator acts as a gatekeeper for the DibiChain data store, in line with the idea of integrating trusted third parties into "trustless" systems in a controlled manner [49].

6   Conclusion

Connecting information across organizations remains a challenge, particularly when private information must be protected to maintain a competitive advantage. For DLT projects, concerns about confidentiality and privacy are among the most common reasons for project abandonment [45, Figure 27]. The challenge of addressing such concerns shows itself clearly in supply chain relationships. A blockchain study by the World Economic Forum finds that in a given supply chain, one or more actors may "try to enforce a lack of visibility about the identity of upstream suppliers, the prices paid by downstream suppliers, the true length of a cash-conversion cycle, the status of regulatory compliance, true levels of demand and available inventory, and details about the production process" [24, p. 7].

We propose the DibiChain protocol as a way of connecting, discovering and exchanging information in a privacy-preserving way. The protocol puts heavy emphasis on data minimization, which in our view should always precede and supplement other protective measures such as access control, data encryption or obfuscation techniques. Consequently, the protocol refrains from assigning persistent user identifiers and does not require users to store private information—in full or in sanitized form—in shared data stores. The DibiChain protocol puts a thin layer of addresses and links above user-operated data silos, exposing just enough information to allow users to discover and exchange relevant information.

Enabling cooperation within and across supply chains becomes increasingly important as we reap the benefits and face the challenges of tightly integrated, global supply chains. The DibiChain protocol aims to offer a novel choice in the tradeoff between privacy and transparency. For use cases which require a high level of privacy and can do without the validity checks and smart contract logic offered by more transparent blockchain solutions, it may provide a viable alternative.

References

1. Abeyratne, S.A., Monfared, R.P.: Blockchain ready manufacturing supply chain using distributed ledger. Int. J. Res. Eng. Technol. **5**(9), 1–10 (2016). https://doi.org/10.15623/ijret.2016.0509001
2. Allen, C.: The path to self-sovereign identity. Pers. Blog (2016)
3. Androulaki, E., et al.: Hyperledger fabric: a distributed operating system for permissioned blockchains. In: Proceedings of the Thirteenth EuroSys Conference (EuroSys 2018), Porto, PT, pp. 1–15. ACM Press (2018). https://doi.org/10.1145/3190508.3190538
4. Back, A.: A partial hash collision based postage scheme. Technical report, Cypherpunks Mailing List (1997)
5. Banker, S.: Blockchain gains traction in the food supply chain. Forbes (2018)
6. Bettín-Díaz, R., Rojas, A.E., Mejía-Moncayo, C.: Methodological approach to the definition of a blockchain system for the food industry supply chain traceability. In: Gervasi, O., et al. (eds.) ICCSA 2018. LNCS, vol. 10961, pp. 19–33. Springer, Cham (2018). https://doi.org/10.1007/978-3-319-95165-2_2
7. Biswas, K., Muthukkumarasamy, V., Tan, W.L.: Blockchain based wine supply chain traceability system. In: Future Technologies Conference (FTC) 2017, Vancouver, Canada (2017)
8. Buterin, V.: Ethereum whitepaper. Whitepaper, Ethereum Foundation (2013)
9. Cachin, C., Vukolić, M.: Blockchain consensus protocols in the wild. Working paper, IBM Research Zurich (2017)
10. Caro, M.P., Ali, M.S., Vecchio, M., Giaffreda, R.: Blockchain-based traceability in agri-food supply chain management: a practical implementation. In: 2018 IoT Vertical and Topical Summit on Agriculture - Tuscany (IOT Tuscany). IEEE (2018). https://doi.org/10.1109/iot-tuscany.2018.8373021
11. Casado-Vara, R., Prieto, J., la Prieta, F.D., Corchado, J.M.: How blockchain improves the supply chain: case study alimentary supply chain. Procedia Comput. Sci. **134**, 393–398 (2018). https://doi.org/10.1016/j.procs.2018.07.193
12. Casino, F., Dasaklis, T.K., Patsakis, C.: A systematic literature review of blockchain-based applications: current status, classification and open issues. Telemat. Inform. **36**, 55–81 (2019). https://doi.org/10.1016/j.tele.2018.11.006
13. Casino, F., Kanakaris, V., Dasaklis, T.K., Moschuris, S., Rachaniotis, N.P.: Modeling food supply chain traceability based on blockchain technology. IFAC-PapersOnLine **52**(13), 2728–2733 (2019). https://doi.org/10.1016/j.ifacol.2019.11.620
14. Castro, M., Liskov, B.: Practical Byzantine fault tolerance. In: Proceedings of the Third Symposium on Operating Systems Design and Implementation, pp. 173–186 (1999)
15. Das, P., Faust, S., Loss, J.: A formal treatment of deterministic wallets. In: Proceedings of the 2019 ACM SIGSAC Conference on Computer and Communications Security. ACM (2019). https://doi.org/10.1145/3319535.3354236
16. Dasaklis, T.K., Casino, F., Patsakis, C., Douligeris, C.: A framework for supply chain traceability based on blockchain tokens. In: Di Francescomarino, C., Dijkman, R., Zdun, U. (eds.) BPM 2019. LNBIP, vol. 362, pp. 704–716. Springer, Cham (2019). https://doi.org/10.1007/978-3-030-37453-2_56
17. Dingledine, R., Mathewson, N., Syverson, P.: Tor: The second-generation onion router. In: Proceedings of the 13th Conference on USENIX Security Symposium - Volume 13, SSYM 2004, USA, p. 21. USENIX Association (2004)

18. Dorri, A., Roulin, C., Jurdak, R., Kanhere, S.S.: On the activity privacy of blockchain for IoT. In: 2019 IEEE 44th Conference on Local Computer Networks (LCN). IEEE (2019). https://doi.org/10.1109/lcn44214.2019.8990819
19. Dwork, C., Naor, M.: Pricing via processing or combatting junk mail. In: Brickell, E.F. (ed.) CRYPTO 1992. LNCS, vol. 740, pp. 139–147. Springer, Heidelberg (1993). https://doi.org/10.1007/3-540-48071-4_10
20. Farkas, C., Ziegler, G., Meretei, A., Lörincz, A.: Anonymity and accountability in self-organizing electronic communities. In: Proceeding of the ACM Workshop on Privacy in the Electronic Society - WPES 2002. ACM Press (2002). https://doi.org/10.1145/644527.644536
21. Federal Office for Information Security: Towards secure blockchains. Report, Federal Office for Information Security (2019)
22. Ferdousi, T., Gruenbacher, D., Scoglio, C.M.: A permissioned distributed ledger for the US beef cattle supply chain. IEEE Access 8, 154833–154847 (2020). https://doi.org/10.1109/access.2020.3019000
23. Finextra: Adoption of DLT presents significant operational challenges for Swift member banks. Finextra (2018)
24. Flanagan, A.J., Maclean, F., Sun, M., Hewett, N., Liao, R.: Inclusive deployment of blockchain for supply chains: Part 4 - protecting your data. Whitepaper, World Economic Forum (2019)
25. Garzik, J.: Public versus private blockchains: Part 1: permissioned blockchains. Whitepaper. BitFury Group (2015)
26. Geng, Y., Sarkis, J., Bleischwitz, R.: How to globalize the circular economy. Nature 565(7738), 153–155 (2019). https://doi.org/10.1038/d41586-019-00017-z
27. GS1: EPC Information Services (EPCIS) standard (Release 1.2). Standards document, GS1 (2016)
28. GS1: EPCIS and CBV implementation guideline (Release 1.2). Technical report, GS1 (2016)
29. GS1: Core Business Vocabulary (CBV) standard (Release 1.2.2). Standards document, GS1 (2017)
30. GS1: GS1 global traceability standard (Release 2.0). Standards document, GS1 (2017)
31. GS1: GS1 general specifications (Release 21.0.1). Standards document, GS1 (2021)
32. Gutoski, G., Stebila, D.: Hierarchical deterministic bitcoin wallets that tolerate key leakage. In: Böhme, R., Okamoto, T. (eds.) FC 2015. LNCS, vol. 8975, pp. 497–504. Springer, Heidelberg (2015). https://doi.org/10.1007/978-3-662-47854-7_31
33. Hackius, N., Reimers, S., Kersten, W.: The privacy barrier for blockchain in logistics: first lessons from the port of Hamburg. In: Bierwirth, C., Kirschstein, T., Sackmann, D. (eds.) Logistics Management. LNL, pp. 45–61. Springer, Cham (2019). https://doi.org/10.1007/978-3-030-29821-0_4
34. Hastig, G.M., Sodhi, M.S.: Blockchain for supply chain traceability: business requirements and critical success factors. Prod. Oper. Manag. 29(4), 935–954 (2020). https://doi.org/10.1111/poms.13147
35. Hewett, N., Lehmacher, W., Wang, Y.: Inclusive deployment of blockchain for supply chains: Part 1 - introduction. Whitepaper, World Economic Forum (2019)
36. Juels, A., Brainard, J.: Client puzzles: a cryptographic defense against connection depletion attacks. In: Conference Presentation, RSA Laboraties (2017)
37. Lamport, L., Shostak, R., Pease, M.: The Byzantine generals problem. ACM Trans. Program. Lang. Syst. 4(3), 382–401 (1982)
38. Lee, T., Pappas, C., Barrera, D., Szalachowski, P., Perrig, A.: Source accountability with domain-brokered privacy. Working paper, ETH Zurich (2016)

39. Leng, K., Bi, Y., Jing, L., Fu, H.C., Van Nieuwenhuyse, I.: Research on agricultural supply chain system with double chain architecture based on blockchain technology. Future Gener. Comput. Syst. **86**, 641–649 (2018). https://doi.org/10.1016/j.future.2018.04.061

40. Ma, Y., Wu, Y., Li, J., Ge, J.: APCN: a scalable architecture for balancing accountability and privacy in large-scale content-based networks. Inf. Sci. **527**, 511–532 (2020). https://doi.org/10.1016/j.ins.2019.01.054

41. Nakamoto, S.: Bitcoin: a peer-to-peer electronic cash system. Whitepaper (2008)

42. Narayanan, A., Bonneau, J., Felten, E., Miller, A., Goldfeder, S.: Bitcoin and Cryptocurrency Technologies. Princeton University Press, Princeton (2016)

43. Naylor, D., Mukerjee, M.K., Steenkiste, P.: Balancing accountability and privacy in the network. ACM SIGCOMM Comput. Commun. Rev. **44**(4), 75–86 (2015). https://doi.org/10.1145/2740070.2626306

44. Pearson, S., et al.: Are distributed ledger technologies the panacea for food traceability? Glob. Food Secur. **20**, 145–149 (2019). https://doi.org/10.1016/j.gfs.2019.02.002

45. Rauchs, M., Blandin, A., Bear, K., McKeon, S.: 2nd global enterprise blockchain benchmarking study. SSRN Electron. J. (2019). https://doi.org/10.2139/ssrn.3461765

46. Rauchs, M., et al.: Distributed ledger technology systems: a conceptual framework. SSRN Electron. J. (2018). https://doi.org/10.2139/ssrn.3230013

47. Reed, D., Sporny, M., Longley, D., Allen, C., Grant, R., Sabadello, M., Holt, J.: Decentralized Identifiers (DIDs) (Version 1.0). W3C working draft, W3C (2020)

48. Sporny, M., Longley, D., Chadwick, D.: Verifiable Credentials data model (Version 1.0). W3C recommendation, W3C (2019)

49. Strehle, E.: Public versus private blockchains. BRL working paper, Blockchain Research Lab (2020)

50. Swan, M.: Blockchain: Blueprint for a New Economy, 1st edn. O'Reilly Media, Inc., Sebastopol (2016)

51. Tian, F.: An information system for food safety monitoring in supply chains based on HACCP, blockchain and internet of things. Ph.D. thesis, WU Vienna University of Economics and Business (2018)

52. Tröger, R., Clanzett, S., Lehmann, R.J.: Innovative solution approach for controlling access to visibility data in open food supply chains. In: Proceedings in Food System Dynamics p. Proceedings in System Dynamics and Innovation in Food Networks 2018 (2018). https://doi.org/10.18461/PFSD.2018.1817

53. Wilhelm, M., Sydow, J.: Managing coopetition in supplier networks: a paradox perspective. J. Supply Chain Manag. **54**(3), 22–41 (2018). https://doi.org/10.1111/jscm.12167

54. Winans, K., Kendall, A., Deng, H.: The history and current applications of the circular economy concept. Renew. Sustain. Energy Rev. **68**, 825–833 (2017). https://doi.org/10.1016/j.rser.2016.09.123

55. Wuille, P.: BIP 0032: Hierarchical Deterministic Wallets. Bitcoin Wiki (2012)

56. Zhang, H.: Vertical information exchange in a supply chain with duopoly retailers. Prod. Oper. Manag. **11**(4), 531–546 (2009). https://doi.org/10.1111/j.1937-5956.2002.tb00476.x

The International Health Data
Workshop (HEDA)

Towards a Resource-Aware Formal Modelling Language for Workflow Planning

Muhammad Rizwan Ali[1] and Violet Ka I Pun[1,2(✉)]

[1] Western Norway University of Applied Sciences, Bergen, Norway
{mral,vpu}@hvl.no
[2] University of Oslo, Oslo, Norway
violet@ifi.uio.no

Abstract. Healthcare industry is in a process of digitalising their activities. One of the most crucial ones is the automation of workflow planning. Workflow planning usually requires domain-specific knowledge, which makes it still a rather manual process requiring domain experts. In addition, workflows in healthcare sectors are mainly cross-organisational. Minor changes in the workflow of a collaborative partner may be propagated to other concurrently running workflows, which can result in substantial negative impacts. In this position paper, we present an initial step of an approach towards automating workflow planning. We show how to connect workflows of collaborative workflows through a resource sensitive formal modelling language. We then use an example to show how the language can be used to model cross-organisational workflows, and we discuss how static analyses can be performed on cost approximation and resource scheduling to facilitate planning automation.

Keywords: Healthcare · Cross-organisational workflows · Resource planning · Formal modelling

1 Introduction

Every industry is, one way or another, undergoing the process of digital transformation, including the healthcare industry. Digital transformation activities in healthcare domain includes pathology imagine analysis, remote patient monitoring through digital wearable devices, digital diagnostics, as well as digitalising *workflow planning*.

Workflows are often *cross-organisational*, especially in healthcare industry, which allow organisations to plan their business workflows across departments within the same organisations or even across multiple organisations. Cross-organisational workflows usually consists of multiple concurrent workflows

Partially supported by *Pathology services in the Western Norwegian Health Region – a center for applied digitization* and *SIRIUS – Centre for Scalable Data Access* (www.sirius-labs.no).

L. Bellatreche et al. (Eds.): MEDI 2021 Workshops, CCIS 1481, pp. 251–258, 2021.
https://doi.org/10.1007/978-3-030-87657-9_19

running in different departments within the same organisation, or in different organisations. For instance, the workflows of diagnosing patients in a clinic may involve a workflow of an external laboratory that examine patients' samples, and a workflow of a courier company transporting patients' samples between the laboratory and the clinic.

In addition, workflow planning usually requires domain-specific knowlege to achieve optimal resource allocation and task scheduling, which makes planning cross-organisational workflows particularly challenging. Furthermore, updating workflows is error-prone: one change in a workflow may result in significant changes in other concurrently running workflows, and a minor mistake could lead to substantial negative impacts, in particular in healthcare domain.

Although digitalising and automating *workflow planning* has been widely investigated, and tools like Process-Aware Information Systems (PAIS) [8] and Enterprise Resource Planning (ERP) systems have been developed to facilitate workflow planning, cross-organisational workflow planning remains a largely manual process as the current existing techniques and tools often lack domain-specific knowledge to support automation in workflow planning and updates.

In this position paper, we present a preliminary step towards automating cross-organisational workflow planning. We propose a resource sensitive formal modelling language $\mathcal{R}$PL with explicit notion of task dependency, which can be used to couple collaborative workflows by means of resources and task dependency. The language is inspired by ABS [12], an active object language [4] extending the Actor [3] model of concurrency with asynchronous method calls and synchronisation using futures. The actor-based concurrency model adopted in $\mathcal{R}$PL is used to capture the interactions between workflow activities in practice: for instance, a doctor can continue to perform treatment on a patient while waiting for laboratory results for the diagnosis of another patient.

The rest of the paper is organised as follows: Sect. 2 introduces the modelling language. Section 3 uses an example to show how the language can be used to model workflows in the healthcare domain. Section 4 briefly discusses the related work. Finally, we summarise the paper and discuss possible future work in Sect. 5.

2   A Resource-Aware Modelling Language

In this section we present a simple modelling language $\mathcal{R}$PL. The language has a Java-like syntax and actor-based concurrency model, and uses *cooperative* scheduling of method activations to explicitly control the internal interleaving of activities inside a concurrent object group, which can be picturised as a processor containing a set of objects.

We use the simple example presented in Fig. 1 to explain the language. The code snippet captures a simple diagnosis workflow

```
1  [Doctor ↦ 5, Nurse ↦ 7]
2  class Clinic() {
3    Pathology lab = new Pathology();
4      ...
5    Unit diagnose(Patient p) {
6      hold((Doctor,1), (Nurse,1));
7      ... // Check the patient
8      Fut<Int> f = lab!examine(p);
9      release((Doctor,1), (Nurse,1));
10     wait f?;
11     Int x = f.get;
12     hold((Doctor,1));
13     this.report(x) after f?; //Write report
14     release((Doctor,1));
15  }}
```

Fig. 1. Diagnosis in a clinic

$$P ::= R \ \overline{Cl} \ \{\overline{T \ x}; \ s\}$$
$$Cl ::= \textbf{class} \ C \ (\overline{T \ x}) \ \{\overline{T \ x}; \ \overline{M}\}$$
$$M ::= Sg \ \{\overline{T \ x}; \ s\}$$
$$Sg ::= T \ m(\overline{T \ x})$$
$$B ::= \textbf{Int} \mid \textbf{Bool} \mid \textbf{Unit} \mid C$$
$$T ::= B \mid F\langle B \rangle$$

$$e ::= x \mid g \mid \textbf{this}$$
$$g ::= b \mid e? \mid g \wedge g$$
$$s ::= x = rhs \mid \textbf{skip} \mid \textbf{if} \ e \ \{s\} \ \textbf{else} \ \{s\} \mid \textbf{while} \ e \ \{s\}$$
$$\mid \textbf{return} \ e \mid \textbf{wait}(g) \mid \textbf{hold} \ \overline{(r, e)} \mid \textbf{release} \ \overline{(r, e)}$$
$$\mid s \ ; \ s$$
$$rhs ::= e \mid \textbf{new} \ C(\overline{e}) \mid \textbf{new local} \ C(\overline{e}) \mid e.\textbf{get}$$
$$\mid e.m(\overline{e}) \ \textbf{after} \ \overline{e} \mid e!m(\overline{e}) \ \textbf{after} \ \overline{e?}$$

Fig. 2. Syntax of $\mathcal{R}$PL

in a clinic. While Line 1 models the available resources, the rest defines a class Clinic that diagnoses patients. A Doctor and a Nurse (resources) are first acquired on Line 6 before checking the patient p. After checking the patient, the doctor sends a sample to the lab for examination through an asynchronous method invocation on Line 8. While waiting for the lab to send back the result (Line 10), the resources are released such that they can diagnose the other patients (Line 9). When the result is ready and retrieved (Line 11), a doctor is acquired to write the report (Lines 12–13), and is released (Line 14) afterwards.

Figure 2 shows the syntax of the core language. A program P consists of resources R, a set of class declaration $\overline{Cl}$, plus a main method body. Resources R is a partial mapping which associates resource identities r to expressions e. Declarations of classes and methods are standard. The language supports basic types B, and *future* type $F\langle B \rangle$, which is similar to any explicit future construct. Statements s include assignments, conditionals, recursion, return, and sequential composition, which are standard. The **hold** and **release** statements handle resource acquisition and release. The **wait** statement releases the control of the processor until the guard g is fulfilled, which can be either a boolean expression or a resolved future. The right-hand side rhs of assignments includes guards g, variables x and self-identifier **this** as expressions e, creating new object in remote and local processors, and getting a future value. Objects in $\mathcal{R}$PL can communicate with each other either synchronously with $e.m(\overline{e})$ **after** $\overline{e?}$ or asynchronously $e!m(\overline{e})$ **after** $\overline{e?}$ *after* the futures $\overline{e}$ are resolved.

3 An Illustrative Example

This section presents a simple motivating example to explain how $\mathcal{R}$PL can be employed in modelling cross-organisational workflows in the healthcare domain. Figures 3 and 4 depict a cross-organisational workflow of handling patients upon their arrival in BPMN [18], which is consisting of three concurrently executing workflows. Figure 5 shows the workflow modelled in $\mathcal{R}$PL.

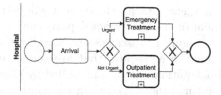

Fig. 3. Workflow of hospital admission

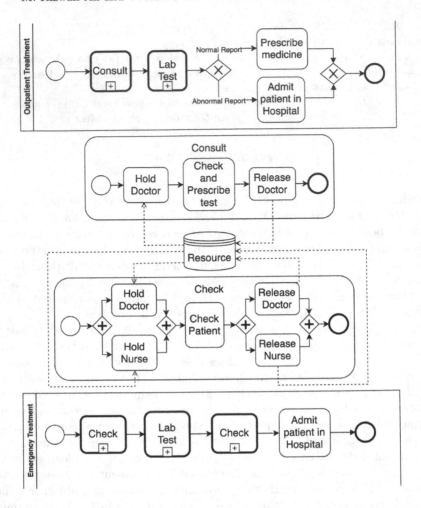

Fig. 4. Workflow of emergency department

Figure 3 shows the hospital admission workflow, which is modelled in $\mathcal{R}$PL by Lines 2–12 in Fig. 5. The workflow connects the ones in Emergency and Outpatient departments. When a patient arrives at the hospital, depending on the his/her emergency status, the patient will be forwarded to either the Emergency department or the Outpatient department.

Figure 4 illustrates the workflows in the Outpatient and Emergency departments in a hospital that are connected to a database containing the Resource information, which is modelled by Line 1 in $\mathcal{R}$PL in Fig. 5. The first box in Fig. 4 captures the workflow in the Outpatient department that performs Treatments to patients (modelled in $\mathcal{R}$PL by Lines 14–26 in Fig. 5). The Treatment workflow in Fig. 4 shows that doctor Consultation will be first provided to the patient (wrt. Line 20 in Fig. 5). Then, some prescribed tests will be made by the lab

```
1   [ Doctor ↦ 5 , Nurse ↦ 7]
2   class Hospital() {
3       Pathology lab = new Pathology( );
4       ED e = new ED(lab);
5       OPD o = new OPD(lab);
6       Unit arrival (Bool urgent) {
7           Fut<Int> f;
8           ... //check the status of the patient
9           if (urgent) { f = e!treat() after (); } // Send the patient to emergency department
10          else { f = o!treat() after (); } // Send the patient to outpatient department
11          wait (f?); Int x = f.get;}
12  }
13
14  class OPD(Pathology lab) {
15      Unit consult() { // Consultation
16          hold(Doctor, 1);
17          //Doctor check the patient and prescribe some test
18          release((Doctor, 1)); }
19      Unit treat() {
20          this.consult() after ();
21          Fut<Bool> g1 = lab!test() after ();
22          wait (g1)?;
23          Bool rep = g1.get;
24          if (rep) { ... } // Issue prescription and discharge the patient
25          else { ... }} // Admit patient in hospital
26  }
27
28  class ED(Pathology lab) {
29      Unit check(Int i, Int j) {
30          hold((Doctor, i),(Nurse, j));
31          // checking patient
32          release((Doctor, i),(Nurse, j));}
33      Unit treat() {
34          this.check(1,2) after ();
35          Fut<Bool> h1 = lab!test() after ();
36          wait (h1?);
37          Bool rep = h2.get;
38          this.check(1,1) after h1?;} // Admit patient in Hospital
39  }
```

Fig. 5. Merging emergency and outpatient department workflow

(wrt. Line 21 in Fig. 5).[1] Depending on the test result, the patient will either be given a prescription or be admitted to the hospital (wrt. Lines 24–25 in Fig. 5). Consultation is a sub-workflow of Treatment, depicted by the second box in Fig. 4, and modelled in $\mathcal{R}$PL by Lines 15–28 in Fig. 5. In this workflow, one Doctor will be acquired (wrt. Line 16 in Fig. 5) as a resource to check the patient and to prescribe necessary tests, and will be released (wrt. Line 18 in Fig. 5) afterwards.

The workflow of the Emergency department, captured by the last box in Fig. 4, performs Treatments to patients that are in emergency state. Lines 28–39 in Fig. 5 model this in $\mathcal{R}$PL. In this Treatment workflow, a preliminary health Check will be performed on the patient (wrt. Line 34 in Fig. 5). Then, some laboratory tests are made by LabTest (wrt. Line 35 in Fig. 5) followed by a second round of health Check (wrt. Line 38 in Fig. 5). Then, the patient is admitted to the hospital. Health Check is a sub-workflow of Treatment in Emergency department, depicted by the third box in Fig. 4, and modelled in $\mathcal{R}$PL by Lines 29–32 in Fig. 5.

---

[1] For simplicity, we do not show the workflow of test and its implementation.

In this workflow, one doctor and one nurse are allocated (Line 30 in Fig. 5) as resources to check a patient. They will be released (Line 32 in Fig. 5) at the end of the workflow so that they are available for other patients.

4   Related Work

Extensive research has been conducted in modelling business process workflow, for example, BPEL [16], BPMN [18], (coloured) Petri-Nets [1]. BPEL [16] and BPMN [18] have been developed to specify business processes to model workflow behaviour. While the former is an executable language allowing simulating process behaviour, the latter captures business process descriptions with a graphical notation. Research has been performed on formalising both BPEL as well as BPMN by means of (coloured) Petri-Nets [5,11]. Formal techniques based on e.g., pi-calculus [2,15], timed automata [10], CSP [19,20] have been developed to analyse and reason about models of business process workflows. Compared to our approach, the main focus of these techniques is on intra-organisational workflows and have limited support for coordinating tasks and resources in workflows that are across organisational.

Approaches have been proposed to merge business process models, e.g., [9] presents an approach to merge two business processes based on Event-driven Process Chains (EPCs) [17], which has been implemented in the process mining framework ProM [7], and [14] describes an operator that takes a pair of business processes as input and generates a configurable business process. To the best of our knowledge, these techniques do not consider connecting workflows across organisations.

In [21], the authors present a brief review of intra-organisational modeling techniques and propose two types of architectures, interaction models and routing approaches, to combine inter-organisational workflows. While the former proposes plans for cooperating processes to interact with each other, the latter provides assistance to route cross-organisational workflows in a uniform way.

An automated technique is proposed in [13] to merge collaborating processes in inter-organisational workflows. Instead of connecting those processes with resources and task dependency, the technique is composed of algorithms that connect the nodes of collaborating processes to produce an integrated process.

In contrast to the work discussed above, our work targets cross-organisational workflows involving multiple concurrent workflows from the collaborative partners, where a change in one workflows may have substantial impacts on the others through the resources that connect the workflows or through task dependency.

5   Conclusion

We have presented in this paper a formal language $\mathcal{R}$PL that can be employed to model cross-organisational workflows consisting of concurrently executing workflows. We use an example to show how the language can be used to capture the collaboration between workflows collaborate via resources and task dependency.

This language is the first step towards automating cross-organisational workflow planning. As for the immediate next steps, we plan to enrich the language such that the resource features, e.g., the experience and specialities can be explicitly specified. We also plan to develop a technique to associate workflow resources to ontology models. As for the long-term future work, we plan to develop analyses to estimate resource allocation and task scheduling, by e.g., constraint solving. Furthermore, we intend to develop verification techniques to ensure the correctness of workflow models in $\mathcal{R}$PL with respect to cross-organisational workflows. A natural starting point is to investigate how to extend KeY-ABS [6], a deductive verification tool for ABS, to support $\mathcal{R}$PL. We foresee that these analyses can eventually contribute to automating planning for cross-organisational workflows.

References

1. van der Aalst, W.M.P.: The application of Petri nets to workflow management. J. Circ. Syst. Comput. **8**(1), 21–66 (1998)
2. Abouzaid, F.: A mapping from pi-calculus into BPEL. In: International Conference on Concurrent Engineering. Frontiers in Artificial Intelligence and Applications, vol. 143, pp. 235–242. IOS Press (2006)
3. Agha, G.: Actors: A Model of Concurrent Computation in Distributed Systems. MIT Press, Cambridge (1986)
4. de Boer, F., et al.: A survey of active object languages. ACM Comput. Surv. **50**(5), 1–39 (2017)
5. Dijkman, R.M., Dumas, M., Ouyang, C.: Semantics and analysis of business process models in BPMN. Inf. Softw. Technol. **50**(12), 1281–1294 (2008)
6. Din, C.C., Bubel, R., Hähnle, R.: KeY-ABS: a deductive verification tool for the concurrent modelling language ABS. In: Felty, A.P., Middeldorp, A. (eds.) CADE 2015. LNCS (LNAI), vol. 9195, pp. 517–526. Springer, Cham (2015). https://doi.org/10.1007/978-3-319-21401-6_35
7. van Dongen, B.F., de Medeiros, A.K.A., Verbeek, H.M.W., Weijters, A.J.M.M., van der Aalst, W.M.P.: The ProM Framework: A New Era in Process Mining Tool Support. In: Ciardo, G., Darondeau, P. (eds.) ICATPN 2005. LNCS, vol. 3536, pp. 444–454. Springer, Heidelberg (2005). https://doi.org/10.1007/11494744_25
8. Dumas, M., van der Aalst, W.M.P., ter Hofstede, A.H.M.: Process-Aware Information Systems: Bridging People and Software Through Process Technology. Wiley, New York (2005)
9. Gottschalk, F., van der Aalst, W.M.P., Jansen-Vullers, M.H.: Merging event-driven process chains. In: Meersman, R., Tari, Z. (eds.) OTM 2008. LNCS, vol. 5331, pp. 418–426. Springer, Heidelberg (2008). https://doi.org/10.1007/978-3-540-88871-0_28
10. Gruhn, V., Laue, R.: Using timed model checking for verifying workflows. In: Cordeiro, J., Filipe, J. (eds.) Computer Supported Activity Coordination, Proceedings of the 2nd International Workshop on Computer Supported Activity Coordination, pp. 75–88. INSTICC Press (2005)
11. Hinz, S., Schmidt, K., Stahl, C.: Transforming BPEL to Petri nets. In: van der Aalst, W.M.P., Benatallah, B., Casati, F., Curbera, F. (eds.) BPM 2005. LNCS, vol. 3649, pp. 220–235. Springer, Heidelberg (2005). https://doi.org/10.1007/11538394_15

12. Johnsen, E.B., Hähnle, R., Schäfer, J., Schlatte, R., Steffen, M.: ABS: A core language for abstract behavioral specification. In: Aichernig, B.K., de Boer, F.S., Bonsangue, M.M. (eds.) FMCO 2010. LNCS, vol. 6957, pp. 142–164. Springer, Heidelberg (2011). https://doi.org/10.1007/978-3-642-25271-6_8
13. Kunchala, J., Yu, J., Yongchareon, S., Liu, C.: An approach to merge collaborating processes of an inter-organizational business process for artifact lifecycle synthesis. Computing **102**(4), 951–976 (2019). https://doi.org/10.1007/s00607-019-00770-z
14. La Rosa, M., Dumas, M., Uba, R., Dijkman, R.: Merging business process models. In: Meersman, R., Dillon, T., Herrero, P. (eds.) OTM 2010. LNCS, vol. 6426, pp. 96–113. Springer, Heidelberg (2010). https://doi.org/10.1007/978-3-642-16934-2_10
15. Lucchi, R., Mazzara, M.: A pi-calculus based semantics for WS-BPEL. J. Log. Algebraic Methods Program. **70**(1), 96–118 (2007)
16. Matjaz, J.B., Mathew, P.S.: Business Process Execution Language for Web Services BPEL and BPEL4WS. Packt Publishing, Birmingham (2006)
17. Mendling, J.: Event-driven process chains (EPC). In: Metrics for Process Models. LNBIP, vol. 6, pp. 17–57. Springer, Heidelberg (2008). https://doi.org/10.1007/978-3-540-89224-3_2
18. Object Management Group: Business Process Modeling Notation (BPMN) version 2.0 (2011)
19. Wong, P.Y.H., Gibbons, J.: A process semantics for BPMN. In: Liu, S., Maibaum, T., Araki, K. (eds.) ICFEM 2008. LNCS, vol. 5256, pp. 355–374. Springer, Heidelberg (2008). https://doi.org/10.1007/978-3-540-88194-0_22
20. Wong, P.Y.H., Gibbons, J.: Property specifications for workflow modelling. Sci. Comput. Program. **76**(10), 942–967 (2011)
21. Xu, L., Liu, H., Wang, S., Wang, K.: Modelling and analysis techniques for cross-organizational workflow systems. Syst. Res. Behav. Sci. Off. J. Int. Fed. Syst. Res. **26**(3), 367–389 (2009)

Systematic Literature Review of Methods for Maintaining Data Integrity

Marten Kask[(✉)], Gunnar Piho, and Peeter Ross

Tallinn University of Technology, Tallinn, Estonia
{marten.kask,gunnar.piho,peeter.ross}@taltech.ee

Abstract. Diverse data is collected in health care for secondary usage. However, this data is collected by various parties and processed by numerous information systems. Hence, to get reliable results, the data integrity must be maintained. This paper aims to discover applications that are introduced to ensure the integrity of the data collected in different fields including the medical field. The Systematic Literature Review method is used in this research to map the appropriate methods for future studies.

Keywords: Data integrity · Systematic literature review · Health data

1 Introduction

There are various health data collected that are processed by several information systems. The data includes patients' privacy [15,28] and as it is subsequently processed to provide medical care, including making diagnoses and for research purposes. It is defined that data integrity measures sanity of the data, i.e., it is originated from a legitimate source [6] and is reliable and trustworthy [17].

Integrity is also one of the CIA (Confidentiality, Integrity, Availability) triads where the system attacks are usually targeted [36]. When the integrity is attacked, generally content of the data is changed for the benefit of the attacker. Furthermore, it is important to address the issues of maintaining data integrity as it can remain undetected and therefore, affect the entire dataset [10]. These aspects describe well why it is necessary to maintain the data integrity to get reliable results. Therefore, the purpose of this review is to discover methods that are described for maintaining the integrity of the collected data that could be taken as a basis for the future research.

2 Systematic Literature Review Process

Basis of this review is the instructions composed by Kitchenham and Charters [13]. According to the guidelines, the three phases of the review described below were followed.

© Springer Nature Switzerland AG 2021
L. Bellatreche et al. (Eds.): MEDI 2021 Workshops, CCIS 1481, pp. 259–268, 2021.
https://doi.org/10.1007/978-3-030-87657-9_20

1. Step: Planning the Review. In this stage, the following research question was formulated:

RQ1: What methods are used to maintain data integrity?
In addition, the reviewing protocol was conducted with the following details:

- covered years: 01/2019-02/2021
- selected digital libraries: IEEExplore and ACM Digital Library
- keyword to search: "data integrity"
- studies to select: full-text studies in English

These covered years, libraries and keyword were selected for the time being to initiate the research. A broader study is planned in the future.

2. Step: Conducting the Review. In the beginning, IEEExplore returned 1261 and ACM Digital Library 598 results. After reviewing the studies by abstracts, 113 articles were initially selected. In the next step, the full texts were examined to identify duplicates and exclude papers that are too distinct from the research objectives (e.g., were mainly focusing on integrity on some technical component's data). Also, some not specifically health data related studies were included for analyzing in the future whether the technology could be adapted for health data as well. Finally, 33 articles were selected to be analyzed and synthesized further.

3. Step: Reporting the Review. In the last step, the results that are outlined in the upcoming sections were reported.

3 Results

The concluding selection of literature is provided in Table 1. In addition, it is generally characterized according to the research question which method for maintaining the integrity was used and which data domain was examined. As noticeable, the majority of the researches describe blockchain-based solutions, i.e., applications that base on a distributed data structure that is used to store information that cannot be deleted or modified [18]. However, there are several other methods that are further examined in the following sections.

Table 1. Selection of literature.

Article	Library	Characteristic	Domain
Patil et al. (2020) [21]	IEEExplore	Blockchain	Undefined
Li et al. (2020) [16]	IEEExplore	Blockchain	Undefined
Shu et al. (2021) [29]	IEEExplore	Blockchain	Undefined outsourced data
Reniers et al. (2020) [24]	ACM Digital Library	Blockchain	Undefined
Wibowo et al. (2019) [36]	IEEExplore	Blockchain	Local Tax Big Data
Sivagnanam et al. (2019) [30]	ACM Digital Library	Blockchain	Research data
Ramkumar (2019) [23]	IEEExplore	Blockchain	Undefined
Cherupally et al. (2021) [5]	IEEExplore	Blockchain	Internet of Things
Manu et al. (2020) [17]	IEEExplore	Blockchain	Sensor data
Morano et al. (2019) [18]	IEEExplore	Blockchain	Vehicle driver data
Wang et al. (2020) [33]	ACM Digital Library	Blockchain	Undefined
Kanimozhi et al. (2019) [10]	IEEExplore	Blockchain	Undefined
Yang et al. (2020) [37]	ACM Digital Library	Blockchain	Undefined
Kim et al. (2021) [12]	ACM Digital Library	Blockchain	A personal information-sharing model
Al-Abbasi et al. (2019) [3]	IEEExplore	Blockchain	Undefined
Sun et al. (2020) [31]	IEEExplore	Blockchain	Electronic Medical Record
Ismail et al. (2020) [7]	IEEExplore	Blockchain	Electronic Health Record
Ismail et al. (2020) [8]	IEEExplore	Blockchain	Electronic Health Record
Rituraj et al. (2020) [25]	IEEExplore	Blockchain	Electronic Health Record
Ashraf Uddin et al. (2020) [4]	ACM Digital Library	Blockchain	Electronic Health Record
Nirjhor et al. (2021) [19]	IEEExplore	Blockchain	Electronic Health Record
Ajay et al. (2020) [2]	IEEExplore	Blockchain	Electronic Health Record
Jabbar et al. (2020) [9]	IEEExplore	Blockchain	Electronic Health Record
Rahman et al. (2019) [22]	ACM Digital Library	Blockchain	Electronic Health Record
Koscina et al. (2019) [14]	ACM Digital Library	Blockchain	Health Data
Wang et al. (2019) [35]	IEEExplore	Blockchain	Personal Health Record
Roisum et al. (2019) [26]	IEEExplore	Fake data insertion	Undefined
Wang et al. (2020) [34]	IEEExplore	Privacy-preserving publicly verifiable databases	Undefined
Abu Rayyan et al. (2019) [1]	ACM Digital Library	Automatic auditing mechanism	End-user data
Parthiban et al. (2019) [20]	IEEExplore	Additional auditing algorithm	Enterprise Resource Planning
Verma et al. (2020) [32]	IEEExplore	Cryptography	e-Healthcare Monitoring System
Kim et al. (2019) [11]	IEEExplore	Keyless signatures infrastructure	Precision Medicine System
Shekhawat et al. (2019) [27]	IEEExplore	Encryption	Big Data in the cloud-based environment

3.1 Blockchain-Based Solutions

Several studies described application where the issue of improving the preservation of integrity for data stored in the cloud. For example, Patil et al. [21] introduced a cloud-based data provenance framework that uses blockchain to trace data record operations. They developed an application for storing confidential files using the Ethereum blockchain. It logs the provenance data, and its hash is stored on an Ethereum based distributed ledger. Other authors [16] have presented IntegrityChain, a decentralized outsourced storage framework that is intended for assuring data confidentiality and integrity at the same time. These authors addressed the importance of remote-stored data because the data owners lose physical control over their data when outsourcing their storage.

What is more, Shu et al. [29] have proposed a blockchain-based decentralized public auditing scheme to replace a centralized third-party auditor that is generally used to verify the outsourced data integrity on behalf of users. A protocol for auditable data sharing that uses blockchain has been written [24]. Yet, it is highlighted that the limitation of that protocol is a need for data owners to be online and respond to requests for obtaining decryption keys.

Various researches have been conducted to enhance data security in big data analysis. Wibowo and Sandikapura [36] have analyzed the blockchain-based Local Tax Big Data analysis focusing on maintaining the level of trust in data validity. They concluded that the blockchain implementation is suitable for the Local Tax Big Data as data security and even interoperability. Another approach is provided in work related to the protection of integrity and provenance of research data [30]. Open Science Chain project has been introduced to provide a framework for tracking and verifying independently scientific data regardless of the domain. After researchers log information about their scientific data, an immutable proof of storing the data is created when its unique identifiers and ownership info are stored on the blockchain. This application also allows other researchers to verify the authenticity of the data. There are blockchain-based frameworks to maintain data integrity for the large-scale real-world information systems presented as well [23].

Additionally, the importance of integrity verification is essential for IoT devices, as well as its applications, use data stored in a cloud [5]. However, IoT devices have more advanced requirements for data processing due to their low storage and computational ability. This is not fully aligned with the blockchain attributes that require some computational power. Thus, DAG (Directed Acyclic Graph) based distributed ledger technology-based solution is proposed that is more lightweight and scalable compared to the usual blockchain solutions. Furthermore, there is integrity verification explicitly included for its cloud-stored data. One body area sensor network-related study [17] has introduced blockchain to avoid aggregated sensor data from being tampered. However, the other study [18] has analyzed the blockchain technology to be used for storing vehicle driver data. Further research [33] has demonstrated a lightweight blockchain system vChain to ensure query integrity where it is not necessary to maintain a full copy of the blockchain. Data integrity has been addressed in the fields of cloud and fog computing as well, where blockchain has been integrated to detect data corruption at the time of occurrence instead of explicit verification requests [10].

To improve data integrity even further, a solution that combines secure multi-party computation with the blockchain has been described in research [37]. When recommending blockchain for guaranteeing data integrity [12], it is mentioned that data standardization should be further studied to handle data integrity in an integrated manner. In addition, there have been further reviews that address the blockchain security architecture [3].

Blockchain-Based Health Data Integrity Solutions. Because of the sensitive nature of health data, improvement of its integrity has been a topic for a number of blockchain-related studies. J. Sun et al. [31] have constructed secure storage and efficient sharing of electronic medical records in IPFS (InterPlanetary File System) using blockchain technology. It provides efficient access control for EHRs (electronic health record) so that the private data is not accessible for unauthorized persons. IPFS is used to ensure the secure storage of the records, and blockchain technology ensures originality and traceability of the data. Another blockchain-based health records management is BlockHR [7,8]. Blockchain is used in this context to support carrying out tracking activities related to false billing, forged diagnostics, and data breaches. Besides, distributed nature of the blockchain is used to maintain the newest information about a patient in each participating hospital. It uses the permissioned network Hyperledger Fabric.

Blockchain is introduced in a cloud-based secure personal health record management system proposed by Rituraj and Naveen Kumar [25]. They approach the necessity of the integrity to deny health care providers accessing and modifying personal health records after they have finalized providing the service. Uddin and Stranieri et al. [4] have analyzed several different types of health record repositories and have outlined that blockchain-based system does not allow unauthorized access because of patient-driven data management. Moreover, if the health data is shared cross border, its confidentiality and integrity are still maintained. In another electronic medical record associated work [19], data integrity has been achieved by using blockchain-based two-factor authorization.

Wider scope of medical data is discussed in a study [2] that proposes a secure architecture for inter-healthcare EHR exchange. They describe a blockchain-based (Ethereum) architecture that detects and avoids malicious activities. Integrity and consistency of health record requests and responses are verified. It is also summarized that many other types of research have been focusing on single health records, but the proposed inter-healthcare system concentrates on security when there are two or more healthcare systems involved. BiiMED is a blockchain (Ethereum) based framework, "Enhancing Data Interoperability and Integrity in regard to EHR sharing" is introduced by Jabbar et al. [9]. That solution uses a decentralized trusted third-party auditor to guarantee data integrity.

An architecture for tamper-proof EHR management system that uses blockchain is described in [22]. This approach differs from others as instead of creating a new blockchain-based system, it introduces a wrapper layer named "blockchain handshaker" between the existing system and a public blockchain network to reduce costs. Additional architecture is introduced in [14] that gives an overview of a federated blockchain-based architecture stated to be GDPR compliant. A distributed architecture for personal health record sharing with data integrity verifiable is described in a study [35] where hash values of personal health records are stored in blockchain. To improve the data integrity verification efficiency, dedicated smart contracts are proposed.

3.2   Other Solutions

Besides blockchain, other solutions have been introduced to protect data integrity as well. It is presented that some fake semantic data can be inserted before outsourcing information to the cloud [26]. This data is generated deterministically but is semantically indistinguishable. Also, as the fake data can be regenerated by functions, there is no need to store it by data owners locally. The privacy-preserving publicly verifiable database has presented [34] to be a solution that guarantees integrity and privacy of queried results.

A strategy to bring the data integrity to end-users [1] is described by Abu-Rayyan et al. They propose an automatic auditing mechanism that monitors database activities and stores an integrity loss rate associated with the database. These rates would be made accessible to the end-users who can use them for decision-making. It is also proposed that on top of existing data auditing algorithms, another CampusStack algorithm could be implemented to improve integrity [20].

Another approach is presented in a study [32] that describes public key cryptography and identity-based public key cryptography for maintaining integrity in e-healthcare monitoring system. Using Keyless Signatures Infrastructure has been proposed for a precision medicine system to validate integrity [11]. One paper described three techniques to be used to maintain the integrity of big data in the cloud: homomorphic encryption, order-preserving encryption schemes and attribute-based encryption [27].

4   Conclusion and Future Work

At the beginning of this paper, the importance of health data integrity is addressed leading to the conduction of this systematic literature review. Guidelines composed by Kitchenham and Charters were followed while composing this research: research question was formulated, and review protocol created.

It was determined that there are many blockchain-based solutions studied. However, these solutions tend to differ from each other, e.g., some of the applications are aimed at devices that require solutions that use lightweight computing. On the other hand, others are aimed at a more specific fields like healthcare.

In addition to the blockchain, some other methods for maintaining data integrity have been researched. Basically, there are solutions that use cryptography or some data auditing algorithm. Furthermore, there are specific tools developed too, for example, privacy-preserving publicly verifiable databases or inserting fake data into the cloud.

Moreover, it can be outlined that the amount of health care data-related studies which are related to data integrity confirm the importance of the topic.

Also, one research openly stated that most researches related to health data integrity tend to focus on single records rather than set-ups where two or more healthcare systems are involved.

Thus, it is worth aiming for the concepts of two and more healthcare systems in future research when health data integrity is considered. This paper is also limited with a small number of libraries; thus in the prospective studies, PubMed, SpringerLink and Science Direct should be considered in the earlier years. In addition, it is planned to discover other relevant systematic literature reviews, compare and analyze the findings. Many papers covered in this literature review had a low TRL (technology readiness level). Hence, in future works, the TRL of the each analyzed study should be determined, and then it can be focused on researching more advanced solutions.

Acknowledgments. This work has been partially conducted in the project "ICT programme" which was supported by the European Union through the European Social Fund.

References

1. Abu Rayyan, L., Hacid, H., Leoncé, A.: Towards an end-user layer for data integrity. In: IEEE/WIC/ACM International Conference on Web Intelligence, WI 2019, pp. 317–320. Association for Computing Machinery, New York (2019). https://doi.org/10.1145/3350546.3352538
2. Ajayi, O., Abouali, M., Saadawi, T.: Secure architecture for inter-healthcare electronic health records exchange. In: 2020 IEEE International IOT, Electronics and Mechatronics Conference (IEMTRONICS), pp. 1–6 (2020). https://doi.org/10.1109/IEMTRONICS51293.2020.9216336
3. Al-Abbasi, L., El-Medany, W.: Blockchain security architecture: a review technology platform, security strength and weakness. In: 2nd Smart Cities Symposium (SCS 2019), pp. 1–5 (2019). https://doi.org/10.1049/cp.2019.0190
4. Ashraf Uddin, M., Stranieri, A., Gondal, I., Balasubramanian, V.: Dynamically recommending repositories for health data: a machine learning model. In: Proceedings of the Australasian Computer Science Week Multiconference. ACSW 2020, Association for Computing Machinery, New York (2020). https://doi.org/10.1145/3373017.3373041
5. Cherupally, S.R., Boga, S., Podili, P., Kataoka, K.: Lightweight and scalable DAG based distributed ledger for verifying IoT data integrity. In: 2021 International Conference on Information Networking (ICOIN), pp. 267–272 (2021). https://doi.org/10.1109/ICOIN50884.2021.9334000
6. Garagad, V.G., Iyer, N.C., Wali, H.G.: Data integrity: a security threat for internet of things and cyber-physical systems. In: 2020 International Conference on Computational Performance Evaluation (ComPE), pp. 244–249 (2020). https://doi.org/10.1109/ComPE49325.2020.9200170
7. Ismail, L., Materwala, H.: BlockHR: a blockchain-based framework for health records management. In: Proceedings of the 12th International Conference on Computer Modeling and Simulation, ICCMS 2020, pp. 164–168. Association for Computing Machinery, New York (2020). https://doi.org/10.1145/3408066.3408106

8. Ismail, L., Materwala, H., Khan, M.A.: Performance evaluation of a patient-centric blockchain-based healthcare records management framework. In: Proceedings of the 2020 2nd International Electronics Communication Conference, IECC 2020, pp. 39–50. Association for Computing Machinery, New York (2020). https://doi.org/10.1145/3409934.3409941

9. Jabbar, R., Fetais, N., Krichen, M., Barkaoui, K.: Blockchain technology for healthcare: enhancing shared electronic health record interoperability and integrity. In: 2020 IEEE International Conference on Informatics, IoT, and Enabling Technologies (ICIoT), pp. 310–317 (2020). https://doi.org/10.1109/ICIoT48696.2020.9089570

10. Kanimozhi, E.A., Suguna, M., Mercy Shalini, S.: Immediate detection of data corruption by integrating blockchain in cloud computing. In: 2019 International Conference on Vision Towards Emerging Trends in Communication and Networking (ViTECoN), pp. 1–4 (2019). https://doi.org/10.1109/ViTECoN.2019.8899394

11. Kim, D., Jo, J., Kwak, J.: KSI based sensitive data integrity validation method for precision medicine system. In: 2019 International Conference on Platform Technology and Service (PlatCon), pp. 1–5 (2019). https://doi.org/10.1109/PlatCon.2019.8668964

12. Kim, J., Kim, M.: Intelligent mediator-based enhanced smart contract for privacy protection. ACM Trans. Internet Technol. **21**(1) (2021). https://doi.org/10.1145/3404892

13. Kitchenham, B., Charters, S.: Guidelines for performing systematic literature reviews in software engineering (2007)

14. Koscina, M., Manset, D., Negri Ribalta, C., Perez, O.: Enabling trust in healthcare data exchange with a federated blockchain-based architecture. In: IEEE/WIC/ACM International Conference on Web Intelligence - Companion Volume, WI 2019 Companion, pp. 231–237. Association for Computing Machinery, New York (2019). https://doi.org/10.1145/3358695.3360897

15. Lai, C., Wan, J., Zheng, D.: Dual privacy-preserving health data aggregation scheme assisted by medical edge computing. In: 2020 IEEE/CIC International Conference on Communications in China (ICCC), pp. 154–159 (2020). https://doi.org/10.1109/ICCC49849.2020.9238932

16. Li, Y., Yu, Y., Chen, R., Du, X., Guizani, M.: IntegrityChain: provable data possession for decentralized storage. IEEE J. Sel. Areas Commun. **38**(6), 1205–1217 (2020). https://doi.org/10.1109/JSAC.2020.2986664

17. Manu, S.R., Bhaskar, G.: Securing sensitive data in body area sensor network using blockchain technique. In: 2020 5th International Conference on Communication and Electronics Systems (ICCES), pp. 1–5 (2020). https://doi.org/10.1109/ICCES48766.2020.9137912

18. Morano, F., Ferretti, C., Leporati, A., Napoletano, P., Schettini, R.: A blockchain technology for protection and probative value preservation of vehicle driver data. In: 2019 IEEE 23rd International Symposium on Consumer Technologies (ISCT), pp. 167–172 (2019). https://doi.org/10.1109/ISCE.2019.8900982

19. Nirjhor, M.K.I., Yousuf, M.A., Mhaboob, M.S.: Electronic medical record data sharing through authentication and integrity management. In: 2021 2nd International Conference on Robotics, Electrical and Signal Processing Techniques (ICREST), pp. 308–313 (2021). https://doi.org/10.1109/ICREST51555.2021.9331010

20. Parthiban, K., Nataraj, R.V.: An efficient architecture to ensure data integrity in ERP systems. In: 2019 5th International Conference on Advanced Computing Communication Systems (ICACCS), pp. 236–241 (2019). https://doi.org/10.1109/ICACCS.2019.8728352

21. Patil, A., Jha, A., Mulla, M.M., Narayan, D.G., Kengond, S.: Data provenance assurance for cloud storage using blockchain. In: 2020 International Conference on Advances in Computing, Communication Materials (ICACCM), pp. 443–448 (2020). https://doi.org/10.1109/ICACCM50413.2020.9213032

22. Rahman, M.S., Khalil, I., Mahawaga Arachchige, P.C., Bouras, A., Yi, X.: A novel architecture for tamper proof electronic health record management system using blockchain wrapper. In: Proceedings of the 2019 ACM International Symposium on Blockchain and Secure Critical Infrastructure, BSCI 2019, pp. 97–105. Association for Computing Machinery, New York (2019). https://doi.org/10.1145/3327960.3332392

23. Ramkumar, M.: A blockchain based framework for information system integrity. China Commun. **16**(6), 1–17 (2019). https://doi.org/10.23919/JCC.2019.06.001

24. Reniers, V., et al.: Authenticated and auditable data sharing via smart contract. In: Proceedings of the 35th Annual ACM Symposium on Applied Computing, SAC 2020, pp. 324–331. Association for Computing Machinery, New York (2020). https://doi.org/10.1145/3341105.3373957

25. Kumar, N.: Cloud-based secure personal health record management system using mixnode and blockchain. In: 2020 Fourth World Conference on Smart Trends in Systems, Security and Sustainability (WorldS4), pp. 70–75 (2020). https://doi.org/10.1109/WorldS450073.2020.9210317

26. Roisum, H., Urizar, L., Yeh, J., Salisbury, K., Magette, M.: Completeness integrity protection for outsourced databases using semantic fake data. In: 2019 4th International Conference on Communication and Information Systems (ICCIS), pp. 222–228 (2019). https://doi.org/10.1109/ICCIS49662.2019.00046

27. Shekhawat, H., Sharma, S., Koli, R.: Privacy-preserving techniques for big data analysis in cloud. In: 2019 Second International Conference on Advanced Computational and Communication Paradigms (ICACCP), pp. 1–6 (2019). https://doi.org/10.1109/ICACCP.2019.8882922

28. Shrivastava, S., Srikanth, T.K., Dileep, V.S.: E-governance for healthcare service delivery in india: challenges and opportunities in security and privacy. In: Proceedings of the 13th International Conference on Theory and Practice of Electronic Governance, ICEGOV 2020, pp. 180–183. Association for Computing Machinery, New York (2020). https://doi.org/10.1145/3428502.3428527

29. Shu, J., Zou, X., Jia, X., Zhang, W., Xie, R.: Blockchain-based decentralized public auditing for cloud storage. IEEE Trans. Cloud Comput. (2021). https://doi.org/10.1109/TCC.2021.3051622

30. Sivagnanam, S., Nandigam, V., Lin, K.: Introducing the open science chain: Protecting integrity and provenance of research data. In: Proceedings of the Practice and Experience in Advanced Research Computing on Rise of the Machines (Learning), PEARC 2019. Association for Computing Machinery, New York (2019). https://doi.org/10.1145/3332186.3332203

31. Sun, J., Yao, X., Wang, S., Wu, Y.: Blockchain-based secure storage and access scheme for electronic medical records in IPFS. IEEE Access **8**, 59389–59401 (2020). https://doi.org/10.1109/ACCESS.2020.2982964

32. Verma, G.K., Singh, B.B., Kumar, N., Kaiwartya, O., Obaidat, M.S.: PFCBAS: Pairing free and provable certificate-based aggregate signature scheme for the e-healthcare monitoring system. IEEE Syst. J. **14**(2), 1704–1715 (2020). https://doi.org/10.1109/JSYST.2019.2921788
33. Wang, H., Xu, C., Zhang, C., Xu, J.: Vchain: A blockchain system ensuring query integrity. In: Proceedings of the 2020 ACM SIGMOD International Conference on Management of Data. SIGMOD 2020, pp. 2693–2696. Association for Computing Machinery, New York (2020).https://doi.org/10.1145/3318464.3384682
34. Wang, Q., Zhou, F., Zhou, B., Xu, J., Chen, C., Wang, Q.: Privacy-preserving publicly verifiable databases. IEEE Trans. Dependable and Secur. Comput. (2020). https://doi.org/10.1109/TDSC.2020.3032961
35. Wang, S., Zhang, D., Zhang, Y.: Blockchain-based personal health records sharing scheme with data integrity verifiable. IEEE Access **7**, 102887–102901 (2019). https://doi.org/10.1109/ACCESS.2019.2931531
36. Wibowo, S., Sandikapura, T.: Improving data security, interoperability, and veracity using blockchain for one data governance, case study of local tax big data. In: 2019 International Conference on ICT for Smart Society (ICISS), vol. 7, pp. 1–6 (2019). https://doi.org/10.1109/ICISS48059.2019.8969805
37. Yang, Y., Wei, L., Wu, J., Long, C.: Block-SMPC: a blockchain-based secure multi-party computation for privacy-protected data sharing. In: Proceedings of the 2020 The 2nd International Conference on Blockchain Technology, ICBCT 2020, pp. 46–51. Association for Computing Machinery, New York (2020). https://doi.org/10.1145/3390566.3391664

Medical Data Engineering – Theory and Practice

Ann-Kristin Kock-Schoppenhauer[1]([✉]), Björn Schreiweis[2], Hannes Ulrich[1],
Niklas Reimer[3], Joshua Wiedekopf[1], Benjamin Kinast[2], Hauke Busch[3],
Björn Bergh[2], and Josef Ingenerf[1,4]

[1] IT Center of Clinical Research, Universität zu Lübeck, 23562 Lübeck, Germany
ann-kristin.kock@uksh.de
[2] Institute for Medical Informatics and Statistics, Kiel University and University
Hospital Schleswig-Holstein, 24114 Kiel, Germany
[3] Lübeck Institute of Experimental Dermatology, Universität zu Lübeck
and University Hospital Schleswig-Holstein, 23562 Lübeck, Germany
[4] Institute of Medical Informatics, Universität zu Lübeck, 23562 Lübeck, Germany

Abstract. Data integration and exchange are becoming more crucial
with the increasing amount of distributed systems and ever-growing
amounts of data. This need is also widely known in medical research
and not yet comprehensively solved. Practical implementation steps
will demonstrate the different challenges in the context of the National
Medical Informatics Initiative in Germany. Top-down versus bottom-
up approaches as general methods of standard-based data integration
in healthcare will be discussed and illustrated in the process of building up Medical Data Integration Centers. As practical examples, the use
cases Infection Control, Cardiology, and Molecular Tumor Board, will be
presented. Finally, limitations that prevent the use of theoretically recommended data integration methods in the particular field of medical
informatics are illustrated.

Keywords: Data integration · Medical informatics · Data
management

1 Introduction

The rapid development of emerging information technologies like mobile wear-
ables causes enormous growth in the amount of generated data in several application areas. As the number of interconnected application systems expands, so does
the demand for data exchange. This fact also applies in medicine, but unique characteristics lead to particular challenges where IT applications are needed for both
routine care and academic research and a link between these areas. Supporting
healthcare professionals in a wide range of facilities ensuring routine care, mainly
by operating a hospital information system (HIS) with numerous networked specialized subsystems, is referred to as *eHealth*. The provision of an electronic medical record (EMR) at the clinical workplace using an EMR system is of central importance. Alternatively, the term electronic health record (EHR) is used,

© Springer Nature Switzerland AG 2021
L. Bellatreche et al. (Eds.): MEDI 2021 Workshops, CCIS 1481, pp. 269–284, 2021.
https://doi.org/10.1007/978-3-030-87657-9_21

including additional data, e.g., from other subsystems or even inter-institutional applications. In basic research on physiological and pathological processes, taking into account all interconnected levels of the organism (molecule, cell, tissue, organ, organism, population), medical knowledge is continuously growing. Special disciplines in *Biomedical informatics* such as medical image processing, bioinformatics, or systems medicine develop innovative IT solutions to support diagnostics and therapy with the goal of precision medicine. *Medical Informatics* covers and connects the two specialized fields by building bridges in both directions: On the one hand, making innovative approaches available at the point of care. On the other hand, Medical Informatics provides real-world data across sites for conducting biomedical research, i.e., multi-centric observational studies or enabling approaches using methods from artificial intelligence or machine learning [1]. Working in the healthcare sector with health data poses different challenges depending on the respective focus. Healthcare systems are tailored to national regulations with complex, constantly changing requirements, mainly addressing economic pressure. Administrative purposes dominate characteristics of EHR data, and a wide range of specialized data, e.g., vital signs or medication found siloed in subsystems [2]. Healthcare organizations rely for legal and security reasons on clinical application systems based on proprietary database schemes, resulting in vendor lock-ins. Moreover, almost half of the hospitals in Germany still use paper-based records as their primary type of documentation, with respect to Hübner et al. [3]. Data from source systems must be harmonized and standardized using appropriate data models and terminologies if they are to be used for research [4,5]. Phenotype and genotype data is complex, in part because of individual biological variability and rapidly expanding biological and medical knowledge [6]. Using standardized descriptions for intricate concepts quickly involves several hundred vocabularies and biomedical ontologies, each offering massive granularity [7,8]. Compared to industry and other application areas, data are not provided willingly by customers and delivered directly in cloud solutions of internet companies. There are privacy, ethical, and legal constraints in healthcare when patient data are going to be reused for research purposes. This adds additional privacy, ethical, and legal constraints when reusing healthcare data for research [9]. To address these issues, a broad consent for the patient's allowance to reuse data and biosamples for later yet unknown research purposes, data sharing regulations, and use/access committees for controlling questions of ownership, intellectual property, and proper utilization will need to be established. These and other challenges are being elaborated in the national Medical Informatics Initiative (MII) described in Sect. 3, a project of the Federal Ministry of Education and Research (BMBF) combining forces of all German university hospitals to harmonize and standardize data models in order to establish federated IT infrastructures for clinical research [10]. Medical Data Engineering, an increasingly used term in the Big Data era, encompasses the mentioned aspects for the integrated provision of standardized data under consideration of ethical and data protection-related restrictions. Innovative methods of medical data analysis based on this infrastructure are also elaborated but only mentioned in the descriptions of the use cases.

2   Top-Down- and Bottom-Up-Approaches

Any healthcare data exchange across multiple sites is significantly hindered by autonomously developed, non-interoperable IT systems, which use proprietary data formats and interfaces. Interoperability is broadly defined as "the ability of two or more systems or components to exchange information and to use the information that has been exchanged" [11]. Given the sheer number of specialized application systems and the high volume of (mutable) transactions required, bilateral data integration results in a complete graph. Therefore, a star-shaped network topology in Fig. 1 enables a twofold reduction in complexity:

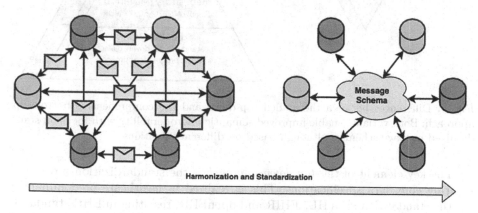

Fig. 1. Data exchange based on standardized message-schema as common lingua franca. Given the number of specialized application systems and the high volume of (mutable) transactions required, bilateral data integration results in a complete graph. Therefore, a star-shaped network topology enables a twofold reduction in complexity: *Technical interoperability* by using interface engines as message-based middleware, the number of interfaces can be reduced from $\binom{6}{2} = 15$ down to 6. Healthcare IT vendors favor a high degree of autonomy, enabled by asynchronous middleware [12]. *Semantic interoperability* in order to reliably interpret exchanged content, standardized message schemes, equipped with standard terminologies, are used as common lingua franca [13].

Older standards still used in healthcare today, such as HL7 v2 for clinical data, DICOM for images, or IEEE 11073 for device data, provide applicable messaging protocols on the technical level but are hardly suited to solve semantic interoperability requirements due to underspecified messaging schemes, e.g., with many optionalities and neglected standard terminologies [13]. More recently, internationally advanced standards such as HL7 FHIR (Fast Healthcare Interoperability Ressources) or openEHR are used for specifying the enormous variety and granularity of medical content by constrained information models with linkages to standard terminologies such as SNOMED CT. Tools including powerful terminology servers are available to validate communicated content according to the specifications [13]. Against this background, two approaches to harmonizing medical data can be distinguished, both of which have their raison d'être: *top-down* versus *bottom-up*, see Fig. 2.

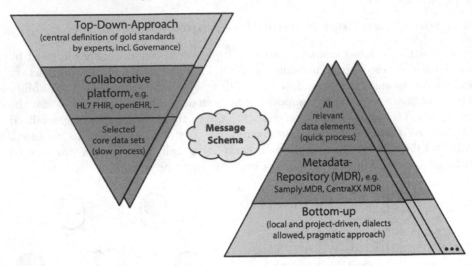

Fig. 2. Differences between the guided top-down and the comprehensive bottom-up approach. Both variants enable improved semantic interoperability with focus on standardized message schemas, although based on different intentions.

The key element of the *top-down approach* is the standardization process of creating core data specifications. This is realized in healthcare predominantly via the standard families HL7 FHIR and openEHR, resulting in EHR standards [13]. Operationally, there is governance for the international harmonization of detailed clinical models as internationally as possible, e.g., with regular balloting meetings for the approval of releases [14]. Collaborations with other de jure standards development organizations, e.g., for topics like terminology or security, ensure the coherence and robustness of the specifications' interrelated parts. Technically, the resource-intensive harmonization process with various feedback loops is supported by collaborative platforms based on proven modeling tools and methods, e.g., Simplifier platform for HL7 FHIR [15] or the Clinical Knowledge Manager from the openEHR community [16].

It should be noted that HL7 FHIR-based content modeling follows an 80/20 rule. This leads to agreed minimum data models tailored to meet individual requirements using profiles and an extension mechanism. Conversely, openEHR aims to provide maximum data models with archetypes, combined and constrained in so-called templates for loading instance data into the openEHR repository. Regardless of these different approaches, the reconciliation process of standard models is time-consuming. Whenever possible, standard specifications adopted in the top-down process are taken into account. Due to restrictions in clinical software and the volatility of healthcare data, a late-mapping approach of source data to standard specifications is strived for as far as possible [17].

The *bottom-up approach* includes all local data elements to reuse and therefore re-purpose metadata in a project-specific context. In contrast to the top-down procedures, data elements are maintained at a local level for numerous research projects. Thus, data elements for routine care or research projects are defined for their single purposes, e.g., employing data dictionaries or metadata repository systems (MDRs). But since the bottom-up approach does not involve the time-consuming but also quality-assuring harmonization of the top-down approach, the context must be documented. ISO 11179-compliant MDRs ensure that metadata is structurally and semantically described and represented based on an agreed metadata schema [18]. The technical hurdle and discrepancy between the spreadsheets preferred by domain experts and MDRs are covered [19]. The main advantage of the bottom-up approach is the individual mapping of the existing, project-specific metadata and the corresponding data sets [20]. Consequently, the loss of information compared to the top-down approach due to necessary compromises is reduced by the direct integration of the elementary data elements, resulting in a higher degree of information mapping.

3 Medical Informatics Initiative

For the past three years, all university hospitals in Germany, together with partner institutions, have joined forces and formed four different consortia to improve data integration and the reuse of medical data from hospitals [10,21,22]. These data integration centers will be established to maintain the necessary infrastructure and establish a federated data platform on a national level. The data integration centers will create the prerequisites for linking research and care data across sites. First results of the MII, with the objective to make data from healthcare and medical research more usable and meaningful, can be seen or have already been published [23–25]. In addition to technical aspects, important issues such as patient consents, use and access restrictions, or core data sets are being discussed and standardized at the national level.

3.1 HiGHmed MeDIC Architecture

The University Hospital Schleswig-Holstein (UKSH), as the second-largest hospital in Germany with its two sites in Kiel and Lübeck, has joined the HiGHmed consortium [21]. Within HiGHmed, a reference architecture for local Medical Data Integration Centers (MeDICs) at all eight HiGHmed sites is specified. The MeDIC concept fosters integrating local, bottom-up fashioned data formats like HL7 v2 into standardized openEHR templates developed in a top-down fashion. The concept is tailored to the hospital settings' special conditions and aims for an overarching harmonization. Patient data and laboratory analyses are mapped to openEHR templates, while, e.g., alignment of local terms with standard terminology for lab results is supported by an MDR. The MeDIC involves two major big data concepts: A block-storage-based data lake as ingesting layer and raw data access and highly-structured data in an openEHR repository representing the data warehouse architecture.

The data lake is a massively scalable block-based storage repository [26], which collects different, heterogeneous information from the primary input

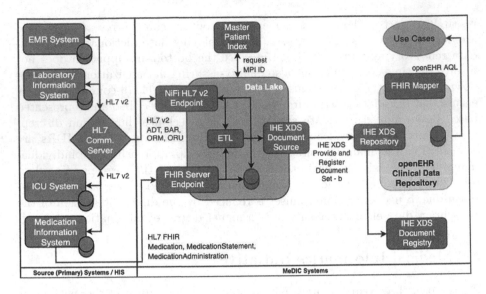

Fig. 3. Overview of the MeDIC architecture including the source systems as used for documentation of patient care.

sources, e.g., the hospital or laboratory information system, enabling online transaction processing (OLTP) capabilities. The data lake integrates existing information streams (see Fig. 3), which flow within the participating hospital and stores the information in raw and unaltered formats. Processing systems can ingest the data without compromising the data structure. The reuse of the same raw data for different use cases is assured without the risk of data corruption. This is crucial since the information within the data lake is sensible and non-anonymized patient data, so handling and processing require particular caution. In order to guarantee extended data consistency, the data lake keeps track of the information for provenance and data lineage [27]. Data are stored in the data lake for the following purposes: (1) all data are available in (2) their original form (3) to be accessible without performance issues on the patient care systems. Performance and accessibility still need to be evaluated in the long term. ETL processes are then used to transfer the medical data to the openEHR repository in a standardized format using a master patient index. This ID is generated for each distinct patient and substitutes the patient ID for data privacy compliance. Common to all HiGHmed use cases that are described below is the reliance on an openEHR-based clinical data repository. OpenEHR is an approach towards standardization of medical records that has seen increasing use as the basis of regional and national medical records infrastructures [16]. It is based on a *reference model* (RM) derived from the CEN/ISO standard ISO 13606-1:2008 [28]. This object-oriented RM consists of a selection of classes that are in relation to each other; the core classes are the Composition (comparable to a document in the paper-based medical record), the Section (grouping entries), the Entry (which contains a medical datum) and the Cluster (which can be inserted into an entry for added information). Based on these RM classes, archetypes are specified by the international community. These archetypes constrain the available RM classes to represent a particular concept. For example, archetypes are available at the Composition level, which represent classes of medical records (e.g., medication plan), or those on the Section or Entry level that represent a particular concept (e.g., blood pressure). Those archetypes are very general and are specified using a maximum dataset mindset. Due to the internationally collaborative process, the archetypes will be broadly and internationally applicable and can be exchanged for purposes of primary and secondary use. OpenEHR makes use of a two-level approach, where templates are specified to further constrain the archetypes for specific use cases. Those constraints may restrict the use of non-applicable data elements, assign appropriate clusters to free slots or bind the values to standard terminologies. Whenever possible, the templates use existing and established archetypes while proposing new archetypes as required to ensure interoperability. Within HiGHmed, the required templates/archetypes are specified using a close collaboration of domain experts, terminologists, and computer scientists. The participating sites then establish ETL jobs from their data lake system towards those templates. In these ETL jobs, local requirements have to be taken into consideration, for example, with regards to the availability of specific data elements or mappings of internal codes used by the respective systems to the standard terminology used within the templates. Within each of the four consortia, use cases have been described to illustrate means and possibilities for data exchange and data integration. In the HiGHmed consortium, the UKSH participates in the use cases *Infection Control*, *Cardiology* and the cross-consortial *Molecular Tumor Board*, which will be described in more detail.

3.2   Use Case Infection Control

The use case Infection Control aims to establish a surveillance system for microbiological infections that occur within hospitals. These infections may be acquired within the hospital or external and, due to the possibility of these infections being resistant to antibiotics, pose a significant threat to the health of the infected patients [21]. Preventing outbreaks of these kinds of pathogens is thus a crucial goal of healthcare providers. The proposed system, called *Smart Infection Control System (SmICS)*, aims to bring the location history and laboratory data of multiple patients together in order to allow for timely decisions limiting the spread of any infection, see Fig. 4. The acquired data are then processed via ETL pipelines and integrated into domain-specific openEHR templates. The data is then queried, analyzed using complex models, and visualized to trace movements of infectious patients and generate hypotheses during outbreaks. This data flow also demonstrates the HiGHmed platform's capability of integrating rich relationships and increased standardization [21]. Since many aspects of the proposed SmICS systems are applicable to the current COVID-19 pandemic, the use case was adopted to meet the current needs. The data models required for SmICS had to be changed substantially since SARS-CoV-2 is a virus, not a living organism,

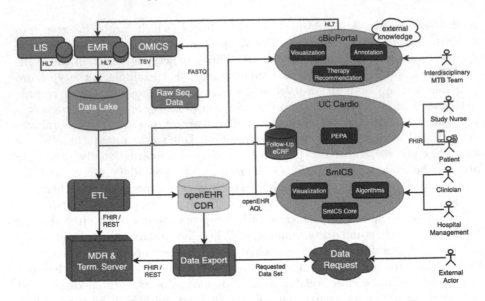

Fig. 4. Data flow from the source systems via the data lake (red) to the HiGHmed infrastructure (grey) and use cases (blue). Primary systems, like LIS and EMR, have internal databases that are only exposed via HL7 v2 interfaces. (Color figure online)

that requires different analyses and treatment. The datasets were defined in a top-down fashion: the microbiological dataset was created, while the dataset for the COVID-SmICS was based on a consensus research dataset called *GECCO* [29]. This dataset was specified in FHIR and transformed to an openEHR representation for the purposes of the SmICS project. The use of GECCO assured that the data collected can be exchanged in other COVID-related projects for country-wide analyses. The knowledge about the COVID-19 disease and treatment is changing rapidly. This is exemplified by the publication of real-world studies regarding the efficacy of vaccinations aftermarket approval [30]. This new knowledge requires that the GECCO dataset is changed appropriately, requiring not only a top-down governance framework but coordinate projects using this data.

3.3   Use Case Cardiology

As the leading cause of death in both Germany and across Europe, Heart Failure (HF) is responsible for a large proportion of hospital admissions, mortality, and morbidity associated with high healthcare costs in Western industrialized nations [31]. Although a range of effective drug treatments is available, the clinical picture of HF is characterized by the ubiquitous risk of decompensation in many cases ending in recurrent hospitalizations. Within the use case *Cardiology*, the aims are to identify disease patterns of HF, detect future cardiac decompensation episodes, and prevent (re-)hospitalizations of high-risk patients.

Therefore, algorithms will be developed to assist both researchers and clinicians based on aggregated, harmonized clinical and patient-generated health data. Considering that the diagnosis of HF requires multi-modal diagnostic procedures, relevant data are spread over multiple heterogeneous information systems in the hospital. Heterogeneous data are often free-text, seldom structured, and semantically meaningful. They are stored in various data types and levels of granularity. Relevant data sources include patients' medical history (echocardiography, ECG, MRI, laboratory findings, or medication data) are HIS, laboratory, and medication information system.

As part of our integration strategy, a process is established providing HL7 v2 messages from EMR system and laboratory information system (LIS) while medication data are exported as FHIR resources. Subsequently, all different types of messages and resources get processed in an ETL pipeline. Within the ETL process, proprietary vocabularies are linked to standard terminologies while additional mapping of data structures towards domain-specific openEHR archetypes is performed. In this use case, a top-down approach is applied, whereas openEHR templates representing sets of research-relevant compositions for HF-related data were specified following guidelines by the *German Center for Cardiovascular Research (DZHK)*. Whereas a large number of data fields in the UKSH HIS are semi-structured, MRI findings are free-text. Therefore natural language processing is part of the ETL process to extract relevant information when transferring values into corresponding openEHR Archetypes [21]. To achieve a more holistic picture of the disease's progression, the combination of patient-reported outcomes (PROs) is evaluated using standardized clinical questionnaires (KCCQ-12) and sensor devices using low-threshold state-of-the-art sensor technologies in follow-up [32]. PROs are of strong interest because they allow conclusions to be drawn about therapy compliance and disease management in a patient's daily routine. Heart rate and physical activity are captured using an Apple Watch Series 4 smartwatch while weight and blood pressure are documented manually into a use case-specific app. Sensor and patient-generated datasets will subsequently be transferred into the Personal Cross-Enterprise Health Record (PEPA) using the app as a gateway [33]. PEPA links to the MeDIC via ETL jobs for integration into the openEHR repository. To track future hospital admissions, follow-up phone calls are performed every six months, including questions of whether any hospitalizations (regardless of their relation to HF) have occurred during the period and to track the survival rate. The surveyed information is manually entered into electronic Case Report Forms.

3.4   Use Case Molecular Tumor Board

Over the last decades, we have seen massive success in understanding genes and signaling pathways of tumors. Simultaneously, the costs and turn-around time for analysis of molecular data such as genomics and transcriptomics, so-called *OMICS* data, was reduced. As a result, molecular tumor boards (MTBs) have been established as interdisciplinary teams, including human geneticists, oncologists, pathologists, medical scientists, bioinformaticians, and data scientists [34]. While traditional guideline-based therapies are discussed in entity-specific tumor boards, MTBs take the specific molecular profile of a patient's tumor into account. The goal is to provide a therapy recommendation by identifying actionable targets for personalized therapies. As such therapy recommendations often include off-label treatments and participation in clinical trials of novel treatments, patients are likely to be enrolled in registry studies to monitor their status by regularly collecting follow-up data [35]. The use case *From Knowledge to Action – Support for Molecular Tumor Boards*, provides additional support from the bioinformatics and medical informatics side to bring the latest research results to patient care [22].

Its major goals include developing best-practice OMICS pipelines to process the sequenced raw data and developing an MTB platform for data visualization, research of feasible clinical trials or therapy options, and structured documentation of therapy recommendations [24]. The MIRACUM-Pipe is developed to provide a fully automated workflow to process sequencing data from raw data to a human-readable and machine-readable format describing the molecular profile. As the amount of raw input data is about 30–40 GB per patient, the processing requires high-performance compute clusters. The *cBioPortal for Cancer Genomics* platform, a special-purpose software driven by a data warehousing approach to analyze and visualize molecular data, was selected as a base [36,37] and extended according to the requirements by Büchner et al. [24]. As this is a field with rapid knowledge growth, variants are annotated using up-to-date external knowledgebases such as OncoKB and Genome Nexus shown in Fig. 4, which will be accessed by the variants' position and altered nucleic acids as human-readable symbols might change [38]. To present a patient at the MTB, the attending physician places an order entry in the EMR system together with information about the patient's current state, prior treatments, and findings. The order acts as a trigger event for the EMR system to send an HL7 message to the data lakes' NiFi HL7 v2 endpoint and staged for further processing. This iteratively developed data model represents the bottom-up approach. Subsequent ETL processes to top-down designed openEHR archetypes and the proprietary data model of cBioPortal are therefore enhanced using an MDR. Structured therapy recommendations from cBioPortal, on the other hand, will be put into an intermediate FHIR store and sent to the EMR system using HL7 v2 messages once they are finalized. This use case is a cross-consortia project at UKSH site deployed on the MeDIC architecture [39].

4   Discussion

The MII project and the local implementation were presented in detail, where theoretical data integration methods characterized by top-down and bottom-up approaches are applied to achieve standards-compliant data harmonization. The question arises whether the approach is without an alternative concerning available approaches, possibly from other application domains.

4.1   Schema-Based Data Integration

Relational databases are used to a large extent for clinical software and have been field-tested for decades. Theoretically, well-known schema-based approaches exist for enabling data exchange and integration challenges [40]. Uniform query interfaces to multiple heterogeneous data sources can be provided by mediated schemes (GAV: global-as-view). Alternatively, data sources can be modeled as views over mediated schemes (LAV: local-as-view). Having studied the involved source data schemes, so-called source-to-target tuple generating dependencies can be derived as first-order logic formula as mapping rules. With that, approaches can profit by reformulating logical queries on target schemes into queries on source schemes. Suitable algorithms such as 'Chase' are available for materialization and exchange queried data to enforce the logical implications of data dependencies. Appropriate mediator architectures that additionally incorporate EHR standards are being explored in several academic projects [41]. However, the following facts hinder schema-based data integration in routine practical applications: 1) Source data schemes are often an intellectual property of the vendors and therefore confidential [42]. 2) Even if the schema is known, access to that knowledge is often denied under medical device regulation. 3) IT staff in the hospital are unlikely to support theoretical data integration approaches based on logical formulas, as appropriate tooling is lacking and legal aspects are not always clarified. 4) Source data models are much more diverse, include unstructured data, and are rarely static in their lifespan. Thus, schema integration approaches are hardly applicable in medical informatics, including relational as well as XML-based schemata.

4.2   Data Integration Approaches Allowing More Flexibility

Numerous advanced methods in data integration address the above limitations, including the need for greater flexibility and consideration of structured and unstructured data [43]. Data integration in the clinical environment is challenging and hampered by ever-changing requirements and standards, and therefore needs to be flexible and adaptable. A major problem here is the above-average occurrence of free-text diagnostic reporting [44]. The need for extracting structured data from free text using appropriate text mining algorithms is very high. However, they have hardly been established for non-English medical texts to date [45].

For flexibility due to constantly changing documentation requirements, the Entity-Attribute-Value (EAV) model is very commonly used in healthcare and medical research [46]. Hereby it is possible to extend the relational data model with static model parts specifically with attributes, which can be added at runtime without relational schema changes, e.g., for medications or laboratory test results. EAV data models are more flexible compared to relational data models due to a targeted relaxation of schema constraints. The flexibility achieved in common EAV data models addresses the massively granular, constantly changing clinical content that can hardly be fixed in static relational schemes. This division of tasks is also found in the openEHR approach called "two-level approach". The difference arises from the fact that in openEHR the static part of the data model is fixed in its RM, and dynamic clinical content such as emergency report is collaboratively standardized in advance via archetypes. Flexibility by relaxing schema-based constraints in the EAV model is pursued to the extreme in Semantic Web approaches. All instance data is provided as Resource Description Framework (RDF) triples schema-less in triple stores.

4.3   Data Integration Using Semantic Web

Semantic Web applications rely on RDF standards and ontology formats such as RDF Schema (RDFS) and the more powerful Web Ontology Language (OWL). SPARQL, an RDF querying language, allows the search and manipulation of distributed networked data sources (triple stores) [47]. There are numerous academically driven applications of the Semantic Web paradigm for healthcare applications. For example, using the Ontology Based Data Access (OBDA) approach, mappings between entities of data schemes and ontologies can be defined to generate materialized, or query virtualized RDF triples. In a Semantic Web context, ontologies are a primary tool for data integration, sharing, and discovery. Many biomedical ontologies such as SNOMED CT can be exploited for Linked Data applications with references to external knowledge bases [48].

This approach seems suitable for the heterogeneous and distributed healthcare sector. However, many of the barriers mentioned in Sect. 4.1 also apply to this approach. And yes, there are meaningful ontologies in the field of biomedical informatics. However, they are not used in a legally mandated way so far. In the real healthcare context, one is confronted with structurally very limited vocabularies such as the diagnoses classification and German procedure classification. Instead of case-hardened applications, mostly prototypical systems are just extensively published than rather used, since there is a limited academic incentive for maintainable, stable, easy-to-use software, and the productive applications are rather engineering than *science* [49]. The current software stacks are only suitable for small data sets; there is no evaluation for extensive data sets or system resilience, which is necessary to withstand the regulations of healthcare IT.

5   Conclusion

The success of the data integration centers described in Sect. 3 as part of the MII for the integrated delivery of health and research data depends on technical, methodological, and organizational issues. Beyond just data integration methodology in accordance with agreed-upon EHR standards, the following challenges prove more serious to overall success: 1) Obtaining data from clinical source systems is extremely difficult due to a lack of comprehensive interfaces. 2) There is resistance to anticipating EHR standards already in clinical source systems (early mapping), which would have advantages concerning data quality over subsequent harmonization along with ETL processes (late mapping). 3) Without the successful implementation of additive requirements such as broad consent, privacy and security, data sharing policies, or trust centers for record linkage, data cannot be made available for integration, especially for legal reasons.

Therefore, the entire process is only as good as the weakest link in the chain. Apart from this, technologies and software in hospitals are always the supporter of the most crucial task: to help patients. Here, the MII with its use cases sets a good example and does not use the information technology methodology as an end in itself.

Acknowledgments. This work is funded by the German Federal Ministry of Education and Research (BMBF) as part of the Medical Informatics Initiative Germany, Grand IDs 01ZZ1802Z and 01ZZ1802T.

References

1. Snyder, J.M., Pawloski, J.A., Poisson, L.M.: Developing real-world evidence-ready datasets: time for clinician engagement. Curr. Oncol. Rep. **22**(5), 1–8 (2020). https://doi.org/10.1007/s11912-020-00904-z
2. Panch, T., Mattie, H., Celi, L.A.: The "inconvenient truth" about AI in healthcare. npj Digit. Med. **2**(1), 1–3 (2019). https://doi.org/10.1038/s41746-019-0155-4
3. Hübner, U., Esdar, M., Hüsers, J., Liebe, J., Naumann, L., Thye, J., et al.: IT-Report Gesundheitswesen, Schwerpunkt - Wie reif ist die Gesundheits-IT aus Anwenderperspektive? Schriftenreihe der Hochschule Osnabrück, Forschungsgruppe Informatik im Gesundheitswesen (IGW) (2020)
4. Lehne, M., Sass, J., Essenwanger, A., Schepers, J., Thun, S.: Why digital medicine depends on interoperability. NPJ Digit. Med. **2**, 79 (2019). https://doi.org/10.1038/s41746-019-0158-1
5. Feldman, K., Johnson, R.A., Chawla, N.V.: The state of data in healthcare: path towards standardization. J. Healthc. Inform. Res. **2**(3), 248–271 (2018). https://doi.org/10.1007/s41666-018-0019-8
6. Council, N.R.: Toward Precision Medicine: Building a Knowledge Network for Biomedical Research and a New Taxonomy of Disease, Washington, DC . The National Academies Press (2011). https://doi.org/10.17226/13284
7. Amos, L., Anderson, D., Brody, S., Ripple, A., Humphreys, B.L.: UMLS users and uses: a current overview. J. Am. Med. Inform. Assoc. **27**, 1606–1611 (2020). https://doi.org/10.1093/jamia/ocaa084
8. Ghazvinian, A., Noy, N.F., Musen, M.A.: How orthogonal are the OBO foundry ontologies? J. Biomed. Semant. **2**(Suppl. 2), S2 (2011). https://doi.org/10.1186/2041-1480-2-S2-S2
9. Hulsen, T., Jamuar, S.S., Moody, A.R., Karnes, J.H., Varga, O., Hedensted, S., et al.: From big data to precision medicine. Front. Med. **6**, 34 (2019). https://doi.org/10.3389/fmed.2019.00034
10. Semler, S.C., Wissing, F., Heyder, R.: German medical informatics initiative. Methods Inf. Med. **57**(S 1), e50–e56 (2018). https://doi.org/10.3414/ME18-03-0003
11. IEEE: IEEE Standard Computer Dictionary: A Compilation of IEEE Standard Computer Glossaries. IEEE Std. 610, pp. 1–217, January 1991. https://doi.org/10.1109/IEEESTD.1991.106963

12. Bezerra, C.A.C., Araujo, A., Rocha, B., Pereira, V., Ferraz, F.: Middleware for heterogeneous healthcare data exchange: a survey. In: ICSEA 2015, pp. 409–414 (2015)
13. Benson, T., Grieve, G.: Principles of Health Interoperability: FHIR, HL7 and SNOMED CT. Health Information Technology Standards, Springer, Cham (2021). https://doi.org/10.1007/978-3-030-56883-2
14. Goossen, W., Goossen-Baremans, A., van der Zel, M.: Detailed clinical models: a review. Healthc. Inform. Res. **16**(4), 201–214 (2010). https://doi.org/10.4258/hir.2010.16.4.201
15. Hong, N., Wang, K., Wu, S., Shen, F., Yao, L., Jiang, G.: An interactive visualization tool for HL7 FHIR specification browsing and profiling. J. Healthc. Inform. Res. **3**(3), 329–344 (2019). https://doi.org/10.1007/s41666-018-0043-8
16. Wulff, A., Haarbrandt, B., Marschollek, M.: Clinical knowledge governance framework for nationwide data infrastructure projects. In: eHealth, pp. 196–203 (2018)
17. LeSueur, D.: 5 Reasons Healthcare Data is Unique and Difficult to Measure (2014). https://www.healthcatalyst.com/insights/5-reasons-healthcare-data-is-difficult-to-measure Accessed 9 Apr 2021
18. Ulrich, H., Kock, A.K., Duhm-Harbeck, P., Habermann, J.K., Ingenerf, J.: Metadata repository for improved data sharing and reuse based on HL7 FHIR. In: MIE, pp. 162–166 (2016)
19. Kock-Schoppenhauer, A.K., Kroll, B., Lambarki, M., Ulrich, H., Stahl-Toyota, S., Habermann, J.K., et al.: One step away from technology but one step towards domain experts-MDRBridge: a template-based ISO 11179-compliant metadata processing pipeline. Methods Inf. Med. **58**(S 02), e72–e79 (2019). https://doi.org/10.1055/s-0039-3399579
20. Mate, S., Kampf, M., Rödle, W., Kraus, S., Proynova, R., Silander, K., et al.: Pan-European data harmonization for biobanks in ADOPT BBMRI-ERIC. Appl. Clin. Inform. **10**(04), 679–692 (2019)
21. Haarbrandt, B., Schreiweis, B., Rey, S., Sax, U., Scheithauer, S., Rienhoff, O., et al.: HiGHmed - an open platform approach to enhance care and research across institutional boundaries. Methods Inf. Med. **57**(S 01), e66–e81 (2018). https://doi.org/10.3414/ME18-02-0002
22. Prokosch, H.U., Acker, T., Bernarding, J., Binder, H., Boeker, M., Boerries, M., et al.: MIRACUM: medical informatics in research and care in university medicine: a large data sharing network to enhance translational research and medical care. Methods Inf. Med. **57**(S 01), e82–e91 (2018). https://doi.org/10.3414/ME17-02-0025
23. Bild, R., Bialke, M., Buckow, K., Ganslandt, T., Ihrig, K., Jahns, R., et al.: Towards a comprehensive and interoperable representation of consent-based data usage permissions in the German medical informatics initiative. BMC Med. Inf. Decis. Mak. **20** (2020). https://doi.org/10.1186/s12911-020-01138-6
24. Buechner, P., Hinderer, M., Unberath, P., Metzger, P., Boeker, M., Acker, T., et al.: Requirements analysis and specification for a molecular tumor board platform based on cBioPortal. Diagnostics **10**(2), 93 (2020). https://doi.org/10.3390/diagnostics10020093
25. Kapsner, L.A., Kampf, M.O., Seuchter, S.A., Gruendner, J., Gulden, C., Mate, S., et al.: Reduced rate of inpatient hospital admissions in 18 German university hospitals during the COVID-19 Lockdown. Front. Public Health **8**, 1018 (2021)
26. Miloslavskaya, N., Tolstoy, A.: Big data, fast data and data lake concepts. Procedia Comput. Sci. **88**, 300–305 (2016)

27. Allen, M., Cervo, D.: Chapter 9 - Data quality management. In: Allen, M., Cervo, D. (eds.) Multi-Domain Master Data Management, pp. 131–160. Morgan Kaufmann (2015). https://doi.org/10.1016/B978-0-12-800835-5.00009-9

28. International Standards Organization: ISO 13606–1:2008 - Health informatics - electronic health record communication - Part 1: reference model. https://www.iso.org/standard/67868.html Accessed 9 Apr 2021

29. Sass, J., Bartschke, A., Lehne, M., Essenwanger, A., Rinaldi, E., Rudolph, S., et al.: The german corona consensus dataset (GECCO): a standardized dataset for COVID-19 research in university medicine and beyond. BMC Med. Inform. Decis. Mak. **20**(1) (2020). https://doi.org/10.1186/s12911-020-01374-w

30. Vasileiou, E., Simpson, C., Robertson, C., Shi, T., Kerr, S., Agrawal, U., et al.: Effectiveness of first dose of COVID-19 vaccines against hospital admissions in Scotland: national prospective cohort study of 5.4 million people. Preprint, February 2021. https://doi.org/10.2139/ssrn.3789264

31. Schmid, T.: Costs of treating cardiovascular events in Germany: a systematic literature review. Health Econ. Rev. **5**(1), 27 (2015). https://doi.org/10.1186/s13561-015-0063-5

32. Faller, H., Steinbüchel, T., Schowalter, M., Spertus, J.A., Störk, S., Angermann, C.E.: Der Kansas City Cardiomyopathy Questionnaire (KCCQ) - ein neues krankheitsspezifisches Messinstrument zur Erfassung der Lebensqualität bei chronischer Herzinsuffizienz: Psychometrische Prüfung der deutschen Version. PPmP - Psychotherapie · Psychosomatik · Medizinische Psychologie **55**(3/4), 200–208 (2005). https://doi.org/10.1055/s-2004-834597

33. Heinze, O., Brandner, A., Bergh, B.: Establishing a personal electronic health record in the Rhine-Neckar region. Stud. Health Technol. Inform. **150**, 119–119 (2009)

34. Singer, J., Irmisch, A., Ruscheweyh, H.J., Singer, F., Toussaint, N.C., Levesque, M.P., et al.: Bioinformatics for precision oncology. Brief. Bioinform. **20**(3), 778–788 (2019). https://doi.org/10.1093/bib/bbx143

35. Hoefflin, R., Geißler, A.L., Fritsch, R., Claus, R., Wehrle, J., Metzger, P., et al.: Personalized clinical decision making through implementation of a molecular tumor board: a German single-center experience. JCO Precis. Oncol., 1–16 (2018). https://doi.org/10.1200/PO.18.00105

36. Cerami, E., Gao, J., Dogrusoz, U., Gross, B.E., Sumer, S.O., Aksoy, B.A., et al.: The cBio cancer genomics portal: an open platform for exploring multidimensional cancer genomics data: figure 1. Cancer Discov. **2**(5), 401–404 (2012). https://doi.org/10.1158/2159-8290.CD-12-0095

37. Gao, J., Aksoy, B.A., Dogrusoz, U., Dresdner, G., Gross, B., Sumer, S.O., et al.: Integrative analysis of complex cancer genomics and clinical profiles using the cBioPortal. Sci. Signal. **6**(269), pl1-pl1 (2013). https://doi.org/10.1126/scisignal.2004088

38. Bruford, E.A., Braschi, B., Denny, P., Jones, T.E.M., Seal, R.L., Tweedie, S.: Guidelines for human gene nomenclature. Nat. Genet. **52**(8), 754–758 (2020). https://doi.org/10.1038/s41588-020-0669-3

39. Reimer, N., Ulrich, H., Busch, H., Kock-Schoppenhauer, A.K., Ingenerf, J.: openEHR mapper - a tool to fusion clinical and genomic data using the openEHR standard. In: Studies in Health Technology and Informatics (2021)

40. Arenas, M., Barceló, P., Libkin, L., Murlak, F.: Foundations of Data Exchange. Cambridge University Press (2014). https://doi.org/10.1017/CBO9781139060158

41. do Espírito Santo, J.M., Medeiros, C.B.: Semantic interoperability of clinical data. In: Da Silveira, M., Pruski, C., Schneider, R. (eds.) DILS 2017. LNCS, vol. 10649, pp. 29–37. Springer, Cham (2017). https://doi.org/10.1007/978-3-319-69751-2_4

42. Dugas, M., Jöckel, K.H., Friede, T., Gefeller, O., Kieser, M., Marschollek, M., et al.: Memorandum "open metadata". Open access to documentation forms and item catalogs in healthcare. Methods Inf. Med. **54**(4), 376–378 (2015). https://doi.org/10.3414/ME15-05-0007

43. Golshan, B., Halevy, A., Mihaila, G., Tan, W.C.: Data integration: after the teenage years. In: Proceedings of the 36th ACM SIGMOD-SIGACT-SIGAI Symposium on Principles of Database Systems, PODS 2017, pp. 101–106. Association for Computing Machinery, New York, May 2017. https://doi.org/10.1145/3034786.3056124

44. Senthilkumar, S., Rai, B.K., Meshram, A.A., Gunasekaran, A., Chandrakumarmangalam, S.: Big data in healthcare management: a review of literature. Am. J. Theor. Appl. Bus. **4**(2), 57–69 (2018)

45. Névéol, A., Dalianis, H., Velupillai, S., Savova, G., Zweigenbaum, P.: Clinical natural language processing in languages other than English: opportunities and challenges. J. Biomed. Semant. **9**(1), 12 (2018). https://doi.org/10.1186/s13326-018-0179-8

46. Dinu, V., Nadkarni, P.: Guidelines for the effective use of entity-attribute-value modeling for biomedical databases. Int. J. Med. Inf. **76**(11–12), 769–779 (2007). https://doi.org/10.1016/j.ijmedinf.2006.09.023

47. Groppe, S.: Data Management and Query Processing in Semantic Web Databases. Springer, Heidelberg (2011). https://doi.org/10.1007/978-3-642-19357-6

48. Kock-Schoppenhauer, A.K., Kamann, C., Ulrich, H., Duhm-Harbeck, P., Ingenerf, J.: Linked data applications through ontology based data access in clinical research. Stud. Health Technol. Inform. **235**, 131–135 (2017)

49. Verborgh, R., Vander Sande, M.: The Semantic Web identity crisis: in search of the trivialities that never were. Semant. Web J. **11**(1), 19–27 (2020). https://doi.org/10.3233/SW-190372

Querying Medical Imaging Datasets Using Spatial Logics (Position Paper)

Gina Belmonte[1], Giovanna Broccia[2], Laura Bussi[2,3], Vincenzo Ciancia[2(✉)],
Diego Latella[2], and Mieke Massink[2]

[1] Azienda Toscana Nord Ovest, S. C. Fisica Sanitaria Nord, Lucca, Italy
[2] Consiglio Nazionale delle Ricerche, Istituto di Scienza e Tecnologie
dell'Informazione "A. Faedo", Pisa, Italy
vincenzo.ciancia@isti.cnr.it
[3] Dipartimento di Informatica, Università di Pisa, Pisa, Italy

Abstract. Nowadays a plethora of health data is available for clinical
and research usage. Such existing datasets can be augmented through
artificial-intelligence-based methods by automatic, personalised annotations and recommendations. This huge amount of data lends itself to
new usage scenarios outside the boundaries where it was created; just
to give some examples: to aggregate data sources in order to make
research work more relevant; to incorporate a diversity of datasets in
training of Machine Learning algorithms; to support expert decisions in
telemedicine. In such a context, there is a growing need for a paradigm
shift towards means to interrogate medical databases in a semantically
meaningful way, fulfilling privacy and legal requirements, and transpar-
ently with respect to ethical concerns. In the specific domain of Medical
Imaging, in this paper we sketch a research plan devoted to the definition and implementation of query languages that can unambiguously
express semantically rich queries on possibly multi-dimensional images,
in a human-readable, expert-friendly and concise way. Our approach is
based on querying images using Topological Spatial Logics, building upon
a novel spatial model checker called VoxLogicA, to execute such queries
in a fully automated way.

Keywords: Open health data platforms · Spatial logics · Model
checking

1 Introduction and Related Work

A number of technologies with proven disruptive impact in Computer Science
have revolved around domain-specific data models and query languages. Let

---

The names of the authors of this paper are listed in alphabetical order.
All co-authors have contributed equally to the work described herein. This work has
been partially supported by the Italian MIUR-PRIN 2017 project IT MaTTerS: Methods and Tools for Trustworthy Smart Systems" and by the POR FESR 2014-2020
project STINGRAY (SmarT station INtelliGent RAilwaY).

© Springer Nature Switzerland AG 2021
L. Bellatreche et al. (Eds.): MEDI 2021 Workshops, CCIS 1481, pp. 285–301, 2021.
https://doi.org/10.1007/978-3-030-87657-9_22

us just name a few. The *Structured Query Language SQL* [12] revolutionised data representation and access, and is nowadays one of the pillars of modern Information Technology. The *eXtensible Markup Language XML*[1] and its query/transformation languages (see e.g. *XQuery* [1] and siblings), provide solid grounds to any modern data-centric or document-centrinc infrastructure. The javascript library *jQuery*[2] is the de-facto standard for traversing HTML documents and identifying elements to be transformed using javascript. These technologies (and many others) have in common the adoption of a concise, unambiguous, declarative *query language* that domain experts, without any particular computer programming skill, can use, enabling widespread adoption of a number of transformative key functionalities. It is not an overstatement to say that without the invention of such fundamental technologies, most of the modern applications of Computer Science as we know them would not exist.

In the medical domain, data may be available in several forms, ranging from diagnostic reports written in natural language to electronic health records, multiomics data, and so on. Among these, *medical images* constitute a large portion of the data that can be related to patients, or used for research purposes. The rise of Artificial-Intelligence (AI) based methods has widely augmented these datasets with computer-generated images (e.g. identifying lesions or regions of interest) or annotations. With respect to Medical Imaging, we mention a notable research effort towards querying and information retrieval (see the literature review in [21] and the citations therein). A major role in this area is currently played by *content-based information retrieval* (CBIR) [4,22,33,34,39].

The survey [27] mentions four key issues for research in the field, among which two are of interest to this paper: *the lack of effective representation of medical content by low-level mathematical features* and *the absence of appropriate tools for medical experts to experiment with a CBIR application*. In the present paper, we present a research line that aims at addressing these issues, among others, by the adoption of a coherent, user-oriented, expert-centric **declarative** computation paradigm. In doing so, we would like to emphasize an underlying problem when managing large, diverse medical imaging datasets: the **lack of a general-purpose query language for images**. Such a language should be able to identify regions of interest either by value, by imaging features (e.g. statistical texture analysis), and by spatial/topological characteristics (relative distance, contact, boolean operations, inter-reachability through other regions). Furthermore, it should make use of a diversity of data sources, ranging from patients datasets, to manually annotated ground truth, to the output of Machine Learning methods, and connect the information therein through expert-driven declarative queries and procedures.

Our proposed approach embraces a classic tenet of AI: that of *spatial logics*, that we shall discuss in the remainder of this work, and that constitutes the core of our initiative. More precisely, our work stems from the so-called *topological spatial logics* [2], where the object of reasoning are points, not regions

---

[1] See https://www.w3.org/XML/.
[2] See https://jquery.com.

(see [16] for an encoding of the *region calculus* of [36] into an extended topological spatial logic). Notably, we propose *model checking* to *automatically* identify sets of points (therefore, ultimately, regions) satisfying user-specified properties. Model-checking (in its "global" variant that we employ) is a fully automated technique that, taking as input a logical specification and a model of a system (in our case such "model" is just a digital image), returns the set of states (in our case, points) that satisfy the specification. This is similar to how other fully-automated methods, such as Machine Learning, are used nowadays, and **significantly diverges from** *deduction*, which is the traditional approach of *Symbolic Reasoning* in Artificial Intelligence.

Several publications related to spatial model checking, and in particular to healthcare-related applications, appeared recently. For instance, in [25], spiral electric waves – a precursor to atrial and ventricular fibrillation – are detected and specified using a spatial logic and model-checking tools. The formulas of the logic are learned from the spatial patterns under investigation and the onset of spiral waves is detected using bounded model checking. In [37] (see also the references in that paper), the authors describe mereotopological methods to programmatically correct image segmentation errors, exploiting a spatial logic called *discrete mereotopology* to integrate a number of qualitative spatial reasoning and constraint satisfaction methods into imaging procedures.

The group of authors of this paper have participated in joint publications on spatial logics and related model-checking approaches. The *Spatial Logic of Closure Spaces* (SLCS) has been defined in [14,15], and used in several applications related to smart cities (see e.g. [13]). Recently, these methods were adapted to the efficient analysis of medical images based on Expert Knowledge [5,8,9]. The Free and Open Source spatial model checker VoxLogicA[3] has been developed to support an innovative methodology to analyse medical images. Such methodology obtained excellent experimental results. More precisely, in [9] the accurate contouring of brain tumour tissue obtained using VoxLogicA has been compared to the best performing algorithms (among which many based on deep learning) on a very relevant public benchmark data set for brain tumours (BraTS 2017 [38]). The obtained results are well in line with the state of the art, both in terms of accuracy and in terms of computational efficiency (on a related note, recent efforts have been devoted to running VoxLogicA on GPUs obtaining a substantial speed-up, see [11]). Furthermore, in [7], VoxLogicA has been used for nevus segmentation, again obtaining results in line with the state of the art. It is also worth noting that the logic SLCS has been adopted, and extended, also in other contexts and by other groups of authors; for instance, for cyber-physical systems ([40]), or for run-time monitoring [6,35].

The intended applications of VoxLogicA are not only novel autocontouring methods, but also the formalization of inter and intra-site workflows and collaboration patterns, and monitoring or *quality assurance* of autocontouring procedures, by encoding well-established protocols or guidelines. In future work, we aim at leveraging the spatial model checker VoxLogicA [9] as the distributed

---

[3] See https://github.com/vincenzoml/VoxLogicA.

execution engine for an Open Platform for collaboration and data management in novel data-centric healthcare applications.

2   Spatial Logics for Medical Imaging

Our approach to the analysis of medical images is based on the fact that a digital image can be seen as a 2D or 3D regular grid, i.e. a graph where each node corresponds to a pixel/voxel and has a fixed number of adjacent nodes. The exact set of nodes adjacent to any given one depends on the particular *adjacency relation* between nodes one chooses. For instance, for 2D images, this set is composed of the pixel itself plus those other pixels with which it shares an edge, if the so called *orthogonal* adjacency relation is chosen, whereas it is composed of the pixel itself plus those other pixels with which it shares an edge or a vertex, if the *orthodiagonal* adjacency relation is considered. As these examples suggest, any adjacency relation must be a reflexive and symmetric binary relation over the nodes of the graph. Graphs, in turn, can be seen as a subclass of *closure spaces*, a generalisation of topological spaces; whenever the edge relation of the graph is an adjacency relation, we speak of *adjacency spaces*[4]. Thus, the theoretical foundations of our approach have their roots in topology and related notions [23]. It is convenient to associate each node of any such graph with some specific information, that can be represented as an *atomic predicate*, possibly expressing a property of some *attribute* of the node. For instance, in the case of black & white digital images, the relevant attribute of any voxel is the *intensity*, which has typically a value in the range 0–255, whereas predicates of interest could express the fact that the voxel is in the border of the image, or that its intensity is lower than a certain threshold.

For the full syntax and semantics of SLCS, we refer the reader to [9,15]. Here we provide an intuitive description of the logical language. SLCS offers specific operators for reasoning about (points in) *closure models*, i.e. closure spaces enriched with atomic predicates. Besides general logical operators like conjunction ($\wedge$), disjunction ($\vee$) and negation ($\neg$), the most basic one for adjacency spaces is the *reachability operator* ρ; the formula $\rho\,\Phi_1\,[\Phi_2]$ is satisfied by a voxel x in an image $\mathcal{M}$ if there is a voxel t in $\mathcal{M}$ and a (possibly empty) sequence of *adjacent* voxels $x_1, \ldots, x_n$ in $\mathcal{M}$ such that x_1 is adjacent to x, x_n is adjacent to t that satisfies Φ_1 and all x_j satisfy Φ_2. For instance, $\rho\,\mathtt{red}[\mathtt{blue} \vee \mathtt{green}]$ means that we are interested in those voxels that can reach any red voxel through a sequence of points that must be blue or green. The *near* operator ($\mathcal{N}$) expresses the fact that any point satisfying $\mathcal{N}\,\Phi$ satisfies Φ or is adjacent to a point satisfying Φ; in fact, $\mathcal{N}\,\Phi$ is equivalent to $\rho\,\Phi\,[\bot]$. Similarly, the formula $\Phi_1\,\mathcal{S}\,\Phi_2$, expressing that fact the the relevant point lays in an area the points of which satisfy Φ_1 and this area is *surrounded* by points satisfying Φ_2, is equivalent to $\Phi_1 \wedge \neg(\rho\,\neg(\Phi_1 \vee \Phi_2)[\neg\,\Phi_2])$.

---

[4] For the purposes of this paper, the terms "voxel", "pixel", "node", and "point" can be considered synonyms.

The *Image Query Language* (ImgQL) comprises SLCS but is enriched with several imaging primitives, among which, more prominently, the Euclidean distance operator $\mathcal{D}^I$ and the statistical similarity operator $\triangle$. Formula $\mathcal{D}^I \Phi$ is satisfied by any point x whose Euclidean distance $d(x, [\![\Phi]\!])$ from the set $[\![\Phi]\!]$ of points satisfying Φ falls in interval I. Intuitively, a point x satisfies the similarity operator $\triangle$ if a *region of interest* around x *correlates* with a *sample area*. More precisely, given a sample area $[\![\Phi]\!]$ specified by formula Φ and a region of interest defined as the *sphere* $S(x,r)$ of given radius r around x, the *cross-correlation*[5] between the histogram of an attribute a of the points in $S(x,r)$ and the histogram of an attribute b of the points in $[\![\Phi]\!]$ is compared with a given threshold c (see [5,9] for further details).

3   The Spatial Model Checker VoxLogicA

VoxLogicA is a model checker for ImgQL. The VoxLogicA type system distinguishes between *boolean-valued* images, that usually are arguments or results of the application of SLCS operators, and *number-valued* images, resulting from imaging primitives. The underlying execution engine is a *global model checker*, that is, the set of all points satisfying a logic formula is computed at once. The computational complexity of the procedure is linear in the number of subformulas times the number of points of the image [15], whereas efficiency-wise, in most cases the computation runs in a matter of seconds, on a high-end desktop computer [9]. Functionality-wise, VoxLogicA specialises the former prototype spatio-temporal model checker topochecker[6] to the case of spatial analysis of *multi-dimensional images*. It interprets a specification using a set of multi-dimensional images[7] as models of the spatial logic, and produces as output a set of multi-dimensional images representing the valuation of user-specified expressions. For logical operators, such images are Boolean-valued, that is, *regions of interest* or *masks* in medical imaging terminology, which may be loaded as *overlays* in medical image viewers. Non-logical operators result in standard, number-valued images. Additionally, VoxLogicA offers file loading and saving primitives, and a set of additional operators, specifically aimed at image analysis, that is destined to grow along with future developments of the tool. The main execution modality of VoxLogicA is *batch execution*. A (currently experimental) *graphical user interface* is under development. A planned future development is *interactive execution*, in particular for semi-automated analysis, by letting a domain expert calibrate numeric parameters in real-time, while seeing the intermediate and final results. Implementation-wise, the tool achieves a two-orders-of-magnitude

---

[5] In ImgQL, the normalised Pearson's correlation coefficient is used; 1 means perfect correlation, -1 means perfect anti-correlation, and 0 indicates no correlation.

[6] See https://github.com/vincenzoml/topochecker.

[7] Besides common bitmap formats, the model loader of VoxLogicA currently supports the NIfTI (Neuro-imaging Informatics Technology Initiative) format (https://nifti.nimh.nih.gov/, version 1 and 2). 3D MR-FLAIR images in this format very often have a slice size of 256 by 256 pixels, multiplied by 20 to 30 slices.

speedup with respect to `topochecker`. Such speedup has permitted the rapid development of a novel procedures for automatic segmentation that, besides being competitive with respect to the state-of-the-art in the field (see Sect. 4), are also easily *replicable* and *explainable* to humans, and therefore amenable of improvement by the community of medical imaging practitioners. `VoxLogicA` is free software and it is available in binary form for the operating systems Linux, OSX, and Windows.

4   Applications in Medical Imaging

In this section, we exemplify the expressive power of the logical language used by `VoxLogicA` by reporting on two case studies. In both cases, only one image per case of the dataset is required to carry on the analysis; however, the tool is also capable of loading multiple images (say, an MRI image and a co-registered CAT image), resulting in multi-modal imaging capabilities. By these examples, we aim at demonstrating that the primitives of spatial logics are very close to the domain of discourse in medical imaging, by the simplicity and conciseness of the presented analysis procedures, that have reached state-of-the-art accuracy.

4.1   Case Study: Brain Tumour Segmentation

Glioblastoma multiforme (GBM) is the most common brain malignancy and is almost always lethal [44]. Survival after 2 years is achieved in only about 9% of patients. Medical images play a crucial role in the characterisation and in the treatment of the disease. The first-line treatment of Glioblastoma is Surgery followed by radiotherapy. Crucial for radiotherapy is the accurate contouring of tissues and organs at risk, employing Magnetic Resonance (MR) and Computed Tomography (CT) images. Recent research efforts in the field have therefore been focused on the introduction of automatic or semi-automatic contouring procedures. More broadly speaking, such procedures can be used to identify particular kinds of tissues, such as parts of the brain (white matter, grey matter) or brain tumour related tissues. Such (semi-)automatic procedures would lead to an increase in accuracy and a considerable reduction in time and costs, compared to the current practice of manual contouring [41]. Automatic contouring of GBM is an open and challenging topic, since GBM is an intrinsically heterogeneous brain tumour, both in appearance, in shape, and in histology. The MICCAI Conference is organising a yearly challenge for brain tumour segmentation, since 2012, providing a common benchmark of brain lesion images, together with their ground truth segmentation approved by experienced neuro-radiologists, in the Brain Tumor Image Segmentation Benchmark (BraTS). One of our specifications in ImgQL has been validated in [9] using the 2017 BraTS dataset [31] containing multi-institutional pre-operative MRI scans of 210 patients affected by high grade gliomas. A priori, 17 cases have been excluded as they present multi-focal tumours or artifacts in the acquisition that the current procedure is not meant to deal with. The executable specification of the segmentation procedure consists of a concise, 30 lines long, text-file where the part concerning segmentation

---

ImgQL Specification 1: Tumour segmentation method

```
1 let pflair = percentiles(flair,brain,0)
2 let hI = pflair >. 0.95
3 let vI = pflair >. 0.86
4 let hyperIntense = flt(5.0,hI)
5 let veryIntense = flt(2.0,vI)
6 let growTum = grow(hyperIntense,veryIntense)
7 let tumSim = similarTo(5,growTum,flair)
8 let tumStatCC = flt(2.0,(tumSim >. 0.6))
9 let gtv= grow(growTum,tumStatCC)
10 let ctv = distlt(25,gtv) & brain
```

---

occupies only 10 lines, as shown in Specification 1, explained by the following steps:

1. Initial identification of the hyperintense regions (lines 2–5) in the MRI (of type FLAIR). These are areas with voxel intensity > 0.95 centile grown up to areas > 0.86 centile (growTum in line 6);
2. Search for voxels with a surrounding histogram similar (cross correlation > 0.6) to the area growTum (tumStatCC in line 8);
3. Identification of Gross Tumor Volume (GTV) by growing growTum up to the tumStatCC area. The GTV is then enlarged by 2.5 cm to simulate the Clinical Target Volume (CTV) in radiotherapy (line 9) (Fig. 1).

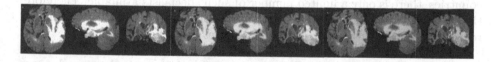

Fig. 1. GTV for patient TCIA_471 from the BraTS 2017 dataset. Leftmost: original image, where the tumour appears hyper-intense. Middle: ground truth in yellow (manually annotated by human experts). Rightmost: VoxLogicA segmentation result of Specification 1 in green (fully automated). (Color figure online)

The segmentation results for the Brats 2017 benchmark are reproduced from [9] in Table 1. The table shows the similarity scores for three commonly used coefficients, namely Dice, Sensitivity and Specificity, for the GTV and CTV areas. These scores indicate the similarity between the area segmented with VoxLogicA Specification 1 compared to the manually annotated images by human experts (i.e. ground truth images). Considering intra- and inter-experts variability of 20 ± 15% and 28 ± 12%, respectively, for manual segmentations [30], Dice similarity scores above 0.8 are considered as very good, and above 0.9 as excellent. The 3D images consist of 240 × 240 × 155 voxels (ca.

Table 1. VoxLogicA evaluation on the BraTS 2017 data set. Adapted from [9].

	Sensitivity (193 cases)	Specificity (193 cases)	Dice (193 cases)	Sensitivity (210 cases)	Specificity (210 cases)	Dice (210 cases)
GTV	0.89 (0.10)	1.0 (0.00)	0.85 (0.10)	0.86 (0.16)	1.0 (0.0)	0.81 (0.18)
CTV	0.95 (0.07)	0.99 (0.01)	0.90 (0.09)	0.93 (0.14)	0.99 (0.2)	0.87 (0.15)

9 M voxels) and the evaluation for each patient takes about 5 s on a desktop computer with an Intel Core I7 7700 processor and 16 GB of RAM.

Once a segmentation of the tumour has been obtained, it can also be used to select images in a dataset, based on some features of interest of the tumour area. For example, one may be interested in images in which the tumour has a volume (in terms of number of voxels it covers) that is larger than a certain threshold (VoxLogicA includes an operator for that). See Sect. 5 for more details.

4.2   Case Study: Nevus Segmentation

Melanoma is the most serious form of skin cancer, the incidence of which has been increasing for many decades [24, 28]. While the disease may be lethal, its correct and early detection, and its consequent treatment, results in no change in life expectancy [32]. Disease recognition is performed through *dermoscopy*, a specialized technique of high-resolution imaging of the skin, allowing specialists to visualize deeper underlying structures of the skin lesions. This technique has been proved to have diagnostic accuracy of up to 84% when carried out by specially trained clinicians [3]. However, one of the main issues is that in many countries, there is only a limited number of such specialists available. Therefore, there is a clear need for automated methods that can help to recognise the disease reliably and at an early stage so that more lives could be saved [19].

The International Skin Imaging Collaboration (ISIC) is a collaboration between academia and industry to find automatic techniques to detect melanoma from dermoscopy images. Since 2016 ISIC organizes challenges titled "Skin Lesion Analysis toward Melanoma Detection" [19]. The first task involved in the challenges, and more in general in the diagnosis of melanoma, is the skin lesion segmentation. In [7] we investigated the feasibility of the application of a procedure implemented in ImgQL for the segmentation of images of nevi from two datasets released by ISIC for the 2016 challenge: a *training* set and a *test* set of 900 and 379 images, respectively. Both datasets contain annotated dermoscopic images and the corresponding ground truth (i.e. a segmentation performed manually by experts) for each image. One of the challenges with such datasets, and, more in general, with dermoscopic images of skin lesions, is their great inhomogeneity. Nevi may show nonuniform colour ranges, their colour may have more or less contrast with the colour of skin, may have different sizes, may have more or less smooth borders, and may be composed of different parts; moreover, the skin may be more or less regular, with the presence of hairs or sebaceous

| (a) | (b) | (c) | (d) | (e) | (f) | (g) | (h) |

Fig. 2. Examples from the ISIC datasets illustrating the inhomogeneity of nevi.

follicles. Furthermore, images may also show heterogeneity due to the dermoscope used: they may be of different size, showing black corners, rings, shadows, or ultrasound gel drops, showing more or less contrast and intensity. Finally, images may also show extraneous elements such as patches or ink marks. The images in Fig. 2 show a few examples of this inhomogeneity.

Due to such great variability in the dermoscopic images datasets, our procedure starts from two basic assumptions: (at least part of) the nevus is in the middle of the image; pixels belonging to the skin are close to the border of the image. Our aim is to distinguish skin tissue from nevus tissue with the help of the texture analysis and other spatial operators. The executable procedure consists of less than 30 lines of code and consists essentially of five parts:

1. *Identify a sample of the skin* by removing the black borders and then taking a small region around the centre of the resulting image.
2. *Identify pixels belonging to the skin* using texture similarity with respect to the previously identified sample.
3. *Preliminary nevus segmentation* via a threshold on the image histogram.
4. *Final nevus segmentation* expanding the result of the previous step using texture similarity.

The segmentation obtained (nevSegm) is compared with the ground truth provided by the ISIC 2016 challenge for both the *training* and *test* sets. For this comparison common similarity indexes were used: Dice, Jaccard, Accuracy, Sensitivity (SE), and Specificity (SP). Table 2 shows the *mean* values for these indexes. The images in Fig. 3 show the resulting images for each step in the segmentation procedure of image ISIC_0008294.

Also in this case, after relevant features of nevi have been identified using voxel-based spatial logics, `VoxLogicA` can be used to query a dataset in order to find images that have specific features (e.g. irregular contour, or large size). See also Sect. 5.

Table 2. Average similarity scores of nevSegm for images of the ISIC 2016 *training* set (all 900 images) and *test* set (all 379 images).

	Accuracy	Dice	Jaccard	SE	SP
nevSegm: Mean *Training* set	0.902	0.818	0.726	0.810	0.965
nevSegm: Mean *Test* set	0.899	0.809	0.717	0.802	0.960

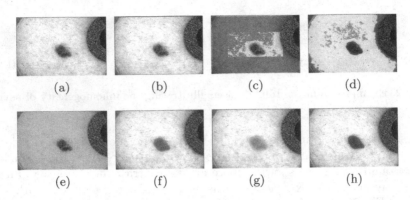

(a)   (b)   (c)   (d)

(e)   (f)   (g)   (h)

Fig. 3. Segmentation of image ISIC_0008294. Figure (a) shows the nevus intensities (greyscale); (b) shows the border of the image (red); (c) shows the sample of the skin (blue); (d) shows the similarity score of each pixels w.r.t. the sample of the skin (variation of the score is shown as the varying intensity of yellow); (e) shows pixels with a similarity higher than 0.05 w.r.t. the sample of the skin (green); (f) shows the pre segmentation of the nevus (magenta); (g) shows the final nevus segmentation (cyan); (h) shows the comparison between the automatic segmentation (cyan) and the ground truth (blue). (Color figure online)

5   Querying Medical Image Datasets

As of today, the toolkit of a Medical Imaging practitioner mostly consists of traditional programming languages, such as the ubiquitous *python*[8]. Programming languages are used in conjunction with libraries of imaging primitives[9], and with Machine Learning (ML) libraries, such as *Keras*[10].

Although such a setup is quite well-established from a programmer's perspective, it is not meant to be used by non-programmers. Domain experts such as Medical Doctors (for instance: Radiotherapists), MRI technologists, Medical Physicists, Healthcare researchers, and even end-users lack a general ability to interrogate medical imaging databases, for instance, in order to search for specific features in images, compose results from different methods to explore the design space of novel analysis techniques, or evaluate the impact of changes in an imaging workflow.

It is worth noting that, even if ML is nowadays a widespread methodology in (medical) image analysis, there are a number of interesting problems that, as of today, are not meant not be addressed using ML alone.

Example 1. As a concrete example, consider **clinical guidelines** (see e.g. [20]). These usually consist of a series of steps and checks that the Radiotherapist

---

[8] See https://www.python.org/.

[9] See, for instance, the *Insight Toolkit (ITK)*, https://itk.org/, also used under-the-hood in VoxLogicA, and the *Open Source Computer Vision Library (OpenCV)*, https://opencv.org/.

[10] See https://keras.io/.

should execute in order to get to an acceptable contouring of a tumour. A hospital may want to perform monitoring and routine checks, and to prepare for changing such guidelines when new ones are published. Before embracing a new set of guidelines, in order to evaluate their impact, the Radiotherapy department might want to investigate how much their standard practice obeys to the new guideline, and how much in practice the old and new guidelines differ on their own patients. A language is needed that can express such guidelines in a concise, human-friendly, expert-oriented way, and that can execute them automatically, highlighting their interpretation on patient images. ML alone cannot currently be used for such tasks, as the encoding of guidelines is, more broadly speaking, a matter of *expert knowledge*. In [43], a model checker is used for the purpose.

Example 2. A declarative, unambiguous, executable encoding of specific guidelines would also be extremely important for **quality assurance** of ML-based methods (e.g., autocontouring for Radiotherapy), enabling those who are responsible for the treatment to monitor and assess the operation of such algorithms in accordance with selected protocols.

Example 3. A research-oriented example is that of **identifying relevant cases to test a research hypothesis**. Imagine for instance, that a researcher needs to check a novel hypothesis relating a spatial feature (say: "the proximity of a brain tumour to the cerebellum"), with an aspect of the treatment (e.g., the survival rate of patients, or the outcome of radiotherapy). For this, it is necessary to filter an existing dataset to find all the cases that satisfy the hypothesis. This is a kind of spatial query on images that cannot be carried on using ML, for the simple reason that there is no training data for detecting such a specific feature as "the tumour is very close to the cerebellum". Traditional programming can be used to identify such cases. However, writing a full program for each such query is not only time consuming, but also practically impossible for researchers who are not expert programmers. Spatial logics instead are very close to the domain of discourse, and permit rapid specification of properties of interest that are related to the spatial distribution of imaging features. Also note that it is not guaranteed that a hand-written program would be efficient enough to analyse the full dataset under time constraints. A specifically designed, declarative, optimizing query engine such as VoxLogicA is better suited for the task. Techniques such as *memoization*[42], automatic parallel execution (see [9]), on-disk caching, and *graphical processing units* (see [11]), are used to speed up computation.

Example 4. Similarly to Example 3, but in a different application context. Healthcare authorities might want to **evaluate the potential impact of new therapies**, by identifying the number of patients that may get benefits. Imaging features could be used to identify such cases; consider e.g. the case of tumours invading specific organs at risk. For instance, consider the query: "find all the cases in which a brain tumour invaded the patient's eye". Once again, there is no training data specific to this query, even if it is likely that Machine Learning will provide in the near future very good methods to identify the simpler concepts of "brain tumour", and "patient's eye'. In this case, a query language would be an excellent solution to coordinate different machine learning algorithms in order to answer more complex, expert-driven questions. More precisely, first, ML-based annotators would be executed on an imaging data set. Then, a VoxLogicA specification can be written that loads the ML-based annotations, and combines them using logical operators.

Example 5. An easy-to-use query system for healthcare datasets definitely creates ethical concerns about its usage. But at the same time, the human readability of the query language makes it *transparent* with respect to such concerns and would ease **ethical scrutiny** when deemed necessary, giving to an ethics committee the ability to know exactly *which questions have been asked to the system, and what do they mean.* Compare and contrast this to a *black-box* method, such as ML; or to the complexity of a traditional computer program interfaced to a database of clinical data.

Example 6. **Remote collaboration in telemedicine** could benefit of an automated system to identify and share regions of interest among several treatment centres. In this case, the flexibility of a query language would be fundamental to integrate different queries into a comprehensive *personalized knowledge base* for each patient. Each centre could contribute a portion of a VoxLogicA specification and practitioners would be entitled to view both the specification and the results in order to quickly gather as much information as available on each patient. As an example, consider queries related to tumour size, past growth, proximity to organs at risk, etc.

6   Outlook: VoxLogicA as a Distributed Query Engine

In the opinion of the authors, the tool VoxLogicA as is, would already constitute a good starting point for querying medical imaging datasets. This is because ImgQL is endowed with *global* operators, e.g. for computing the number of voxels that evaluate to true, that is the *volume*, of a given formula, or for comparing different regions to check if they are included in one another, or are overlapped, or are disconnected etc.[11] By this, using VoxLogicA alone, it is possible to identify in a dataset of medical images those satisfying certain global properties, based on the segmentation provided by the voxel-based properties (such as those described in Sect. 4). For a concrete example, consider e.g. the ability to find all the images of patients where *the brain tumour is larger than x*, or *the oedema is larger than the tumour*, or *the gross tumour volume is very close to the cerebellum*, or, changing the example, where a nevus is *divided into k regions*, and so on. For the nevi segmentation case study, also properties related to the shape and contour of a nevus are very relevant. We also emphasize that the "lower level" information, e.g. the tumour segmentation, or the skull segmentation, could also be the output of Machine-Learning based voxel classifiers, but still, reachability, proximity, overlap, volume of the regions obtained

---

[11] Such operators come from the classical theory of *region calculi*, see [16] for details.

via Machine Learning would be the ingredients of complex queries that could be run using our tool. We note in passing that the current language is textual, although future work could also consider its *visual* counterpart[12]. The reader should keep in mind that VoxLogicA is aimed at a technical audience, namely that of *domain experts* in medical imaging, who generally speaking are engineers, physicists, MDs or technicians, with few programming expertise, but quite a lot of technical competence.

However, a number of research directions could be pursued, in order to turn the current tool into a fully-fledged query engine. In this section we sketch a research roadmap, by describing a number of future improvements, to direct our results more closely to the field of Information Retrieval.

Integration with Clinical Databases. Information systems such as *RIS-PACS* [26] are of vital importance for the functioning of modern healthcare. Therein, all the information available about patients that undergo treatments is archived. In a clinical setting, therefore, a query language for medical imaging would be way more useful if enabled to query such information systems directly.

Indexing. In SQL databases, data is indexed in order to speed up queries. In VoxLogicA, the most expensive queries are related to the computation of distance maps, to connected components and to statistical texture analysis. Therefore, the identification of data structures to be computed in advance from medical images (e.g., when such images are added to a dataset) in order to speed up such operations, would be a relevant research line. In this respect, a first step is to observe that *minimization* may be used to reduce models up-to *logical equivalence*. In [17,18], a minimization algorithm is proposed that minimizes images up-to proximity ("near") and reachability queries.

Distributed Execution. Distributed execution of VoxLogicA queries could be very relevant for broadly known, widespread datasets, such as those that are commonly used for research and benchmarking purposes (see e.g. the BraTS dataset [38]). Also for multi-centric studies, in order to respect privacy and intellectual property concerns, it would be worthwile to implement a fully distributed variant of VoxLogicA that can be used to interrogate remote medical systems and draw statistical conclusions, without having to share the whole dataset across all the participants in a study.

Computational Efficiency. In order to improve efficiency of queries, the strategy that is currently under investigation is that of GPU computing. The current on-GPU implementation of VoxLogicA [11] exploits Graphical Processing Units to improve the performance of image analysis. As software portability is a major issue, VoxLogicA GPU is currently implemented using OpenCL[13], an

---

[12] It is out of the scope of this work to discuss the advantages and disadvantages of visual vs. textual query languages.

[13] See https://www.khronos.org/opencl/.

open standard by *Kronos*, known to be executable on GPUs from any vendor. The prototype is currently being improved. A major bottle-neck is the computation of *Connected Components* of a binary image; this is used to resolve inter-reachability queries on image regions, and it requires iterative calls to the GPU and comparisons between images, which is particularly computationally intensive. However, the speed-up achieved by the propotype is quite substantial, and may become as high as two orders of magnitude, depending on the size and type of the evaluated formula.

Human-Computer Interaction. The experience of our group in using VoxLogicA for medical image analysis against a large dataset, is that a major hurdle is constituted by HCI issues related to the visualization of intermediate results, the interactive construction of queries, and to comparing and exchanging several different versions of the same analysis between a group of interested users. Furthermore, the target group of users for our project is that of healthcare practitioners, where user interfaces for image visualization employ some highly standardised concepts (such as viewing images slice by slice, using *axial, coronal* and *sagittal* projections, or using overlays on images to visualize regions of interest). Such aspects need to be carefully evaluated in order to design a query system for medical images which is effective (see e.g. the usability study in [29], and the cognitive load issues investigated in [10]).

7   Concluding Remarks

In this paper we have sketched our research roadmap to turn the spatial model checker VoxLogicA into a fully-fledged query engine for datasets of medical images. Some of these directions will already be pursued in the immediate future, namely the on-GPU implementation, the Human-computer Interaction aspects, and the minimization procedures. At the horizon, distributed execution, and integration with clinical databases, could be the last steps needed, in order to initiate the technological transfer of our results in this direction.

References

1. XQuery 3.1: An XML Query Language (2017). https://www.w3.org/TR/2017/REC-xquery-31-20170321/
2. Aiello, M., Pratt-Hartmann, I., Benthem, van, J.: Handbook of Spatial Logics. Springer, Heidelberg (2007). https://doi.org/10.1007/978-1-4020-5587-4
3. Ali, A.R.A., Deserno, T.M.: A systematic review of automated melanoma detection in dermatoscopic images and its ground truth data. In: Medical Imaging 2012: Image Perception, Observer Performance, and Technology Assessment, vol. 8318, p. 83181I. International Society for Optics and Photonics (2012)
4. Aswani, N., et al.: Khresmoi: multimodal multilingual medical information search. In: Proceedings of the 24th International Conference of the European Federation for Medical Informatics, p. 12 (2012)

5. Banci Buonamici, F., Belmonte, G., Ciancia, V., Latella, D., Massink, M.: Spatial logics and model checking for medical imaging. Int. J. Softw. Tools Technol. Transf. **22**(2), 195–217 (2019). https://doi.org/10.1007/s10009-019-00511-9
6. Bartocci, E., Bortolussi, L., Loreti, M., Nenzi, L., Silvetti, S.: MoonLight: a lightweight tool for monitoring spatio-temporal properties. In: Deshmukh, J., Ničković, D. (eds.) RV 2020. LNCS, vol. 12399, pp. 417–428. Springer, Cham (2020). https://doi.org/10.1007/978-3-030-60508-7_23
7. Belmonte, G., Broccia, G., Vincenzo, C., Latella, D., Massink, M.: Feasibility of spatial model checking for nevus segmentation. In: Proceedings of the 9th International Conference on Formal Methods in Software Engineering (FormaliSE 2021), pp. 1–12. IEEE (2021)
8. Belmonte, G., Ciancia, V., Latella, D., Massink, M.: From collective adaptive systems to human centric computation and back: spatial model checking for medical imaging. In: Proceedings of the Workshop on FORmal Methods for the Quantitative Evaluation of Collective Adaptive SysTems, FORECAST@STAF 2016, Vienna, Austria, 8 July 2016. EPTCS, vol. 217, pp. 81–92 (2016)
9. Belmonte, G., Ciancia, V., Latella, D., Massink, M.: VoxLogicA: a spatial model checker for declarative image analysis. In: Vojnar, T., Zhang, L. (eds.) TACAS 2019. LNCS, vol. 11427, pp. 281–298. Springer, Cham (2019). https://doi.org/10.1007/978-3-030-17462-0_16
10. Broccia, G., Milazzo, P., Ölveczky, P.C.: Formal modeling and analysis of safety-critical human multitasking. Innov. Syst. Softw. Eng. **15**(3–4), 169–190 (2019)
11. Bussi, L., Ciancia, V., Gadducci, F.: Towards a spatial model checker on GPU. In: Peters, K., Willemse, T.A.C. (eds.) FORTE 2021. LNCS, vol. 12719, pp. 188–196. Springer, Cham (2021). https://doi.org/10.1007/978-3-030-78089-0_12
12. Chamberlin, D.D., Boyce, R.F.: SEQUEL: a structured English query language. In: Rustin, R. (ed.) Proceedings of 1974 ACM-SIGMOD Workshop on Data Description, Access and Control, pp. 249–264. ACM (1974)
13. Ciancia, V., Gilmore, S., Grilletti, G., Latella, D., Loreti, M., Massink, M.: Spatio-temporal model checking of vehicular movement in public transport systems. Int. J. Softw. Tools Technol. Transf. **20**(3), 289–311 (2018). https://doi.org/10.1007/s10009-018-0483-8
14. Ciancia, V., Latella, D., Loreti, M., Massink, M.: Specifying and verifying properties of space. In: Diaz, J., Lanese, I., Sangiorgi, D. (eds.) TCS 2014. LNCS, vol. 8705, pp. 222–235. Springer, Heidelberg (2014). https://doi.org/10.1007/978-3-662-44602-7_18
15. Ciancia, V., Latella, D., Loreti, M., Massink, M.: Model checking spatial logics for closure spaces. Log. Methods Comput. Sci. **12**(4) (2016)
16. Ciancia, V., Latella, D., Massink, M.: Embedding RCC8D in the collective spatial logic CSLCS. In: Boreale, M., Corradini, F., Loreti, M., Pugliese, R. (eds.) Models, Languages, and Tools for Concurrent and Distributed Programming. LNCS, vol. 11665, pp. 260–277. Springer, Cham (2019). https://doi.org/10.1007/978-3-030-21485-2_15
17. Ciancia, V., Latella, D., Massink, M., de Vink, E.: Towards spatial bisimilarity for closure models: logical and coalgebraic characterisations (2020). https://arxiv.org/abs/2005.05578
18. Ciancia, V., Latella, D., de Vink, M.M.E.: On bisimilarities for closure spaces - preliminary version (2021). https://arxiv.org/abs/2105.06690
19. Codella, N.C., et al.: Deep learning ensembles for melanoma recognition in dermoscopy images. IBM J. Res. Dev. **61**(4/5), 5–1 (2017). Special Issue on Deep Learning

20. Combs, S.E., et al.: ESTRO ACROP guideline for target volume delineation of skull base tumors. Radiother. Oncol. **156**, 80–94 (2021)
21. Demner-Fushman, D., Müller, H., Kalpathy-Cramer, J., Antani, S.: A decade of community-wide efforts in advancing medical images understanding and retrieval. Computer. Med. Imaging Graph. (2014)
22. Deserno, T.M., Güld, M.O., Thies, C., Plodowski, B., Keysers, D., Ott, B., Schubert, H.: IRMA - content-based image retrieval in medical applications. Stud. Health Technol. Inform. **107**(Pt 2), 842–6 (2004)
23. Galton, A.: A generalized topological view of motion in discrete space. Theor. Comput. Sci. **305**(1–3), 111–134 (2003)
24. Godar, D.E.: Worldwide increasing incidences of cutaneous malignant melanoma. J. Skin Cancer 2011 (2011)
25. Grosu, R., Smolka, S., Corradini, F., Wasilewska, A., Entcheva, E., Bartocci, E.: Learning and detecting emergent behavior in networks of cardiac myocytes. Commun. ACM **52**(3), 97–105 (2009)
26. Haux, R.: Strategic Information Management in Hospitals: An Introduction to Hospital Information Systems. Springer, New York (2003). https://doi.org/10.1007/978-1-4757-4298-5
27. Long, L.R., Antani, S., Deserno, T.M., Thoma, G.R.: Content-based image retrieval in medicine: retrospective assessment, state of the art, and future directions. Int. J. Healthc. Inf. Syst. Inform. Off. Publ. Inf. Resour. Manag. Assoc. **4**(1), 1–16 (2009)
28. Lozano, R., et al.: Global and regional mortality from 235 causes of death for 20 age groups in 1990 and 2010: a systematic analysis for the global burden of disease study 2010. Lancet **380**(9859), 2095–2128 (2012)
29. Markonis, D., Holzer, M., Baroz, F., Castaneda, R.L.R.D., Boyer, C., Langs, G., Müller, H.: User-oriented evaluation of a medical image retrieval system for radiologists. Int. J. Med. Inform. **84**(10), 774–783 (2015)
30. Mazzara, G., Velthuizen, R., Pearlman, J., Greenberg, H., Wagner, H.: Brain tumor target volume determination for radiation treatment planning through automated MRI segmentation. Int. J. Radiat. Oncol. Biol. Phys. **59**(1), 300–312 (2004)
31. Menze, B.H.e.a.: The multimodal brain tumor image segmentation benchmark (BRATS). IEEE Trans. Med. Imaging **34**(10), 1993–2024 (2015)
32. Mocellin, S., Nitti, D.: Cutaneous melanoma in situ: translational evidence from a large population-based study. Oncologist **16**(6), 896 (2011)
33. Müller, H., Clough, P., Hersh, W., Deselaers, T., Lehmann, T., Geissbuhler, A.: Evaluation axes for medical image retrieval systems: the ImageCLEF experience. In: Proceedings of the 13th Annual ACM International Conference on Multimedia, MULTIMEDIA 2005, pp. 1014–1022 Association for Computing Machinery, New York (2005)
34. Müller, H., Michoux, N., Bandon, D., Geissbuhler, A.: A review of content-based image retrieval systems in medical applications-clinical benefits and future directions. Int. J. Med. Inform. **73**(1), 1–23 (2004)
35. Nenzi, L., Bortolussi, L., Ciancia, V., Loreti, M., Massink, M.: Qualitative and quantitative monitoring of spatio-temporal properties with SSTL. Log. Methods Comput. Sci. **14**(4), 1–38 (2018)
36. Randell, D.A., Cui, Z., Cohn, A.G.: A spatial logic based on regions and connection. In: Proceedings of the 3rd International Conference on Principles of Knowledge Representation and Reasoning (KR 1992), pp. 165–176. Morgan Kaufmann (1992)
37. Randell, D.A., Galton, A., Fouad, S., Mehanna, H., Landini, G.: Mereotopological correction of segmentation errors in histological imaging. J. Imaging **3**(4) (2017)

38. Spyridon (Spyros) Bakas et al. (Ed.): 2017 International MICCAI BraTS Challenge: pre-conference proceedings, September 2017. https://www.cbica.upenn.edu/sbia/Spyridon.Bakas/MICCAI_BraTS/MICCAI_BraTS_2017_proceedings_shortPapers.pdf
39. Tang, L.H., Hanka, R., Ip, H.H.: A review of intelligent content-based indexing and browsing of medical images. Health Inform. J. **5**(1), 40–49 (1999)
40. Tsigkanos, C., Kehrer, T., Ghezzi, C.: Modeling and verification of evolving cyber-physical spaces. In: Proceedings of the 2017 11th Joint Meeting on Foundations of Software Engineering, pp. 38–48. ESEC/FSE 2017. ACM (2017)
41. Vorwerk, H., et al.: Protection of quality and innovation in radiation oncology: the prospective multicenter trial the German society of radiation oncology (DEGRO-QUIRO study). Strahlentherapie und Onkologie **190**(5), 433–443 (2014)
42. Wikipedia contributors: Memoization – Wikipedia, the free encyclopedia. https://en.wikipedia.org/w/index.php?title=Memoization&oldid=1002117560 (2021). Accessed 29 Mar 2021
43. Yousef Sanati, M., MacCaull, W., Maibaum, T.S.E.: Analyzing clinical practice guidelines using a decidable metric interval-based temporal logic. In: Jones, C., Pihlajasaari, P., Sun, J. (eds.) FM 2014. LNCS, vol. 8442, pp. 611–626. Springer, Cham (2014). https://doi.org/10.1007/978-3-319-06410-9_41
44. Zong, H., Verhaak, R.G., Canoll, P.: The cellular origin for malignant glioma and prospects for clinical advancements. Expert Rev. Mol. Diagn. **12**(4), 383–394 (2012)

Evaluation of Anonymization Tools
for Health Data

Olga Vovk[✉], Gunnar Piho, and Peeter Ross

Tallinn University of Technology, Tallinn, Estonia
{olga.vovk,gunnar.piho,peeter.ross}@taltech.ee

Abstract. It is hard to overestimate the value of data in modern health-care practice. On the one hand, we have an opportunity to use the data for health care quality improvement, and, on the other hand, we have privacy challenges. Considering the fact that we are dealing with sensitive personal data, privacy rights must be protected. Data anonymization is a technique to use healthcare data while preserving privacy.

Anonymization is a complex process that requires technical skills, an understanding of privacy requirements, and understanding health data's nature. Numerous anonymization tools are available to automate the anonymization process. Selecting among existing anonymization tools is challenging due to the necessity of collecting, comparing and analysing information on all tools separately.

This research aims to provide a systematic assessment of structured health data anonymization open-access tools and make the selection process easier. This paper describes the tools' advantages and disadvantages and reports whether these tools are sufficient to anonymize health data. In our understanding, based on the presented research, the tool selection process can speed up to 5 times because instead of installing and testing anonymization tools by themselves and collecting all relevant information, one can focus on the most suitable tools based on criteria given in this paper.

This work aims to help readers understand the advantages and disadvantages of free anonymization tools and improve, simplify, and speed up the selection process.

Keywords: Anonymization tools · Health data anonymization · Privacy · Anonymization software

1 Introduction

It is hard to overestimate the value of data in modern health care. According to the World Health Organization (WHO), global growth in the adoption of Electronic Health Records (EHR) over the last five years is 46% [1]. The EHR records

This work has been conducted in the project "ICT programme" which was supported by the European Union through the European Social Fund.

L. Bellatreche et al. (Eds.): MEDI 2021 Workshops, CCIS 1481, pp. 302–313, 2021.
https://doi.org/10.1007/978-3-030-87657-9_23

various measurements from the human body (height, weight, blood pressure), lab tests (e.g. blood tests, tissues samples, DNA), medical imaging (e.g. X-rays, MRI's, Ultrasound images), and different observations. Doctors and practitioners use all this health data in EHR for primary purposes - to diagnose and treat a patient [2]. Before digitalization, the usage of health data for other purposes than primary was significantly limited. However, recent progress in digitalization brings new possibilities, and the research community, healthcare professionals, policymakers can re-use this health data for their professional needs. For example, the re-use of health data can be used is contribute for to health care facility management, policy making, financing and reimbursement, research and innovations (discovering a new treatment and creating digital health apps), and health statistics (defining the prevalence of a particular disease).

When re-using healthcare data for secondary purposes, it is crucial to keep in mind that this data contains sensitive information. Therefore, the health data controllers must follow the data protection measures. Many countries have legal regulation that state the fundamental principles of health data privacy and security: The General Data Protection Regulation (GDPR) in the EU, The Health Insurance Portability and Accountability Act (HIPPA) in the US, The Personal Information Protection and Electronic Documents Act (PIPEDA) in Canada. According to those laws, health institutions must implement proper measures to protect patient's data, e.g. securely store and transfer data, ensure data integrity, protect from unauthorized access and data loss. However, in some instances, data needs to be shared outside the health care institutions, such as for other healthcare institutions, researchers, innovators and the community.

However, in certain cases data needs to be shared outside health care institutions, for example, with other healthcare institutions, researchers, innovators and the community. In all these cases, the healthcare institution transmitting the health data must apply relevant security measures to ensure a proper data protection level and lower the risks.

One of the options to ensure data protection is to anonymize the dataset or, in other words, de-personalise it and exclude all personal information by which the patient can be identified [3]. According to ISO 25237:2017 standard, anonymization is the act of eliminating the links between identifiable data and the data subject [4]. Legal regulations, including those mentioned above, require consent to use the patient's data. However, this requirement does not cover anonymized datasets. We can anonymize datasets manually, create a custom automated anonymization tool, or find and use an existing tool for anonymization. Manual anonymization usually would be challenging due to the enormous scope of anonymized data. Creating a custom algorithm requires significant IT skills. Using existing anonymization tools seems to be a good solution. However, the challenge here is on how to select a proper one.

There is a considerable literature gap in evaluating the quality of the tools for health data anonymization. Choosing those tools may be challenging due to the diversity of tools and the lack of comparison. It is especially challenging to understand the protection level the anonymization tool can provide. The paper "Evaluation of Data Anonymization Tools" [5] compares anonymization tools, but not specifically evaluate healthcare data anonymization tools. It is essential to underline that healthcare data is sensitive data that requires more protective measures than other personal data.

Some papers describe the effectiveness of anonymization tools. For example, "A tool for optimizing de-identified health data for use in statistical classification" [6] and "µ-ANT: semantic microaggregation-based anonymization tool" [7]. Both papers use proprietary databases, but they do not compare results objectively with other similar tools. Those and similar papers are dedicated to the effectiveness of anonymization tools, not comparing to other tools. In contrast, our work provides a systematic assessment of anonymization tools. The objectives of this work are: 1) to test existing tools on the same conditions (computational power and dataset), 2) to compare them, 3) describe the tool's advantages and disadvantages and 4) provide recommendations on whether this tool is sufficient to be used to anonymize healthcare data or not.

The evaluation process used in this paper includes the following parts: general (information about the tools), technical (risk analysis, technical requirements, functionality, usability and performance) and legal (license conditions to usage) parts. In this paper, we provide an overview of available open-access anonymization tools. We also evaluate the functionality, interface and license conditions, data anonymization efficiency and evaluate their sufficiency for using them in healthcare data anonymization. This evaluation helps readers better understand existing anonymization tools, their suitability to be used on health data anonymization and makes tool selection easier.

The structure of the paper is as follows. In section Methods, we formulate research questions and describe methods that we use to answer those questions. In the section Results, we present the main findings of current research by evaluating selected anonymization tools. Finally, in the Discussion and conclusion section, we discuss the evaluation results and summarise our findings.

2 Methods

In this section, we formulate research questions and describe the methods used to answer those questions. This paper aims to answer the following research questions:

RQ1. What are the main open-access tools available for health data anonymization?

RQ2. What are advantages and disadvantages of these tools?

RQ3. What tools are the best to use for health data anonymization?

The paper provides a systematic assessment of anonymization tools that includes an evaluation based on the essential software sustainability criteria. As no universal framework exist to evaluate anonymization tools, we took the "Software Evaluation: Criteria-based Assessment" methodology, proposed by the Software Sustainability Institute (in cooperation with the University of Edinburgh, the University of Manchester, the University of Oxford, and the University of Southampton) [8]. The authors of mentioned research offer to focus on the main criteria (quality, usability, sustainability and maintainability) defined in ISO/IEC 9126-1 Software engineering - Product [9]. We amended the proposed methodology by including the technical and legal parts to suit our needs. In conclusion, our evaluation procedure for selecting the anonymization tools is divided into three categories, as shown in Fig. 1.

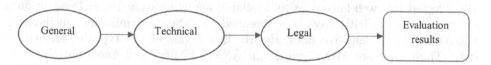

Fig. 1. Evaluation steps

In each category, tools will get a score of compliance to the quality requirement - yes (2 points)/partially (1 point)/no (0 points). Step of the general evaluation of the tool includes: information about the software identity (domain, logo, distinguishable name), available information about version and updates, whether the tool is free to use, information about the published papers about the tool and recognition in academic literature, another relevant information We divided the technical evaluation into 3 parts:

1. Usability
   - Understandability. How straightforward is it to understand the purpose of the software, its essential and advanced functions?
   - Documentation. Does the tool have clear and understandable documentation?
   - Buildability. How straightforward are instructions and easy to install?
   - Learnability. How straightforward is it to learn how to use essential and advanced functions of the tool?
   - Portability. Can the tool be installed and used under different operating systems?
   - Supportability. Is the tool currently supported, and is it likely to be supported in the future?
   - Interoperability. Does the tool meet appropriate open standards and formats?
2. Risk assessment. Is there a functionality that allows evaluating the quality of anonymization and calculates re-anonymization risks in the dataset
3. Functionality. Does the tool supports different anonymization methods, and how flexible it is to change settings?

In the legal category, we evaluate tools license requirements and the permission to use the software in the research projects without any restrictions.

3 Results

This section presents the research results and answers the research questions stated in the previous section. We evaluated the tools in February-March 2021 and used the last available versions.

RQ1. Main open-access tools
We selected five well-known freely available anonymization tools. Description of those tools explicitly says they intended to data anonymization, including anonymization of sensitive data. Health data is one of the types of sensitive data. Those tools are ARX, Amnesia, μ-ANT, sdcMicro and Anonimatron.

Here we provide tools descriptions according to their official web pages. ARX is an anonymization tool for sensitive personal data [10]. Amnesia is a flexible data anonymization tool that removes identifying information from data [11]. μ-ANT (The Microaggregation-based Anonymization Tool) is a software package to anonymize dataset using microaggregation [12]. sdcMicro is R-package to protect (micro-)data and make it available for researchers and public use [13]. Anonimatron is a tool to de-personalize or anonymize data [14].

RQ2. Advantages and Disadvantages of the Selected Tools
All of the selected tools are free, have an open-access, and have an understandable description of their purpose. Even though tools serve a joint mission, they have different general characteristics. 4 out of 5 tools are using Java programming language, sdcMicro is using programming language R. 3 out of 5 selected tools (ARX, Amnesia, sdcMicro) can be installed and used with GUI, others (μ-ANT, Anonimatron) require more technical skills to use them. The oldest tool is ARX, created in 2012, then sdcMicro and Anonimatron (2017), and the most recent ones are Amnesia and μ-ANT (2019).

All of the selected tools have a clear and understandable description of their purpose. They have a distinguishable name, website and Git repository with available information about software. Based on those three criteria (software identity, available information and whether the tool is free to use), all tools we evaluated with a maximum score of 2 points. 3 out of 5 selected tools have scientific publications evaluating their efficiency. We found over 20 scientific publications about the ARX tool, and 4 scientific publications about both the μ-ANT and sdcMicro tool. In this criteria, those three tools received a maximum score, and other tools received zero points. Table 1 concludes the score for selected tools in the general category.

Technical Evaluation
We assessed technical characteristics in 3 categories (usability, risk assessment and functionality), based on 9 criteria. The maximum available score in the evaluation is 18 points. Table 2 shows the score for selected tools in technical evaluation.

Understandability and Documentation. All selected tools we evaluated with the highest score for understandability and documentation.

Buildability. All tools have documentation on installation and usage. Nevertheless, it is worth to mention, that in addition to the regular documentation ARX

Table 1. General evaluation

General criteria	ARX	Amnesia	μ-ANT	sdcMicro	Anonimatron
Software identity (domain, logo, distinct name)	2	2	2	2	2
Available information about version and updates	2	2	2	2	2
Tool is free to use	2	2	2	2	2
Scientific publications	2	0	2	2	0
Total score	**8**	**6**	**8**	**8**	**6**

and Amnesia provide video where explain in details how to install, set up and use their tools. Provided videos make the process of installation and learning more straightforward, especially for inexperienced user.

Portability. All tools, except Amnesia, are available for the most commonly used OS - Windows, Linux and Mac OS X. Currently, Amnesia is available only for Windows and Linux.

Supportability. Only 2 tools (Amnesia and sdcMicro) have recently updated versions, during the last 2 months. Other tools were updated more than 6 months ago.

Interoperability. Most of the tools, except Amnesia, explicitly specify in the documentation what data formats they support for data anonymization. All tools, except Anonimatron, use the most commonly used format, CSV. Simultaneously, Anonimatron supports different database formats commonly used in production software. Table 3 concludes detailed information about supported formats.

Risk evaluation is a significant part of the data anonymization process. The result achieved by anonymization depends not only on the tool's capabilities but also on the user's settings. For this reason, build-in risk evaluation brings valuable information about the quality of data anonymization. It helps users understand the probability of de-anonymizing and finding the right balance between risk and data usability. Unfortunately, only 2 tools have this functionality. ARX has a very well presented risk assessment functionality by showing the distribution of risks in the dataset (records that have the risk of re-identification), the appearance of HIPAA identifiers in the dataset and risks of re-identification different attacker models (prosecutor, journalist and marketer attacker models). Those attacker models show the probability of re-identification data by combining anonymized dataset with other information, such as population register. If the user sees a high risk of data re-identification, anonymization settings must be changed to ensure proper data protection. sdcMicro includes the function that calculates the disclosure risk, which helps calculate the individual and the global risk. However, this function requires more technical skills, e.g. knowledge of the R programming language. μ-ANT can calculate information loss after anonymization, which helps assess data usability but does not substitute the evaluation of re-identification risk.

Functionality for selected tools was evaluated based on availability to use different methods required for anonymization for healthcare data. Table 3 shows what anonymization methods the tools support. All tools, except Anonimatron, use k-anonymity, which is the most well-known anonymization method. In our previous research [15], we identified that k-anonymity, l-diversity and t-closeness are the most well known methods in data anonymization. Current research shows how those methods are implemented in practice, in particular by ARX.

Table 2. Technical evaluation

Technical criteria	ARX	Amnesia	μ-ANT	sdcMicro	Anonimatron
Usability					
Understandability	2	2	2	2	2
Documentation	2	2	2	2	2
Buildability	2	2	1	1	1
Learnability	2	2	1	1	1
Portability	2	1	2	2	2
Supportability	1	2	1	2	1
Interoperability	2	1	2	1	1
Risk evaluation					
Risk evaluation	2	0	0	1	0
Functionality					
Functionality	2	2	1	2	1
Total score	**17**	**14**	**12**	**14**	**11**

Legal Evaluation

All evaluated tools have licenses that specified the conditions of their usage. For all tools, the license allows usage, including for commercial purposes. Nevertheless, licenses have specific prohibitions and requirements presented in Table 4. Mentioned licenses are commonly used with reasonable demands and based on legal requirements. All tools were evaluated with the highest score, as is shown in Table 5.

RQ3. Quality Assessment

The total maximum score that tools can get is 28 points, including 8 points in general evaluation, 18 points in technical evaluation and 2 points in the legal evaluation. Table 6 shows the total score appointed to the anonymization tools in this evaluation.

Table 3. Supported formats and anonymization methods

Criteria	ARX	Amnesia	μ-ANT	sdcMicro	Anonimatron
Supported formats	CSV, MS Excel, MS SQL, DB2, MySQL and PostgreSQL	CSV	CSV, XML	CSV, STATA, SAS, SPSS, R	MySQL, Postgress and Oracle
Anonymization methods	k-anonymity l-diversity t-closeness σ-disclosure privacy β-likeness σ-presence k-map (ϵ, σ)- differential privacy	k-anonymity k^m anonymity	k-anonymity, t-closeness	k-anonymity l-diversity	pseudonymi- zation

Table 4. Legal requirements

Tool	License	License allows	License prohibits	License requires
ARX	Apache License 2.0 [16]	Commercial use Modify Distribute Sublicense Private use Use patent claims Place warranty	Hold liable Use trademark	Include copyright Include license State changes Include notice
Amnesia	Attribution 4.0 International (CC BY 4.0) [17]	Commercial use Distribute Modify	Sublicense	Give credit Include copyright State changes
μ-ANT	MIT License [18]	Commercial use Modify Distribute Sublicense Private use	Hold liable	Include copyright Include license
sdcMicro	GPL-2 general public license [19]	Commercial use Modify Distribute Place warranty	Sublicense Hold liable	Include original Disclose source Include copyright State changes Include license
Anonimatron	MIT License [18]	Commercial use Modify Distribute Sublicense Private use	Hold liable	Include copyright Include license

Table 5. Legal evaluation

Legal criteria	ARX	Amnesia	μ-ANT	sdcMicro	Anonimatron
Total score	**2**	**2**	**2**	**2**	**2**

Table 6. Total score

	ARX	Amnesia	μ-ANT	sdcMicro	Anonimatron
General	8	6	8	8	6
Technical	17	14	12	14	11
Legal score	2	2	2	2	2
Total score	**27**	**22**	**22**	**24**	**19**

Table 6 and Fig. 2 show that ARX received 27 points, the highest score among other tools. sdcMicro received 24 points; both, Amnesia and μ-ANT got 22 points; and Anonimatron received 19 points.

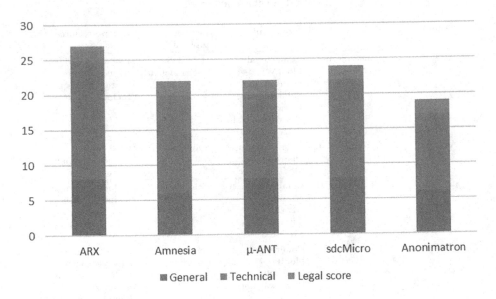

Fig. 2. Anonymization tools

Based on these results, we conclude that ARX is the most suitable health data anonymization tool. This tool provides all required benefits: information about the tool, documentation on installation and usage, including instruction video, supports various data formats and anonymization methods and has risk assessment functionality, which is essential and not supported in other tools.

sdcMicro is the second tool based on our evaluation score. This tool also has many benefits, including functionality to calculate risks. Nevertheless, this tool requires knowledge of R-language and mathematics and is challenging to inexperienced users.

μ-ANT and Amnesia share 3rd place with 22 points. Same as sdcMicro, μ-ANT require technical knowledge and is challenging to use for inexperienced users. In contrast, due to a simple installation and GUI, the Amnesia is suitable for beginners in the field. However, both tools, μ-ANT and Amnesia, are missing the risk assessment functionality to evaluate the correctness of anonymization.

Finally, the Anonimatron got from us 19 points. In our understanding, it does not suit health data anonymization. Unlike other tools, Anonimatron does not work with commonly used formats for health data (e.g. CSV), does not use well-known anonymization methods (e.g. k-anonymity) and does not have the functionality to assess risks. The tool use pseudonymization to modify the database. Anonimatron can create a database that is similar to a real one but does not contain personal information. Developers can use this database for testing purposes. However, this tool is not suitable to work with health data.

4   Discussion and Conclusion

In this paper, we evaluated open-access anonymization tools and analysed their suitability for health data anonymization. Our research shows that ARX is probably the most suitable open-access tool for health data anonymization. ARX got the highest score in general, technical and legal categories. It is available for all commonly used OS and supports the most well-known dataset formats. The tool has various methods that allow customising the anonymization process based on the user's needs. More than 20 scientific publications presented the effectiveness of ARX. This tool is universal, easy to install, and does not require deep technical knowledge to start. Additionally, developers provide detailed videos on usage that speeds up and simplifies the learning process. The most valuable feature from a data protection perspective, missing in many other tools, is build-in risk analysis. This functionality allows estimating the probability of the dataset's re-identification.

Health data anonymization is a complicated task. Most tools show good performance for "flat" data where information has one entry per value, e.g. "name-age-diagnose-procedure". However, actual data is more complex, and some values like name and age can have only one entry (John Doe, 39 years), but multiple diagnoses and procedures (59621000 Hypertension and 162864005 Body mass index 30+ - obesity (finding); 5880005 Physical examinations and 164783007 Ambulatory blood pressure recording). Some patients may not have a record in a particular row, for example, if they don't take any medications. For this reason, before using an anonymization tool, data needs to be pre-processed and put in a proper format.

The other challenge is to use the correct settings within the tool. Users must themself identify that data is considered an identifier, quasi-identifiers, or sensitive data and apply proper anonymization methods respectfully. For this reason, in the anonymization process, users can not entirely rely only on tools. required. Human input is required even in the best anonymization tool and plays a significant role in the anonymization process.

The main limitation of this research is the inclusion for evaluation only free and open-access anonymization tools. In future work, we plan to evaluate commercial tools for data anonymization and special libraries that software developers can use in building their software.

There is a demand for health data anonymization tools, which leads to the improvement of existing tools and the development of new tools. In general, anonymization tools can improve in several ways. We believe that future anonymization tools are easier to use, offer more functionalities, including risk assessment, have a graphical interface that allows easier installation and usage, and require less technical skills. Additionally, anonymization tools can improve by taking into account the complex structure of health data, and they should support more standards and formats used in the health care field, e.g. FHIR, SNOMED CT, ICD-10, HL7, JSON and XML.

References

1. World Health Organization electronic health records. Analysis of third global survey on ehealth based on the reported data by countries (2016). https://www.who.int/gho/goe/electronic_health_records/en/. Accessed 18 Apr 2021
2. Safran, C., et al.: Toward a national framework for the secondary use of health data: an American medical informatics association white paper. J. Am. Med. Inform. Assoc. **14**(1), 1–9 (2007)
3. Fernández-Alemán, J.L., Señor, I.C., Lozoya, P.Á.O., Toval, A.: Security and privacy in electronic health records: a systematic literature review. J. Biomed. Inform. **46**(3), 541–562 (2013)
4. ISO 25237:2017, Health informatics – Pseudonymization (2017)
5. Vinogradov, S., Pastsyak, A.: Evaluation of data anonymization tools. In: Proceeding International Conference on Advances in Databases, Knowledge, and Data Applications (DBKDA), pp. 163–168 (2012)
6. Prasser, F., Eicher, J., Bild, R., Spengler, H., Kuhn, K.A.: A tool for optimizing de-identified health data for use in statistical classification. In: 2017 IEEE 30th International Symposium on Computer-Based Medical Systems (CBMS), pp. 169–174. IEEE (2017)
7. Sánchez, D., Martínez, S., Domingo-Ferrer, J., Soria-Comas, J., Batet, M.: μ-ant: semantic microaggregation-based anonymization tool. Bioinformatics **36**(5), 1652–1653 (2020)
8. Software Sustainability Institute software evaluation. Criteria-based assessment. https://www.software.ac.uk/resources/guides-everything/software-evaluation-guide. Accessed 20 Mar 2021
9. ISO. International Organization for Standardization. http://www.iso.org/. Accessed 20 Mar 2021
10. ARX. https://arx.deidentifier.org/. Accessed 23 Mar 2021
11. Amnesia. https://amnesia.openaire.eu/. Accessed 23 Mar 2021
12. μ-ANT (the microaggregation-based anonymization tool). https://github.com/CrisesUrv/microaggregation-based_anonymization_tool. Accessed 23 Mar 2021

13. sdcMicro. https://github.com/sdcTools/sdcMicro. Accessed 23 Mar 2021
14. Anonimitron. https://realrolfje.github.io/anonimatron/. Accessed 23 Mar 2021
15. Vovk, O., Piho, G., Ross, P.: Anonymization methods of structured health care data: a literature review. In: Attiogbé, C., Ben Yahia, S. (eds.) MEDI 2021. LNCS, vol. 12732, pp. 175–189. Springer, Cham (2021). https://doi.org/10.1007/978-3-030-78428-7_14
16. The Apache Software License (ASL). The Big DFSG-compatible Licenses. Debian Project. http://www.apache.org/licenses/. Accessed 20 Mar 2021
17. Creative Commons. https://creativecommons.org/licenses/by/4.0/. Accessed 20 Mar 2021
18. MIT. https://www.mit.edu. Accessed 20 Mar 2021
19. GPL FAQ: Does using the GPL for a program make it GNU Software? GNU project. Free software foundation. https://www.gnu.org/licenses/gpl-faq.html#DoesUsingTheGPLForAProgramMakeItGNUSoftware. Accessed 20 Mar 2021

Usages of the ContSys Standard: A Position Paper

Kristian Kankainen(✉) iD

Department of Health Technologies, Tallinn University of Technology,
Ehitajate tee 5, 19086 Tallinn, Estonia
kristian.kankainen@taltech.ee
https://www.taltech.ee/en/department-health-technologies

Abstract. This position paper presents preliminary findings from an ongoing systematic literature review over the usages of the ContSys standard ISO 13940 [7]. I show that the literature reveals several patterns of how "A system of concepts for the continuity of care" is understood and applied.

Keywords: ContSys · ISO 13940 · Standards adoption

1 Introduction

There can exist several understandings of what the ISO 13940 e.g. ContSys standard's "A system of concepts for the continuity of care" is useful for. This position paper presents the preliminary findings of the author's literature review on how the ContSys standard has been understood and applied.

Work on the concepts underlying continuity of care began in 1998 as an European pre-standard, with the goal to establish a common conceptual framework for continuity of care across national, cultural and professional barriers [17].

The international standard was released in 2015 and contains definitions for approximately 150 concepts and their inter-relations using UML (Unified Modelling Language). The concepts cover the following topics healthcare actors, healthcare matters, activities, process, healthcare planning, time, responsibilities and information management. The concepts give a basis for content and context in healthcare services and in practice the standard is aimed to be used whenever requirements for information in healthcare are specified [7].

The terms used in the standard have no actual value outside the framework, still, during the times before the standard's conception, there was a need felt to clearly define terms such as *continuity of care, shared care, seamless care,* and *integrated care* [17].

Continuity of care is defined as *efficient, effective, ethical care delivered through interaction, integration, co-ordination and sharing of information between different healthcare actors over time.* The system of concepts is focused on the clinical process, which it defines as *a set of interrelated or interacting*

© Springer Nature Switzerland AG 2021
L. Bellatreche et al. (Eds.): MEDI 2021 Workshops, CCIS 1481, pp. 314–324, 2021.
https://doi.org/10.1007/978-3-030-87657-9_24

activities that use inputs to deliver an intended result [7]. Even though it is designed to support the care process, the standard does not define it nor does it have any regulatory impact on the delivery of care [17].

2   Method

As this position paper presents preliminary results from an unfinished literature review, no real method can be said to have been followed. I plan to use Kitchenham and Charters guidelines for the systematic literature review [13].

A maximalistic search strategy was agreed on to only use Google Scholar and search separately for the terms "iso 13940", "cen 13940", and "contsys". The otherwise popular databases PubMed, IEEE, Science Direct, and SpringerLink databases yielded very few and unconvincing search results. See Fig. 1 for overview of the review process so far and its search result counts. Articles has been excluded if not in English, if unrelated or mere descriptions rather than usages of ContSys. The 22 articles that has been included so far are summarized in Table 1.

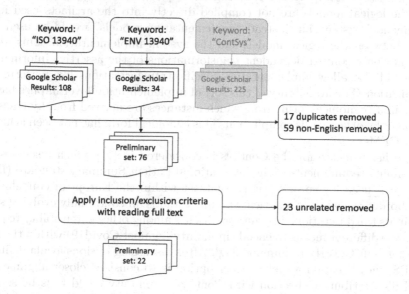

Fig. 1. Counts of found, excluded and preliminary included articles in the preliminary selection process.

3   Results

3.1   Using the Standard as a Conceptual Model

The ISO 13940 standard is used in [19] for defining the usage contexts for Clinical Element Models (CEM), like problem lists, health issues, and health issue threads. CEMs are similar to detailed clinical models and archetype models, and

Table 1. Articles included so far in the literature review categorized by usage.

Usage	Included articles
Using the standard as a conceptual model	[12, 15, 19],
Shortcomings of the standard	[5, 6]
Ontological perspective	[16, 20]
Extending the standard	[2–4, 10, 21, 22],
Seen but unused possibilities of the standard	[18, 26]
Concurrent Use Initiative	[1, 9, 11, 14, 23–25]

are used to model 'assertive' information, e.g. "to assert that the patient has [x]". These assertions can be expressed in multiple contexts, such as discharge diagnoses, cause of death, complication of surgery, problem list. Transformation of the assertive information between contexts using should ideally be lossless. The work discusses the importance of having an "implementation layer", which means that the logical models are not compiled directly into the artifacts used in an implemented system, but instead "implementation models" would be used as a buffer between the logical models and the system implementation. This would allow not only context-dependent transformations of the assertive information, but would also allow implementation-specific transformations like performance optimization. The availability of this sort of implementation layer implies having CEMs in a "canonical form" from which instances are derived from by transformation or by other words compilation. This canonical form has not been achieved yet by CEMs.

Another use-case for the ContSys is considered in [12] which discusses the extensibility requirements of the International Patient Summary standard (IPS). The IPS is used for normalizing the dataset within the European Guideline on cross-border exchange of a patient summary and is an continually evolving standard in its third iteration. The authors discuss among other extensibility requirements the different means to encode immunity (against Covid19) within the IPS, e.g. a kind of 'COVID-19 immune flag'. After discussing options available inside the IPS, they mention as yet another option is to consider closer alignment of the IPS's Attribute Collection with ContSys. Immunity could thus be seen as "an aspect of a person's health state, perceived or recorded as a health matter; conversely 'lack of immunity' could be recorded as a specialization of 'problem'". The authors explain the difference in location where the fact is stored reflects that the IPS is a snapshot, recording the relevant data about patients' healthcare at a point in time. The authors also state that testing is needed to understand the impact of changing the scope of the IPS Attribute Collection to include health matters.

Another use case found in the literature is for creating a data quality assured registry for the reuse of information on infant feeding from birth until two years old [15]. The authors propose a 13-step construction process and use the ContSys for defining task-relevant data. The incorporation of organizational context to the information model enabled the authors to integrate elements with same meaning from different data sources, facilitate the definition of Data Quality metrics independent of the overall level of analysis required for the reuse of the fact of study, and also incorporate clinical researchers into the construction process. As a result of contextualising the data with ContSys concepts enabled the replication of the methodology and its use in multi-centre population studies, even with different organizational contexts.

3.2   Shortcomings of the Standard

In [6] the authors compare the applicability of the Observational Medical Outcomes Partnership's Common Data Model (OMOP CDM) and the ContSys for transforming quality registry data and making the data FAIR (Findable, Accessible, Interoperable, and Reusable). The data was taken from the Dutch National Intensive Care Evaluation and mapped to both data models. Their findings was that both models could be used, but that the OMOP platform offers more tools and guidance for mapping data and that the lack of guidance for ContSys (e.g. sparse definitions and term explanations of the standard) can result in the same data being mapped differently by different persons. A crucial finding was that the ContSys can represent negative findings while OMOP CDM can not.

Cillessen and Hofdijk discuss in [5] the importance of the problem list. They emphasizes that the transformation of the problem list, away from an institutional level to a holistic list at the patient level across the network, is an essential component for person-centered care. Problems should be linked to plans via assessments to achieve goals. Currently problem lists are isolated inside institutions.

They suggest to use the SOAP (Subjective/Objective/Assessment/Plan) note format and point out that shared decision making can be interpreted as the assessment phase of the SOAP concept, resulting in the update of the plan, fitting in the overarching care plan.

They find that ideally, the problem list is to serve as a dynamic "table of contents" of the patient's chart and should serve as a multi-disciplinary index of the health issues. But to interpret various problems and track progress, the concept of 'problem' has a wider scope than diagnosis.

3.3   Ontological Perspective

According to the pilot study [16] the ContSys provides domain-specific terms with definitions and relationships, but states that it was not developed as an ontology. They suggest that the ContSys standard would benefit from a formal ontological analysis. Their hypothesis is that such analysis would help to further formalize the meaning of the concepts and ease the adoption, support further evolution and assist maintenance of the standard.

The study focused on the concepts *Health issue* and *Health state* and placed them under the top-level ontology BioTopLite2 (BTL2). They suggest that the rooting of the ContSys in an ontological framework also has the potential to detect logical contradictions in the standard.

The chapter on "New Research Initiatives Influencing Knowledge Networks Through the Center for eIntegrated Care" in [20] refers to the work on ContS-Onto as "A research initiative engaged in the development of an Ontology of Continuity of care based on an ISO Standard ISO 13940".

3.4   Extending the Standard

[22] describes the methodology proposed by the UNINFO Working Group in Italy to extend the ContSys standard to social concepts. It provides an example of the definition of the individual care plan established in the social context to track the activities (both needed and provided) related to one or more social needs of a specific subject of care. Moreover, as different services can be planned and provided by a multidisciplinary team composed of both health and social care professionals, an integrated plan is envisioned. The adoption of the integrated model could facilitate the interoperability between systems as well as the coordination and cooperation activities of the different actors involved in the provision of services in a comprehensive continuity of care process

[21] proposes a conceptual model that combines the main concepts of health with social care and assistive domotics linked to the healthy behavior and lifestyle components in a continuity of care perspective. The proposed conceptual model is based on ContSys and extends it with contexts covered, the stakeholders involved as well as information systems and devices to be integrated in a home setting. The flow of the data produced by the devices included in the architecture depends on the type of user, his/her needs, the context of the service provided (i.e. social, clinical, assistive domotics) as well as the type of the device used.

The work [10] have proposed amending the standard with terms of measures for patients medication adherence, which the authors state is "currently in progress in ISO TC 215". The authors' motivation comes from the lack of agreed upon terms for measures of medication adherence in a big data perspective.

A big line of work by Bernd Blobel has been found around the new standard ISO 23903:2021 Health informatics—Interoperability and integration reference architecture – Model and framework (IRA), that was released in April 2021. The main aim of this new standard is to provide a reference architecture that supports integrating specifications between different domains, e.g. with their domain specific methodologies, terminologies and ontologies [8].

In [3] Blobel brings into attention that in 2015 the ISO/CEN/TC251 decided to mandatorily include the IRA in their new standards and revisions of old, including also the ContSys. In the future the standards will provide only their basic models and refer to the IRA. In addition, Blobel mentions that top level ontologies are currently turned to ISO standards.

It has earlier been pointed out by Blobel in [2] that "The increasingly complex interoperability challenge cannot be met starting from an information object point of view, as most of the existing approaches [...] do. When constructing a picture of the real world from those information artefacts, we will result in the tragic situation of creating an excellent map, however the landscape is wrong".

Blobel [4] sees the sharing of concepts with the help of openEHR Archetypes and ContSys as an evolutionary step from structured messaging towards cooperation between applications, but critiques it as being restricted to computer-to-computer communication, representing information based either on the domain independent Reference Model of Open Distributed Processing (RM-ODP) or domain-specific information models. Because these "approaches require a priori sharing the underlying knowledge such as instantiated concepts and terminologies including the applied syntactical and procedural rules". The IRA model would instead enable to interrelate domain-specific structure and behaviour by ontologically representing its concepts and relationships. According to Blobel, "Interoperability is not first a technological challenge, but requires domain-specific and especially social competencies" and for this the integration of different actors using their own languages, methodologies, terminologies, ontologies requires harmonization and also translation or transformation between the actors' languages. "The interoperability approach must advance from interoperability between computer systems towards a business process specific cooperation of actors representing the different domains participating in the business case as well as the actors' individual conditions [and environmental context]."

Blobel places the subject of care in the middle as the controller of this process. "For that purpose, all interoperability levels [...] must be provided by all participating systems cooperating on this level" and states that "It is impossible to represent such [...] systems by one domain's terminology/ontology or – even worse – by using [information and communications technology (ICT)] ontologies." and concludes that "an adaptive approach is required to sharing and harmonizing ICT, domain and personal ontologies, and conditions at runtime".

3.5 Seen but Unused Possibilities of the Standard

To lower the learning curve for software engineers to be able to employ Health Level 7 (HL7) standards, the authors of [18] have aligned the meta-models of many HL7 standards with the meta-model for the Universal Modelling Language (UML). Their work has created what they call Model Driven Health Engineering by extending the Navigational Development methodology used in Model Driven Engineering.

Their hypothesis is that a UML translation of the standards is helpful for developers as developers are able read UML, but are often not proficient with the HL7 standards.

The paper states as possible future work that "Aligning the concepts used in HL7 standards with this [ContSys] kind of system of concepts is a complex and tedious task" but adds that in a potential complementary research line, the already found relations in their reference model could play the role of aligning concepts and make the aligning "more simple and maintainable."

In [26] the authors see as the main interoperability problem that predefined headers for Electronic Health Record (EHR) information models are rarely shared and mention that a wise usage of the ISO 13940 combined with other standards targeted for EHR content standardization can contribute to a more harmonized data capture. The authors instead describe as a short-term strategy a method for using shared Archetypes and openEHR templates for modifying user-created data input forms in vendor systems. Their spreadsheet-based method is suggested to be used as a way to "translate" annotated openEHR templates to a form that resembles what current EHR system administrators are familiar with and using today.

3.6   Concurrent Use Initiative

The combination of the ContSys standard in conjunction with two other standards, the ISO EN 13606 Health informatics - Electronic health record communication (EHRCom) and the ISO EN 12967 Health informatics - Service architecture (HISA), form what is called the Concurrent Use initiative, which was started in 2012 by CEN with the ambition to see how they could be used together to make a contribution to interoperability within their combined scope [11].

Many of the works refer to the Concurrent Use initiative by simply naming the three standards [9,23,24], and [1].

While [25] report plans for a new Bulgarian NHIS system, with the main purpose to replace the old financial report mechanism with activity-based funding. Moreover to the Concurrent Use Initiative, they mention also to base the NHIS on the ISO/TS 29585 standard Health informatics - Deployment of a clinical data warehouse. In their work, the ContSys is said to underpin the NHIS Correspondents Zone with the purpose to ensure semantic interoperability of information exchanged between correspondents through the whole information lifecycle.

[14] describes a reconstruction of an EHR system previously used in two regions in Japan, to be connectable nation wide. The old system used an in-house XML-based formalism for describing clinical models (called Medical Markup Language), this was replaced with openEHR archetypes. The article mentions openEHR/ISO 13606 as a "standard that enables interoperability of clinical concepts and has been widely adopted to build other standards", where these other standards are mentioned the ContSys and Detailed Clinical Models. Later on, they describe the system's interoperability to be based on using archetype artifacts without modifications from the openEHR Clinical Knowledge Manager repository, albeit they report that out of 99 developed archetypes, only 69 archetypes (e.g. 70%) could be used without modification and 22 had to be specialized and 8 newly designed.

4   Discussion and Future Work

4.1   Using the Standard as a Conceptual Model

I find the idea (from [19]) to use transformations for presenting singularly modeled assertive clinical information in multiple contexts enumerated in the ContSys (like problem lists, health issues, and health issue threads) to be powerful.

As the contexts enumerated in the ContSys should hold universally, I see this approach has the potential to be used for integrating assertive clinical information also on an inter-organizational level. The approach would thus depend on the availability of suitable transformations for each data source. This I find similar to the successful results found in [15] for integrating same meaning elements by incorporating organization context into their information models.

4.2 Shortcomings and Modifications

Although comparing ContSys and the Observational Medical Outcomes Partnership's Common Data Model (OMOP CDM) can seem unintuitive, as ContSys is a conceptual model and the CDM is a relational database schema, it can't be denied that this kind of comparison has been found in the literature. To me only one of the shortcomings brought out in [6] is real: the lack of documentation and this can result in different understandings of the ContSys. Still I don't see the OMOP CDM as a replacer for the ContSys, as the CDM has a too narrow purpose of use, e.g. to integrate different data sets in a traditional data extract, transform, and load process, not continuity of care. The fact that the ContSys can represent negative findings while OMOP CDM can not, only proves the point.

The discussion (in [5]) around the importance of the problem list as a pivotal structure in the transition away from an institutional level to a holistic list at the patient level across the network resonates for me much with Blobel's proposition, to put the patient in control in the center between many domains.

It is unclear to me whether this is a shortcoming of the standard, as [17] states that ContSys' concept of Health Issue "broadens the common concept of 'health problem' to encompass issues that should not actually be labelled as 'problems'". Moreover, [17] states that Health Issues have a label given by the healthcare professional currently in charge and that the label can change over time and vary between healthcare professionals.

Seen from this perspective, the ContSys has the potential to function as the "dynamic table of contents" with alignments between local problem lists and shared health issues stored in a patient-owned data repository. Investigating how the SOAP (Subjective/Objective/Assessment/Plan) concept can be operationalized is of big interest to me.

4.3 Ontological Perspective

The works on progressing an ontological perspective to the standard show many benefits. But the efforts seem to struggle in finding or agreeing upon a single top-level ontology. This makes it uncertain whether ontologizing the ContSys is worth more than the academical exercise. Still, the work referred to in [20] seems to be the project lead by Subhashis Das entitled "A Common Semantic Data Model (CSDM) for complex Healthcare Network". It seems to be under active development and the results of it is of big interest to me. Also, Blobel points out (in [3]) that the ISO is standardizing top-level ontologies, but it is unknown whether or in which way this affects the coming revision of ContSys that ought to be based on the Interoperability Reference Architecture.

4.4   Extending the Standard

The different proposals to extend the ContSys for other domains seem for me to prove the point made by Blobel and the work on Interoperability Reference Architecture, that an a priori sharing of the underlying knowledge will never suffice, but instead a sharing of concepts between domains by transformational or translational means during runtime is needed.

With the big line of work on the Interoperability and integration reference architecture (IRA) and seeing from the perspective of the subject of care, Blobel brings forth the importance to integrate multiple different domains, all having their own specifics and languages, and also stresses on the need to be able to translate or transform between the domains during runtime. This opinion of course shows the limits of the ContSys which represents only a single domain, but it is still unclear in which way the Interoperability and integration reference architecture standard will change the ContSys.

4.5   Seen but Unused Possibilities

The mentioning of ContSys as a possible but not implemented solution is taken as statements of approval and positive adoption of the standard.

I see value in the hypothesis stated in [18] that the developers are often more proficient with their own vocabularies than with healthcare standards. That they mention the ContSys in this context shows real potential for the standard's conceptual system as a vocabulary for communication between developers and stakeholders. This I feel resonates also with the ContSys' original idea that its system of concepts "should not differ in nature from those that are used to structure and organise the data locally in the Electronic Health Record" [17].

4.6   Concurrent Use Initiative

Since most papers mentioning the Concurrent Use Initiative were descriptions of planned national health information systems, I take the Concurrent Use Initiative as an important catalyst to bring forth systems with any interoperability requirements built-in. But the concept of Concurrent Use Initiative seems to have been or will soon become superseded by the Interoperability and integration reference architecture (IRA).

5   Conclusion

I see the ContSys as a domain description that ought to apply universally to procedures across healthcare providers. Thus I see potential in using the standard as a vocabulary for a kind of (user) interface for anchoring data between global and local views. This might be similar to the method of providing labels for problems in problem lists.

Integrating local and global views has two common strategies depending on which of the levels is used for actually storing the data, and which is used as a view to the stored data. These strategies are Local-as-view and global-as-view.

I feel there is inevitably a conflict coming from having many stakeholders to data, each with a certain right to their own global view and each with their own processes.

As the ContSys only describes, but does not define a process of care, it could be used as a basis for a global data model, providing the vocabulary for data stakeholders to map their data. Still, as processes vary between the data stakeholders, this will the result in a fragmented coverage. Thus, the potential for ContSys is not so much in semantic labels to conform to, but defining a certain granularity of data for data stakeholders.

References

1. Abishev, O., Spatayev, Y.: The future development of digital health in Kazakhstan. Eurohealth **25**(2), 24–26 (2019). World Health Organization. Regional Office for Europe. https://apps.who.int/iris/handle/10665/332524
2. Blobel, B.: Standardization for mastering healthcare transformation - challenges and solutions. Eur. J. Biomed. Inform. **13**(1) (2017). https://doi.org/10.24105/ejbi.2017.13.1.3. International Journal of Medical Research & Health Sciences
3. Blobel, B.: Challenges and solutions for designing and managing pHealth ecosystems. Front. Med. **6**, 83 (2019). https://doi.org/10.3389/fmed.2019.00083
4. Blobel, B., Ruotsalainen, P., Lopez, D.M., Oemig, F.: Requirements and solutions for personalized health systems. Stud. Health Technol. Inform. **237**, 3–21 (2017)
5. Cillessen, F., Hofdijk, J.: Transition requirements from problem list to an overarching care plan for the support of person-centered care. Stud. Health Technol. Inform. **272**, 292–295 (2020). https://doi.org/10.3233/SHTI200552
6. de Groot, R.: OMOP CDM compared to ContSys (ISO13940) to make data FAIR. OHDSI symposium, p. 4 (2020)
7. ISO Central Secretary: Health informatics — System of concepts to support continuity of care. Standard ISO 13940:2015, International Organization for Standardization, Geneva, CH (2015)
8. ISO Central Secretary: Health informatics — Interoperability and integration reference architecture – Model and framework. Standard ISO 23903:2021, International Organization for Standardization, Geneva, CH (2021)
9. Kalra, D.: Electronic health record standards. In: Haux, R., Kulikowski, C.A. (eds.) IMIA Yearbook 2006: Assessing Information - Technologies for Health, vol. 45, pp. 136–144. Schattauer GMBH-Verlag, Stuttgart (2006)
10. Kardas, P., et al.: The need to develop standard measures of patient adherence for big data: viewpoint. J. Med. Internet Res. **22**(8) (2020). https://doi.org/10.2196/18150
11. Kay, S.: Towards concurrent use of ContSys, 13606, and HISA. Technical report, CEN TC251, Madrid, March 2013
12. Kay, S., Cangioli, G., Nusbaum, M.: The international patient summary standard and the extensibility requirement. Stud. Health Technol. Inform. **273**, 54–62 (2020). https://doi.org/10.3233/SHTI200615

13. Kitchenham, B., Charters, S.: Guidelines for performing systematic literature reviews in software engineering. Technical report EBSE 2007–001. Keele University and Durham University Joint Report (2007)
14. Kobayashi, S., Kume, N., Nakahara, T., Yoshihara, H.: Designing clinical concept models for a nationwide electronic health records system for Japan. Eur. J. Biomed. Inform. (2018)
15. García-de León-Chocano, R., Sáez, C., Muñoz-Soler, V., García-de León-González, R., García-Gómez, J.M.: Construction of quality-assured infant feeding process of care data repositories: definition and design (Part 1). Comput. Biol. Med. **67**, 95–103 (2015). https://doi.org/10.1016/j.compbiomed.2015.09.024
16. Martínez-Costa, C., Kay, S., Oughtibridge, N., Schulz, S.: ContSys under Ontological Scrutiny. In: MIE, p. 999 (2015)
17. Mennerat, F., Booth, N.: Concepts underlying continuity of care - the system of concepts described in ENV 13940a. J. Innov. Health Inform. **10**(1), 31–38 (2002). https://doi.org/10.14236/jhi.v10i1.237
18. Olivero, M.A., Domínguez-Mayo, F.J., Parra-Calderón, C.L., Escalona, M.J., Martínez-García, A.: Facilitating the design of HL7 domain models through a model-driven solution. BMC Med. Inform. Decis. Mak. **20**(1), 96 (2020). https://doi.org/10.1186/s12911-020-1093-4
19. Oniki, T.A., Coyle, J.F., Parker, C.G., Huff, S.M.: Lessons learned in detailed clinical modeling at Intermountain Healthcare. J. Am. Med. Inform. Assoc. JAMIA **21**(6), 1076–1081 (2014). https://doi.org/10.1136/amiajnl-2014-002875
20. Hussey, P., Kennedy, M.A. (eds.): Introduction to Nursing Informatics. Health Informatics, 5th edn. Springer, Cham (2021). https://doi.org/10.1007/978-3-030-58740-6
21. Pecoraro, F., Luzi, D., Pourabbas, E., Ricci, F.L.: A conceptual model for integrating social and health care services at home: the H@H project. In: 2016 IEEE 18th International Conference on e-Health Networking, Applications and Services (Healthcom), pp. 1–6, September 2016. https://doi.org/10.1109/HealthCom.2016.7749489
22. Pecoraro, F., Luzi, D., Pourabbas, E., Ricci, F.L., Rossi Mori, A.: Extending contsys standard with social care concepts: a methodology proposed by the UNINFO working group in Italy. Stud. Health Technol. Inform. **270**, 223–227 (2020). https://doi.org/10.3233/SHTI200155
23. Rosa, M., Faria, C., Barbosa, A.M., Caravau, H., Rosa, A.F., Rocha, N.P.: A fast healthcare interoperability resources (FHIR) implementation integrating complex security mechanisms. Procedia Comput. Sci. **164**, 524–531 (2019). https://doi.org/10.1016/j.procs.2019.12.215
24. Soman, S., Ranjan, P., Srivastava, P.K.: A distributed architecture for hospital management systems with synchronized EHR. CSI Trans. ICT **8**(3), 355–365 (2020). https://doi.org/10.1007/s40012-020-00301-8
25. Stanev, I., Koleva, M.: Bulgarian health information system based on the common platform for automated programming. In: MCIS 2016 Proceedings, p. 8 (2016)
26. Sundvall, E., Terner, A., Broberg, H., Gillespie, C.: Configuration of input forms in EHR systems using spreadsheets, openEHR archetypes and templates. Stud. Health Technol. Inform. **264**, 1781–1782 (2019). https://doi.org/10.3233/SHTI190645

Author Index

Printed in the United States
by Baker & Taylor Publisher Services